Spiritual *Choices*

The Problem of Recognizing Authentic Paths to Inner Transformation

Spiritual Choices

The Problem of Recognizing Authentic Paths to Inner Transformation

Edited by
Dick Anthony,
Bruce Ecker,
and Ken Wilber

Paragon House Publishers

New York

Published in the United States by

PARAGON HOUSE PUBLISHERS
90 Fifth Avenue
New York, New York 10011

Third printing

Library of Congress Cataloging-in-Publication Data

Spiritual Choices.

   Bibliography:
   Includes index.
   1. Spiritual life—Congresses. 2. Religions—
Congresses. I. Anthony, Richard, 1939–   . II. Ecker,
Bruce.   III. Wilber, Ken.
BL624.S675   1986   291.4   86-5027
ISBN 0-913729-14-0
ISBN 0-913729-19-1 (pbk.)

Acknowledgments

Grateful acknowledgment is made for permission to reprint the following published materials:

"A Question of Balance: Health and Pathology in New Religious Movements" by Frances Vaughan, from the *Journal of Humanistic Psychology*, 23 (3), Summer 1983. Reprinted in modified form by permission of the *Journal of Humanistic Psychology*.

"On Spiritual Authority: Genuine and Counterfeit" by John Welwood, from the *Journal of Humanistic Psychology*, 23 (3), Summer 1983. Reprinted in modified form by permission of the *Journal of Humanistic Psychology*.

"Meher Baba—an interview with Dick Anthony" first appeared as "The Outer Master as the Inner Guide: Autonomy and Authority in the Process of Transformation," in the *Journal of Transpersonal Psychology*, 14 (1), 1982. Reprinted in modified form by permission of the *Journal of Transpersonal Psychology*.

"A Ten-Year Perspective" by Ram Dass (Richard Alpert), from the *Journal of Transpersonal Psychology*, 14 (2), 1982. Reprinted in modified form by permission of the *Journal of Transpersonal Psychology* and the author.

Drawings of Zen Buddhist meditation posture, from *Zen Training: Methods and Philosophy* by Katsuki Sekida, edited by A. V. Grimstone; New York: John Weatherhill, Inc., 1975. Reprinted by permission of the publisher.

Diagram of "The Psychic Life Cycle", from Figure 5 in *Ego and Archetype* by Edward Edinger, reproduced by permission of the C. G. Jung Foundation for Analytical Psychology, New York.

Quotations of Meher Baba (© Adi K. Irani) are reprinted by permission of the Avatar Meher Baba Perpetual Public Charitable Trust, Ahmednagar, M.S., India.

Contents

Preface

This book is largely the result of a seminar, led by Dick Anthony, that attempted to develop criteria that would aid people in making spiritual choices intelligently. In that seminar two previously separate scholarly traditions, transpersonal psychology and the scientific study of religion, were brought into dialogue in an effort to illuminate these issues. The Anthony typology, comprising Part 1 of the book, represents a summary of research on the new religions from within the scientific study of religion and was used as a device to structure discussion within the seminar. The transpersonal psychologists in the seminar developed the essays included in this volume in response to Anthony's presentation of his point of view. We have in turn used the perspective provided by the typology in commenting on their efforts, as well as on those essays that were contributed by transpersonal writers who did not participate in the seminar. So the dialogue initiated between the two fields within the seminar continues in this manuscript and perhaps moves towards some kind of synthesis. (Other books stimulated by the seminar include Ken Wilber's *A Sociable God*, which originally was written as his contribution, and Dick Anthony and Ken Wilber's *Polarity vs. Progress: Alternative Images for the Process of Transformation*, in preparation. The Introduction includes further description of the seminar.)

Ultimately it is up to the reader to decide whether the cross-fertilization of the two fields is helpful in resolving spiritual dilemmas. To us it seems that the sophistication regarding cultural influences upon spiritual interpretation—and misinterpretation—provided by the scientific study of religion is a useful corrective to the essentially individualistic point of view provided by transpersonal psychology. Transpersonal psychology's explicit documentation of the continuity between psychological and mystical stages of development, on the other hand, fruitfully transcends the religious reductionism which has been such a problem for the scientific study of religion.

In such a complex collaborative effort as this one, it is difficult to know where to begin—or end—in acknowledging aid, but we would at least like to hit the high spots. Claude Welch, who was then President of the Graduate Theological Union in Berkeley, and Jacob Needleman, who was Director of GTU's Center for the Study of New Religious Movements, were each helpful in giving advice and support with respect to the Spiritual Choices seminar. The National Endowment for the Humanities provided the seminar's funding. Paul Schwarz, administrative coordinator for the Center, handled the seminar's practical arrangements. Esalen's Michael Murphy gave useful advice on the composition of the seminar, encouraged several of his colleagues to participate, and with James Hickman provided the space in San Francisco where the meetings were held. Pam Blair typed the transcripts of the meetings as well as much of the manuscript of this book. Vicki Klubok typed the rest of the manuscript. Samuel Bercholz, the president of Shambhala Publications, provided helpful advice with respect to the plan of organization of this manuscript. We are grateful to Laurel Hulley for insightful readings of Part 1 and of the editorial commentaries, resulting in numerous enhancements of both style and substance, and for contributing key points to the discussion of the Gurdjieff work in Part 1. Louise Barrie gave useful advice for the revision of the Conclusion and in collaboration with Steven Barrie-Anthony generally provided aid and comfort to her husband, Dick Anthony, during the course of this project. William Eastman of the State University of New York Press and James Ellison of Paragon House Publishers gave helpful advice with respect to revision of the manuscript. Harvey Cox made useful suggestions concerning revision of the manuscript and strongly urged that we add the Conclusion. To our line editor, Alex Holzman, goes our appreciation for meticulously polishing the entire volume and for prompting valuable clarifications by helping us view it through a reader's eyes.

Finally, the reader may be curious to know how the work was apportioned among the three editors. The book began when Anthony dictated its plan of organization and the first draft of the present version of the Anthony typology in a long memo. The editors reached agreement on material to be included from among a selection provided by Anthony. Ecker extensively reorganized and edited the original draft of the typology article and added important elaborations of his own to the explication of the typology categories. The rest of the articles and interviews were edited by Ecker in collaboration with Wilber. Working from outlines and passages dictated by Anthony, Ecker produced a nearly final version of the Introduction and working drafts of the prefaces and commentaries for the articles and interviews, incorporating his own elaborations as well as suggestions from Wilber in the process. Anthony wrote the Conclusion, directed and participated in the final revision of the manuscript as a whole so as to ensure its continuity of argument and style, and provided the scholarly footnotes and references throughout.

D. A.
B. E.
K. W.

Introduction:

The Spiritual Seeker's Dilemma

Never in recorded history has there been so abundant an assemblage of systems promising psychological and spiritual inner development as is currently available in North America. To shop in today's psychospiritual "supermarket" is to encounter a confounding diversity of offerings. For the individual with a genuine hunger for truth, reality, spirit, soul, self, God, oneness, freedom, being, and meaning, the task of choosing among these offerings is intricate and subtle, and not without an element of peril.

It has been said that in the field of business, a person is well advised to risk very little; that in personal life and relationships it is necessary to risk more; and that in the field of spirituality, we have no choice but to risk everything. Discrimination in matters spiritual is, therefore, of paramount importance.

Academic and journalistic opinion regarding the proliferation in America of psychospiritual orientations and groups has divided primarily into two camps: critical opposition and uncritical, enthusiastic welcome. The critics view the development of the new religions as an expression of two pathological syndromes in present American society: narcissism on the one hand, and authoritarianism (or brainwashing) on the other, the latter being particularly at issue in the controversy over cults and deprogramming.[1] In contrast, the supporters[2] see the trend as heralding the spiritual rebirth of Western culture and a new age of love and wisdom in which masculine and feminine, mind and heart, inner and outer will be balanced as never before.[3]

The editors of this volume identify with neither the blanket reductionism of the opposition nor the wide-open ecumenism, eclecticism, and optimism of the supporters. We feel that the new cultural pluralism presents the individual with unprecedented opportunities as well as perils, and so calls for refined discriminations. How can we tell the excesses of the exploitative "master" from the unconventional behaviors of the genuine master who has transcended ordinary consciousness and sees and knows what others do not? What is spiritual authenticity and how can we distinguish it from shallow, pseudomystical rationalizations of self-interest? How can we recognize signs of psychological pathology in a group or leader, and so avoid involvements that maintain and even exaggerate members' psychopathology under the guise of higher development? The various spiritual and psychological systems and teachings differ in so many ways that it often seems impossible to make meaningful comparisons among them. How, then, can we orient ourselves to discriminate helpful from harmful involvements?

These are the key questions this volume addresses. In Part 1, Dick Anthony and Bruce Ecker present a systematic framework of concepts and criteria designed to help both the seeker and the observer come to terms with these questions and make the kinds of refined discriminations that are needed. An editorial commentary following each of the articles and interviews in the rest of the book demonstrates the use of the assessment framework from Part 1 over a broad range of approaches to inner transformation. Part 2 examines five widely differing psychospiritual involvements in some depth. In Part 3, four transpersonal psychologists suggest criteria for distinguishing genuine masters from charlatans and helpful from harmful involvements. The problem of ego inflation in the spiritual context also receives a close look. A final overview in Part 4 consists of an exchange of ideas between philosopher Jacob Needleman and the editors concerning major themes in the volume, followed by the Conclusion.

Simply stated, our point of view is that mysticism is valid—that human beings can and do attain direct, transcendent consciousness of ultimate reality—but that distortions of mysticism abound and can be dangerous. In describing how these distortions occur in specific groups and movements, we have necessarily drawn upon our own understanding of the texts of the mystical traditions as well as upon our direct experiences of sustained involvement in the mystical-spiritual orientations that we personally practice.* We are participant-observers in the new religions, the only approach we feel can adequately encompass both the theoretical and the experiential aspects of involvement—as is essential in devising any sound assessment framework. The challenge that faces the participant-observer in spiritual involvements is, of course, the need for what Soren Kierkegaard termed "mastered irony," the ability temporarily to step away from one's own cherished commitments in order to see other points of view and to assess one's own point of view *as if* it were not one's own.[4] While this is our intended *modus operandi* here, our biases and intuitive preferences do enter the picture. We have attempted to indicate explicitly those places where this occurs.

Spiritual Choices carries further the kind of inquiry that first emerged in 1970 with Jacob Needleman's book, *The New Religions*.[5] The task of discriminating between authentic and pseudo-mysticism is squarely in the province of transpersonal psychology, that young discipline which views human development as extending beyond the stage of the sturdy, rational ego into the states and stages described by the various mystical-spiritual traditions. However, transpersonal psychologists have been shy of tackling this task.[6] As Steven Hendlin[7] has noted, transpersonal psychology's commitment to oneness and to the social scientific validation of the transcendental dimension has made the field too uncritically welcoming of every approach that labels itself "spiritual." Transpersonal psychology has been especially reluctant to examine critically specific groups and forms of practice, fearing perhaps to infect the fledgling pluralistic spirit of the new age with the old age blight of competitive, judgmental oneupmanship. Such examination requires developing an atmosphere of open dialogue and ironic detachment in which rigorous, critical exchange serves the developing discrimination of all— a process that would strengthen, not weaken, the pluralistic base. It is in that spirit that we offer this volume. We raise key issues, not for the purpose of settling them definitively but as a stimulus to the reader's own process of inquiry.

Involvement with a group, spiritual master, or formal tradition is not, of course, the only way to nurture an active spirituality. Many people who are unaffiliated with such involvements are nevertheless deeply committed to spiritual inner development, spiritual values, and spiritual practice, while perhaps informally drawing upon and identifying with

*Dick Anthony and Bruce Ecker are disciples of Meher Baba; Ken Wilber is a student of Zen and Vajrayana Buddhism.

one or more traditions in a uniquely personal way. The value of this book should be no less for these people than for those who are interested in formal participation. The subtleties of spiritual discrimination are the same in either case. Both the free agent and the group member or disciple face the constant possibility of self-deception. Both have to distinguish between experiences, influences, and attitudes that foster transcendental awareness and those that only mimic doing so.

This book emerged from a seminar that took an unusual approach to the problem of discerning between helpful and harmful involvement in the new religions. The seminar was created by Dick Anthony as part of a visiting scholars program of the Center for the Study of New Religious Movements at the Graduate Theological Union in Berkeley, an ecumenical divinity school that conducts joint Ph.D. programs in religion with the University of California at Berkeley. The Center for the Study of New Religious Movements was established as a non-partisan clearinghouse for research and scholarship upon nontraditional contemporary religions and consciousness groups. Jacob Needleman was its overall director and Dick Anthony was for several years its research director.

During the year in which most of the interviews and articles in this volume were generated, the visiting scholars program[8] focused on spiritual authoritarianism and mental coercion (or brainwashing). Participants included: Nevitt Sanford, a clinical psychologist who co-authored *The Authoritarian Personality*, a landmark study of authoritarianism; Benetta Jules-Rosette, an anthropologist who is an expert on African religion; and Connie Jones, a sociologist of religion who has specialized in feminist religious concerns. As part of the year's activities Dick Anthony moderated a biweekly seminar that worked toward developing criteria to aid prospective members of new religious movements in discriminating legitimate spiritual authority from spiritual tyranny. The seminar secondarily focused on the issue of "reductionism," or the explaining away of religious significance when studied from secular psychological and social science perspectives.

To aid in the exploration of these themes, a group of transpersonal psychologists and theologians was invited to participate in the seminar, along with representatives of more reductionist perspectives.[9] The conventional approach to the social scientific study of religion is to contrast the supposedly rational-objective, debunking theoretical orientations of psychologists and sociologists on the one hand with the supposedly naïve and biased views of the proponents of religion or enlightenment on the other. By bringing exponents of orthodox, conventional viewpoints into sustained dialogue with exponents of transpersonal (non-reductionist) orientations, Anthony hoped to transcend this polarization.

During much of the year the seminar was structured around a two-hour group interview of a member or former member of a new religious group. At the end of the interview, the guest would leave and another hour was spent in discussion. At a certain point it became useful to interview people who were also members of the seminar. About two-thirds of the way through the year, Anthony conceived the idea of having the seminar interview its own participants as a way of making the implicit, reductionist assumptions in the format more explicit. When the seminar concentrated upon interviewing "outsiders" who were then asked to leave before their contributions were discussed, it had been natural for semiconscious reductionist assumptions to persist unquestioned; the person being interviewed had no chance to refute them. If the seminar were to interview its own participants, Anthony reasoned, such biases would be more exposed. Consequently, he volunteered to be the first interview subject under the new format. The interview, in which Anthony invites the seminar members to attempt a reductionistic interpretation of his experience in relation to Meher Baba, is included in Part 2.

At the end of the seminar, participants were asked to write essays on the criteria defining the nature and limits of valid religious authority.[10] Some of the papers by the transpersonal writers are included in *Spiritual Choices*. Entries in the book that were produced independently of the seminar are the interview of Jacob Needleman and the articles by Steven Tipton and Gary Rosenthal. All of the interview transcripts have been edited for continuity, clarity, and grammar.

The task of this book is difficult in a way that mirrors the difficulty faced by the seeker. Our subject matter goes beyond any kind of truth that can be uniformly and definitively formulated. We aim, rather, to promote a spirit of sharpened inquiry, discrimination, and critical awareness regarding guides and paths to higher consciousness. The new religions no longer merit attention merely by virtue of their countercultural contrast with an unsatisfying cultural mainstream, as in the 1960s. They must now stand up to more sophisticated scrutiny and prove their intrinsic value, and in this they differ widely. We draw upon both transpersonal psychology and the social scientific study of religion to provide frames of reference for perceiving and evaluating groups and leaders. The contributors to this volume have identified what, to them, seems important and relevant to the task—just as the reader has to do for himself or herself.

Let us consider a very simple but useful framework for classifying spiritual masters and teachers based on four conceivable levels of spiritual authority. The reader may or may not agree that all four types actually exist, but let us for the moment consider the following types of spiritual guides:

1. The false guide with mundane consciousness only, who poses as having transcendent consciousness or a divine connection. Such a guide may be sincere and self-deluded, or willfully deceitful and hypocritical.
2. The guide who has attained certain realms or levels of transcendence and so has extraordinary knowledge, powers, and personal qualities that clearly go beyond mundane, physical consciousness; but who has not yet gone beyond egotism and personal desire, and so is capable of self-delusion and maleficence, and of posing as being what he or she is not, either in self-delusion or willful deceit.
3. The advanced guide whose gnosis is beyond personal desire and self-delusion, and whose mind encompasses other minds, but who is not consciously one with infinite being.
4. The fully realized or fully enlightened guide who is consciously one with infinite being and with all beings and things, on all levels of consciousness, and is conscious of being the *true nature* of matter, energy, and mind.

The seeker's dilemma is that he or she is not capable of distinguishing *for certain* among the four kinds of guides, let alone among the different kinds of help they offer. The seeker is not qualified to make choices that must be made. It is impossible for one who is lodged in mundane consciousness to evaluate definitively the competence of any guide to transformation and transcendence, without having already attained to an equal degree of transcendence. No number of "objective" criteria for assessment can remove this "Catch-22" dilemma. Therefore the choice of a guide, path, or group will remain in some sense a subjective matter. Subjectivity, however, has many modes, from self-deluding emotionality to penetrating, illuminative intuition. Perhaps the first job of the seeker would best be to refine that primary guide, one's own subjectivity. There are, certainly, many ways of doing so in the post-1960s cultural milieu, for subjectivity has now become a socially valid basis for determining how to live.

Let us now conclude our Introduction with a look at the new cultural context in which Americans are experimenting with alternative religious systems, and finally with an examination of some serious problematic developments in several new religious groups that bring into focus the need to better discriminate between safe, genuine spiritual authority and dangerous imitators. The cultural setting is of more than academic interest because prevailing cultural attitudes and values heavily condition and distort our interpretation of spiritual systems. Here and throughout *Spiritual Choices* we alert the reader to specific distortions that the present cultural milieu tends to engender.

The Spiritual Search in Post-1960s America

There exists today both a popular and scholarly consensus that American society underwent an important revolution in values during the 1960s, a revolution whose most visible aspect was the hippie movement, and whose influence has quickly spread throughout the social order.[11] The main question is not *whether* this momentous change of American culture has occurred, but what constitutes its meaning and value. The controversy over this question is nowhere livelier than with regard to that aspect of the post-1960s milieu termed the new religions, the widespread mushrooming of all manner of native and imported psychospiritual doings.[12] While our task in this volume is to consider the spiritual efficacy, not the societal significance of the new religions, the cultural context is nevertheless important.

The crucial aspect of the cultural change for our purposes is the shift from objectivistic to subjectivistic ways of organizing experience. Within the pre-1960s mainstream American world-view, the meaning of individual life was objective, *i.e.*, it was externally determined. It inhered in one's completion of duties and attainment of status within the social world. Fulfillment and the value and meaning of life were determined not by reference to one's personal estimation or *experience* of value or meaning, but rather by reference to position within the status hierarchy. In the post-1960s period the reverse has become true for an increasing part of the population. More and more the meaning of human life is taken to be something that can be evaluated only by the person living the life, and this evaluation most often is based on an experiential sense of self-fulfillment or lack of self-fulfillment. The key-word of the new world-view is self; the key-word of the old world-view was status.[13]

It is beyond our scope here to go into the historical currents underlying the pre- and post-1960s attitudes in any detail. Suffice it to say that the pre-1960s attitudes expressed the objectivist philosophical positions of positivism and utilitarianism,[14] whose roots may be found in the Enlightenment of the late eighteenth century as well as in the veneration of a world-view based upon the assumptions of Newtonian physics, which pervaded that century. The subjectivist orientation of the post-

1960s period has roots in the counter-rational tradition that arose in coun-terpoint to the Enlightenment.[15] Amazingly, the 300-year-long hege-mony of objectivism in popular culture seems—to many observers—to have crumbled in the 1960s. This is not to say that objectivism has van-ished, but it now is widely regarded as only one frame of meaning among others by which a person can choose to live.

Prior to the 1960s, subjectivist orientations were at the cultural periphery and defined themselves to a great extent in a way that took for granted the domination of the utilitarian-positivist perspectives. The cul-tural significance of subjectivist orientations—in the arts, philosophy, and religion—was not necessarily their innate or inherent attractiveness, but rather their existence as alternatives to a mainstream that was viewed with dissatisfaction or contempt. For many people, personal identity was based on establishing a sharp contrast between one's own values and those of the mainstream. This contrast identity theme in large measure defined the counterculture. However, now that the objectivist stance has lost its pretension to exclusive validity, the various subjectivist orienta-tions must demonstrate their value in terms of intrinsic merits; it is no longer sufficient to be a mere alternative to the corrupt central tendency of objectivism. Since the 1960s, it has become widely recognized by par-ticipants in both transpersonal therapies and non-mainstream religions that dangers exist, that one must not simply assume that life will become a utopia by rejection of the positivist orientation and the affirmation of a subjectivist one. Some sort of discrimination among alternatives within the subjectivist world-view is desirable and needed.

As a specific example of how the cultural change has altered attitudes and colors our view of spiritual involvement, let us consider the partic-ular issue of *authority*. Until recently *paternalism* was the dominant style of authority in Western industrialized countries.[16] Paternalism operates within the success ethic, a framework in which one's position in the sta-tus system is taken as indicative of one's degree of moral virtue. Individ-uals grant authority to people who are higher up in the system's hierar-chy. Because they assume that the attitude of higher-ups toward those lower in status is benevolent, they regard higher-ups as similar to benev-olent fathers to whom obedience is owed and from whom, if they are obedient, will come benevolent attention to their well-being. This hier-archical status system is objective in the sense that it operates according to well-defined criteria, known to all concerned, which state who has authority relative to whom, and who is, and who is not, owed obedience by whom.

In contrast to the scheme of paternalist authority, *autonomous* authority develops within a subjectivist or existential value system. Here it is assumed that people generate their own sense of the meaning of things. Objective authority cannot exist in such a value system since meaning has become subjective. An implicit assumption about what is meaningful does, however, inform this framework: that it is meaningful to find meaning, to create and sustain a sense of the meaningfulness of one's own existence. And so people come to value not their position within the status system, but their capacity to find meaning in life and to give their own style of being in the world integrity and internal coherence. The social status system is now based upon shifting impressions of the other's holistic integrity. A key indicator of that holistic integrity is a person's capacity to be self-sufficient—not to need or be dependent upon other people to tell one the meaning of things, but rather to find meanings within one's own holistic, inner process. The bottom line is that people gain authority in their interactions with others to the extent that they seem autonomous and free from the need for other people.

The shift from paternalistic to autonomous authority has been occurring for a long time, first in artistic and intellectual circles, followed by dissemination into the popular value system in ever-widening circles, until finally, in the 1960s, there came a critical transition, and what had been the perspective of small subcultures became a mass perspective, and continues to be so. Spiritual seeking in the new religions occurs within the context of this societal shift from paternalistic to autonomous authority, and in many groups the seeking is largely a search for that capacity to find meaning autonomously, within one's own experience, rather than having meaning conferred externally.

Yet in practice autonomous authority is often extremely shallow and based upon nothing more than one's choice to act as if one had it. In its shallow versions, the striving for autonomous authority involves group members in a game of continuous oneupmanship, with each individual trying to appear less needy and impressively to have "gotten one's act together." This leads to a sense of isolation and a feeling that people cannot be open and honest about their uncertainties, human frailties, emotional needs, and woes—in short, about their present state of development, with all its limitations. People need some way of relating to a source of knowing that goes beyond what they already possess, and they need to be open about that need. The issue then becomes how people can admit to having that healthy need and seek help without opening themselves up to manipulation and exploitation by those who are merely pretending to have achieved genuine autonomous authority. In other words, the seeker's dilemma is how to continue to develop autonomous authority *and* to get help from someone who has a greater degree of truly autonomous authority than does the seeker. The seeker has to sail between the Scylla of groups in which the search for autonomous authority is believed futile and is therefore relinquished in favor of group identity and submission to paternalistic authoritarianism, and the Charybdis of groups in which members are educated in the *simulation* of real autonomy, generating not autonomy but aloofness, atomistic individualism, and existential isolation. How does a seeker recognize and search out assistance from someone who has become truly autonomous by realizing his or her own ultimate self or being? For that is the state of true, radical autonomy, which achieves both independence and benevolence toward the seeker without paternalism, without requiring the seeker to define himself as "one-down" in order to merit the helping relationship. The authentic spiritual master supports the seeker's development toward attaining the same real autonomy the master enjoys. Our shifting cultural images of autonomy, however, more often than not are shallow caricatures that fail to have any vital relation to this true autonomy. Compared to these caricatures, the process of attaining genuine autonomy with the help of an authentic spiritual master can *seem* to head in quite the wrong direction.[17]

The cultural transition from positivist-objectivist-collectivist ways of determining the meanings of things to holist-subjectivist-individualist ways involves an epistemological revolution, a qualitative change in how we know. The new, epistemologically individualist world-view plus the new, spiritually pluralistic environment have produced a new salvational dilemma, namely, that of finding one's own spiritual path, subjectivistically, from amongst a wide range of psychospiritual systems, strategies, and personalities.

The new salvational dilemma has been put into bold relief by a steady sequence of problematic developments—first the rise of psychedelic utopianism with its mistaken reliance on hallucinogenic drugs to produce a personal and social world of love and freedom; then the dramatic eruption of leadership pathology in groups such as the San Francisco Psychosynthesis group, Synanon, and the People's Temple; plus ongoing controversies over the methods of *est*, Scientology, Reverend Moon, Guru Maharaji, and Bhagwan Shree Rajneesh, to name a few. The distinctive problems of the epistemologically individualist world-view have emerged in a wide range of groups, some of which have been particularly problematic or controversial. We next review these cases, which together form the immediate background and stimulus for this book.

THE PEOPLE'S TEMPLE

By far the most disastrous of the problematic developments occurred in Jonestown, Guyana, in 1978, when Jim Jones brought years of increasingly bizarre, authoritarian abuse to a horrible crescendo with the mass suicide-murder of approximately 900 of his followers. Jones's personal magnetism and tremendous energy had, for many years, a convincingly altruistic, humanitarian quality. His social and religious idealism and his responsiveness to community and individual needs were powerfully inspiring to many. It is because the People's Temple had seemed such a positive force that the tragedy assumed broad significance for all of the new religions and made *spiritual tyranny* a central concern of transpersonal psychologists. Such spiritual tyranny now seemed to constitute a far greater danger because it was more subtle and insidious than had previously been assumed. Though Esalen Institute had earlier sponsored a conference on spiritual tyranny with transpersonal psychologists in attendance, it was the Jonestown tragedy that made the transpersonal community take seriously the perils of the new religions, including groups based on transpersonal ideals.

The uniqueness of the People's Temple may have been the degree to which members cut themselves off from social, emotional, and physical resources outside the group. They found themselves in a torrid, concentration-camp environment, surrounded by the Guyana jungle. Malnutrition, disease, and mandatory labor left them physically exhausted, and psychological submission to Jones left them emotionally exhausted as well. As a result of accepting Jones's sociopolitical ideology, they were deeply alienated from and fearful of the larger American society they had left. With the murder of a visiting congressman by Jones's lieutenants, the imminent doom of the group seemed a foregone conclusion, and Jones's longstanding agenda of a "noble death" seemed preferable to the nightmare of readjusting to life without the group. To "die with dignity," in Jones's words, was a "revolutionary act" that symbolically affirmed their eternal affiliation with the Good and allowed them to elude the collapse of their meaning system and sense of group identity.

SYNANON

Founded in 1958 by Charles E. (Chuck) Dederich, Synanon has gone through three major phases with distinctly different purposes.* Until 1967 it was a residential rehabilitation facility for drug addicts, with therapy centered around an intensive group encounter session that came to be known as the "Synanon game." In the traditional, most common form

---

*This description of the evolution of Synanon is compiled from two sources, personal accounts of former members—for example, William Olin, *Escape From Utopia: My Ten Years in Synanon* (Santa Cruz, CA: Unity Press, 1980)—and United States government reports associated with Civil Action No. 82-2303 of the U.S. District Court for the District of Columbia. The editors make no independent claims for the accuracy of these reports and sketch them here only to show the sort of issues raised about Synanon within the climate of opinion in which our seminar occurred.

of the game, group members verbally attacked each of the players in turn, focusing on personal faults and failures to conform to Synanon norms and regulations. Addicts who completed the rehabilitation program were returned to the outside world.

In 1966 Synanon began to operate "game clubs" for nonresidents and non-drug abusers who came to a Synanon facility to be in the Synanon game. There were five Synanon houses (three in California, one each in New York and Detroit) which, by 1967, had a total of 3,400 game club members, according to Synanon claims.

Beginning in 1967 Synanon reoriented its residential facilities away from drug rehabilitation and became a cradle-to-grave utopian commune. The program to return addicts to the outside world was abolished, and residents were encouraged to stay and work toward establishing the utopian Synanon vision. The main facility was relocated from urban Santa Monica to a 3,300-acre property in rural Marin County, north of San Francisco. Recruitment concentrated on middle-class professionals who had no addiction problems and were attracted to Synanon's values and communal lifestyle. Synanon stood for nonviolence, and to some members embodied the best elements of all the religions. It described itself as an alternative to the social unrest of American society at large, and also as a social revolution that would change the larger society.

Until about 1971, according to ex-members, there was a great deal of love, laughter, and personal growth. For many members Dederich had renewed their sense of self-worth as well as their social and moral inspiration, and so had won their unquestioning loyalty and devotion. He was regarded as infallible. Members would do anything asked of them so that Dederich would not withdraw his love. By 1973 Synanon had developed into a wealthy, fully self-contained, self-supporting commune, including a private school system. Its reported net income for 1972 alone was $5.4 million, a result of a number of large business operations.

But as early as 1972, it began to appear to some members that Dederich's decisions were clearly not in the followers' best interests. He began major experiments in social reorganization in 1973, such as separating parents from their children at the age of six months and rearing children in dormitory settings. Then, at Dederich's initiative, the board of directors voted unanimously in 1974 to proclaim Synanon a religion. According to its critics, disaffected ex-members, and a United States government report, Synanon's posture now became increasingly paramilitary, in contrast to its previous adherence to the principle of absolute non-violence. Dederich and other Synanon executives began explicitly to encourage physical violence against Synanon's "enemies." A partial listing of the extensive allegations in the federal report[18] includes: a large number of kidnappings, vicious beatings at gunpoint, and an attempted murder (the highly publicized incident in which a rattlesnake placed in his mailbox bit an attorney)[19]; the formation of the Synanon Imperial Marines and Synanon National Guard,[20] including the development of a weapons arsenal; the waging of a "holy war" against "enemies" and "the ungodly" (mainly attorneys, the media, and any government official or agency that criticized or opposed Synanon) through massive lawsuits, harassment, threats of violence, and actual violent acts. The Synanon leadership also is alleged to have manipulated members in extreme ways, including Dederich's 1976 requirement of "vows of childlessness," involving abortions for all pregnant women and vasectomies for all men in Synanon, and Dederich's October 1977 requirement that all marriages and couple relationships in Synanon were to be dissolved immediately, with new partners to be arranged under the direction and approval of Synanon. Another charge focuses on the allegedly illegal disbursement of $6.8 million from Synanon accounts to the few Synanon elite. Given these reports Synanon appears to have become by small increments a group whose practices were volatile, violent, and exploitative.

SCIENTOLOGY

The evolution of L. Ron Hubbard's Scientology movement has in certain respects been similar to that of Dederich's Synanon.* Both organizations initially offered innovative psychotherapy techniques, then were transformed into a religion under the increasingly authoritarian control of the charismatic founder, and entered into escalating conflict with the wider society. The resemblance between the two groups stops there, however. It does not extend to particulars of ideology and practice.

Hubbard's movement formally began in 1950 as Dianetics, an approach to psychotherapy arguing that optimal human functioning and health are prevented by "engrams," unconscious reactive patterns generated in moments of trauma. An engram includes all of the emotions, thoughts, and sensory perceptions that occur at the time of the traumatic event. The psychotherapeutic process of consciously cancelling engrams

---

*This sketch of Scientology is drawn from a study that is widely considered to be a reliable, scholarly account of the movement: Roy Wallis, *The Road to Total Freedom: A Sociological Analysis of Scientology* (London: Heineman Educational, 1976). Again, as with our report of the allegations concerning Synanon, we make no independent claims for the accuracy of this account, but are sketching it here merely to indicate the sort of issues raised about Scientology within the climate of opinion in which our seminar occurred.

is termed "auditing," and the desired state in which one's entire lifetime of engrams has been disarmed is termed "clear."

Hubbard's previous work writing science fiction gave him access to an extensive network of readers, and within about a year of announcing the formation of Dianetics, there were practicing autonomous groups in the United States and Britain. These groups accorded Hubbard no permanent claim to authority, and regarded themselves as competent to develop the theory and practice of Dianetics and to challenge Hubbard's views and actions. When the number of people involved in Dianetics began to drop considerably, Hubbard inaugurated Scientology, a new gnosis that provided a transcendental legitimation for his authority. Hubbard claimed he had gained access to a transcendental realm never before revealed, and now offered a knowledge that would enable human beings consciously to regain their spiritual true nature, as never before on earth. This state of Total Freedom is attainable by cancelling the engrams generated not only in this life, but all previous lives. Neither Gautama Buddha nor Jesus Christ had reached this state, according to Hubbard. Rather, "they were just a shade above clear."[21]

With the introduction of Scientology, Hubbard began to organize his following as a congregation responsive to his charismatic authority, subordinating other potential leaders and expelling those who refused to accept his sole authority. The transition to Scientology (which subsumed and retained Dianetics) occurred at a time when the movement was internally endangered by defection and schism, and externally attacked by the press, medical organizations, and governments. Hubbard's response to these difficulties was to assert increasingly authoritarian control within his movement and increasingly hostile and aggressive measures against the surrounding society. Severe actions against Scientology by the American, British, and Australian governments convinced Hubbard that a major conspiracy was determined to render his organization defunct. In Australia for example, a formal government report virulently attacked Scientology, and in the United States the Food and Drug Administration carried out a raid for the purpose of seizing Hubbard's "E-meters," electronic devices used in the process of auditing. (The introduction of E-meters had made auditing a less subjective and intuitive affair, and had changed it from an interpersonal technique requiring diffuse professional skills to an objective, measurable process that almost anyone could learn.)

Numerous individuals and organizations believed by Scientologists to be actively hostile to the movement became the victims of anonymous or pseudonymous defamations (often in the form of defamatory telephone calls to employers, lenders, neighbors), theft of documents, spying, and forgery. For some time it was Scientology's practice to declare certain individuals "fair game." Totalitarian-like internal control measures included "disconnection," or the ordering of a member to sever relations with family members, their spouse, friends, etc., and "security checking," a mandatory confessional procedure.

By 1968 governmental actions against Scientology, including bans in Australia, had become so extensive that a multinational ban seemed an imminent possibility. In November 1968 the Church of Scientology issued a *Code of Reform*, described as a response to public criticisms, which cancelled the Fair Game list, disconnections, and security checking as a form of confession. This more-or-less ended the period of escalating conflict. However, the movement's basic structure retains some totalitarian features, according to Wallis[22]: the leadership seeks not merely to make the theory and practice of Scientology available as a service, but to maximize the commitment of large numbers of members who see their own salvation closely linked with the achievement of organizational ends specified by the leadership. Members are not organized communally, but rather face the authority structure of the movement as isolated individuals. The majority of Scientologists are exposed and committed only to the movement's propaganda representations, and remain unaware of the inner leadership's purposes and power-seeking orientation.

PSYCHOSYNTHESIS

Beginning in the early 1970s, a group coalesced in San Francisco around psychosynthesis, a psychological system first formulated by Robert Assagioli in 1910.* Assagioli was dissatisfied with Freud's system, in

---

*This sketch of the evolution of the San Francisco psychosynthesis group is based largely upon an interview with two former members conducted by the Center for the Study of New Religious Movements seminar. The two former members continue to use psychosynthesis as a therapeutic orientation and believe it to be valuable for that purpose. From their point of view the problems that developed in the San Francisco psychosynthesis group are sociological ones to which any closely knit group of psychotherapeutic professionals might be prone unless specific precautions are taken; excellent psychological and transpersonal theory (which they believe psychosynthesis to have) is by itself not a sufficient safeguard. For a similar argument with respect to psychoanalytic societies see Robert Lifton, *Thought Reform and the Psychology of Totalism* (New York: W. W. Norton, 1969), Chapter 23, in which Lifton, a prominent psychoanalyst, warns against totalistic or authoritarian tendencies that sometimes creep into psychoanalytic professional organizations unless safeguards against them are consciously maintained.

part because of its apparent failure to recognize man's higher or spiritual aspects. Psychosynthesis does this, although Assagioli explicitly stated that his system is not a religion. The San Francisco psychosynthesis group was comprised largely of highly educated professionals in psychology, education, medicine, and law. In gradual, almost imperceptible increments over a period of years, this sophisticated group and its leader evolved from wholesome dedication to a psychology that affirmed the best in people into a highly isolated, authoritarian, messianic, fear-driven cult.

The leader, a transpersonal psychologist whom we shall call "Smith,"[23] had spent more time studying with Assagioli than had any others, but to a degree repudiated him after his death in 1974. There followed a slow buildup among group members of a very coherent, airtight, paranoid world-view, prescribed by Smith, who could generate compelling experiences of love and intimacy at the same time as he intensified his methods of indoctrination and authoritarian control of group members. Members had all had personal experience of psychosynthesis as an effective, affirmative system for facilitating inner growth, which evidently provided some plausibility both for Smith's strong sense of mission and for the group's shared sense of being a chosen few who were in a unique position to help the world. The desire to make the world a better place by putting spiritual values into effective practice was very strong among group members.

Smith spoke as though he had full knowledge of members' past lives. He asserted that the group had been together as a group many times before. Members' individual spiritual fates were inseparably linked to the group, as their souls were part of the group soul. Later Smith introduced the theme of the existence of absolute evil in the world. Thereafter, members' "evil parts" and "bad energy" were under endless inquisition. Any deviation from Smith's authority meant that one was feeding one's evil part, and therefore getting cut off from one's soul. To leave the group meant damnation.

Members who were too consistently dominated by their evil part were put in quarantine, sometimes for months, in which they were allowed contact only with Smith and his four or five directors. Smith's main technique for individual indoctrination was the "processing session," in which he would subject the member to up to eight hours of emotional catharsis and visualization programming in order to bring about the feelings, attitudes, and perceptions that he wanted to instill. Often other members would be watching; sometimes it was done over the telephone.

Relationships between spouses within the group and with parents and other family outside the group were severed in order to break off evil influences. Finally there was to be no contact at all outside the group: evil influences would pull them from the path. Within the group, the growing, fearful preoccupation with the evil part in everyone led to panoramic mutual mistrust, with each member seeing all others as predominantly evil. Members immediately reported each other's infractions, and would do anything to redeem themselves and regain Smith's love once they had been identified as dominated by their evil part. Smith kept total control by requiring that members submit every aspect of their lives for approval by himself and his directors (who would periodically be reshuffled, having themselves manifested bad energy).

Secret contact with friends or relatives outside the group made it possible for one or two members, with great inner struggle, to break out beyond the wall of terror that had been erected. A chain reaction of defections and disclosures occurred in 1980, culminating in the dissolution of the group and the graduate school it had established. Smith and a group of about six others left the San Francisco area in secrecy.

THE UNIFICATION CHURCH

Reverend Sun Myung Moon's Unification church has been at the center of the "brainwashing" and deprogramming controversy. The anti-cult movement that developed in the 1960s and 1970s arose in response to the Unification church and a number of other groups which it claimed had in common various practices, such as authoritarian and manipulative leadership, communal and totalistic social organization, aggressive proselytizing, and systematic programs of indoctrination. The controversy over these groups hinges on the question of whether or not members are lured in against their will and become psychological slaves bereft of all capacity for independent choice and action. The anti-cult movement maintains that this is indeed the case; psychological and sociological research studies generally indicate otherwise.[24]

CHOGYAM TRUNGPA, RINPOCHE

Chogyam Trungpa is a Tibetan Buddhist spiritual master who was prepared from childhood to be the abbot of a number of monasteries there. In 1959 he fled the Chinese communist takeover of Tibet and in 1970 came to America, where he is now widely known. He is regarded by followers as an incarnation of an earlier master, the Trungpa Tulku, and continues Tibet's 1200-year-old Vajrayana Buddhist tradition, a Tantric tradition of "crazy wisdom," as Trungpa calls it.

Trungpa's spiritual authority is controversial for well-known reasons: sex with disciples (both men and women), hard drinking, and the following incident, reported by Peter Marin in the February 1979 issue of *Harper's* magazine. The incident occurred in the fall of 1975 at an annual retreat ordinarily open only to Trungpa's regular disciples: "A woman is stripped naked, apparently at Trungpa's joking command, and hoisted into the air by [Trungpa's] guards, and passed around—presumably in fun, though the woman does not think so." Two special guests—a couple, and *not* regular disciples—have already retired to their room, wary from having heard rumors of sexual carrying-on at these occasions. Later Trungpa notices their absence and requires them to join the group. They refuse, and Trungpa, drunk, eventually orders their room broken into, through the window. This happens, and the man attacks the invaders with a broken bottle. He cuts several people, and after shouts and screams, realizes what he has done and stops fighting. The couple is brought before Trungpa. They refuse his request that they strip, and he orders his guards to strip them. They stand huddled together naked, and Trungpa seems satisfied. Others begin to strip, then many others. Trungpa says, "Let's dance," and the crowd does so. The couple returns to their room.

The next day, Trungpa meets with the couple and says that nothing like it will happen again. They decide to stay on. The man "explains later: They were, after all, about to receive the Tantric teachings, and he did not want to miss them."

Tantric strategies for achieving enlightenment involve sexual and emotional energies in ways that often offend Western morality. Numerous other Eastern masters who have been caught indulging mundane appetites are violating their own moral teachings. Trungpa's behaviors are not self-contradictory in this way. He claims that they are consistent with the Tantric tradition that, instead of resisting certain "base" impulses, one should utilize them as an avenue of higher spiritual growth. This approach makes it particularly challenging to distinguish between authentic and debauched, exploitative masters.

BHAGWAN SHREE RAJNEESH

The teaching of Rajneesh, an Indian with a mainly Western following, emphasizes the cathartic expression of accumulated, long-suppressed urges and emotions, particularly sexuality and aggression, as an avenue of transcendent liberation. The convergence of mystical and psychotherapeutic themes in Rajneesh's teaching attracted many human potential workers—encounter group leaders, bodywork practitioners, Esalen staff members—who went to Rajneesh's Poona, India ashram during the 1970s.

The conspicuous presence throughout Poona of high-libido, orange-garbed Rajneesh devotees—orange being the color traditionally worn in India by wandering ascetics and spiritual renunciates—proved too jarring and offensive to the local cultural sensibilities. Political pressures against Rajneesh grew even without public awareness of the physical violence that was occurring regularly as part of the catharsis work in ashram encounter groups. Participants were encouraged to act out their aggressive impulses, occasionally resulting in broken arms and legs. Richard Price, a co-founder of Esalen Institute who had practiced Buddhist meditation for many years and was a prominent Gestalt therapist and group leader, discovered the violence soon after he arrived in Poona in early 1978. Some of Price's account of what he witnessed has been published in an English journal:

> A woman who had her arm broken was repeatedly kicked. A young man twice hit a sixty year old woman in the face. And on and on. There were 18 fights in the first two days alone—then I stopped counting. I did prevent one young man from hitting a 61 year old man with his fist. Stopping him was strictly against the "rules".
>
> After the end of the "encounter" group a woman in the so-called "primal" group had her leg broken, a few days after the broken arm incident. . . . On inquiry many other incidents came to light—injuries physical, mental and spiritual.[25]

This account corroborates others published in 1978 in Germany, alleging broken ribs[26] and two separate incidents of a group leader promoting a vicious mood and getting the group to attack one member,[27] in one case a woman whose clothes were torn off and who was bloodied by blows and kicks.

After his return to the U.S., a number of letters went back and forth between Price and the person in charge of the Rajneesh encounter groups. The latter acknowledged the violence, but argued that any injury that could heal was not extreme, and that the violence was therapeutic. Nevertheless, the Rajneesh Foundation in Poona stated on March 18, 1979, "As of January this year specific instructions have been issued to all group leaders to no longer allow participants to use fighting as a means of discharging repressed emotions, or for any other purpose."

Uninhibited sexuality also has had a major part in Rajneesh's teaching, both in principle and practice. One devotee published a vivid account of orgiastic group sex in the Poona ashram.[28] A former devotee known to the editors reports periods in which devotees were urged to have sexual intercourse immediately with any person towards whom the desire arose. Lack of privacy was no obstacle; a couple would copulate freely in a room with others present.

With public pressure mounting against him, in June 1981 Rajneesh left India for the United States, where he again provoked civil opposition by purchasing a huge tract of land near a small town in Oregon and encouraging his large following to take up residence. Outnumbering local residents in town elections, devotees won key offices of the town government, threatening in effect to take over the town politically. Rajneesh's flamboyant style and his pronounced interest in wealth and luxury—such as a large fleet of Rolls Royce automobiles (the reported number of them grew from twenty-eight to over ninety during 1983–1985)—exacerbated the situation and weakened his plausibility as a spiritual figure in the eyes of many.[29] In September 1985 eight of the highest officials in Rajneesh's organization, including his personal secretary, abruptly absconded to Europe amidst charges of attempted murder, arson, and diverting tens of millions of dollars to Swiss bank accounts. Rajneesh described them as "turning a meditation camp into a concentration camp" and claimed that the alleged activities occurred totally without his awareness. Then, on October 28, 1985 he was apparently attempting to leave the USA for Bermuda to avoid prosecution for violating immigration laws when federal agents arrested him. Plea bargaining led to the return of Rajneesh to India seventeen days later.

TRANSCENDENTAL MEDITATION (TM)

One of the age-old, time-honored forms of meditation in the East is *mantra* meditation, the mental repetition of a special syllable or syllables—the mantra—that resonantly attunes the individual mind to a particular domain or plane of transcendental existence. Transcendental Meditation (TM) is a form of mantra meditation that has been successfully popularized and commercialized in the West since the 1960s by the Maharishi Mahesh Yogi, an Indian guru. The Maharishi and his meditation technique have come to seem problematic in several ways:

1. The Beatles' disillusionment with the Maharishi during their stay with him in India in 1968 involved allegations that Maharishi had sex with a visiting American student.
2. Many serious students of Eastern meditation regard the TM technique as a trivialization of authentic mantra meditation. They argue

that by being prepackaged and made easy enough for an international staff to quickly teach to the paying public, the technique necessarily is made superficial. Authentic meditation practice requires direct, long-term contact with a realized master who can competently and safely guide the individual practitioner's unique, idiosyncratic inner development. Critics also charge that TM has used Harvard research findings on the physical effects of TM as corroboration of its transcendental, transphysical efficacy. This, they charge, is a confusion of two separate issues. Finally, they note that TM presents itself as an individually customized process, yet there are only a small number of mantras that are given to the many thousands of practitioners.

3. There is much anecdotal evidence in the psychotherapeutic community that TM practice can bring repressed material into awareness and create considerable mental and emotional difficulties which TM trainers are unable to resolve with the standardized platitudes that they often use. In such cases it is common for TM practitioners to break off their involvement and seek psychotherapy. This criticism ties in with the argument that TM fails to provide direct guidance by a master who is competent to guide the student's inner development.

4. In the late 1970s, TM advertisements and training programs began to offer instruction in developing *siddhis* (pronounced sid'-hees), which are occult powers such as levitation and flying. All the major systems of mystical spirituality agree that such powers do exist, but maintain they have nothing to do with attaining gnosis or realization of ultimate spiritual reality. For a group to appeal to new members on the basis of their attraction to such occult powers signals a sharp divergence from spiritual values. Although the TM movement's nominal metaphysical position is that the *siddhis* are merely a byproduct of TM meditation and serve as indicators of progress, not as an end in themselves, why, then, do they spotlight them? The focus on *siddhis* began after mass interest in TM began to decline, which leads some observers to speculate that the organization attempted to renew TM's mass appeal by shifting its image from a human potential, "optimum health" sort of involvement to a more transpersonal one, in the direction of magic and occultism.

5. Lastly, the TM organization seems to hold a kind of grand vision of TM as a world force. This vision contains theocratic overtones, synthesizing governmental, educational, and transcendental interests. However benign such a vision may be, the "world mission" theme

represents a potential source of volatility and tyranny in any group. Some ex-members of the TM organization complain of a totalistic or cultist trend, with some workers developing lifestyles that are immersed in the TM world and cut off from the larger society.

It was with these groups and events in mind that the seminar at the Center for the Study of New Religious Movements studied the problem of recognizing authentic, trustworthy spiritual authority. Since the seminar ended in 1981, additional allegations and controversies have developed over the conduct of other highly regarded spiritual masters, most notably Baba Muktananda, the Hindu master of the Siddha Yoga path who had a large American following before his death in 1982; Richard Baker, until 1984 abbot and *roshi* (Zen master) of the San Francisco Zen Center; and Da Free John, the American-born "Adept" who does not exclusively identify himself, his teachings or his following of over 1,000 devotees with any single spiritual tradition.

The Winter 1983 edition of the magazine *CoEvolution Quarterly* featured articles documenting the controversies surrounding the first two men. Allegations against Muktananda first became widely known in 1981 when one of his American swamis sent a letter to numerous professors, psychologists, schools, and centers (including the Center for the Study of New Religious Movements). Two other Americans who had for many years been in Muktananda's inner circles left him in late 1980, and later, after Muktananda's passing, began publicly to disclose what they knew. The central charge against Muktananda is that he regularly had sex with female disciples in their teens and early twenties. Two of these young women have confirmed the allegations, in each case describing their sexual encounters with Muktananda as a molestation or even rape. Because Muktananda's spiritual teaching strongly emphasized celibacy, some people in the transpersonal community find the apparent hypocrisy more than the master's apparent promiscuity *per se* most objectionable. Other allegations include Muktananda's encouragement of physical violence and terror tactics, and financial chicanery involving millions of dollars in Swiss bank accounts.

Those in Muktananda's inner circles who have remained loyal to him and to his successors claim to have no personal knowledge of his sexual habits. They do not deny the possibility of sexual relations with devotees. Even if this did occur, it is acceptable, in their view, because Muktananda as a transcendentally enlightened master was beyond considerations of good and evil; it is both futile and inappropriate for the unenlightened devotee to judge his actions. Any sexual contact with devotees could only have benefitted them. An opinion sometimes heard among outside observers in the transpersonal community is that the revelations mean Muktananda clearly did not have perfect enlightenment, but he did such a great deal of good in his lifetime that his good reputation should not be completely dismissed due to the excesses of his latter years. Other opinions are considerably harsher. Certainly this case shows that in making spiritual choices there is a critical need for criteria that can penetrate good reputations and alert the seeker to hidden exploitation.

At the San Francisco Zen Center, the problems that came to a head in 1983 likewise involve a number of master-disciple sexual affairs, as well as a complex pattern of alleged misuses of authority and charisma, both psychologically and financially.

The controversy over Da Free John—who claims to have attained full realization of ultimate spiritual reality—came to public attention in April 1985 when major San Francisco newspapers gave front-page coverage to a female devotee's $5 million lawsuit against him. The suit alleges that the devotee, who was a member of Da Free John's community from 1976 to 1984, was "forced to consume alcohol . . . and was required to partake in various sexual acts commanded by 'the Master'"; that she was the victim of a "plan and scheme to unlawfully hold and imprison" her for eight days on Da Free John's Fiji island in March 1984; that she was beaten "with the support and backing" of other community members, in particular being "violently struck" by her husband "many times over a prolonged period of time, concluding in June 1984."[30]

Representatives of Da Free John's community deny these charges, while acknowledging that from 1974 until 1976 their master involved devotees "in an experiment of intense experiencing of both worldly pleasures and spiritual joys."[31] These worldly pleasures admittedly included sexual experimentation, alcohol consumption, and wild parties—activities that ended in 1976, according to official accounts. However, a number of other former devotees claim first-hand knowledge that such activities and extravagant lifestyles continued in Da Free John's inner circle until at least 1983. According to these claims, in 1983 Da Free John was regularly having devotees perform sexual acts in front of him.[32,33] During a two-month period in 1976, Da Free John allegedly had movie cameras set up in a basement room and ordered devotees to be filmed in sexual acts. "I saw the women crying hysterically afterwards," says one woman who claims to have been one of Da Free John's "wives" at the time, and who says also that she saw his wife, Nina, come out of his house with a large patch of hair ripped out of her head, and a black eye.[34]

Among the approximately forty devotees who currently (1985) live with Da Free John in the South Pacific on a Fiji island, are nine female devotees whom the disaffected former members describe as his "wives."

Community representatives acknowledge only that Da Free John has a "certain relationship with nine women."[35] The husband of the woman filing the lawsuit has stated that there is "nothing orgiastic" about Da Free John's relationship with these women, and that "It's an absolute love commitment, a stable situation." Regarding his wife's charge that he sexually assaulted her at Da Free John's command, he maintains that the master "never commanded either of us to do anything."[36]

Spokespersons of Da Free John's community explain that his teachings are similar to the "crazy wisdom" traditions of Tibetan Buddhism, in which a spiritual teacher may trick and humiliate followers for their spiritual growth.[37] "From our point of view, Da Free John is an enlightened person, which means he is free of the conventional neurosis of ordinary people and lives in a continuous condition of communion with the Living God. . . . His marriage is unconventional and his personal life is unconventional."[38] " . . . he is no mere charismatic leader who is blindly followed . . . Our way of life encompasses an entirely affirmative, nonrepressive attitude toward work, sexuality, body, and mind. Thus, it embodies active participation in society. . . . Everyone is fully expected to live a normal, productive life and to maintain loving relationships with family and friends."[39]

The editors of this book agree that it remains to be seen where the uprush of novel religiosity in America will lead. How much of the present interest stems from real spiritual hunger—the deep yearning and love for truth, ultimate being, God—and how much from psychological "deficiency motivation" or the essentially secular desire for a more comfortable life? How much, indeed, are narcissism or authoritarian submissiveness motivating our interest and distorting our judgment? Can we tell the pearl from the glass bead? Or will we miss the real item, or misuse it, to experience in years hence a backlash of cynicism against things spiritual? A new, holistic paradigm indeed seems to be emerging, but will it be built out of real or pseudo-resolutions of our human dilemmas? The tendency to subtly twist and usurp spiritual teachings for unspiritual ends is so universal that these distortions can reconstitute themselves in any human culture, even a culture dominated by transpersonal ideals.

If transpersonal psychology, as a field of useful scholarship that addresses the transcendental dimension of man, is going to progress—given that the culture as a whole has shifted from an objectivist to a pluralistically subjectivist situation—then the transpersonal ideas must not merely attract people away from conventional roles and mindsets, but actually help people discriminate between different forms of subjectivist or mystical involvements and identities. The issues raised by the critiques of narcissism and cultic authoritarianism seem to be the perfect proving ground for the transpersonal field. If it can help people to discriminate between helpful and less-than-helpful involvements, either in therapy or in spiritual groups, then transpersonal psychology will have proven itself.

Our basic viewpoint—that mysticism is valid, though usually and sometimes dangerously distorted—is not original. A number of contemporary scholars, such as Jacob Needleman,[40] Robert Ornstein,[41] and Steven M. Tipton[42] share this viewpoint and have offered their own criteria for recognizing what is and what is not an authentic approach to spiritual transformation and higher consciousness. They all contribute, as we hope the present volume will, to the sharpening of the new spiritual sensibilities in North America.

As Toynbee[43] and others have described, the disintegration of a civilization tends to be accompanied by a great influx of "seeds," new forms of religion which in effect compete to lead cultural renewal; and out of this competition there arises some system that slowly becomes the framework for the next cultural epoch. In Augustinian Rome, for example, Christianity was just one of many competing mystery cults. It eventually became the basis for the Christian civilization of the Middle Ages, a civilization which now seems to be in a final period of decline similar to that of Augustinian Rome. A great deal may be at stake in how America cultivates the abundance of spiritual seeds that have been sown in its soil.

Notes

1. Works that criticize most new religions as being narcissistic and/or authoritarian include Christopher Lasch, "The Narcissist Society," *New York Review of Books*, Sept. 30, 1976, pp. 5–12; Edwin Schur, *The Awareness Trap: Self-Absorption Instead of Social Change* (Chicago: Quadrangle, 1976); Ann Braden Johnson, "A Temple of Last Resorts: Youth and Shared Narcissism," in Marie Coleman Nelson (ed.), *The Narcissistic Condition: A Fact of Our Lives and Times* (New York: Human Sciences, 1977); Tom Wolfe, "The Me Decade and the Third Great Awakening," in *Mauve Gloves & Madmen, Clutter & Vine* (New York: Bantam, 1977); Peter Marin, "The New Narcissism: The Trouble with the Human Potential Movement," *Harpers, 251,* 1505 (Oct. 1975), pp. 45–56; and Nathan Adler, *The Underground Stream: New Life Styles and the Antinomian Personality* (New York: Harper/Torchbook, 1972).

Works that criticize most new religions as being "cults" that practice "brainwashing" include Margaret Singer, "Coming Out of the Cults," *Psychology Today*, 12: 8, 72–82; Richard Delgado, "Religious Totalism," *University of Southern California Law Review*, 15: 1, 1–99 (1977); and John Clark, "Cults," *Journal of the American Medical Association*, 242: 3, 279–281 (1978).

For a general survey of the scholarly literature on brainwashing in the new religions see Dick Anthony, "The Fact Pattern Behind the Deprogramming Controversy," *New York University Review of Law and Social Change*, 9, Spring 1980. Thomas L. Robbins and Dick Anthony, in "The Limits of 'Coercive Persuasion' as an Explanation for Conversion to New Religious Movements," *Journal of Political Psychology*, Summer 1980, critique the brainwashing explanation of conversion to cults.

2. See, for example, Marilyn Ferguson, *The Aquarian Conspiracy: Personal and Social Transformation in the 1980s* (Los Angeles: J. P. Tarcher, 1981); Theodore Roszak, *The Making of a Counter Culture: Reflections on the Technocratic Society and its Youthful Opposition* (Garden City, NY: Doubleday/Anchor, 1969); and Charles A. Reich, *The Greening of America* (New York: Random House, 1970).

3. For an overview of adulatory versus critical literature on the new religions see Thomas Robbins and Dick Anthony, "New Religious Movements and the Social System: Integration, Disintegration or Transformation," *The Annual Review of the Social Sciences of Religion*, vol. II, 1978, 1–25.

4. Søren Kierkegaard, *The Concept of Irony* (1841) (Bloomington: Indiana University Press, 1965).

5. Jacob Needleman, *The New Religions* (New York: Doubleday & Co., 1970).

6. The major exception has been the work of Ken Wilber, whose "Pre/Trans Fallacy" initiated the "critical movement" in transpersonal psychology. See *Eye to Eye* (Garden City, NY: Anchor/Doubleday, 1983) and *A Sociable God* (New York: McGraw-Hill, 1983). For an amusing yet substantive approach by a lay author, see Rick M. Chapman, *How to Choose a Guru* (Berkeley: White Horse, 1981) first published in 1973 by Harper & Row.

7. Steven J. Hendlin, "Pernicious Oneness," *J. Humanistic Psych.*, 23, 61–81, Summer 1983.

8. Supported by a grant from the National Endowment for the Humanities.

9. Seminar members were Dick Anthony, Arthur Deikman, Etta Deikman, James Fadiman, Bruce Fireman, Durwood Foster, Robert Frager, Arthur Hastings, Connie Jones, Bennetta Jules-Rosette, Michael Murphy, Claudio Naranjo, Jacob Needleman, Lewis Rambo, Paul Reisman, Nevitt San-

ford, Paul Schwartz, Ted Stein, Frances Vaughan, John Welwood, Ken Wilber, and Philip Zimbardo.

10. These essays were presented at a national conference on the topic of legitimate versus illegitimate religious authority in new religious movements, which was conducted by the Center for the Study of New Religious Movements in June of 1981. (The conference was funded by the Rockefeller Foundation.)

11. Survey research studies that document the shift in American values since the 1960s include: Daniel Yankelovich, *New Rules: Searching for Self-Fulfillment in a World Turned Upside Down* (New York: Random House, 1981); *The Connecticut Mutual Life Report* (Hartford: Connecticut Mutual Life Insurance Co., 1981); Robert Wuthnow, *The Consciousness Reformation* (Berkeley: University of California, 1976); and Charles Glock and Thomas Piazza, "Exploring Reality Structures," in Thomas Robbins and Dick Anthony (eds.), *In Gods We Trust: New Patterns of Religious Pluralism in America* (New Brunswick, NJ: Transaction, 1981).

Interestingly, the 1960s shift in values has continued to occur in the 1970s and 1980s in spite of the highly visible resurgence of conservative political and religious attitudes, e.g., Reaganism, the Moral Majority, supply side economics, the growth of fundamentalist churches. Both modernist values and neo-conservative ones seem to be growing in popularity but within different segments of the population. This polarization of values has been occurring at the expense of a centrist synthesis of liberal political and religious attitudes—welfare state capitalism, mainstream denominational Christianity—that had gained hegemony in American life in the 1930s with Roosevelt's New Deal and remained dominant until the 1960s.

The split in values of course began before the 1960s and has been given different names by different observers. David Reisman has referred to inner-directed versus other-directed values in *The Lonely Crowd: A Study of the Changing American Character* (Garden City, NY: Doubleday, 1954); D. Miller and Guy E. Swanson, to entrepreneurial versus bureaucratic values in *The Changing American Parent* (New York: Wiley, 1958); Daniel Bell, to industrial versus post-industrial values in *The Winding Passage* (New York: Basic, 1980); Clark Roof, to localist versus cosmopolitan values in *Community and Commitment: Religious Plausibility in a Liberal Church* (New York: Elsevier, 1978); Alvin Gouldner, to traditional, old class versus new class values in *The Future of Intellectuals and the Rise of the New Class* (London: Oxford University Press, 1979); and Dick Anthony and Thomas Robbins, to dualistic versus monistic values in "Spiritual Innovation and the Crisis of American Civil Religion," *Daedalus, 111* (1), 215–234, Winter 1982. Each of these distinctions has much in common with the others and seems roughly equivalent to the distinction between objectivist and subjectivist ways of organizing experience, which we develop in the following pages. The distinction between objectivism and relativism is developed persuasively by Richard Bernstein in *Beyond Objectivism and Relativism: Science, Hermeneutics and Praxis* (Philadelphia: University of Pennsylvania, 1983) and by George Lakoff and Mark Johnson in *Metaphors We Live By* (Chicago: University of Chicago, 1980). The terms have much in common with Isaiah Berlin's terms rationalism and counter-rationalism, which we discuss in note 15.

12. The growth of Oriental-mystical orientations has been well documented in a series of national surveys. Andrew Greeley in *Sociology of the Paranormal: A Reconnaissance* (Beverly Hills, CA: Sage, 1975) found that thirty-five percent of the American population claim to have had "mystical" experiences. Linda Bourque and Kurt W. Back in "Can Feelings Be Enumerated?", *Behavioral Science, 15,* 1970, pp. 487–496 found that the percentage of people reporting mystical experiences grew steadily during the 1960s (twenty-one percent in 1962, thirty-two percent in 1966, and forty-one percent in 1967). Fifteen percent of respondents from a random sample of the San Francisco area reported involvement in Oriental religions—see Robert Wuthnow, "The New Religions in Social Context," in Charles Glock and Robert Bellah (eds.), *The New Religious Consciousness* (Berkeley: University of California, 1976). The corresponding figure for a sample of college students in the Montreal area was thirty-four percent—see Frederick Birk and William Reimer, "A Comparative Analysis of New Religious and Parareligious Movements in the Greater Montreal Area," presented at the 1974 Annual Convention of the Association for the Sociology of Religion; and twelve percent of all Americans reported having participated in Oriental religion according to Gallup Poll results, *Religion in America Annual, 1977–1978.*

   Moreover, the nature of Christian religious commitment has been changing since the 1960s toward a more supernaturalistic, less secular, rationalistic form of belief. Before that period most scholars of religion had assumed that secularization of religious attitudes was an irreversible aspect of modernization. Belief in the supernatural (for example, an afterlife, the devil, a transcendent God) had steadily declined in mainstream denominations throughout the twentieth century as religion in America increased its emphasis on rational ethical themes and deemphasized faith "in things unseen"—see Charles Y. Glock and Rodney Stark, *Religion and Society in Tension* (Chicago: Rand McNally, 1965) and *American Piety: The Nature of Religious Commitment* (Berkeley: University of California, 1968). Since the 1960s, however, the mainstream liberal denominations—which tend to emphasize ethical themes at the expense of the supernatural—have declined while evangelical and fundamentalist churches have grown—see W. C. Roof and C. B. Hadaway, "Shifts in Religious Preference in the Mid-Seventies," *Journal for the Scientific*

Study of Religion, 16, 4: 409–412, 1978; Dean Kelley, "Why Conservative Churches Are Still Growing," *Journal for the Scientific Study of
Religion, 17,* 165–172, June 1978; and Reginald Bibby and Merlin B.
Brinkerhoff, "Circulation of the Saints Revisited: A Longitudinal Look
at Conservative Church Growth," *Journal for the Scientific Study of
Religion, 22,* 253–262, 1983. One survey found that thirty-four percent
of the American population claimed to have experienced the born-again
phenomenon and considered themselves to be evangelical or fundamentalist Christians in 1977, whereas only twenty percent did so in 1963
(Gallup Poll results, *Religion in America Annual,* 1977–1978). In light of
these shifts, it is not surprising that two consecutive American presidents
have considered themselves born-again Christians (Carter, elected in
1976, and Reagan, elected in 1980 and 1984).

13. Yankelovich (op. cit.) is particularly illuminating regarding this distinction. See also: Ralph Turner, "The Real Self: From Institution to
Impulse," *The American Journal of Sociology, 81,* 989–1016, March
1976; Steven M. Tipton, *Getting Saved from the Sixties* (Berkeley: University of California, 1982); and Robert Bellah, Richard Madsen, William
M. Sullivan, Ann Swidler and Steven M. Tipton, *Habits of the Heart*
(Berkeley: University of California, 1985). Our assertion of a continued
shift from a status orientation (a culture of role) to a culture of self since
the 1960s may seem surprising in view of the widespread careerism of
the 1970s and 1980s. As these authors make clear, however, the new style
of careerism is a fulfillment rather than a contradiction of the culture of
self and has strong continuity with the value shifts of the 1960s. Anthony
and Ecker enlarge upon the distinction between the culture of role and
the culture of self in their article discussing the Anthony typology.

14. Positivism is a philosophical system in which the only valid basis of
knowledge is the "positive" data of sense experience, that is, material,
observable, objective facts which can be scientifically related to each
other through general laws. Utilitarianism, in our present context, is the
doctrine that the worth or value of anything is determined by its usefulness. Utilitarianism is closely linked to consequentialism, which holds
that the value of an ethical or moral position is to be determined according to the concrete effects that result from it rather than by standards of
intrinsic worth.

15. See Isaiah Berlin's *Against the Current: Essays in the History of Ideas*
(New York: Viking, 1980) for one of the most illuminating discussions of
the dialectical relationship between the "rationalism" that gained hegemony in Western culture with the Enlightenment and the many
"counter-rational" (Berlin's term) perspectives that developed in opposition to it. The most notable of the counter-rational perspectives
include: the Romantic and Modernist movements in literature and in the
other arts; existentialist philosophy, originating with Kierkegaard and
Nietzsche; phenomenology, originating with Husserl; natural language

philosophy, originating with Wittgenstein and Austin; dialectical approaches such as those of Hegel and Marx; and hermeneutics, whose most persuasive current exponents are Gadamer and Ricoeur. Most of these artistic and philosophical positions have been converted into counter-rational minority positions in the human sciences (which are dominated by rationalist positivism and utilitarianism). In social and political theory these include Schutzian phenomenology; ethnomethodology; symbolic interactionism; the natural language approach of Peter Winch and his followers; Robert Bellah's hermeneutic sociology; and neo-Marxist critical theory, developed most coherently by members of the Frankfurt school, including Adorno, Horkheimer, Marcuse, and currently Habermas. In the psychotherapeutic professions, counter-rational positions include those of humanistic and transpersonal psychology and existential psychiatry.

For excellent surveys of contemporary anti-positivist positions in social and political science, see Richard Bernstein, *The Restructuring of Social and Political Theory* (Philadelphia: University of Pennsylvania, 1976) and *Beyond Objectivism and Relativism: Science, Hermeneutics and Praxis* (Philadelphia: University of Pennsylvania, 1983). For a discussion of anti-positivist orientations in the scientific study of religion see Dick Anthony, "A Phenomenological-Structuralist Approach to the Scientific Study of Religion," *ReVision*, 5 (1), Spring 1982, and Dick Anthony, Thomas Robbins and Robert Bellah, *Between Religion and the Human Sciences: Toward the Non-Reductionistic Study of Religion* (Berkeley: University of California, forthcoming). For the commonly held view that the counter-culture of the 1960s developed largely as a result of mass exposure to the various types of counter-rational positions, see Daniel Bell, *The Cultural Contradictions of Capitalism* (New York: Basic, 1976); Marshall Berman, *All That Is Solid Melts Into Air: The Experience of Modernity* (New York: Simon and Schuster, 1982); Morris Dickstein, *Gates of Eden: American Culture in the Sixties* (New York: Basic, 1977); and Frank Musgrove, *Ecstasy and Holiness: Counterculture and the Open Society* (Bloomington: Indiana University, 1974). For counter-rational influences upon the development of interest in contemporary nontraditional religion see Robert Wuthnow, *The Consciousness Reformation* (Berkeley: University of California, 1976) and *The Post-Christian Periphery* (Berkeley: University of California, 1978).

16. Our contrast between paternalistic and autonomous authority was stimulated by Richard Sennett's use of this distinction in *Authority* (New York: Random House, 1981). Our treatment of these issues differs considerably from his, however. The reader should also be aware that the shift from paternalistic to autonomous authority is occurring at different rates in different segments of the population. Autonomous authority is most influential within the "other-directed" (Reisman, op. cit.), "bureaucratic" (Miller and Swanson, op. cit.), "cosmopolitan" (Roff, op. cit.),

"post-industrial" (Bell, op. cit.) "new class" (Gouldner, op. cit.), which we have argued involve a subjectivistic mode of interpreting reality. Paternalistic authority remains more at home within the "inner-directed," "entrepreneurial," "localist" "old class" which we have argued favors an objectivistic style.

17. For discussion about the apparent conflict between healthy autonomy and surrender to genuine spiritual authority, and the resolution of that conflict, see the interview of Dick Anthony on Meher Baba and the editorial commentary that follows it, as well as the article by John Welwood.

18. "Defendant's Statement of Material Facts," U.S. District Court for the District of Columbia, Civil Action No. 82-2303 (The Synanon Church, plaintiff, versus the United States of America, defendant).

19. Additional homicide conspiracies are described in "Exhibit Volume XII" of the same Civil Action cited in the previous footnote.

20. According to the Justice Department's "Statement of Material Facts," Synanon's Chief of Security wrote to the top leadership in September, 1977, that "I now understand, gut level, that we are willing to handle essentially any incident on our property, including ones calling for us to use premeditated deadly force, without calling the police . . . and that we establish intense weapons training of all our reserves as a top priority" (p. 90).

21. *Ability, 81* [c. 1959], 6; cited in Roy Wallis, op. cit., 104.

22. Roy Wallis, op. cit., 180, 188, 189.

23. The pseudonym is used here because, while we question the wisdom of protecting this individual in this manner, there is a consensus among transpersonal psychologists close to the situation not to stigmatize "Smith" permanently.

24. For a review of the arguments on both sides of the controversy and extensive references to the research literature, see Thomas Robbins and Dick Anthony, "Deprogramming, Brainwashing and the Medicalization of Deviant Religious Groups," *Social Problems* (Feb. 1982), 29, 283-297; and Dick Anthony, "The Fact Pattern Behind the Deprogramming Controversy", *Review of Law and Social Change* (1980), 9, 73-90. For participant observation accounts of the Unification Church that emphasize reasons for conversion other than "brainwashing" see Thomas Robbins, Dick Anthony, et al., "The Last Civil Religion: Reverend Moon and the Unification Church," *Sociological Analysis, 34* (2), April 1978, and Dick Anthony and Thomas Robbins, "The Effect of *Detente* on the Growth of the New Religions: Reverend Moon and the Unification Church," in *Understanding the New Religions*, Jacob Needleman and George Baker (eds.), New York: Seabury, 1978.

25. In David Boadella, "Violence in Therapy," *Energy and Character 11*, January 1980, pp. 1-20 (Dorset, England).

26. Jorg Andrees Elten in *Der Spiegel*, *35*, August 28, 1978.
27. Eva Renzi, "Let Me Go, I Want to Get Out of Here," *Stern Magazin*, *35*, August 1978; and Jorg Andrees Elten in *Der Spiegel*, *43*, October 22, 1979.
28. Ma Satya Bharti, *The Ultimate Risk: Encountering Bhagwan Shree Rajneesh* (London: Wildwood House, 1980).
29. For a critique of Rajneesh as a Tantric spiritual master, see Benjamin Walker, *Tantrism: Its Secret Principles and Practices* (Wellingborough, England: Aquarian, 1982).
30. Lawsuit allegations quoted from the *San Francisco Examiner*, April 3, 1985, A10.
31. Quoted from an official summary of Da Free John's teachings entitled, "The Four Fundamental Questions."
32. *San Francisco Chronicle*, April 4, 1985, p. 16.
33. *San Francisco Examiner*, April 5, 1985, p. A12.
34. *San Francisco Chronicle*, April 4, 1985, p. 16.
35. *San Francisco Examiner*, April 14, 1985, p. A22.
36. *San Francisco Examiner*, April 7, 1985, p. B4.
37. *San Francisco Chronicle*, April 5, 1985, p. 18.
38. *San Francisco Examiner*, April 7, 1985, p. B4.
39. *San Francisco Examiner*, April 14, 1985, p. B9.
40. Jacob Needleman, *Lost Christianity* (New York: Doubleday, 1980).
41. Robert Ornstein, *The Mind Field* (London: Octagon, 1976).
42. Steven M. Tipton. *Getting Saved from the Sixties: Moral Meaning in Conversion and Cultural Change* (Berkeley: University of California Press, 1981).
43. Arnold J. Toynbee, *A Study of History: The Disintegrations of Civilization* (New York: Oxford University Press, 1939); *An Historian's Approach to Religion* (New York: Oxford University Press, 1979); *Christianity and Civilization* (Wallingford, PA: Pendle Hill Publications, 1983).

Part One

THE ANTHONY TYPOLOGY:

A Framework for Assessing Spiritual and Consciousness Groups

The Anthony Typology:

A Framework for Assessing Spiritual and Consciousness Groups

by Dick Anthony and Bruce Ecker*

The world's diverse mystical traditions share a common purpose: to bring people to the highest state of spiritual realization that human beings can achieve. The seeker in present-day America has access to many of these traditions and faces the challenge of coming to terms with a great diversity of approaches. There are no clear-cut, stereotypic features by which authentic mystical-spiritual involvements can reliably be recognized. The inner processes of spiritual realization are subtle, paradoxical, and, like a labyrinth, branch off into many false avenues. It is a matter of fine discrimination to recognize which spiritual groups and

*Dick Anthony is a psychologist who specializes in the study of new religious movements from an interdisciplinary perspective. For further biographical information see the preface to Anthony's interview in Part 2, and also the text of that interview.

Bruce Ecker is a psychotherapist whose practice in Berkeley, California includes individual, couple, family, and group work. His graduate training and his subsequent clinical and theoretical work in transpersonal psychology follow a fifteen-year career as an experimental physicist, which included numerous professional publications and conference addresses nationally and internationally. The interplay of psychological and spiritual dynamics has for many years been one of his major areas of study.

leaders are competent to guide the seeker along an avenue of actual, transcendental realization.

The Anthony typology[1] is a conceptual framework designed to assist
in assessing the spiritual validity and helpfulness as well as the potential
harmfulness of a broad range of groups and leaders who claim to offer
higher consciousness, enlightenment, salvation, or transformation. The
typology includes an examination of how mystical teachings become distorted when interpreted through the lens of present-day American values
and cultural assumptions.

In addition to describing the spiritual sensibilities of the various kinds
of groups that comprise the new religions, the typology is intended as a
stimulus to the spiritual sensibilities of the reader. One's ability to sense
the quality of a group's spiritual efficacy is, of course, limited only by
one's own spiritual discrimination.

INTRODUCTION TO THE TYPOLOGY

The Anthony typology assesses a spiritual group along three descriptive dimensions: its *metaphysics*, its central mode of *practice*, and its
interpretive sensibility. The typology resolves each of these basic dimensions into bipolar categories: metaphysics is described in terms of *monism* or *dualism*, practice in terms of *technical* or *charismatic* type, and
interpretive sensibility in terms of *unilevel* versus *multilevel* sensibilities.
Figure 1 diagrams the interplay of the three bipolar dimensions, forming
an eight-cell typology. Each cell represents a general type of spiritual
group, identifiable by certain characteristics.

Monism-Dualism Dimension:

The distinction between monistic and dualistic world-views corresponds roughly to a distinction between Eastern and Western religions.
In monistic world-views, all individuals are inherently one with the Godhead and will ultimately enjoy that condition consciously. Dualistic
world-views, however, maintain that not all individuals ultimately
achieve salvation; one must qualify by surviving a competitive salvational
ordeal or selection process. Those who do not will receive eternal
damnation.[2]

Monistic orientations maintain there is one and only one ultimate,
absolute essence which is the true nature of all apparently separate
beings and things. Such monistic traditions as Hinduism, Buddhism, and
Sufism affirm both the immanence and the radical transcendence of this

Figure 1:

THE ANTHONY TYPOLOGY

		Monism	Dualism
Multilevel	*Charismatic*	(Multilevel monistic charismatic groups)	(Multilevel dualistic charismatic groups)
	Technical	(Multilevel monistic technical groups)	(Multilevel dualistic technical groups)
Unilevel	*Charismatic*	(Unilevel monistic charismatic groups)	(Unilevel dualistic charismatic groups)
	Technical	(Unilevel monistic technical groups)	(Unilevel dualistic technical groups)

ultimate spiritual reality, and point to a state of conscious, mystical one-ness with it as the goal of the tradition. This orientation tends to view time, the material world, and discursive reasoning as illusory. Morality has a pragmatic but not an ultimate metaphysical basis. Thus the dual-istic distinction between good and evil is at bottom also illusory, and all people and beings are destined for the final state of conscious unity, albeit through an enormously complex process. Most monistic systems embrace cyclical theories of culture (such as the *yuga* system in Hinduism) and affirm the idea of reincarnation, in support of the view that all beings eventually achieve monistic realization. Religious figures tend to be what

Max Weber calls "exemplary" rather than "ethical" prophets. Their influence occurs mainly through the power of the example that they set rather than through systematic ethical teachings or prescriptions. A primary example is the Buddha.

The dualistic traditions include the orthodox mainstreams of what are considered to be the Western religions: Judaism, Christianity, Islam. Within the dualistic traditions almost all of the themes of the monistic tradition are reversed; time is real, not illusory, as are good and evil, contributing to a heightened sense of "contingency," of individual destinies dividing into two primary directions symbolized by the themes of heaven and hell. A person is always at risk with respect to unavoidable, dire choices which will define his or her ultimate identity and state. Morality, here, is close to the essence of the religious quest: the attempt to be good, or qualified for salvation, rather than bad, or disqualified and excluded from salvation. Salvation in the dualistic traditions is usually conceived in terms of permanent enjoyment of *proximity* to God, with persistence of individual identity, in contrast with the monistic goal of the realization of Godhead as one's own true nature, with cessation of separate selfhood.

The prophets in dualistic traditions are "ethical" prophets who propose new ways of organizing social life. The prophetic message tends toward utopian or millennarian thinking with eschatology, the idea that history is coming to a dramatic end, the primary theme. Ethical prophets usually propose some way of contributing to the eschatological resolution of history.

Both the monistic and dualistic ideas can become problematic in groups that interpret them rigidly and literally. Literal dualism, emphasizing the contrast between good and evil, can, by promoting repression of aspects of the self considered negative and evil, result in the projection of these aspects onto an external contrast group, which then appears to epitomize evil. Thus literal dualism promotes the formation of an in-group whose members share a particular style of repression and projection. In-group members see themselves as having conclusively resolved the problem of good and evil, and as being in a cosmically significant battle with the evil out-group—the felt duty of the insiders being somehow to vanquish the out-group and bring about both the eschatological resolution of history and the harmonious period that is promised after the "end times." This dynamic has characterized much of the history of the Western dualistic traditions, though we do find within them individuals who attained and expressed the highest degrees of spiritual realization, such as Francis of Assisi, Teresa of Avila and Meister Eckhart in the Christian world.

The problematic tendencies of overly literal monistic groups are different; we describe them later. In some respects, monism and dualism form a continuum on which the user of the typology must place the spiritual group in question. For example, the International Society for Krishna Consciousness (ISKON), popularly known as Hare Krishna, stridently repudiates some elements of strict monism. Krishna consciousness devotees reject notions of complete metaphysical oneness as "maya impersonalism" and affirm the ultimate separateness of individual souls from the transcendent identity of Krishna, the Personality of Godhead. ("Krishna consciousness" does not denote becoming or merging in Krishna.) Yet they accept the illusory nature of the phenomenal world (maya) as well as karma and reincarnation. It is arguable that these monistic elements derive from the premise of metaphysical unity, and we therefore classify the group as monistic even though it also embraces certain dualistic elements.

In addition, various "consciousness" groups that might be called "quasimonistic" we include as monistic for purposes of the Anthony typology. Such orientations as the Human Potential movement and the est training[3] often do not have explicitly elaborated monistic world-views, such as formal conceptions of metaphysical unity or doctrines of karma, but their practitioners generally do accept monistic assumptions such as the relativism of mundane "reality," the primacy of "consciousness," the premium on exploration of the inner self, and the importance of direct experience as opposed to intellectual formulations and dogma.

Technical-Charismatic Dimension:

These categories indicate the nature of a group's practice. In technical groups, techniques—any repetitive mental or physical processes that can be taught through explicit articulation and instruction—are the basis of seeking spiritual transformation. Common examples include most forms of meditation (such as mantra meditation and visualization meditation), chanting, hatha yoga, and pranayama (breath yoga). In charismatic groups, spiritual attainment is sought primarily through direct, personal relationship with the leader. Because the leader is regarded as a direct link with, or embodiment of, divine authority, knowledge, and love, contact with such a person is itself considered transformative, particularly sustained contact involving devotion, love, remembrance, attention, and obedience. Both the technical and charismatic approaches can be authentic avenues to spiritual realization. Both, too, are subject to distortions that are potentially harmful, although in characteristically different ways.

While many groups are distinctively technical or charismatic in their practice, some combine both forms, or change over time, or involve different members with different approaches. For example, followers of Sri

Chinmoy meditate on the spiritual master's picture. And in the Divine Light Mission of Guru Maharaj-Ji, some devotees are intensely devoted to the guru as the "Lord of the Universe," while others are primarily concerned with "The Knowledge" and the meditation technique taught by the guru. In most of these composite cases, however, one of the two modes is regarded as primary and essential, the other secondary and instrumental, for achieving spiritual transformation. Our assignment of a group to a practice category is always based on what the group's operational metaphysical world-view deems to be the essential mechanism or methodology of transformation.

Unilevel-Multilevel Dimension:

These terms describe a group's sensibilities regarding the nature of spiritual transformation and attainment. As described by the mystical traditions that map the levels of transformation in some detail—for example, various traditions within Hinduism, Sufism, and Buddhism—even the lower levels of true spiritual transformation involve a radical, permanent change in the sort of being that one perceives and feels oneself to be. One experiences that one's existence is independent of the physical body, for example. *Unilevel* groups err toward trivializing and misreading the nature of genuine spiritual transformation. Although we shall later explore the different kinds of unilevel distortion encountered in many of the new religions, suffice it here to say that groups with unilevel sensibilities confuse the attainment of authentic spiritual transcendence or realization with the attainment of mundane psychological, sensory, or material conditions, such as financial success, interpersonal satisfaction, inducement of special inner sensations or moods, commitment to a certain set of beliefs. Unilevel sensibilities include what Trungpa[4] has termed "spiritual materialism," the self-serving distortion of spiritual teachings.

Multilevel groups do not confuse mundane and transcendental consciousness and so foster genuine spiritual inner development. Our frame of reference for defining unilevel versus multilevel sensibilities is the collective teachings of the great mystical traditions—those mentioned above as well as others, including Zen Buddhism, Christian mysticism, and Taoism. All of these traditions stress that spiritual development requires sharp discrimination to avoid the many false trails at every step of the way. The multilevel category of Anthony's typology is based upon a set of key values, attitudes, and discriminations culled from the mystical traditions. Groups that effectively foster these pro-transformative values, attitudes, and discriminations are multilevel groups; groups that diverge from them are unilevel groups; and some groups combine unilevel and multilevel features.

In practice, unilevel groups fail to be effective catalysts for spiritual transformation because of two characteristic flaws that cause them to confuse transcendent and mundane experience. First, they are overly literal and "definitive" in their interpretation of language and texts, with too little appreciation of symbolic and metaphoric levels of meaning. This is the problem of *univocality*. Second, they harbor the attitude that the value as well as the proof of spiritual transformation lies in predictable, observable consequences in the mundane sphere. This is the problem of *consequentialism*. Univocality and consequentialism are closely linked and tend to occur together. They are the defining features of the unilevel category.

The terms multilevel and unilevel can be used to describe either a specific group of practitioners *or* a spiritual system in the abstract. But it is a particular person's or group's interpretation of spiritual teachings that the Anthony typology designates as being either unilevel or multilevel, for different groups can put any one body of mystical teachings into practice in either unilevel or multilevel ways, no matter how multilevel the teaching is in itself. For example, while Zen Buddhism is a multilevel orientation in principle, we are interested in whether a particular Zen master and students are actually engaged in multilevel practice. Zen, like any spiritual system, is subject to unilevel distortion. The terms unilevel and multilevel refer to a group's *actual* rather than professed sensitivity to higher levels of being.

Unilevel groups blur crucial distinctions between levels of spiritual knowledge and authority. They confuse mystical gnosis or the direct experience of spiritual reality with exposure to the words and symbols given by the enlightened one who has had that ultimate gnosis; and they confuse the non-ordinary meanings of the enlightened one's words and symbols with the mundane meanings of their own unenlightened interpretations of those words and symbols. The territory is confused with the map, and the interpretation of the map is confused with direct knowledge of the territory; thus the reader of the map is confused with the one who has arrived at the territory. The univocal attitude is one of "knowing for sure." Group members do not question their ability to read the map and fail to see their interpretations as a fallible production separate from the group's guiding symbol system or teachings, which are idolized. Unilevel groups in effect collapse the three-level hierarchy of spiritual authority (gnosis, symbol, and interpretation) into a self-confirming amalgam, and so are unable to detect their own distortions. They become vulnerable to distortion caused by shifting trends in cultural attitudes to which the leaders unconsciously subscribe, and by any psychopathological agendas that the leaders may have.

Multilevel groups preserve the three-level hierarchy and take for granted that their own interpretations of spiritual teachings are fallible. Members know that they do *not* "know for sure." *Belief* in the group's world-view, while useful, is considered as counting relatively little toward spiritual realization. Believing in spiritual ideology may even be detrimental from the multilevel standpoint if it promotes a false sense of knowing truth. Spiritual symbol systems and teachings are regarded as containing many levels of meaning, which become apparent only when the individual develops the appropriate level of transcendent awareness. Moreover, each level of meaning points beyond itself toward ultimate spiritual reality. Thus from the multilevel point of view there is nothing like a "definitive" understanding of spiritual teachings, except for the understanding that comes with ultimate or final enlightenment.

In unilevel groups, members' spiritual experiences tend to be used as proof of the group's "correct" world-view or of the individual's spiritual status and progress. Multilevel groups read much less significance into isolated mystical experiences and are wary of confusing them with ultimacy, or even with an enduring transformation of the individual. In contrast to unilevel perspectives,which tend to trivialize or concretize spiritual attainment, there is, in multilevel groups, an appreciation of ultimate spiritual gnosis as being so awesome, so vastly beyond the normal, mundane realm of comprehension, that to glimpse something of it experientially is to become aware of how *little* one knows, sees, and feels relative to what is possible.

The unilevel-multilevel dimension is the typology's measure of a group's discrimination regarding spiritual transformation and realization. In a later section we discuss the differences between unilevel and multilevel sensibilities in key areas of group practice, such as morality, ingroup/out-group boundaries, attitudes toward spiritual advancement, etc. Familiarity with these differences enables the prospective member to be alert to many indications that can signal a psuedo-transformative involvement.

Anthony's categories of multilevel versus unilevel spirituality have important precedents and parallels in the work of earlier writers on religious authenticity versus inauthenticity. These include Kierkegaard's *dread* versus *despair;* William Blake's *double vision* versus *single vision;* William James's *twice-born* versus *once-born;* and in the contemporary period, Wilfred Cantwell Smith's *faith* versus *belief* and Robert Bellah's *prophetic* versus *celebratory* civil religion.[6] All these thinkers draw upon a traditional, basic contrast between worldly-mindedness and transcendent awareness; Anthony's unilevel-multilevel dimension is novel in that non-mainstream groups occupy both the authentic (multilevel) and inauthentic (unilevel) categories.

Studies of actual groups show that those belonging to certain cells in Figure 1 are more prone to problematic and possibly harmful developments than are groups in other cells. We have already noted the heightened vulnerability of unilevel groups to domination by changing cultural fashions and leaders' psychopathology. In metaphysics, dualism tends to be more problematic, owing to the dire contingencies with which individuals are faced in that world-view. Dualism produces greater psychological tensions and hence more extreme styles of coping, in general, than does monism—although monism, as we show later, can go awry in ways of its own. Regarding style of practice, the charismatic orientation tends to be the more problematic because it is inherently more subjectivistic as well as more dependent on the soundness and stability of the spiritual leader or master. The technical orientation is generally more stable by virtue of its objectively defined structure of exercises or practices, and the discipline they require. However, this is not to say that charismatic orientations are fundamentally faulty for lack of discipline; great masters such as Ramakrishna and Francis of Assisi prove otherwise.

The identification of certain categories in the Anthony typology as being more frequently problematic does not mean that all groups in these categories are problematic or harmful. It does mean that greater caution and greater discrimination are warranted—especially when more than one of the problematic categories are involved. In particular, problems of authoritarianism occur primarily in unilevel charismatic groups, which tend to segregate members from society and family; and problems associated with narcissism[7] develop mainly in unilevel monistic technical groups. We shall explain these correlations later.

The typology is not intended as a rigid construct that mechanically reveals the true characteristics of group members or groups. It is important to note that while unilevel groups are, by definition, on a false trail in terms of *mystical* inner development, they are not necessarily always harmful or devoid of value. In their influence on members' *psychosocial* development, some unilevel groups can be argued to be beneficial. The important point is that the typology's negative evaluations refer in a general way to how prone certain types of psychospiritual orientation are to harmful distortion with respect to spiritual values and principles. The assignment of a particular group or system to a unilevel, "problem" cell in the typology does not necessarily mean that this group is harmful or pathological in all respects. But before we discuss in detail how the typology categories map the characteristics of specific spiritual and consciousness groups, let us first examine, in general, how distortions occur in America's new religions and review some of the main themes of inauthenticity that tend to develop among them.

STYLES OF DESCRIBING REALITY

If there is any one feature common to the various psychospiritual systems, teachings, groups, world-views, etc., it is a central interest in something called "reality." This interest may be explicit or implicit, and reality may be construed as spiritual or psychological, objective or subjective; but the group or system exists, in principle, as a way for members to attain some sort of optimum relationship with reality, however construed. One way to begin to understand the psychospiritual panorama, therefore, is to examine styles of describing reality.

Linguists, sociologists, literary scholars, and philosophers generally agree that there are two basic styles of language use: univocal and multivocal (not to be confused with the unilevel and multilevel categories in the typology, although they are related in ways that will become apparent). Very simply, the univocal style is denotative and involves precise, single meanings of words, as in scientific discourse. The multivocal style is connotative and emphasizes multiple meanings of words—many voices—so that meanings shade off into each other, and the meaning of a word cannot be understood except in relation to its unique context; because statements have no independent, free-standing meanings, it is impossible for them to be definitively paraphrased or translated. Multivocal language is *symbolic*, in contrast to the *literal* sense of the univocal style. The univocal style reflects a rational-linear-analytical orientation; the multivocal style reflects a holistic-synergetic-relativistic orientation. Multivocality is illustrated most characteristically by poetry, mystical religious writing, and to some extent all imaginative writing. Its style is epitomized by modernist works such as the novels of James Joyce or Marcel Proust, or the plays of Samuel Beckett, Jean Anouilh or Eugene Ionesco.

While these two approaches to language have clear value in their separate, paradigmatic contexts—univocality in science and multivocality in modernist art and literature—disagreement arises when we try to understand or affirm where the home of reality is, and of sense and wisdom about human life. Here there is real controversy and difference of opinion. Mystics and existentialist philosophers argue that human reality is unique and individual, that its meaning cannot definitively be captured in terms of general, rational constructions. They usually affirm the multivocal use of language as most nearly approximating knowledge or wisdom about the human condition. On the other hand, rationalist philosophers and theologians argue that words can be used to construct an unambiguous representation of the world that is objectively true, independent of the observer's point of view; and that people who maintain otherwise are simply prisoners of their own subjectivity.

Those who interpret religious ideas univocally believe that there is one interpretation which is straightforward, correct, and not relative to any context, such that anyone who truly understands the ideas understands them in this particular way, the correct way. But hermeneutics, the science of interpreting the meaning of an author's words and images and explaining it to others, argues that interpretation of texts is *always* influenced by our cultural conditioning. And never is this more the case than when we fail to take the cultural relativity of an interpretation into account and believe that we understand a set of ideas in a timelessly correct fashion. It is precisely when we believe that our interpretations are direct, straightforward, and not influenced by our historical situation that they are most influenced by it, because that influence is now unconscious. So when we say that people interpret religious ideas univocally or literally, we mean that they *believe* that they are interpreting them literally and infallibly, and that therefore their interpretation is simplistic and overly influenced by unconscious cultural tendencies. We believe that unwittingly the univocal style is every bit as subjective as the multivocal.

Psychospiritual teachings can be viewed as strategies for resolving profound, universal human dilemmas at their roots. However, any individual's view of both the dilemmas and the purported methods of resolving them is deeply influenced by the particular cultural matrix in which he or she exists. Without sufficient awareness of the cultural influence— consisting of a world-view comprised largely of semiconscious and unconscious beliefs, attitudes, and values—we may think we are autonomous and objective in our choice of psychospiritual orientation, when actually we are succumbing to cultural conditioning and subscribing to a pseudo-universal pseudo-resolution of misperceived dilemmas. Both univocal and multivocal styles of expressing and interpreting meanings are fallible in this way. To be able to recognize the deep structure of human dilemmas and to choose among real rather than pseudo-resolutions of them requires an awareness of our culturally derived assumptions that allows us to work with and beyond them. This applies not only to individuals but to transpersonal and humanistic psychology as well. If psychology adopts too atomistic or individualistic a conception of human nature, the resultant ignorance of the cultural relativity of our situation and the depth of its effect upon us can cause psychology to trivialize itself with a kind of pseudo-universality, a mistaking of passing fashions in psychology for universal truths of human nature. Psychology, including transpersonal psychology, may be no less vulnerable than religion to confusing its own *surface structures* with the *deep structures* of human make-up.

What is the relationship of the univocal and multivocal styles of language and interpretation to Anthony's unilevel and multilevel categories? The univocal style applied to religious themes always produces unilevel religion; literalistic, definitive interpretations of religious meanings always confuse transcendental and mundane realms of being. The multivocal style applied to religious themes produces *either* unilevel or multilevel religion, depending on whether the multivocal interpretations preserve the distinction between transcendent and mundane consciousness. Multilevel multivocality interprets mystical-religious statements without assuming that the multivocal meanings refer to ordinary experience. Unilevel multivocality, on the other hand, confuses transcendent experience with nonrational aspects of mundane experience. For example, the view that one transcends or escapes the duality of good and evil by rejecting all moral rules is a multivocal interpretation (a repudiation of rational-literal prescriptions) that constitutes a *unilevel* religious attitude; the mere ideological repudiation of moral rules cannot produce the kind of transcendence described by spiritual masters. In contrast, a stance illustrating multilevel multivocality is the view that moral rules are important as general guidelines, but that ordinary people cannot conclusively determine the moral character of any specific act by others (except in some extreme cases, such as the Holocaust) because the morality of the act depends on the total context of the situation, including the actor's motives and other hidden, inner factors not rationally knowable to others, but only to the transcendent consciousness of a genuine master, or to God.

FIVE CONFUSIONS

What are the chief fallacies that present-day North American culture tends to foster in our interpretation of spirituality and spiritual development? Let us examine five key confusions sometimes encountered in the new religions as well as in the transpersonal school of psychology. These are specific forms of the basic unilevel error of reading transcendence into mundane experience, as it occurs in unilevel *monistic* groups.[8]

1. The confusion between spiritual perfection and worldly skill.
2. The confusion between ordinary and transcendent types of nonrational experience, or between transcendence and regression.
3. The confusion of the transcendence of good and evil with antinomianism.
4. The confusion of detachment with dissociation and repression.
5. The confusion of detachment with potent or effective attachment.

1. *The confusion between spiritual perfection and worldly skill:*
Descriptions of the spiritually perfect or fully realized master's consciousness have no concrete reference points within the experience of imperfect individuals. Such descriptions can be partially understood only by intuitive leaps or glimpse-experiences of some transcendent state. Even those glimpses are only metaphors, pointing in the right direction but not providing actual experience of the master's state.

The distinction between perfect spiritual gnosis and all other levels of consciousness is a real one in both monistic and dualistic mystical traditions. For example, in Christianity the writings of the mystics St. Teresa of Avila, St. John of the Cross, and Meister Eckhardt describe stages leading to final conscious union with Christ; and various traditions within Sufism, Buddhism, and Hinduism describe an ultimate state of perfect consciousness that radically transcends all intermediate stages and all degrees and forms of mundane excellence, genius or talent.

However, the distinction between spiritual perfection and worldly excellence or talent is difficult to make in the contemporary American context, partly because of the cultural emphasis on autonomy as a key motif. Along with this emphasis on personal autonomy, many people now distrust paternalistic authority, and believe that its obligatory, hierarchical status system is false, that it is not truly benevolent, and that it involves some form of exploitation.[9] In the cultural spirit that came to the fore in the 1960s, association tends to be voluntary and free of moral obligation or commitment. Commitments are now established by means of conscious, voluntary contracts full of escape clauses. A person's authority is based mainly on his or her ability to define the terms of these involvements and to enter and withdraw from them at will.

Given this new means of defining and experiencing authority, any sort of commitment between people that implies a non-contractual, nonspecific need to obey another person as part of the relationship is considered, on its face, illegitimate, undesirable, and suspect. The idea of a master having perfect consciousness is uncomfortable and unwelcome—and therefore not taken seriously—because the perfection implies total faith, surrender, and obedience to the master, no matter what one is told to do.

Another cultural bias against the concept of spiritual perfection is the "idea of progress"[10] combined with the world-view of scientism. With this bias the ideal spiritual master is construed as the equivalent of a scientific genius, a path-finder making discoveries within consciousness that can then be articulated in a rational-discursive, univocal fashion, comprehensible to anyone capable of understanding language in a precise, univocal way. Viewed in this way, spiritual realization becomes the discovery and mastery of the special effects of which the mind and body are capable; a master is one who possesses psychophysical capacities that excel the commonly recognized human potential. Thus, spiritual mastery is seen as only a matter of *relative* excellence; the idea of "perfection" does not really apply. This represents a unilevel misreading of the nature of spiritual realization because it confuses the transcendence of all phenomenal limitations with "advanced" abilities vis-à-vis phenomena.

These unilevel conceptions of spiritual mastery restrict master-disciple relationships to what we term the *apprenticeship model*—a valid and even time-honored form of spiritual pursuit, but one which differs considerably from other important forms, particularly the traditional form of relationship to a perfectly enlightened master. The apprenticeship model views the master or teacher as a kind of technologist of consciousness, an advanced expert relative to the student, but imperfect, still in the process of his or her own inner development and therefore still possibly having certain fallibilities, personality distortions, or ego indulgences. These limitations are seen as separate from, and not interfering with, the master's ability to teach what consciousness skills he or she does have. There is an assumption that the basis of spiritual development is technique. The master instructs the student in exercises such as meditation, breathing practices, and visualization. The student expects to learn the teacher's inner skills and attain a comparable state of consciousness during this lifetime.

Given the currently widespread American themes of autonomy and scientism, the apprenticeship model is a culturally preferred and comfortable interpretation of spiritual mastery and the master-disciple relationship. It certainly prevails among transpersonal psychologists and is undoubtedly a fair representation of many authentic teacher-student arrangements, but—and this is the point—it is by no means a general truth of mystical spirituality. It does not apply to many masters such as Rumi, Marpa, Hafiz, Ramakrishna, Meher Baba—masters whose ways of working with disciples contradict virtually every assumption of the apprenticeship model.

2. *The confusion between ordinary and transcendent types of non-rational experience, or between transcendence and regression.*

Extremes of ordinary emotion or of sensory stimulation can be confused with the transcendence of rationality described by the mystics. Lacking experience of authentic states of transcendent consciousness, it is tempting to define as "mystical" those elements of normal consciousness such as rage, eroticism, grief, and other emotions, which most closely, though misleadingly, mimic transcendence of the ordinary plane through sheer subjective intensity. In the Romantic tradition especially, experiences which are emotional, sensual, impulsive and unpredictable are seen as transcending rationality.[11] This attitude, which stems in our cultural arena from the nineteenth-century Romantic poets and flourished again in the 1960s counterculture, receives further support from a popularized Freudianism, in which the unhealthiness of repressing emotion is taken to mean that the "primary process" themes of emotionality, sensuality, and impulsivity "transcend" the rational mode of the ego or the socially conformist mode of the superego. However, *spiritual* transcendence is not correctly identified with one particular side of any mundane polarity with which we grapple—reason versus emotions, subjectivity versus objectivity, individuality versus collectivity. Spiritual transcendence means consciousness of a unity of existence in which such polar splits are fully and irreversibly integrated and synthesized. To identify emotional release or any particular feature of mundane experience or behavior with spiritual transcendence is a basic unilevel error, and is both univocal and consequentialistic. It is univocal as a literalistic interpretation of spiritual meanings in terms of ordinary experience; and it is consequentialistic in that the value of spiritual transformation is thereby regarded not as intrinsic, but as deriving from the desirability of its mundane consequences, such as the emotional catharsis in which transformation is supposed to result.

3. *The confusion of the transcendence of good and evil with antinomianism:*

Historically, antinomianism in Christianity has been the rejection of moral rules based on the doctrinal position that faith alone, not obedience to the moral law, is necessary for salvation. Today, some spiritual seekers sometimes regard the repudiation of moral norms as a way of achieving monistic transcendence of the duality of good and evil. The monistic view is that the duality of good and evil, like all dualities, is ultimately an illusion, and unilevel monistic antinomianism maintains that moral precepts generate and sustain the dualistic illusion of good versus evil. To repudiate moral rules transcends that dualism, in this view, by liberating consciousness from involvement with the split categories of good and evil. However, while the problem of good and evil is one of the basic, universal dilemmas facing human awareness, the mere rejection of moral norms is a false solution that amounts to a regressive avoidance of the issue, not the transcendence of it. The unilevel fallacy here is in equating transcendence with what is really a psychological strategy within ordinary consciousness. Later we shall describe our view of how struggle with the moral dimension of experience promotes the process of authentic spiritual transformation.

4. *The confusion of detachment with dissociation and repression:*

Detachment is accorded great importance in many systems of spiritual practice. However, what is practiced as "detachment" in the contemporary American context frequently represents the ego defense mechanisms of dissociation and repression, the splitting-off and "burial" of uncomfortable thoughts and feelings. Whereas true detachment is an aspect of real transcendence of the opposites of experience (pleasure and pain, success and failure), pseudo-detachment is merely a psychological coping device, and the confusion of the two—again, the mistaking of a psychological maneuver for an attribute of transcendent consciousness— is another example of the unilevel misinterpretation of spiritual teachings.

There are many specific forms of the confusion of detachment with dissociation and repression; here we consider two that illustrate how this confusion serves culturally dictated themes.[12]

First is the confusion of detachment with indifference to the sufferings of others, rationalized by interpreting suffering in terms of karmic laws: those who are suffering have, like all people, merited or "chosen" the conditions in which they find themselves, are themselves causing it, and will eventually learn to transcend or give up that causation and allow themselves to become happy and successful; but the process of first choosing and then giving up suffering is part of their karmic education, and is good for them in the long run. Threfore, enlightened people who observe others suffering have no moral or spiritual obligation to help relieve them of it. In fact, it would be detrimental to them to do so. This form of pseudo-detachment fosters callousness and indifference to the people with whom one is competing. It is a cultural adaptation to the capitalist competitive environment. The detachment of the fully enlightened master who perceives the karmic dynamics directly is different. The master never withdraws from participating in the suffering of those whom he or she is viewing. Whenever possible the master aids in the resolution of the karmic dilemmas in which the sufferer is stuck. The master's genuine detachment allows full involvement in all circumstances, and the master's transcendent view of the situation and altruistic participation in it resolves the apparent contrast between detachment and active benevolence. The follower who allows thoughts about karma to serve as the rationale for indifference to the sufferings of his or her fellows is practicing an epistemological sleight of hand by claiming an existential point of view which is not, in fact, authentic for him or her. The follower's own consciousness is still heavily conditioned by pleasure and pain, joy and sorrow. An honest orientation would involve concern and empathy for the suffering of others and, while accepting suffering as a result of karma, would view karmic determination as a process that one is not yet able to fully understand or apply to the problem of suffering. The multilevel aspirant should, in response to honest feelings, work to relieve the suffering of others while continuing efforts to understand both suffering and karmic determinism, but should not claim more understanding on the basis of a univocal grasp of the *words* than his or her existential condition warrants. Only when karmic determinism permeats the follower's apprehension of his or her situation should he or she view others primarily through its lens.

Detachment can also be confused with a particular kind of indifference to one's personal situation. In this case the pseudo-detachment involves "living in the moment" and adjusting to any material situation, in the same apparent way that a master does. One is "detached" from self-concern and gives up trying to play or organize life in the temporal, material, rational fashion. This strategy legitimizes cultural alienation, and it attempts to avoid the anxiety inherent in conventional responsibilities and commitments. It readily masquerades as detachment from worldly ambition and money, and as "living in the present." But this reaction against commitment does not represent "being in the present" in a mystical sense. For one who has not attained transcendent reality, pretended indifference to personal circumstances involves the repression of appropriate, real self-concerns. The resulting despair and insecurity require further repression, often achieved through immersion in increasingly intense experience such as various kinds of conflict (political causes, rebellion against authority figures), alcohol, drugs, promiscuity, or violence—all to avoid the emotional difficulty of having to master the practical skills of a material and social world in which one feels alienated. But real self-concerns cannot be disowned or transcended by rendering them unconscious. They must consciously be considered if they are to be eventually transcended.

5. *The confusion of detachment with potent or effective attachment.*

The freedom of the genuine master appears closely linked to his detachment, which remains unshaken in every material situation because of his inner contact with the source of all satisfaction. Seen through unilevel sensibilities, the radical detachment of the authentic master may be translated into the belief that the master is happy and satisfied because he or she can control or have power over material circumstances and arrange them to a preferred pattern. This interpretation implies that a measure of the disciple's spiritual development is his or her ability to achieve vocational preferences and make money—an identification of spiritual virtue with worldly status, but in a different way than in the "Protestant ethic," which stresses material and emotional asceticism as instrumental to success. The confusion of detachment with potency involves the attempt to control circumstances by dropping all judgment and practicing an open, "detached" attention. In a way, this is a variation on the unilevel approach to going beyond good and evil: one suspends judgment of good or bad as an aid to improving perception of the actual situation and acquires control over it by initially giving in, by yielding and blending harmoniously rather than attempting to impose one's will or judgment. Only then does one see how to exert force or influence and change the situation.

Thus in the confusion of detachment with potent attachment, there is a relative degree of detachment in service of basic aims to which one is nevertheless attached. The fallacy lies not in the procedure itself—as an elegant *modus operandi* it has its charms—but in the idea that any of this constitutes the true detachment of spiritual transcendence. True detachment means unshakable inner poise in the midst of the most intense action and in the face of the gravest disasters. It requires a profound transcendence of self-interest, which is not true of the procedure of harmonious efficacy described above.

Moreover, in blending with a material situation which happens to be degraded, one easily becomes degraded oneself, and one's supposed mastery over the situation may be pure illusion. Such mastery or control can be a disguised or deluded surrender to one's base self, reminiscent of what Freud described as rationalization and Marx described as false consciousness, an opiate, an agent of alienation. "Detachment" in service of potent attachment becomes a new way of rationalizing participation in an alienating, competitive social milieu—again, adaptation rather than transcendence, the basic unilevel fallacy.

These five confusions illustrate the unilevel misinterpretation of spiritual themes, and prepare the ground for a more thoroughgoing discussion of the Anthony typology of nonmainstream religious groups. That discussion will be most profitable if we first review briefly the historical background of unilevel and multilevel sensibilities in the Western dualistic tradition of Christianity, for our cultural orientation in late twentieth-century America has crystallized out of the Western experiment with dualism.

THE HISTORICAL CONTEXT OF
UNILEVEL AND MULTILEVEL SENSIBILITIES
IN AMERICA'S NEW RELIGIONS

It will be helpful here first to review some of our terms. Univocality and multivocality are general styles of interpreting language and meaning. Unilevel and multilevel refer to the interpretation of *religious* themes. The univocal style, with its clear-cut, straightforward, literalistic interpretations, when applied to religious themes produces unilevel religion in which transcendental meanings are lost behind mundane, concrete, rational interpretations. The multivocal style, applied to religious themes, produces either unilevel or multilevel religion, depending on whether it distinguishes appropriately between transcendent and mundane consciousness.

The roots of the univocalization or rationalization of religion in the West extend back to Old Testament Judaism. Ancient Israel, unlike its neighboring societies, worshipped a radically transcendent God who was immune to manipulation by his followers and made severe ethical demands upon them. There was thus a profound metaphysical gulf between man and God, and a thoroughly demythologized cosmos between them. In contrast to religions that emphasize a more interactive process between man and transcendent realms, the ancient Hebraic focus on correct ethical conduct in this world as a form of loving obedience to a distant divinity is regarded by historians and sociologists of religion as a distinctly rationalist trend.[13]

The Old Testament conception of God was largely carried over into Christianity. However, the Roman Catholic Church implemented a progressive remythologization of the cosmos, which became peopled by angels and saints who could mediate with God. Mary was elevated as a mediator and co-redeemer with Christ. In addition to having access to saintly mediation, the individual could also get a favorable, personal response from God through the rituals of confession and the other sacraments (penance, the Eucharist, baptism).

Confession, the sacraments and the system of saints reduced the pressure on individuals with respect to whether they were good or evil. These holy rituals and mediators were seen as insuring individual salvation and so helped ease the potentially severe ethical pressures of Judeo-Christian dualism, as well as the consequent pressure towards repression and projection of evil attributes. Furthermore, what might be termed "salvational individualism" did not exist. One sought salvation not so much as a meritorious individual, but as a member of a corporate body, the Church. All of these factors made a certain amount of imperfection and acting-out tolerable, since salvation was determined not by brittle rules, but by connection to a network of responsive relationships that extended into the transcendent realm. A person's salvational status could not be definitively determined by reference to any clear-cut, rational formula, ethical or otherwise. This multivocality of the Christian religious consciousness in the Middle Ages offset the Old Testament trend towards univocality.[14]

The univocal attitude, however, was a theme within formal theology, though it generated few concrete implications for practical life and existed in a complementary relationship to the generally multivocal style of practical life.[15] A person's salvational status or relationship to transcendence, to Christ, was not dependent on doctrinal belief as a univocal ideational attitude. It was more a matter of experiential faith, the total response and whole-hearted absorption that places all of oneself in personal relationship to spiritual truth.[16]

The Roman Catholic Church in the Middle Ages tended to reduce ethical pressures to such an extent that society would have deteriorated in its commitment to spiritual values if this tendency were left unchecked. This provoked the formation of sects that sought to renew ethical pressures and create reforms, and the dialectic between the mainstream Church and peripheral sects persisted throughout the Middle Ages. A theoretical tradition amongst scholars of the sociology of religion sees this dialectic as the primary motif within the history of religion, particularly Western religion.[17]

The sectarian impulse based on dualistic ethical perfectionism led periodically to escalating tension and conflict. In terms of the repression-projection dynamic, ethically zealous reformist sects constituted ingroups that perceived the mainstream Church as a wayward out-group responsible for the spiritual degeneration of society. The Church-sect tension had to be neutralized in some way and the medieval Church accomplished this and moderated the overly intense ethical pressure within the sects through reabsorbing them into the mainstream as either monastic orders or lay brotherhoods—in a sense, "co-opting" them. The Church gave them power, made them part of the mainstream, and was to some extent reformed by them, so that the sectarian pressure actually had a kind of cybernetic feedback effect by continuously "correcting" the direction of the mainstream. Of course, the Church-sect conflicts were not always resolved in this way; sects were sometimes dispersed through excommunication and even persecution for heresy, and in the later Middle Ages such persecution resulted in widespread executions. (Likewise, the tense dialectic between Christianity and Islam throughout much of the later Middle Ages, as well as the anti-Semitism and scapegoating within Christian societies, had as their source the repression-projection dynamic that tends to accompany dualistic religions.)

The sectarian impulse throughout the Middle Ages was an urge to concretize the ideal, to achieve an *equation of fact and value*.[18] The medieval Church managed to contain the sectarian impulse until the compromise between univocality and multivocality finally ruptured in the sixteenth century with the Protestant Reformation. Univocality then began to dominate multivocality in the everyday realm of practical life. The Protestant Reformation marked the triumph of sectarianism and the beginning of univocal-rational culture as we know it.

A primary influence upon the development of a univocal cultural sensibility was the notion that the Bible had one fixed meaning throughout history. The early Protestants assumed not only one fixed meaning, but also that scripture was transparent to the understanding of anyone capable of reading it. This assumption of scriptural perspicuity was a natural handmaiden to notions such as the priesthood of all believers and the deemphasis of the sacraments, both of which were intrinsic to Protestantism. The Protestant Reformation exchanged the authority of the medieval Church as a mediating institution between man and God for the fixed authority of the written word. If biblical meaning were not univocally fixed once and forevermore, then there would remain no inerrant link between man and God. Other Protestant cultural themes such as ethical precisionism and the predestination of individual fate by an inscrutable watchmaker God flow naturally from such biblical literalism.[19]

The values and themes of the Reformation achieved full hegemony in Northern European culture in the late eighteenth century as a result of their complex interaction with the themes of the Enlightenment. What the Enlightenment chiefly added to the rationalist formulation of the Protestants was the empiricist-positivist theme—the view that knowledge is to be derived only from sensory experience combined with the process of discursive reason. When applied to the question of individual fate such an empiricist orientation tends toward the view that spiritual stature will be reflected in observable material or social status, a notion that had some influence among American Puritans under the heading of the "doctrine of assurance." Within this doctrine the interlinked spiritual and social stature were still held to be predestined by God. When material failure is assumed to be a sign of eternal damnation, however, powerful practical motivation is established for the individual to attempt anxiously to succeed in worldly terms. From this point it is a relatively short step to the Enlightenment's rejection of the doctrine of predestination and its affirmation of the typically capitalist notions of free will and mastery. Thus, the interaction of the Reformation and the Enlightenment gave birth, via the American and French revolutions, to the "spirit of capitalism" and its success ethic—the notion that the individual's moral value is reflected in worldly success.[20]

Of a piece with the rational-empiricist orientation in post-Reformation culture was the rise of individualism. The Reformation rejected the "institutional salvation" model of the medieval Church and shifted the emphasis onto individual autonomy. As viewed through rational-empiricist eyes, the world becomes atomistic, populated by radically separate objects and beings. The spirit of capitalism is, of course, highly infused with individualism. Similarly, the important theme of utilitarianism—the view that the worth or value of anything is determined by its utility— meshes naturally with the emphasis on material progress and the equation of fact and value.

Sociologists have described the post-Reformation cultural gestalt as a "culture of role."[21] One's functional position or status in the collectivity defined one's sense of personal identity and worth. Individualism was encouraged, yet the scheme of individualistic worth, the scale of status, was dictated by the group, the social collectivity. The univocal equation of fact and value on which these developments were based violated or transgressed traditional, multilevel religious principles in at least three ways. First, from a religious point of view, the name of the equation is *idolatry*, a condition of relating to the concrete symbol of transcendence as if it were ultimacy itself. Second, this equation presumes to assess the whole person based upon manifest appearances, behaviors, and specific acts, which violates the traditional view that final judgment is God's prerogative, the province of transcendent consciousness. Third, the equation eliminates the traditional distinction between appearance and reality, in effect collapsing the hierarchy of ontological levels by interpreting the lower in terms of the higher, such as in equating worldly success with moral stature.

When the univocal "culture of role" (rationalist, materialist, individualist, utilitarian-positivist) became established in Northern Europe (and then North America) in the late 1700s, there soon appeared multivocal counter-tendencies, stimulated by the swing of the mainstream into univocality and unilevel religion. Multivocal sensibilities remained peripheral counter-tendencies in philosophy, the arts, the sciences, and religion

for nearly two hundred years[22] until erupting in America in the 1960s
with sufficient force to bring an end to the hegemony of univocal attitudes. A pluralistic environment has resulted, visible in the mushrooming
of the new religions, many of which represent an enthusiastic pursuit of
multivocal monism in reaction to the dissatisfying, univocal dualism of
the old order.

However, as we have seen earlier, multivocality is in itself no guarantee of spiritual authenticity, as it can take both unilevel and multilevel
forms. Many, perhaps most, of the new monistic groups that have
emerged are unilevel, possibly because the unilevel sensibilities of the
old order, consisting largely of unconscious cultural biases and presup-
positions, have been carried over into the new groups. However, this unilevel carry-over, this epistemological sameness, is well hidden by the dramatic differences of spiritual imagery and themes in the new religions. If
this unilevel carry-over is indeed often the case—and in our view it is—
then one of the main tasks of transpersonal psychology should be to provide the public with practical assistance in the tricky task of recognizing
multilevel or genuinely transformative spiritual involvements. The
Anthony typology, to which we now return in depth, is one framework
of ideas to assist in this task. It describes how the unilevel misinterpretation of spirituality breeds problematic attitudes in groups, and how
multilevel orientations can be recognized.

THE ANTHONY TYPOLOGY IN DEPTH

We can now continue our earlier discussion of the Anthony typology
with a more thorough consideration of its categories and of the interplay
among the unilevel-multilevel, monistic-dualistic, and technical-charismatic bipolar dimensions.

Figure 2 names specific groups that in our judgment exemplify the
various cells of the typology. Some explanation is warranted regarding
the assignment of groups in the chart. The widespread emergence of the
new religions in the 1960s accompanied and mirrored a shift in the value-
structure of American culture. Ever since, all fields of cultural analysis
have focused on the new religions as a key testing ground on how American society could, or should, evolve. Those fields include sociology, psychiatry, social and clinical psychology, and the scientific study of religion
(a cross-disciplinary academic field involving sociology, anthropology,
psychology, linguistics, and philosophy). The anti-modernistic, neo-conservative movement in each field has been especially active in
promoting the documentation and intellectual scrutiny of the new reli-

Figure 2:

THE ANTHONY TYPOLOGY WITH ILLUSTRATIVE GROUPS

		Monism	Dualism
Multilevel	*Charismatic*	Meher Baba Neem Karoli Baba Da Free John[1] Baba Muktananda[1] ┌----Sri Chinmoy	(See note 3)

Multilevel	*Technical*	[Zen Buddhism]
		Tarthang Tulku (Tibetan
		  Buddhism)
		Chogyam Trungpa[1]
		  (Tibetan Buddhism)
		Swami Satchidananda
		  (Integral Yoga)
		[Shabd Yoga]
			[The Gurdjieff work]
			[Subud]

Unilevel	*Charismatic*	Bhagwan Shree Rajneesh ┌-Guru Maharaj-Ji Charles Manson Messiah's World Crusade	Unification Church ┌---Synanon People's Temple
Unilevel	*Technical*	Transcendental Meditation └---The *est* Training[2] └---Scientology Hare Krishna------------------	Norman Vincent Peale Robert Schuller Terry Cole Whittaker

Notes:

Square brackets indicate spiritual systems as distinct from specific groups of practitioners.

Dashed lines indicate a second typology category that represents an important aspect of a group's orientation.

1. The involvements offered by Da Free John, Baba Muktananda (who died in 1982), and Chogyam Trungpa appear to be multilevel except for certain aspects of each master's career that for us are problematic, especially incidents that could be seen as sexually hedonistic and could be taken as indicating a less than ultimate degree of spiritual realization. See the Introduction for an account of the controversy involving each of these masters.

2. The *est* Training is not offered as a spiritual avenue, yet is described as producing "transformation" and "enlightenment" and so is included here. For an explanation of what we see as its unilevel and multilevel elements, see the editorial commentary following the interview of Werner Erhard in Part 2. (The format of the training was revised and its name changed to the Forum in early 1985.)

3. While some traditions within orthodox Catholicism can be placed in the multilevel, charismatic, dualistic category, we do not happen to know of any *non-mainstream* spiritual groups that can be included here. Some monastic orders (exemplified in the contemporary period by, for example, Thomas Merton and Mother Teresa of Calcutta) focus on relationship with the person of Jesus, the Christ, as the essential condition for spiritual transformation, and do so in a context of multilevel spiritual sensibilities.

gions, particularly with respect to alleged brainwashing and other authoritarian abuses in cults. The controversy over cults and deprogramming has also stimulated a great deal of responsible journalistic scrutiny and informed intellectual comment on the world-views and practices of new religious movements (in, e.g., *The New York Review of Books* and *The Partisan Review*). In short, the high degree of cultural significance ascribed to the new religions from all quarters, pro and con, has led to a great deal of descriptive documentation. The assignment of groups to typology categories in Figure 2 is based largely on these sources of information, plus our own direct familiarity with the groups in question.

Unilevel Groups:

Unilevel groups confuse real and pseudo-transcendence of mundane consciousness. Spiritual themes receive consistently mundane interpretations that in effect subordinate them to personal desire, personal efficacy, security, self-concept, emotional compulsion, and competitive advantage. Unilevel interpretations foster an idolatry of the self, often in subtle, unconscious, and covert ways.

Generally this self-idolatry results from univocal or literalistic interpretations of religious statements, as if they were scientific statements with decisive, unambiguous meanings. As a rule, this occurs in a manner determined by prevailing cultural biases. In the American setting it is most often *consequentialism* that distorts spiritual-mystical interpretations, resulting in the unilevel view that the truth of religious ideas is found in their concrete consequences, particularly in their contribution to personal efficacy.

As we have noted, the term unilevel refers to a collapsing down into one level of what should be recognized as a multilevel hierarchy of types of spiritual knowledge. At the top of this hierarchy is ultimate spiritual gnosis of reality or divine being. Below this are the whiffs and glimpses of spiritual transcendence that come from transient mystical experiences, from personal contact with a genuinely enlightened master, or from the teachings of such a master. At the bottom of the hierarchy are interpretations of such teachings through the associations, categories, and meanings available to mundane consciousness—the level on which doctrine, dogma, and most theology exists.

Unilevel orientations blur the distinctions between these levels. For example, *believing* is confused with *knowing*: belief, an element of speculative interpretation in mundane consciousness, is mistaken for authoritative gnosis or direct knowledge of spiritual truth, which occurs only in transcendent consciousness.

This is not to say that all unilevel involvements are without value or are necessarily detrimental to members. While it is the case that virtually all of the blatantly harmful groups have been unilevel ones, a wide range of psychological and social benefits can result from participation in groups that we would consider unilevel, such as renewed vocational motivation, cessation of drug use, relief of neurotic distress, decrease in moral confusion and anomie, suicide prevention, and increase in social compassion and social responsibility.[23] Classifying a group as unilevel implies only that the group's claims regarding *spiritual* benefits—transcendence, transformation, enlightenment, or salvation—are in some significant way fallacious. Thus, although a consciousness group may consistently and impressively enhance its members' psychological well-being, it remains in our view unilevel if it does not promote spiritual transcendence or enlightenment as meant by the mystical traditions, yet claims to do so.

Unilevel Dualism:

Univocal literalism applied to the themes of the Western dualistic traditions produces unilevel dualistic groups. Primary examples are the People's Temple, Synanon (up to 1978, under Charles Dederich) and the Unification Church. As a rule, unilevel dualistic ideas carry to a rigid extreme the emphasis on a collective or group-oriented sense of identity that characterizes the dualistic traditions.

Authoritarianism in the new religions occurs most readily in this orientation because the collectivistic theme of commitment to an idealized social whole comes at the expense of individualism. Unilevel dualistic groups that explicitly combine religious and sociopolitical themes have been described as "civil religion sects,"[24] including the three groups mentioned above. Such sects view the surrounding, mainstream culture as corrupt and intrinsically threatening both to the group and to its purpose of reestablishing a virtuous society. Civil religion sects tend to hold utopian, absolutist, theocratic ideologies and to isolate themselves from the surrounding culture in alternative communities—self-sufficient mini-societies that are intended as examplary models and seedpoints for future American society. Members are encouraged or required to break off outside social and vocational involvements and to devote all of their energies working for the group's utopian vision. But although these groups often do create a large, complex community with formidable resources, they achieve social cohesiveness only by requiring a high degree of social and psychological uniformity, which provokes charges of cultism, authoritarianism, and brainwashing, and has elicited the anti-cult tactic of coercive deprogramming.[25] The high degree of submission to authority plus the relative social isolation of the group ties its fate to the mental health of the leader, usually a charismatic figure. The unilevel, dualistic, charismatic type of group is the most problem-prone and potentially perilous kind in the Anthony typology.

Civil religious sects articulate a dualistic moral idealism similar to some forms of traditional American civil religion. They seek the redemption of the nation through the imposition of univocal moral rules that definitively distinguish good from evil people and good from evil nations. Based on its univocal sensibilities, the group accords itself an exclusive association with the supreme good and contrasts itself with all who are evil, namely those who differ from the group's beliefs, rules, and allegiances. This contrast identity is a key aspect of unilevel dualistic groups.

It is outside our scope here to analyze the psychological dynamics that produce a contrast identity orientation—self-esteem and belongingness needs, reaction formation, repression and projection of the shadow— but it is noteworthy that a group with a highly polarized contrast identity may actually perceive the corruption of mainstream culture more-or-less accurately and insightfully. It is the group's view of itself as entirely without corruption that is pathological and an indicator of potential trouble. Such groups cannot promote authentic inner transformation because they do not help people to integrate all aspects of the psyche. Rather, they encourage repression and projection of psychical aspects considered "bad," and rigid identification with the opposite, "good" attributes.[26]

The mainstream American society is not, as a rule, receptive to the attempts of a civil religion sect to reform it, and becomes decreasingly tolerant as the group provokes increasing confrontations. This leads to serious problems for the group because the plausibility of its role and world-view is undermined as the larger society successfully resists its grandiose schemes.[27] The organization then tends to disintegrate, usually after a passage through highly volatile, desperate conditions, which in the case of the People's Temple at Jonestown erupted into a major catastrophe of mass murder and suicide. Synanon was on a course of increasingly violent confrontation with mainstream society until its leader was arrested in 1978.

The example of the People's Temple as well as the allegations against Synanon have lent a sense of urgency to the analysis of civil religion sects. How likely is it that other such sects will go to disastrous extremes in pursuit of their "missions"? Will the Unification Church, for instance, become immersed in tragedy as were the People's Temple and Synanon?[28] The chief diagnostic indicator of potential tragedy, in our opinion, is the combination of a contrast identity, isolation, and paranoid preoccupation with persecution. This configuration prevailed in Jonestown and Synanon but does not describe the Unification church.[29] Unlike the People's Temple, Reverend Moon and his devotees do not view their cultural environment, the non-communist world, as totally evil. Although it is corrupt and in danger of losing God's grace, it is also capable of redemption and spiritual revitalization. The Moonies see themselves as bearing the responsibility for bringing about the New Kingdom by winning over the masses, and pursue an optimistic activism that distinguishes them from the followers of Jones. The latter anticipated neither divine intervention in their behalf nor victory through their own efforts, and consequently became increasingly volatile and susceptible to despair.

Unilevel Monism:

Whereas Western dualistic traditions have been inherently collectivistic—the Islamic, Christian, and Jewish themes all involve one's membership in the divinely favored group as a necessary condition for salvation—Eastern monistic traditions such as Mahayana Buddhism and Vedanta Hinduism regard social identity as ultimately being part of the world of illusion, with salvation an individual affair. Monistic systems typically view history as cyclical rather than directional, and see time as illusory, so that the world does not change in any way that fundamentally affects spiritual salvation. The only real progress in spiritual development occurs on the individual level by transcending the conditioning influences of the outer, collective world, especially its prescriptions for the individual sense of identity.

When seen through the unilevel lens of American utilitarian-materialist, literal interpretation, these monistic ideas encourage an excessive individualism and become vehicles for the American themes of autonomy, control, and what sociologists call "voluntarism," the belief that human beings have free will to determine their own destiny. There is something of a paradox here; prominent, deterministic elements such as the law of karma in Eastern monistic systems could be expected to make adherents passive or even fatalistic, but as interpreted by Americans (such as Emerson, Thoreau, other Transcendentalists, New Thought and Unity)[30] the monistic ideas have become vehicles for voluntarism rather than fatalism.

We have seen that unilevel dualism generates an excessively group-oriented basis for identity, and so is prone to authoritarian developments that neglect the individual. Unilevel monism swings to the opposite extreme of excessive autonomy and individuality, and so is prone to narcissistic tendencies that neglect the welfare of society. This polarization of the individual versus the collective, or self versus society, illustrates a general characteristic of unilevel interpretations—the accentuation of polar opposites, with one pole regarded as the seat of truth, transcendence, or salvation. According to monistic mystical traditions, however, such polarization of qualities is the very basis of illusion; spiritual enlightenment involves penetrating realization of the illusoriness of the opposites of experience. Ideally, to approach this realization, human consciousness and sense of identity should be neither excessively individualistic nor excessively collectivistic. Rather, the whole dimension of self/society, if it were to be non-neurotic and non-problematic, would fade into the background of consciousness and would cease to be rigidly tied to self-concept definition. The degree of the individual's emphasis on self versus society would shift flexibly according to the situation, rather than cling to any one fixed position.

Another important polarity that the individual ultimately transcends, according to monistic teaching, is that of good and evil. Since the Eastern systems tend to see collective social reality as illusion, with salvation occurring only individually, salvation therefore involves the transcendence of society's moral rules, the socially conditioned notions of good and evil. To the American's utilitarian-individualist mentality, this appears to mean that all social rules, moral and pragmatic, imprison one in a rigid, inflexible, overly mechanical and predictable consciousness that prevents creative new solutions to problems. In this unilevel view the chronic determinism of karma only operates to the extent that one remains a prisoner of cultural or social conditioning. Freedom from that determinism, and true creativity, autonomy, and voluntaristic free will— mastery—requires that one reject and transcend the conventional rules and constraining commitments of social reality. This maximizes individual satisfaction.

Monism thus interpreted promotes a style of mastery that entails the repudiation of binding commitments—deep, long-lasting, intense commitments, whether to society as a whole, particular social groups, families, marital partners, or children. One works out specific and time-limited arrangements or contracts with others, the intent being to achieve maximal satisfaction for all parties involved, while minimizing binding commitments.

The American unilevel version of monism also involves what the sociologist Émile Durkheim called the "infinity of desire." Desire is potentially infinite when satisfaction is interpreted in an excessively individualistic way. Because an individual can always imagine ways in which his or her self-satisfaction could improve relative to any specific arrangement, he or she always feels deprived and wants to evade each established contract. There is a continuous attempt to improve contractual arrangements, all of which seem limiting and frustrating relative to some imagined future state of grandiose satisfaction.

In a sense, all of American culture is imprisoned by the "infinity of desire," and so unilevel monist approaches are popular because of the need somehow to maximize individual satisfaction. Unilevel monism both expresses the individualism of American culture and in turn intensifies it. The *est* Training, Scientology, Transcendental Meditation and many human potential offerings are examples of popular involvements that have significant aspects catering to unilevel monistic sensibilities. These systems actually do promote satisfaction and increase people's pleasure and efficacy in the material world in some respects, because unilevel monistic ideas lend themselves to practical application in the American culture, and people do become more satisfyingly effective in the world as a result. But these are short-term, pragmatic advantages, and the overall dilemma of the infinity of desire remains, producing anomie or existential nausea.

Unilevel, consequentialist interpretations of psychospiritual progress generate expectations of rapid, dramatic transformations of the highest order. Adherents claim that the two-weekend *est* training, for example, produces enlightenment for all who take it.[31] Unilevel monistic groups often sell their programs on a short-term schedule, consonant with the unilevel monistic preference for autonomy over commitment to long-term involvements. Participants sign up and pay for the expertise provided by these groups on a session-by-session basis. In Scientology, for example, the process of auditing is charged for by the hour.

We considered earlier how unilevel dualistic groups encounter plausibility problems that put the group as a whole in question, sometimes precipitating desperate actions. In unilevel monistic systems, on the other hand, the organizations are able to maintain the plausibility structure because participants in fact *do* experience short-term gains. Only later do they find that they don't know how to account for the long-term ineffectiveness of the ideas. They tend to think in terms of a failure of individual understanding or will, and the organizations escape blame. Individual self-blame preserves group plausibility in any kind of group, but the short-term format of involvement in many unilevel monistic groups makes this dynamic especially effective.

Unilevel Monism, Psychotherapy, and the Guru-Therapist Syndrome:

When unilevel monistic assumptions influence humanistic and transpersonal psychotherapy, the therapy—individual or group—

tends to adhere (though not in all cases) to a short-term format and to produce some potent, unusual experience—emotional catharsis, for example—so that clients leave thinking that their lives have been dramatically altered, when actually their dilemmas have not been resolved. The therapists and therapy organizations seldom become aware of any problematic aspects of the therapies they use. While human potential techniques in the workshop format can produce enduring resolutions of some clients' issues, the pseudo-resolutions produced in a unilevel monistic framework soon fail either to provide satisfaction or dispel the person's dilemma and distress, and so contribute to existential despair.

The flaws of therapy in this framework emerge more visibly in situations that prolong the therapy relationship. For instance, when one of the members of the first year-long residential program at Esalen Institute committed suicide, group leaders realized that workshops oriented excessively towards sharp confrontation and dramatic catharsis were not really helpful. They also realized that there were no long-term marriages among the Esalen staff; staff members tended to be unable to maintain commitments to loved ones and family. There seemed something wrong with a set of ideas that supposedly promoted universally benign change and transcendence, but failed as a framework for stable family life.

The problems generated by unilevel monistic assumptions in the human potential movement also become evident when they are utilized within an ongoing, one-to-one therapy relationship. The excessive emphasis on autonomy and control results in minimal attention to the evolving relationship between therapist and client and, in particular, in a neglect of transference.[32] The neglect of the client's transference results also from the wildly optimistic view of therapy that the unilevel monistic framework often engenders, assuming that the client will be changed quickly by therapeutic techniques that are so potent as to make the relational aspect of therapy unimportant. But the techniques are usually not that potent, which becomes evident when the therapy is long enough. After an initial phase of positive transference in which the techniques seem impressive and the therapist is idealized by the client as a guru figure,[33] a period of disillusionment sets in when the client becomes aware that problems are persisting, though perhaps in a superficially changed form. The therapist now appears something other than a miracle worker, and this disillusionment ushers in the client's negative transference. In therapy based on unilevel monistic assumptions, the negative transference tends to develop especially quickly and intensely because the therapy rarely can produce the dramatic, immediate, and enduring changes that are expected. Furthermore, the therapist in this framework is not prepared to recognize, let alone work with the negative transference, and so there are many abrupt and unhappy terminations of therapy in the human potential movement, and much jumping from therapist to therapist.

"Tantric Freudianism" as a Unilevel Monistic Motif:

Known for its unorthodox and sometimes seemingly scandalous approaches to what other traditions regard as our "lower" nature—desires, passions, and urges of all kinds, sexual and otherwise—the Tantric tradition of India and Tibet has become popular among spiritual seekers in America and Europe. Tantrism everywhere is highly vulnerable to misinterpretation and degeneration into a pseudo-spiritual rationalization of libertinism and power-greedy occultism.

Tantrism is a distinct type of mystical sensibility that exists independently of, but enters into, other mystical traditions. There are many Tantric sects within both Hinduism and Buddhism. In addition, the Tantric sensibility has had a great influence on Taoism and Shingon, a major religious sect of Japan. Most spiritual traditions require the aspirant straightforwardly to turn away from dark to light in order to achieve transcendent realization, but Tantrism regards itself as a way of power that seeks to utilize all aspects of experience, good and evil, virtues and vices, for the purpose of achieving enlightenment. Tantrics consider this to be the most direct approach possible, the "Short Path." The passions and the forces of darkness and delusion "are yoked like snarling tigers to the adept's carriage. The dangers of such a course are obvious."[34] Despite these dangers, the Tantric sects of Asia differ widely with respect to indulgences in libertinism and the use of occult power for selfish ends. At one end of the spectrum are sects, such as those of Tibet's Vajrayana Buddhism, whose doctrines take an impeccable stance against such indulgences.[35] There are even some Tantric sects in Tibet, India, China, and Japan that give little or no attention at all to erotic themes. At the other end of the spectrum are many sects whose philosophies and practices are appallingly degenerate, carrying to grotesque extremes the unilevel view that antinomian acting-out is necessary for achieving mystical realization.[36]

The popular understanding of Tantrism in America and Europe is usually distorted toward the degenerate forms. The acting out of socially prohibited desires and impulses, especially formerly repressed sexual and aggressive urges, is viewed as transcending one's socially conditioned, limited identity, revealing good and evil in their true light as arbitrary cultural constructs. The tendency to interpret Tantrism in this unilevel way is probably much increased in the West by the support unilevel Tantrism finds in popular but erroneous notions of the Freudian theory of repressed sexuality or libido. In pop Freudianism, the dramatic, cathartic release of repressed sexual and emotional impulses is seen as the route to freedom and transcendence of psychosocial conditioning. The convergence of pop Freudian and unilevel Tantric sensibilities is obvious. "Tantric Freudianism" denotes this hybrid as a unilevel monistic motif that in varying degrees influences many groups, perhaps most notably the approach of Bhagwan Shree Rajneesh.[37] Popular stereotypes of Zen Buddhism also suffer this distortion.[38] Tantric Freudianism can serve as a rationalization for flamboyant acting-out and impulsivity, including substance abuse or other modes of escapist immersion in sensual pleasure.

While the coming-to-consciousness of inadequately assimilated, repressed sexual-emotional contents can indeed be instrumental to the resolution of psychological disturbances, in itself it by no means constitutes what the major mystical traditions mean by transcendent consciousness, no matter how extraordinary and liberating the cathartic release or accompanying acting out may be. Catharsis is no guarantee even of the psychological resolution of conflicts, and can have serious disadvantages as a psychotherapeutic technique.[39]

In orthodox Freudianism and in higher Tantrism, it is the prohibition against awareness of repressed impulses that is lifted, not the prohibition against acting them out. Both traditions involve techniques for making unconscious impulses conscious and assimilating the psychic energy carried in them (although these techniques and the depths to which they penetrate are very different in the two traditions). The advantage of awareness without acting out is that the energy can be separated or transformed from its investment in primitive urges—primitive in the sense of keeping the individual from entering into social harmony (Freudianism) or spiritual realization (Tantrism).

From the viewpoint of mystical spirituality, the problem with yielding to passionate lustful, aggressive, or covetous urges is that these urges lock one more strongly into the illusory ego-state of separate, isolated "I"-consciousness. The other person, toward whom these urges are directed, becomes an external object who is used and has significance only insofar as he or she fulfills or frustrates one's cravings. The spiritual value of consciously restraining these urges that embody unenlightened self-interest is to make the opposite trend, empathy or compassion, possible. In empathy the recognition of the other as a "thou" or keenly feeling being makes a claim on the heart that limits how far one is willing to indulge self-interest at the other's expense. Empathy goes beyond mere self-restraint into self-forgetting or true attenuation of self-preoccupation.[40] The farther reaches of self-forgetting penetrate the illusion of separateness more and more, until the illusion vanishes altogether in ultimate realization of spiritual reality in its seamless oneness. Thus, to act regularly on passions and desires that implicitly regard others as objects is to pursue a course inherently contrary to the essential process of spiritual realization.[41]

The above discussion provides a basis for discriminating between authentic and degenerate Tantric practice. To sharpen the picture further, let us briefly examine the pragmatics of dealing with passions and desires in a Tantric tradition we regard as an exemplary form of higher Tantrism, Vajrayana Buddhism.[42] In Vajrayana as in all Buddhism, it is understood that desire is the cause of suffering (this is the second of the Buddha's Four Noble Truths) and is a major obstacle to enlightenment. However, as a Tantric approach Vajrayana differs from non-Tantric Buddhist sects in that, rather than striving to *extinguish* desires and passions and as a result lose the great amounts of energy in them, its strategy is to *transmute* desires and passions so that their full force and energy are harnessed in service of the aspirant's intensive striving for enlightenment in this lifetime. To transmute a desire totally and irreversibly in this way is to "vanquish" it; the desire is undone, its energy completely reclaimed. Vanquishing is held as the best outcome if it can be safely done, but this is not always possible, since dangerous frustration and serious mental disturbance can result if one too long avoids yielding to an intense, persistent, unvanquished desire. Therefore, failing to vanquish, the desire must be "ennobled," a process similar to but somewhat broader than Freudian sublimation. In ennobling, the desire persists but its force is transferred from the objects or images that were its initial focus to objects or images identified with the spiritual goal. Specific meditation techniques exist for this purpose. Note that both vanquishing and ennobling require keeping desires in awareness in order to work with them; the aspirant must not repress or deny them on the one hand, or indulge them on the other. The aspirant is not always able to sustain these difficult conditions, and failing to achieve continued non-indulgence, retreats into a third approach, "yielding in special ways." This means either closely observing the act, its causes and results so that lessons are drawn that make the desire less compelling, or else using special techniques of attention and visualization during the act in an attempt to prevent the indulgence from deepening the grip of the desire. In no case should the aspirant simply indulge in gratification of the desire in its own terms. Yielding, the least preferred way of working with the passions from the Vajrayana point of view, is utilized only when unavoidable and even then is guided by techniques aimed at the eventual vanquishing of passions.

In contrast to the approach just outlined, degenerate or unilevel Tantric groups typically seek an ongoing, intense stimulation of passions and desires with unrestrained indulgence or acting out, based on the false premise that rule-breaking and sheer intensity of emotion foster mystical realization.

Technical and Charismatic Styles of Practice in Unilevel Groups:

Earlier we described the tendency of unilevel dualism to produce problems for a group as a whole, while unilevel monism tends to produce problems for the individual. An exception to this pattern emerges on the monistic side when we consider the technical-charismatic variable of the typology. The monistic groups that have avoided problems for the organization as a whole are ones in which the group's practice orientation is primarily technical, such as est, Transcendental Meditation, and Esalen-style human potential involvements. The potential of unilevel monistic systems for volatility and impulsive, dramatic acting out is moderated when they have a structuring discipline of techniques. The techniques involve a considerable degree of disciplined attention to immediate, pragmatic means-ends relationships, which operates as something of a control on the impulsivity and grandiosity that can develop when participants regard themselves as transcending conventional moral norms.

Unilevel monistic charismatic groups, on the other hand, lack the disciplining influence of techniques and can foster dramatic acting out and ventilation of emotions through impulsivity, as illustrated in the extreme by the homicidal activities of Charles Manson and his followers,[43] and by the broken legs and arms that were regarded as acceptable side-effects in Rajneesh encounter groups. Whether monistic or dualistic, unilevel charismatic groups tend to enter into conflict, as a group, with the larger society. As we have seen, the unilevel dualistic groups that are the most problematic are the groups that are the most charismatic, such as Jim Jones's People's Temple and Synanon, which despite extensive use of techniques, became increasingly charismatic under Chuck Dederick.[44] By contrast, unilevel dualistic technical groups seem benign—witness the positive thinking groups such as congregations influenced by Norman Vincent Peale, Unity, and other Christian technique-oriented groups, including Pentecostal groups that emphasize speaking in tongues and catharsis.

The charismatic orientation tends to be highly problematic in all unilevel groups because unilevel sensibilities fail to provide a check on any grandiose delusions entertained by the leader. The group remains gullible as the leader's fantasy becomes more and more inflated, fed by members' adulation, homage, or worship. In unilevel charismatic groups the fate of the group hangs upon the mental health of the individual who is leading it. As his or her own mental state becomes increasingly unstable, so does the fate of the group.

Unilevel Groups, Belief and Self-Concept:

In general, unilevel religion and unilevel psychospiritual orientations centrally involve an idolatry of explicit formulations (texts, ideology) that the group regards itself as definitively understanding. They view their formulations as being ultimate, and so in effect their commitment is to the formulation, the belief system, rather than to a genuinely transcendental truth.

Both monistic and dualistic unilevel orientations involve this basic univocality, but in quite different ways. Most unilevel dualistic groups overtly and explicitly emphasize conversion to belief in the group's definitive formulation. In unilevel monistic groups, the members' commitment to a belief system is frequently covert and disguised as participation in a "science of consciousness," by which they "see for themselves" through experimentation with their consciousness as individuals that the group's metaphysics are true. For example, the Divine Light Mission of Guru Maharaj-Ji has used techniques that produce retinal luminosity with closed eyes, auditory signals, and tastes in the mouth. There follows a huge leap from these empirical events to the all-enveloping world-view they supposedly demonstrate. Members slip into belief in an entire cosmic scheme on the basis of very limited "evidence." This unilevel monistic emphasis on concrete, experiential "proof" of a transcendental belief system reflects the materialist, consequentialist value orientation of American culture, and again illustrates the cultural distortion of mystical teachings.

As a rule, unilevel systems make definitive assessments of people's spiritual status or degree of attainment using conversion to the group's belief system or ideology as the major criterion. Unilevel groups typically assign momentous spiritual significance to change in belief. When converted to the group's beliefs, a person supposedly is conclusively established as saved or enlightened as opposed to those others who are unenlightened, fallen, or damned. We have described the unilevel attitude as essentially an idolatry of the self, a witting or unwitting exploitation of spiritual themes for mundane and self-serving purposes. Commitment to the specific belief system is taken as evidence that the self is somehow superior to other selves. Consequently, unilevel groups tend to define sharp, categorical differences between insiders and outsiders, establishing a rigid boundary between believers and non-believers, enlightened and unenlightened. This sharp boundary is an important mark of groups with unilevel sensibilities. However, there is a subtlety here. By "boundary" we are not referring to whether formal membership is sharply defined, or whether meetings are closed and secret. These are not in themselves the essence of the unilevel boundary; rather, the issue is whether group members regard themselves as having a definitively superior and privileged spiritual status relative to humanity at large simply by virtue of their commitment to the group's practices and belief system.

Belief is something more than just entertaining an idea. It is the commitment to being a certain kind of person—the kind who would affirm that idea.[45] In effect, beliefs are not so much conceptual entities that you *receive*, as much as decisions about yourself that you *make*. The overarching significance of unilevel belief is that by subscribing to the group's beliefs, members achieve highly positive beliefs about themselves: they are good, superior, saved, advanced, enlightened. This enhancement of members' positive self-concepts is a primary, if usually unconscious, function of involvement in unilevel groups. By encouraging members to identify rigidly with a highly positive self-concept, unilevel groups foster the repression of what in Jungian psychology is called the shadow, the aspects of oneself that conflict too much with one's self-concept and arouse too much anxiety and disorientation to face and accept. Such groups therefore cannot assist people to integrate consciously all aspects of the psyche, as is required if one is to move beyond mundane ego-consciousness. Authentic spiritual inner development becomes a possibility in multilevel groups, where the individual's commitment to the group is based not on belief but on faith, a distinction of the first magnitude in religious life that has been blurred in the contemporary United States.

Multilevel Groups:

What is needed to transcend rigid, literalistic religion is not abandonment of religious forms, beliefs, or guiding structures, but abandonment of *certainty* about one's interpretations of them. In a multilevel group interpretations of spiritual teachings and symbols are understood as being necessarily fallible, yet the aspirant makes a deep commitment to the guiding forms of his or her particular path. Descriptions of transcendent consciousness are not interpreted in terms of mundane experience.

One of the essential aspects of spiritual development is the attenuation of the many forms of preoccupation with the self-concept and self-interest—a gradual release from involvement with all sense of "I," "me," "my," and "mine." Multilevel groups recognize not only the primacy of this task, but also its exceedingly subtle and elusive nature. On the whole they avoid getting caught in the unilevel "idolatry of the self."

Multilevel groups do not proselytize by appealing to self-interest, self-image, or fascination. They do not promise dramatic progress, vivid experiences, personal efficacy or power, secret knowledge, bliss, psychic abilities, wealth, health, or romance. One may assume, of course, that various self-serving motives accompany any line of action—including joining a multilevel group—but the attraction to multilevel orientations tends to be on the basis of a recognition of their intrinsic truth value. Even if less noble motives are simultaneously present, to join seeking some higher truth for its own sake is to create an allegiance that involves, from its beginning, a gesture of self-transcendence. Thus, popular notions of self-improvement do not apply to multilevel involvements. The seeker of self-improvement is in a way the opposite of the seeker of self-transcendence, developing and cultivating the psychophysical self-identity rather than shedding it. The distinction is an important one. Conventional societal indicators of social and psychological self-improvement generally prove irrelevant to spiritual development in multilevel groups.

Monism and dualism, considered in the context of multilevel sensibilities, contrast much less than their unilevel versions, though some scholarly experts on mysticism such as R. C. Zaehner and Rudolf Otto have argued that there is a clear distinction between Eastern and Western mysticism.[46] One difference often cited is that Western mysticism involves an exalted apprehension of God while Eastern mysticism involves union with God. In that sense, then, Western mysticism remains dualistic. But there are also many convergences between Eastern and Western systems of mysticism, to the point where many thinkers, for instance Aldous Huxley, affirm an essential sameness.[47]

When religious systems are interpreted univocally and regarded as sets of *beliefs*, their differences are maximized; spiritual reality, at the level of ultimate, direct realization, is essentially one, but *formulations* of that reality differ according to the cultural matrix in which they are embedded.[48] A Westerner and a person from an Eastern culture could have identical experiences of ultimate mystical realization, but the metaphors and frame of reference they use to convey something of ultimate reality to the unenlightened will necessarily draw upon the stock of images available to the home culture. That accounts for both the similarities and the differences between multilevel religions from East and West. The similarities derive from the fact that the same reality is being poetically and symbolically described; the differences derive from the different vocabulary of metaphor in different cultures. People whose consciousness is lodged on the physical plane and deeply conditioned by their culture can begin to come into felt relationship to transcendental reality only through the metaphors that speak to them. The use of metaphoric pointers towards transcendent reality is for the purpose, after all, of communicating a sense of that reality to the unenlightened. The people who are enlightened certainly do not need the teachings and symbol systems because they have the reality itself, which is transcendent. The enlightened one knows that "the map is not the territory." The maps he or she offers for the benefit of the unenlightened do not definitively or comprehensively or in any sufficient sense capture the gift of that reality. That essence is ineffable. But because these maps are intended to aid people in pursuing the experience of the reality, they are constructed in the language of the cultures themselves, and so differ from culture to culture. It appears possible to distinguish the surface structure or culture-specific forms used to describe ultimate spiritual gnosis from the deep structure or cross-cultural invariants.

Thus, multilevel groups do not place central emphasis on *beliefs*. They do not encourage the attitude that their belief systems definitively or exhaustively embody ultimate spiritual truth. Multilevel groups instead regard sacred scripture, the teachings and utterances of enlightened masters, and the like as having a potency, a multivocal and often metaphorical potency, to foster certain kinds of inner transformation if properly assimilated. In contrast to unilevel groups, belief systems in multilevel groups do not idealize members' self-concepts. Therefore, multilevel groups do not assign greater ontological worth to insiders than to outsiders. In fact they discourage all definitive moral judgments or evaluations of either oneself or others as total persons. Multilevel morality has a different basis.

Multilevel sensibilities affirm the metaphorical nature of religious language and avoid literal, univocal interpretations. Religious teachings and symbol systems serve as vehicles for approaching transcendence, but are in no sense equated with transcendent reality itself. (Unilevel monistic groups may explicitly affirm the same attitude, but they trivialize that affirmation in actual fact by covertly giving central importance to belief.) Multilevel groups relate to the metaphorical/poetic/symbolic character of religious systems in a truly operational way. Members realize that their approach to their symbol system is always a matter of interpretation, and their interpretations, they know, may be and in fact almost certainly are mistaken since aspirants in multilevel groups do not regard themselves as enlightened. Consequently they realize that any overt contrast between their symbol system and other symbol systems is dependent upon uncertain interpretation, and that to use their identification with their symbol system as proof of their superiority to outsiders and their systems is folly. The multilevel attitude is that individual members are not qualified in any objective sense to make statements about the superior validity of any religious system until they achieve transcendental gnosis. Until then, they cannot make those kinds of judgments. And since the enlightened masters within these traditions discourage religious exclusivity and emphasize the need to find oneness rather than "manyness," students and disciples have no grounds (other than raw egotism) for affirming divisive attitudes towards other groups.

It cannot be overemphasized that the tendency towards unilevel self-idolatry persists far into the process of authentic spiritual transformation and is constantly present and active even in multilevel groups. An important aspect of multilevel spiritual practice is the process of recognizing the unilevel or pseudo-transformational postures that one has unwittingly brought into the involvement. Discovering one's own unilevel tendencies and learning not to be seduced by them requires a continual refinement of awareness and discrimination. While unilevel tendencies become institutionalized in unilevel groups, they do not dominate in multilevel groups because of a shared appreciation of the key distinctions between actual gnosis of spiritual reality, experiential glimpses, symbols, and teachings that point to that reality, and interpretations of those symbols, teachings, and glimpses. The defining feature of a multilevel group is an active awareness of these distinctions, which minimizes the degree to which unilevel distortions can grow before they are recognized and greatly reduces the potential for a group's spiritual system to serve as a vehicle for self-idolatry. In unilevel groups the epistemological hierarchy is collapsed to one level. This is a result of the univocal, positivistic notion that there is only one correct way to understand religious meanings and symbols, and that once one has that understanding and accepts it as truth, one has achieved salvation or enlightenment and stands apart from the common run of humanity.

Still, any multilevel group has, as a rule, certain unilevel twists to which it is particularly susceptible and which therefore must be remedied in some way as they occur. As an example let us consider the Gurdjieff work, a multilevel dualistic technical orientation when appropriately pursued. This system was brought to the West by G. I. Gurdjieff, a native of Armenia, who died in 1949. Gurdjieff's system includes teachings and practices derived from various esoteric traditions within Eastern Orthodox Christianity, Sufism and Zoroastrianism. The transformative efficacy of this approach depends upon long-term involvement in a competently led Gurdjieff group, an essential condition without which Gurdjieff's teaching is merely a body of interesting ideas. One of the special strengths of the Gurdjieff perspective is its vigilance against the unilevel error of interpreting transcendence where there is only mundane consciousness. In this perspective the chief requirement for developing the needed discrimination and avoiding unilevel self-delusion is a willingness to experience one's own mundane consciousness consciously, for what it is—uncertain, crowded with insubstantial, false selves, and virtually devoid of anything truly "higher" and enduring. The Gurdjieff work has three principal points of susceptibility to unilevel distortions:

1. Gurdjieff's metaphysics holds that man does not automatically possess a "soul," or "kesdjan body." It is developed over time only by special forms of inner struggle, which the Gurdjieff work is meant to support. But the Gurdjieffian diagnosis of man as he is—asleep, soulless, and fully controlled by biological, psychological, social, and cosmic forces—can be used to justify a denial of the intrinsic worth of others and oneself, stemming from the view that until people develop to a certain level of consciousness—the awakened state of having a "real I"—they are basically automata and not truly human selves at all. This attitude can rationalize the exploitation and manipulation of others. One may disregard morality in dealing with beings who are really just mechanical systems. In this unilevel distortion, one's lack of empathy for others as feeling beings is legitimized as reflecting one's ability to discriminate lower from higher development. Moreover, Gurdjieff groups that mismanage this aspect of the teaching tend to produce a low sense of self-worth in neophyte and low-status members, since they believe themselves in some sense subhuman. The view that the spiritual worth and final spiritual destiny of the individual are fundamentally in doubt is the defining feature of dualistic orientations in the Anthony typology.[49]

2. Gurdjieff's approach stresses giving only the necessary degree of attention and energy to one's "negative" emotions and tendencies, an inner practice of some subtlety. It can degenerate into repression of feelings in general (dualistic systems have a particular tendency to foster repression) and a stiff, mental tenor of life. Here, avoidance of one's emotional dimension is mistaken for transformational endeavor.

3. The Gurdjieffian vigilance against false spiritual hopes and false sense of transcendence can lead to an excessive downplaying and neglect of members' spiritual feelings and aspirations. Being ordinary and mastering the ordinary state can become so much the focus and apparent aim of the work that it becomes unclear why one is doing it, so remote does the spiritual possibility seem. In this unilevel distortion genuine spiritual yearning, which involves an active intuition of spiritual reality, is mistaken for mundane imagination and emotionality.

These three unilevel twists often occur even in competently led

Gurdjieff groups, but only as stages through which relatively inexperienced members pass in the course of maturation. But in less competently led groups, these three trends are the end product rather than temporary phases that lead beyond themselves.

Multilevel groups, then, are not free from the problem of unilevel tendencies, but are able to overcome them. Let us look now at additional ways in which multilevel groups differ from unilevel ones. In unilevel groups, mystical experiences tend to be interpreted as proof of the correctness of the belief system, and hence of the spiritual status of the individual and the group. But in multilevel perspectives genuine mystical experiences are regarded as valuable *glimpses* of transcendent consciousness; they do not imply any conclusive spiritual attainment.[50] In this sense, again, people in multilevel orientations do not see sharp boundaries existing between their groups and other people. Both insiders and outsiders are far from attaining ultimate spiritual realization, which so vastly transcends all other levels and kinds of experience that everything that is not "That" is more similar to everything else that is not "That" than it is to ultimacy. The seeker within a multilevel group feels a commonality with all of struggling humanity (including members of unilevel groups). He or she is not particularly concerned with his or her own relative degree of imperfection because relative to the goal of realization of the ultimate truth, all imperfection is the same. It is all not "That."

Thus multilevel groups affirm a vast difference between ordinary mundane consciousness and the state of full mystical enlightenment, which is attained by a rare realized master. The mystical traditions describe intermediate stages of transformed consciousness, but for our present purpose we need only consider the two extremes of ordinary and fully realized consciousness, and the radical transformation of consciousness in going from one to the other. Multilevel groups do not trivialize that distinction; unilevel groups do. The *est* training, for example, has been criticized along these lines because its creator, Werner Erhard, has maintained that the two-weekend training produces enlightenment, or at least what would be termed enlightenment in Zen Buddhism.[51] In Scientology a certain number of hours of auditing brings one from a deluded state to the state of "Clear," which is supposed to be equivalent to the consciousness of the Buddha. In a Rajneesh ashram the emotional upheaval and sense of catharsis that occurs at the end of chaotic meditation is equated with *samadhi*, a transcendent state of consciousness.

Multilevel groups, on the other hand, do not see authentic transcendence as so readily attainable. The unenlightened state is assumed, and there is no expectation of quick transcendence, or even any steady progress towards it. Multilevel groups sustain the allegiance of individuals who value the authenticity of the approach rather than the expectation of rapid progress. For if direct consciousness of ultimate spiritual reality is the only goal that has inherent, timeless truth, if all other games or involvements are inherently relative, fleeting and deluded, then the only enterprise that makes any sense is to strive towards that goal to the best of one's ability, but without, paradoxically, any sense that one has a sure capacity or power to get any closer to it. But that is of no matter, since, as Buddha said, any length of time is short; the important thing is to turn towards the spiritual goal and to act in a way that seems to have most promise for bringing one closer to it. To this end, multilevel groups regard the moral dimension of experience as an important area of spiritual practice.

Morality in Multilevel Groups:

Moral rules in multilevel groups are not regarded as metaphysically ultimate injunctions, as they are in unilevel dualistic religion. Rather, moral rules have a two-sided pragmatic function. They help the aspirant to go beyond ego-consciousness by preventing behaviors that sustain or exacerbate it; and they "prime the pump" by fostering attitudes and values that begin to anticipate some of the attributes of transcendent consciousness.

In using the Anthony typology, the ability to recognize the multilevel attitude toward morality is an important area of discrimination. The multilevel assumption is that spiritual aspirants, in contrast to enlightened masters, seriously need guidance on how to steer among the apparent opposites of good and evil tendencies in ways that promote spiritual realization. Group members do not assume that they have gone beyond good and evil simply by virtue of commitment to the group's world-view and practices. Moral rules and principles are regarded as being necessary to guide the social practice of the unenlightened until they transcend all finite identifications and become a perfect embodiment of pure love, when such rules will no longer be necessary. This view of morality can be found throughout the literature of the mystical traditions. For instance, in the aphorisms of Patanjali,[52] the central text of Raja Yoga, Patanjali argues that the practices of yoga start only after moral practice has been established, and that the yogic practices assume the aspirant's obedience to the traditional moral maxims. In traditional Zen Buddhism (as distinct from popularized or "beat" Zen), the application of moral rules in day-to-day living is a key aspect of the student's practice.[53]

Among the teachings and utterances of historical masters—Buddha, Chuang Tzu, Ramakrishna, Hafiz, Rumi, Kabir—there is a consensus that the transcendence of conventional morality in ultimate enlightenment amounts to being more attentive to the welfare of others, not less. In the state of final enlightenment there is no sense whatsoever of separative "otherness" in relation to anyone or anything, so that pure, unconditional love becomes an intrinsic aspect of the enlightened consciousness. This love expresses itself in the most supremely intelligent way in each situation, always bringing about the maximum benefit for those with whom one comes in contact. One sense, then, in which ultimate enlightenment transcends conventional morality is that it far surpasses it. Another sense in which one goes beyond good and evil in ultimate enlightenment is that one no longer has a self-concept, and so is not what Meher Baba calls a "prisoner of the good," following moral rules self-servingly as a way of supporting a positive self-image. On the contrary, the separate self, the ego-self, has radically dropped away. In multilevel groups, members realize that they have not achieved final enlightenment, and that selfishness, self-concern, fear, neediness, play large and even dominating parts in their make-up. Therefore they cannot afford to abandon traditional moral rules that limit self-interest.

Multilevel groups, then, accept the restrictions of moral rules without becoming imprisoned in a positive self-concept as the result of obedience to them. One way they accomplish this is through an ongoing comparison of their personal degree of inner development with descriptions of the ultimate state. Multilevel approaches involve valid strategies for glimpsing real transcendence, and these glimpses reveal mundane consciousness, which is the members' normal state, as a kind of delusion. Following moral rules as a strategy for minimizing that delusion is not identified in any way with the attainment of some high position on the ladder of spiritual development. Obedience to moral precepts is recognized as simply a minimal condition for being a seeker at all. One is so far from the goal that despite glimpses of greater being and despite a multilevel perspective, one is essentially the same as any other person trapped in this predicament of mundane, egoic consciousness.[54]

What happens when moral rules conflict? For example, suppose a child is starving and the mother has no resources for providing food. After unsuccessfully trying all conventionally acceptable ways of obtaining food, the mother steals bread to feed the child. Obviously, this is a case where the moral imperatives of "thou shalt not steal" and caring for a dependent child conflict, and one has to make a choice.

In multilevel orientations, the fabric of moral themes and their possible conflicts is accepted as being so complex that in any specific situation, an outside observer cannot possibly judge accurately all of the relevant factors. The universal human dilemma faced in multilevel systems
is that it is impossible to codify morality in a rational, unambiguous, general formulation that would enable one to know the optimally moral act
in each specific situation by referring to the formulation. This view of
authentic moral choice as an intrinsically personal and non-routine act of
judgment has a substantial basis in the history of Western thought. Both
Aristotle and Kierkegaard, for example, affirmed that moral choice in
actual, concrete situations is inherently dialectical, a balancing act that
strives to achieve the "golden mean" between opposed excesses. Since
situations are always unique, one must always choose anew, as if for the
first time. One must choose wisely, but with no real assurance that one
will be able to do so, since moral choice cannot, in the end, be decided
according to mechanical principle. Hence Kierkegaard describes the
"authentic" individual as living in "fear and trembling," a condition of
"dread," caught between the opposites; and to replace authentic choosing with a rational formulation or belief system that tells one what to do
(the unilevel solution, in our terminology) is to deaden self-awareness and
abandon one's own being, a condition of "despair."

A multilevel view assumes that despite their most sincere efforts,
people of mundane consciousness necessarily miss the golden mean to
one degree or another all of the time. Sin is relative, not a matter of black-
and-white contrast with virtue. Compared to the perfect morality of the
fully enlightened being, who always fulfills the Dharma and enacts the
golden mean, relative sin is the constant state of all who are unenlightened. Therefore, one cannot definitively establish one's own moral virtue
by contrasting it with another's inferior moral stature, even if the contrast
involves some apparently conclusive difference, such as some crucial act
that the other has performed that is regarded as sinful. Although the
members of multilevel groups strive earnestly to live up to their system's
moral imperatives, they do not believe that they therefore are capable of
judging other people who do not obey these imperatives. Only when seen
from the viewpoint of transcendent consciousness—God's or the enlightened master's—is the moral condition of individuals clearly and certainly
known.

The moral sensibility in multilevel groups differs from the sociological notion of obedience to moral rules as a price that members pay to
belong to a society, with a consequent right to judge and punish those
who disobey. Multilevel groups are not that kind of club. They are highly
moral, yet do not define their boundaries according to whether people

appear to obey or violate rigid moral formulas. This helps their members attenuate separative and elitist attitudes and gradually evolve toward conscious oneness with all humanity and all existence.

Lest there be any impression that morality in multilevel systems is a matter of "anything goes," again we stress that quite the opposite is true. Members accept both their full obligation to moral law and the dilemma of not always knowing how to fulfill it. Multilevel systems often involve codes of specific moral rules to which members take vows of obedience, as for example in Zen Buddhist, mystical Christian monastic, and certain Sufi orders. In general, behavioral conformity to these rules is expected to be as definite as in any unilevel group, although the way members view the significance of the conformity is quite different.

Multilevel Faith Versus Unilevel Belief:

In unilevel groups, *believing* is confused with *knowing*. In multilevel groups, the distinction between believing and knowing is clear. The authenticity and transformative efficacy of a person's religious commitment does not stand or fall on the possession and accurate grasp of a correct set of concepts; while concepts can help orient the seeker toward spiritual reality, they fail, in themselves, to capture it. So, while multilevel group members accept conceptual maps as valuable, and in this sense do entertain beliefs, they know that they do not know truth definitively through such devices—which is to say, through the intellect. Their religious commitment is based on a different kind of knowing, which has traditionally been called faith.

Faith is an enormous subject, and we aim here only to sketch the important distinction between faith, a primary characteristic of multilevel orientations, and belief, a primary characteristic of unilevel ones. Wilfred Cantwell Smith's *Faith and Belief*[55] presents a persuasive examination of the faith/belief distinction in Buddhist, Islamic, Hindu, and Christian instances.

According to Smith, belief is a modern orientation that has come into widespread use as an aspect of the univocal rationalization of culture. Belief, in the modern sense, is an attitude toward propositions about reality—rather than toward reality itself—wherein the believer affirms that propositions that might be false are in fact true. The belief orientation assumes that the propositions under consideration have a clear, univocal meaning that is understood in the same way by anyone with minimum linguistic competence. The primary existential issue with respect to such propositions, then, is whether they are true or false rather than whether the individual's understanding of them is adequate. Smith contends that such an epistemological orientation toward religious concepts did not exist prior to the Enlightenment in any of the above religious traditions, and that it exists today as the central orientation only within the Christian tradition in the West.

Interestingly, according to Smith the modern concept of belief did not even have linguistic representation in English prior to the Enlightenment. The English word "belief" then meant something akin to love and commitment, so that a statement such as, "Believe in Him and you will be saved" meant that you would achieve salvation if you loved and were faithful to Christ. Belief was an existential orientation toward persons or institutions rather than an epistemological orientation toward propositions. The meaning of "belief" gradually changed from its traditional to its modern sense as the prestige of the positivistic attitude spread from science to other cultural areas such as religion and politics. Thus, when we read an English version of the Bible such as the King James, which was translated before the modern period, the frequently occurring word "belief" means something quite different to us than it did to its original translators. Although the word "belief" was often used, the modern concept of belief appeared seldom if at all in this or any other traditional sacred text.

Faith, Smith explains, is primarily an orientation toward ultimate spiritual reality—rather than toward propositions about that reality—in which a person achieves an organismic affirmation of not only the existence but also the benevolence of transcendent being. Within the four religious traditions Smith explores, it is taken for granted that the stock of images, concepts, and practices within each tradition is useful as an aid to the achievement of such faith. In this sense the body of received doctrine is considered to be true; it aids in the attainment of that faith without which life is hollow and meaningless. The question of the empirical truth or falsity of the statements embodying such doctrines—that is, the question of "belief"—typically does not arise because it is the truth of individual lives rather than the truth of propositions that is considered the fundamental religious issue. Faith is the hallmark of this existential truth or authenticity.[56]

This is indeed how religious concepts are utilized in multilevel groups, where they form an ideational framework that guides members toward more direct modes of spiritual knowledge. Of course, the members of any group, multilevel or unilevel, *operationally* accept their particular religious forms (texts, symbols, practices, and the like) as true. How, then, can a seeker distinguish multilevel faith from unilevel belief? Unilevel groups interpret spiritual ideas and symbols in terms of mundane meanings that are well-defined, wholly understandable rationally, and therefore closed. We have seen that for the person of unilevel belief, conceptual uncertainty threatens the very basis of the religious involvement, and so the conceptual posture tends to be rigid and well-protected by psychological defense mechanisms. This is the literalism or univocality that characterizes the way unilevel groups regard their forms as "true," and it is a key indicator for the seeker. We have cited a number of examples, including the five confusions described earlier (pp. 46–52). In contrast, in multilevel groups the acceptance of religious forms as "true" is not literalistic, because this is the open-ended, multivocal acceptance of the transcendent dimension on its own terms, as it were, with no pretense of definitively understanding that which is accepted as true. Thus the multilevel acceptance of religious forms draws upon and is an expression of faith. The relationship between faith and critical reason has been described by Meher Baba:

> True faith is grounded in the deeper experience of the spirit and purified intuition. It is not to be regarded as the antithesis of critical reason, but as its guide. . . . Many forms of credulity cannot be removed except by the free working of critical reason. However, critical reason can clarify only those forms of faith that are not based on pure intuition. True faith, grounded on pure intuition, is an imperative which cannot be made subject to reason; for it transcends the limits of the mind and is fundamental and primary. . . . True faith is a form of sight, not blindness, and need not be afraid of the functioning of critical reason.[57]

Technical and Charismatic Styles of Practice in Multilevel Groups:

We have described how multilevel groups face and accept the spiritual seeker's condition of unenlightened ego-consciousness—of walking, as it were, in the dark, on uneven ground, carrying a candle (consciousness) that usually illuminates the terrain barely if at all, yet sometimes blazes briefly, giving a helpful glimpse-experience of greater vision and surer treading. We now need to examine how the technical and charismatic forms of practice operate in this multilevel context.

In multilevel technical groups such as Zen Buddhism (monistic) and the Gurdjieff work (dualistic), techniques do not have a short-term, clear-cut relationship to the process of enlightenment. One simply does them as a way of conscious living. Distortions that prevail in unilevel groups—attachment to or idolatry of techniques, the tendency to value the aid to transcendence as if it were actual transcendence—do not prevail in multilevel technical groups, although they may occur in individuals at early phases in the course of spiritual maturation. Practitioners in multilevel technical groups do not expect to achieve enlightenment solely as a result of technique. Rather, techniques are seen as part of a much larger process of spiritual inner development, and often have multiple or paradoxical purposes. The point is that multilevel technical groups trivialize neither the great complexity and duration of the process of ultimate spiritual realization, nor the fact that with or without techniques, one is unable, as a separate, ego-bound individual, to bring about one's own enlightenment. The image of a snake eating its own tail is sometimes used to make the point that a technique—the snake's mouth—can undo much of the egoic or "lower" self. But the mouth cannot then finally eat itself, and one's egotism becomes invested in the spiritual technique and the attainments it yields. This is a tendency common to both multilevel and unilevel groups. Spiritual inflation and egotistical motivation can fuel technical spiritual practices and deliver the aspirant to impressive stages of experience beyond mundane physical awareness. However, when based on egotism these attainments and experiences constitute a binding addiction rather than a liberation, and the person's motivational structure must sooner or later collapse. In multilevel technical situations, one is expected to recognize dramatic experiential consequences of the techniques as being yet other forms of illusion, and one ruthlessly evades attachment to them. The possibility of self-delusion due to mistaking intermediate for ultimate consciousness of spiritual reality persists far into the journey. The best safeguard may be close guidance from a highly enlightened master.

Psychospiritual practice in multilevel technical groups usually occurs within a time-tested, highly evolved tradition that makes the shared wisdom and examples of centuries or millennia of advanced practitioners available to present aspirants. Obvious examples are the various branches of Buddhism, certain Sufi orders, and certain yogic traditions within Hinduism, such as Raja Yoga. Such traditions use very subtle distinctions and discriminations to guide members' daily practice as well as their interpretations of texts and symbols. This traditional context serves to limit the degree to which changing cultural sensibilities can distort the group's perception of its path. It preserves a multilevel, multivocal appreciation of spiritual meanings and serves as a corrective to univocal, rational-discursive-literal interpretations that tend to arise in the modern context.

The role of the spiritual master in multilevel technical orientations goes well beyond conventional concepts of "teacher," "instructor" and "expert." What the master communicates and reveals is much deeper and subtler than formal instruction in techniques. The master is firmly established in an intermediate or advanced level of transcendental consciousness and can *directly impart* transcendental experiences to the disciple.[58] But in a multilevel technical approach the master in effect guides from the side, and leaves the whole responsibility for achieving spiritual progress to the disciple. Progress made is in direct proportion to the disciple's exertion and utilization of the master's guidance.

In the multilevel charismatic situation, the basic strategy of spiritual development is quite different. Multilevel charismatic involvements are unfamiliar and in some respects foreign to contemporary Western sensibilities, and tend to be interpreted reductionistically even in transpersonal circles. We therefore need to describe this category of the typology in some detail.

By definition, the multilevel charismatic approach relies on the transformative potency of a personal relationship to a master who is regarded as God-conscious. In multilevel charismatic monistic frameworks, the ultimate state is viewed as one in which consciousness directly experiences Godhead as its own true nature: the God-realized master has penetrated all limited identifications with matter, energy, and mind and is fully conscious of *being* the formless, divine reality. In this state no trace of an egoic, separate self sense remains; the manifest personality is a direct expression of and direct link with divine Being. The consciousness that looks out through the eyes of a God-realized master is, according to multilevel charismatic monistic orientations, none other than the infinite, transcendental self—the innermost reality of all apparently separate beings and things. The master is both an external person and the indwelling divinity within the disciple.

The disciple becomes aware of the master's presence within, and the task of spiritual practice is then to keep the master's company, internally, throughout the situations of daily experience. This requires the disciple to develop remembrance of and attention to the master, which gradually brings about a thoroughgoing integration of the disciple's personality, since all aspects of oneself now have to become somehow compatible with the master's company. This complex task challenges the whole structure of ego-based living, but the disciple is motivated by the supreme value of the master's contact and by the love that the master elicits—the love of God-unconscious for God-conscious, as one master puts it.

Spiritual progress in this approach is strictly a matter of deeper or closer inner communion with the master. The main obstacle is self-preoccupation and self-interest. Drawing closer to the master involves effacement rather than advancement, removal rather than gain. The disciple continually discovers and surrenders old patterns of thought, feeling and action that obstruct the inner contact or generate resistance to the master's guidance or orders. The ego is gradually attenuated, and the master's presence—the disciple's true self—becomes more and more the inner reference point of consciousness, replacing "I", "me" and "my." Eventually the final veil of ego is lifted by the master, giving God-realization—union with the ultimate spiritual reality, which is the master's conscious self. The process is usually regarded in multilevel monistic groups as requiring many lifetimes.

Whereas in multilevel technical situations the master assists from the side and responsibility for achieving spiritual illumination rests with the disciple, in multilevel charismatic situations the master is the central focus and final goal of spiritual practice, and the disciple is responsible for working towards deeper self-surrender to the master. The master bestows spiritual transformation and gnosis upon the disciple when the latter is ripe for it. Self-surrender in multilevel charismatic involvements is not a matter merely of symbolic or ritualistic gesture, but of actually relinquishing attachment to mental, emotional, and behavioral patterns that make one unavailable for the master's inner contact.

Western culture stresses individual autonomy and views charismatic master-disciple relationships suspiciously. The distinction between unilevel and multilevel charismatic involvements tends to seem insignificant in this context, especially since the concept of monistic God-realization is largely unknown and seems implausible here. Viewed through the Western sociocultural lens, multilevel monistic charismatic situations appear to be idolatrous on the one hand and psychologically regressive and authoritarian on the other. It seems to be idolatry to consider someone to be God personified, and indeed it *is* idolatry to do so—unless the person actually is God-realized. Idolatry occurs when a valued object or a symbol of spiritual ultimacy is regarded as being ultimacy itself, but if the God-realized state actually exists—and in our opinion it does—then a God-realized master is *both* the symbol of ultimacy and ultimacy itself. To recognize and honor the divinity of such a master is not idolatrous.

Surrender and obedience to such a master differs fundamentally from the unilevel charismatic syndromes of authoritarianism and the exploitation of disciples' neurotic dependency needs. Not that disciples in multilevel charismatic situations are free of such tendencies; it is the master who is free of any tendency to exploit these traits. Rather than exploiting disciples' dependency needs or sheltering them from their struggles with life, the multilevel charismatic master repeatedly throws the disciple back onto his or her own resources to "find" the master internally and receive the master's guidance. The master orchestrates this ongoing, complex process in a way that reveals and resolves neurotic distortions and deepens the experience of contact with the master's transcendental being. This process also teaches the disciple to discriminate between internal guidance from the master and mundane, subjective promptings born of desire, imagination, and social conditioning.

Mystical glimpse experiences in multilevel monistic charismatic situations tend to involve the master as both the trigger and the content of the experience; the disciple becomes aware of some transcendent dimension of the master's being. Since the master is the disciple's own real self, the experience not only brings the disciple into closer relationship with the master, but also brings the disciple's ego into conscious relationship to the disciple's innermost being.[59]

How can disciples be certain that the master has realized the ultimate monistic state? The multilevel attitude is that without being God-realized themselves, disciples do not and cannot have definitive knowledge of the master's divinity. All they know is what they experience of the master's effect on them. But this includes an intuitive recognition or inner glimpse of the master's spiritual stature, a felt knowing of the master's divinity that is not ultimate knowledge, but goes beyond emotionalism and ideological belief. It is the master who provides these glimpse experiences, including the discovery of the master's inner presence. Such experiences, which often play a key part in convincing the prospective disciple of the master's authenticity, are distinguishable from the psychic or occult effects of a lesser master because they do not fascinate; rather, they touch the heart and impart a deep feeling of coming home to oneself. Intuitive conviction and faith towards the master in a multilevel charismatic group is not a product of social consensus in the group, but derives directly from contact with the master. Also, the master passes the crucial test of time. As years and decades go by, the master's external personality remains fully plausible as an embodiment of ultimate truth, love, light, knowledge, power. The result is that the disciple perceives the master's transcendence as clearly more real and stable than the disciple's own ego-state. One sees that one's doubts are more a reflection of the instability and limitations of one's own consciousness than of the master's.

We have been examining the multilevel charismatic approach as practiced in monistic frameworks. Contemporary masters who represent this form of involvement include Meher Baba, Neem Karoli Baba, Da Free John, Baba Muktananda, and Sri Chinmoy. However, opinion is by no means uniform, and the plausibility of some of these masters as fully realized beings remains controversial.[60] Historical examples include Ramakrishna Paramahansa, the late nineteenth-century Hindu master of Bengal, and Shams-e-Tabriz, the thirteenth-century Persian Sufi master whose relationship with his great disciple, Jalālu'-Din Rumi, is one of the most famous instances of the multilevel charismatic situation.[61]

The history of Christian mysticism provides us with examples of multilevel charismatic spirituality in a dualistic framework. The love of Jesus, the Christ, draws the lover—the "bride of Christ"—into ever more complete surrender of the ego-life, leading to deeper degrees of conscious internal communion with Christ. It is love, surrender, and obedience in relation to Jesus, the only supreme agent of divinity in this tradition, that is spiritually transformative and salvational. The lives and experiences of Teresa of Avila, John of the Cross, and Francis of Assisi, for example, have provided the West with stunning demonstrations of the potency of charismatic love for a divinely conscious master. The spiritual practice of Therese of Lisieux is an important example from the early twentieth century, and in the contemporary period the entire world is aware of Mother Teresa of Calcutta, whose visible work radiantly expresses the relationship she experiences with Christ.

Among the new religions in America there are, to our knowledge, no groups that represent a multilevel charismatic dualistic involvement though there are, of course, certain monastic orders within the Catholic church that are dedicated to mystical spirituality of this kind. The non-mainstream "charismatic movement" among born-again Christians is, in our view, a unilevel (because fundamentalist or univocal) orientation. This is certainly not to say that born-again Christian involvements are devoid of religious value. However, as a rule these groups encourage rigid, polarized psychological postures in members, and so do not foster the reconciliation of opposites required for transcendence of the mundane ego-state.[62]

We have already noted how the multilevel technical and multilevel charismatic situations differ regarding the master's role in bringing about the disciple's enlightenment. In the multilevel technical case, the disciple has to achieve mystical gnosis directly through his or her own efforts, with the master guiding the way; in the multilevel charismatic case, the disciple has to surrender more and more profoundly to the master, who bestows deepening inner contact with divine presence and is responsible for bestowing ultimate spiritual realization when the disciple is finally ripe for it. In accordance with these differences, the two approaches differ in the degree of authority that is given to the master by the disciple. In the multilevel charismatic situation, the disciple regards the master as having unbounded authority that is worthy of unconditional obedience and surrender. In multilevel technical involvements, the master's authority has limits and the disciple retains a sense of being independent of the master, and ultimately on his or her own.

Obviously the emphasis on self-surrender makes charismatic involvements potentially more dangerous than technical orientations. By definition, a multilevel charismatic situation is one in which the master is

God-realized and therefore beyond any form of exploitation. But the prospective disciple has no way of knowing for certain if the master is indeed God-realized. In our view, one should accept a charismatic master's authority only if, after a period of "testing" the master to the best of one's abilities—we have suggested many criteria—one wholeheartedly can regard him or her as worthy of unconditional obedience and surrender, and as being *completely* plausible as a living embodiment of ultimate spiritual truth, love, being. One should test especially for whether the master's character leaves no doubt that he or she is worthy of total, unguarded commitment.[63] The prospective devotee who, after stringent scrutiny of the master's character, cannot regard the master in this way, unreservedly, should not accept the master's authority at all. The greatest danger is in allowing one's own wish-fulfillment to create the master's "divinity" and override an instinctive sense that the master falls short of ultimate spiritual transcendence.

Recognizing an authentic multilevel charismatic involvement is further complicated by the widespread view that the multilevel charismatic situation is inherently a kind of self-deception. This attitude, which prevails in transpersonal circles, has several causes. First, there is widespread disillusionment with many spiritual figures whose private behaviors eventually came to light and made a farce of their public image as the God-realized guru. Second, sophisticated Westerners are extremely wary of how unconscious, infantile wishes for an all-nurturing, all-knowing parent can lead us to project these God-like qualities onto a less-than-divine guru figure, but it amounts to mere religious prejudice when used to debunk the very concept of a God-realized master and the unique implications of a relationship to someone in that ultimate state. And third, the master-disciple relationship in the multilevel charismatic situation seems to violate deeply held Western values affirming individual autonomy and freedom from the dictates of others. While all three of these objections are borne out in unilevel charismatic involvements, the multilevel case, however rare, is an essentially different matter, one whose intrinsic significance awaits widespread Western discovery.

ULTIMATE ENLIGHTENMENT AND MASTER-DISCIPLE SEXUAL RELATIONS

Sexual contact between spiritual master and disciple is a deeply problematic issue that has yet to be seriously examined by transpersonal psychologists, despite the continuing discovery of such activity. For example, revelations documented in the Winter 1983 edition of *CoEvolution Quarterly* involve Baba Muktananda, the Hindu master who died in 1982 and who had a large American following, and Richard Baker, who resigned as abbot and *roshi* (Zen master) of the San Francisco Zen Center. (Sexual controversies also have compromised at least two other Zen *roshis* in other cities.) In April 1985 a number of former devotees of Da Free John publicly alleged that he routinely ordered followers to engage in sexual acts in front of him.[64] The central issue is this: Does a master's sexual behavior have implications regarding the master's level of spiritual realization and trustworthiness?

The answer to this question depends on one's model of the state of ultimate enlightenment. For example, we saw that in the unilevel model of Tantric Freudianism the idea that the fully enlightened master is beyond considerations of good and evil implies that the master's promiscuous sexual acts are exemplary, boldly transcending conventional morality, and demonstrating how to be promiscuous in a perfect, liberating, conscious, non-exploitative way. Our own understanding of the unitive heights of spiritual gnosis is that the fully truth-realized master has shed all limited identifications with matter, energy, and mind and directly experiences being the infinite, eternal, formless reality or Godhead, the true nature of all beings and things on all planes of existence. This is a permanent state of infinite completeness, freedom, knowledge, power, and bliss. Such a master can be termed "perfect" and is radically free of identification with the opposites, such as masculine-feminine, strength-weakness, success-failure, beauty-ugliness. Sexual desire, which is based on the duality of feminine and masculine qualities, could not exist in this fully truth-realized state. This multilevel monistic view of ultimate gnosis (which paraphrases the teachings of Vedanta Hinduism, Persian Sufism, and Mahayana Buddhism) implies that a perfectly enlightened master would not have sex with disciples because of his or her own desire. Such desire simply would not arise.

There are, however, three arguments offered to explain why a perfect master might engage in sexual relations with disciples: (1) to serve as a role-model for transcending conventional morality and going beyond the duality of good and evil; (2) to play in freedom with sexual energy as cosmic recreation; (3) to initiate directly the disciple into higher consciousness, or otherwise benefit the disciple's inner development, through the avenue of sexual, or *kundalini,* energy. Our view of spiritual perfection considers all three possibilities to be implausible. The role-model concept fails because the master's only purpose as role-model is to promote spiritual realization in others. Indulgence in sexual promiscuity does not do so and is no improvement over sexual repression as far as mystical realization is concerned. It is a unilevel fallacy to view the mere violation of conventional morality as a transcendence of good and evil; both promiscuity and repression are non-transcending strategies that exhaust themselves and leave deep dissatisfaction. Furthermore, promiscuity often rebounds into repression, and vice versa, each strategy reactivating the other and neither promoting a happy integration of sexuality and transformative spirituality.

That sex with disciples could represent the master's own cosmic enjoyment, free of attachment or desire, is equally implausible. The perfect master's infinite bliss is based on direct experience of being, in truth, the formless spiritual reality. The notion that physical sex would enhance a perfect master's already limitless ecstasy is inconsistent with this understanding of ultimate gnosis. Finally there is the view that a master might utilize the energies of sexual intercourse to foster a disciple's attainment of transcendent awareness. Whether or not this is a real possibility, actual experience shows that the chances of deception and self-deception in this matter are so great as to be almost a guarantee that a master's sexual advances constitute not authentic Tantric mysticism—which in its higher forms makes sexual energy serve spiritual ends through meditation, not physical sex[65]—but spiritual fraudulence and exploitation. Most female disciples who describe the effects of sexual intercourse with a master report not inner spiritual progress but deep psychological wounds and spiritual disillusionment and derailment.[66]

A spiritual master who sexually exploits a trusting disciple is comparable to a parent who sexually molests a child. Erotic feelings, tensions, and dependencies are a normal part of children's healthy development, but the sexually exploitative parent (or master) massively compounds these erotic tensions, failing to meet the unguarded child's (or disciple's) critical need for a way of resolving them and severely undermining his or her self-esteem. To be thus betrayed and used as an object by the very person from whom one most needs deep regard, understanding, and support, and who represents one's whole world of meaning, does great psychological harm with long-lasting emotional repercussions.

A master who has sex with disciples is in all likelihood not at the highest levels of enlightenment, not beyond self-interest, and therefore not a trustworthy candidate for the profound surrender and obedience of the charismatic form of spiritual practice. The technically-oriented apprenticeship relationship is, in our opinion, the only situation where the appropriateness of such involvement is even arguable. In the apprenticeship relationship, the disciple consciously retains responsibility for judging what is acceptable in the experiences that the master offers, and

so presumably can make up his or her own mind about the appropriateness of such activity given a particular, concrete situation. Even here,
however, the power differential inherent in any teaching situation makes
it likely that a sexual relationship between a teacher and student will
involve the egotistic exploitation of the latter by the former. Therefore
we recommend extreme caution on the part of the disciple.

SUMMARY

The Anthony typology encompasses many different aspects of the
world-views, interpretations, and practices of spiritual groups. It is a conceptual gestalt that eludes simple summary. The tables and chart that
follow are intended only as reference aids for using the Anthony typology. They are necessarily incomplete and rely upon the previous detailed
discussion of the typology.

The tables review the main features of the typology's three bipolar
dimensions—the monism-dualism dimension that describes a group's
metaphysics, the unilevel-multilevel dimension that describes interpretive sensibility, and the technical-charismatic dimension that describes
mode of practice. The final chart reviews some of the key characteristics
of the eight kinds of spiritual groups that the typology defines.

Figure 3:

METAPHYSICS DIMENSION

Monism	Dualism
The existence of separate beings and things is illusory.	The world is real.
The true nature of all is the formless Reality or Godhead.	Individuals have different final spiritual destinies.
All apparently separate beings will eventually experience ultimate realization, in which the separate self illusion vanishes and consciousness realizes its infinite true nature.	Separate selfhood persists even in ultimate spiritual gnosis.
	One's final status depends on fulfilling moral and/or metaphysical criteria.

Figure 4:

INTERPRETIVE SENSIBILITY DIMENSION

Unilevel	Multilevel
Univocal and consequentialist sensibilities generate "definitive," mundane interpretations of spiritual themes.	Non-definitive understanding of spiritual themes; multivocal interpretations preserve transcendental meanings without mundane skew.
Collapsed hierarchy of spiritual authority (gnosis vs. teachings vs. interpretations).	Distinct hierarchy of spiritual authority (gnosis vs. teachings vs. interpretations)
Conversion to the group's belief system gives entry into spiritually exalted status; membership implies definitive spiritual superiority.	Acceptance of group's beliefs does not confer exalted status; no definitive criteria for knowing the moral or spiritual stature of others.
Expectations of rapid, dramatic spiritual attainment	Spiritual attainment seen as a lengthy process that is largely beyond conscious control
Plays into members' desire for positive self-concept ("idolatry of the self")	Attenuates preoccupation with self-concept, positive or negative.
Polarization of opposites (good/bad, autonomy/surrender, success/failure, etc.) and identification of transcendence with one pole.	Dialectical interplay of opposites leading to a higher synthesis consciously realized.

Figure 5:

PRACTICE DIMENSION

Technical	Charismatic
Reliance on techniques as the essential means of spiritual attainment. A technique is any well defined, repetitive mental or physical activity that is regarded as being instrumental to the achievement of transformation.	Reliance on personal relationship to a spiritually realized person as the essential means of spiritual attainment.

PARTIAL REVIEW OF GROUP CHARACTERISTICS IN THE ANTHONY TYPOLOGY

		Monism	Dualism
Multilevel	*Charismatic*	Glimpses of master's unity with essential Self reconcile autonomy with surrender. Monistic/charismatic definition of spiritual ideals minimizes collectivistic authoritarianism and repression/projection dynamic. Point of vulnerability: misinterpretation results in narcissistic self-idolatry.	Glimpses of Christ's love for essential Self reconcile surrender with autonomy. Dualistic/charismatic collectivism of Catholic orders minimizes narcissistic hyper-individualism. Point of vulnerability: too much authority granted collectivity can reduce transformative potency of master-disciple relationship.
	Technical	Master's competence in transmitting skills and inspirational potency in embodying their effects resolve split between transcendence and materiality in modern life. Point of vulnerability: overly technical emphasis in contemporary culture may vitiate inspirational effect of master.	Same as multilevel monistic technical, but heightened sense of dualistic contingency results in heroic efforts. Points of vulnerability: outsiders may be defined as beneath spiritual/ethical concern, and neophytes may be overwhelmed at awesomeness of task.
Unilevel	*Charismatic*	Repudiation of moral norms, informal social structure, and peripheral status of techniques yields tendency towards either "borderline" impulsivity, small-scale sociopathy, or narcissistic stagnation, depending upon direction of psychopathology of leader.	Authoritarian collectivism/utopianism. Repression/projection dynamic: adversary relationship with surrounding society. Tendency towards mass extra- or intra-punitive action.
	Technical	Adaptation of mystical techniques for enhancing mundane personal effectiveness and well-being. Tendencies towards hyper-individualism, narcissism, and repudiation of moral norms.	"Positive Thinking" reinterpretation of Christian ethics. Christ viewed as Super-Capitalist. Success and virtue synonymous. Moral absolutism. Repression/projection dynamic directed at non-mainstream groups and Communists.

Notes

1. This typology was originally developed by Anthony as a device for summarizing several years of his and his team's research into the mental health effects of the new religions. The research was conducted under the auspices of the Department of Psychiatry, School of Medicine, University of North Carolina at Chapel Hill and was funded by United States Public Health Service Grants. Anthony first communicated the typology in his summary progress reports to the agency and subsequently has used it as a general framework for summarizing research on the new religions in a series of review articles usually co-authored by Thomas Robbins, a key member of his research team. These include: Dick Anthony and Thomas L. Robbins, "A Typology of Non-Traditional Religious Movements in Modern America," presented at the Annual Meeting of the American Association for the Advancement of Science, 1977; Thomas L. Robbins, Dick Anthony and James Richardson, "Recent Theory and Research on Today's New Religions," Sociological Analysis, Vol. 34, No. 2, April 1978; Thomas L. Robbins and Dick Anthony, "The Sociology of Contemporary Religious Movements," in Annual Review of Sociology, Vol. 5, Palo Alto: Annual Reviews, 1979; Dick Anthony, "The Fact Pattern Behind the Deprogramming Controversy," New York University Review of Law and Social Change, 9, 73–90, 1980; Dick Anthony and Thomas L. Robbins, "Contemporary Religious Movements and Cults—the United States," in Mircea Eliade et al. (eds.), Encyclopedia of Religion (New York: Free Press, forthcoming); and Thomas L. Robbins and Dick Anthony, " 'Cults' in the Later Twentieth Century," in Charles H. Lippy and Peter W. Williams (eds.), Encyclopedia of Religion in America (New York: Scribners, forthcoming). Each of these articles includes updated research in the field and cites hundreds of references. For ease of readability the authors have chosen to include in this presentation of the typology only a representative selection of these references. The reader interested in exploring the full range of research and scholarship upon which the typology is based should consult the above articles. In this presentation Anthony has considerably expanded the structure of the typology relative to its earlier versions. Bruce Ecker has contributed important elaborations to the explication of the typology categories and is also jointly responsible for the literary form of this version.

2. By "dualistic" and "dualism" we are referring to *ethical* dualism, *i.e.*, absolutist conceptions of good and evil, not to *ontological* dualism, which merely contrasts the mundane and transcendental realms (e.g., monistic Hinduism and Buddhism can be said to be ontologically dualistic). The Western mainstream of Judeo-Christian ethical dualism has involved a single transcendent, personal God who "legislates" to his creation, and whose revealed will forms a basis for conceptions of absolute good and evil. Only people who embrace good and reject evil are granted salvation.

Evil has often been embodied in a subordinate demon (Satan) who competes effectively with the omnipotent creator prior to the final apocalypse.

3. Known as the Forum, with a new format, as of January 1985.

4. Trungpa, Chogyam, *Cutting Through Spiritual Materialism* (Berkeley: Shambhala, 1973).

5. Wilfred Cantwell Smith, *Faith and Belief* (Princeton, NJ: Princeton University Press, 1979).

6. Robert N. Bellah, *The Broken Covenant: American Civil Religion in Time of Trial* (New York: Seabury, 1975).

7. Note that "narcissism" denotes a specific type of psychological condition, only one symptom of which is the outwardly apparent self-love and self-involvement that constitute the popular stereotype. Essentially narcissism involves a basic sense that one's self is unlovable and insubstantial. The outward symptoms reflect attempts to fill or distract from a chronic inner emptiness—cf. Heinz Kohut, *The Restoration of the Self* (New York: International Universities Press, 1977).

8. For another extensive analysis of the confusion of types of experience, see Ken Wilber, "The Pre/Trans Fallacy," in *Eye to Eye* (New York: Doubleday/Anchor, 1983).

9. See the Introduction and the interview of Dick Anthony.

10. The "idea of progress" is a dominant root metaphor structuring Western consciousness since the Renaissance and is the subject of an extensive literature. For a fuller discussion of its role in Western culture see Dick Anthony and Thomas L. Robbins, "Religion, Rationality and the Idea of Progress," *Society*, Nov.-Dec. 1979.

11. Søren Kierkegaard's description of this Romantic or "aesthetic" (his term) style in his 1843 work *Either/Or*, vols. I and II (Princeton, NJ: Princeton University Press, 1959) still has not been surpassed for penetrating insight. Kierkegaard argued that the bad faith, inauthenticity, or "despair" (his term) of such universalized relativism lies in its covertly ideological nature. The Romantic ideologue or "dandy" attempts to evade the dread inherent in an authentic experience of the normal human condition by adopting a systematic program of planned spontaneity and hedonism. By attempting the "construction" of a self through rational calculation of hedonistic consequences, the person adopting the aesthetic strategy confuses persona with self and puts authentic freedom or spontaneity at an impossibly great remove. Our critique of today's new religions in terms of the unilevel/multilevel distinction is similar to Kierkegaard's exposure of the spiritual flaws in the aesthetic strategy. For a useful discussion of the genetic relation between the elite aesthetic perspective of Kierkegaard's time and the mass aesthetic perspective of today see John Douglas Mullen, *Kierkegaard's Philosophy: Self-Deception and Cowardice in the Present Age* (New York: New American Library, 1981).

12. See also the Ram Dass article in Part 2.

13. The overview of Western religious evolution in this section is greatly influenced by the views Max Weber expressed in his scattered writings on the topic. A good brief source for Weber's perspective is Wolfgang Schluchter's article, "The Paradox of Rationalization: On the Relation of Ethics and World," in Guenther Roth and Wolfgang Schluchter (eds.), *Max Weber's Vision of History: Ethics and Methods* (Berkeley: University of California Press, 1979), 11–64.

14. An excellent description of the multivocal tendencies of the Middle Ages is in J. Huizenga, *The Waning of the Middle Ages* (New York: Doubleday/Anchor, 1954). See especially Chapter XV, "Symbolism in Its Decline," 200–214.

15. There is a line of argument—which we find persuasive—to the effect that communication technologies have a determining effect upon the epistemological rules that define the styles of consciousness of historical eras—cf. Neil Postman, *The Disappearance of Childhood* (New York: Laurel/Dell, 1982) and Donald M. Lowe, *History of Bourgeois Perception* (Chicago: University of Chicago, 1982). From this point of view, oral cultures are inherently multivocal whereas print cultures are univocal. Given this argument, the Christian Middle Ages was an intermediate culture that may be referred to as "scribal" in that the illiterate masses existed in a largely oral/multivocal epistemological space, while the literate clergy (the scribes) existed within a chirographic approximation of a print/univocal epistemological space. Moreover, chirographically based literacy retained many characteristics of oral culture—books were normally read aloud in a communal context, manuscripts had many variant forms, and authorship was essentially collective—which would presumably explain the mixed univocal/multivocal style of formal theology.

16. See Chapter 5, "Credo and the Roman Catholic Church," in Wilfred Cantwell Smith, *Faith and Belief* (Princeton: Princeton University Press, 1979). See also Smith's *Belief and History* (Charlottesville, VA: University Press of Virginia, 1977).

17. A good introduction to this theoretical tradition—"sect/Church theory"—is Roland Robertson, *The Sociological Interpretation of Religion* (New York: Schocken, 1970). For a novelistic depiction of sect/Church tensions see Umberto Eco, *The Name of the Rose* (New York, Warner, 1983).

18. A common complaint about the modern scientistic worldview is that by emphasizing an epistemological ideal of pure objectivity it produces an unbridgeable gulf between fact and value, thus producing existential nausea, angst, anomie. The phrase "the fusion of fact and value" is often used from this point of view to indicate the harmonious integration of subjectivity and objectivity and is taken to be a good thing. It is also argued that the medieval Christian worldview involved this fusion and that one of the advantages of contemporary mysticism is that it can reestablish a

fusion of fact and value even in the face of modern scientism (see for instance Claire Myers Owens, "The Mystical Experience: Facts and Values," in John White (ed.) *The Highest State of Consciousness*, (Garden City: Doubleday/Anchor, 1972), 135–152.

Medieval sects, however, believed themselves to be pre-millenial exemplars for the coming post-millenial Utopia or heaven on earth foretold in the New Testament. They considered their communities to be definitive of or equivalent to ethical value, rather than as merely attempting to establish the coherent relationship between ethical value and communal life as implied in the phrase "fusion of fact and value." The equation of fact and value, then, involves the idolatrous identification of the material *status quo* with transcendence itself, which we take to be a defining attribute of unilevel religion.

19. See Kai Erickson, *Wayward Puritans* (New York: Wiley, 1966) for an excellent study of the relationships between biblical literalism, moral precisionism (*i.e.*, the view that every detail of human behavior is to be regulated by absolute moral rules given by God), and the repression-projection dynamic in producing both literal and figurative "witch hunts" within American society. Erickson writes: " . . . the Puritans had an instrument of authority to offer which governed their lives as firmly as all the bishops in Christendom—the Holy Writ itself. Perhaps the most important difference between the Puritans and their Anglican countrymen was that they regarded the Bible a complete guide to Christian living, a digest of all the statutes and regulations necessary for human government. The scriptures not only supplied rules for the broader issues of Church polity but for the tiniest details of everyday life as well" (p. 47).

20. This view of the effect of the Reformation upon the development of the "spirit of capitalism" is heavily influenced by Max Weber's classic study, *The Protestant Ethic and the Spirit of Capitalism* (New York: Scribners, 1958) and by the similar thesis expressed in R. H. Tawney's *Religion and the Rise of Capitalism* (New York: Meuler, 1926). We are also indebted to a more contemporary study of the influence of the Scottish Enlightenment upon the development of capitalism: Albert O. Hirschman's *The Passions and the Interests: Political Arguments for Capitalism Before Its Triumph* (Princeton, NJ: Princeton University Press, 1977). Also, George Marsden, in *Fundamentalism and American Culture* (Oxford: Oxford University Press, 1980), offers a useful overview of the relationship between biblical literalism and the Enlightenment in the shaping of the positivist/utilitarian strains in American culture. For other informative sociological discussions of the problems of utilitarian/positivist culture see: Alvin W. Gouldner, "Utilitarian Culture and Sociology," Ch. 3 in *The Coming Crisis in Western Sociology* (New York: Basic, 1970) and Robert N. Bellah, *The Broken Covenant: American Civil Religion in Time of Trial* (New York: Seabury, 1975). An excellent and very original critique from the point of view of the philosophy of ethics is Alasdair MacIntyre's *After Virtue: A Study in Moral Theory* (South Bend, IN:

University of Notre Dame Press, 1981). In addition, it might be argued that the debunking of utilitarian/positivist or "bourgeois" culture is the primary preoccupation of artistic modernism. For a valuable survey of anti-bourgeois themes in modern American literature see Ernest Earnest, *The Single Vision: The Alienation of American Intellectuals* (New York: New York University Press, 1970). See also Daniel Bell, *The Cultural Contradictions of Capitalism* (New York: Basic, 1976).

Finally, it has been argued by an influential critical tradition (originating within modern Marxist thought) that the intolerance of ambiguity inherent in bourgeois ideology becomes authoritarianism, ethnocentrism, or dogmatism (of the left or the right) when subjected to social or psychological strain. See T.W. Adorno et al., *The Authoritarian Personality* (New York: Norton, 1950); Milton Rokeach, *The Open and Closed Mind: Investigations into the Nature of Belief Systems and Personality Systems* (New York: Basic, 1960); and David Loye, *The Leadership Passion: A Psychology of Ideology* (San Francisco: Jossey-Bass, 1977).

21. For a good discussion of the transition from a "culture of role" to a "culture of self" in post-1960s values, see Ralph Turner, "The Real Self: From Institution to Impulse," *American Journal of Sociology, 81*, 989–1016, March 1976.

22. See Isaiah Berlin's *Against the Current: Essays in the History of Ideas* (New York: Viking, 1980) for one of the most illuminating discussions of the dialectical relationship between the "rationalism" that gained hegemony in Western culture with the Enlightenment and the many "counter-rational" (Berlin's term) perspectives that developed in opposition to it. The most notable of the counter-rational perspectives include: the Romantic and Modernist movements in literature and in the other arts; existentialist philosophy, originating with Kierkegaard and Nietzsche; phenomenology, originating with Husserl; natural language philosophy, originating with Wittgenstein and Austin; dialectical approaches such as those of Hegel and Marx; and hermeneutics, whose most persuasive current exponents are Gadamer and Ricoeur. Most of these artistic and philosophical positions have been converted into counter-rational minority positions in the human sciences (which are dominated by rationalist positivism and utilitarianism). In social and political theory these include Schutzian phenomenology; ethnomethodology; symbolic interactionism; the natural language approach of Peter Winch and his followers; Robert Bellah's hermeneutic sociology; and neo-Marxist critical theory, developed most coherently by members of the Frankfurt school, including Adorno, Horkheimer, Marcuse, and currently Habermas. In the psychotherapeutic professions, counter-rational positions include those of humanistic and transpersonal psychology and existential psychiatry.

For excellent surveys of contemporary anti-positivist positions in social and political science, see Richard Bernstein, *The Restructuring of Social and Political Theory* (Philadelphia: University of Pennsylvania,

1976) and *Beyond Objectivism and Relativism: Science, Hermeneutics and Praxis* (Philadelphia: University of Pennsylvania 1983). For a discussion of anti-positivist orientations in the scientific study of religion see Dick Anthony, "A Phenomenological-Structuralist Approach to the Scientific Study of Religion," *ReVision, 5* (1), Spring 1982, and Dick Anthony, Thomas Robbins and Robert Bellah, *Between Religion and the Human Sciences: Toward the Non-Reductionistic Study of Religion* (Berkeley: University of California, forthcoming). For the commonly held view that the counter-culture of the 1960s developed largely as a result of mass exposure to the various types of counter-rational positions, see Daniel Bell, *The Cultural Contradictions of Capitalism* (New York: Basic, 1976); Marshall Berman, *All That Is Solid Melts Into Air: The Experience of Modernity* (New York: Simon and Schuster, 1982); Morris Dickstein, *Gates of Eden: American Culture in the Sixties* (New York: Basic, 1977); and Frank Musgrove, *Ecstasy and Holiness: Counterculture and the Open Society* (Bloomington: Indiana University, 1974). For counter-rational influences upon the development of interest in contemporary nontraditional religion see Robert Wuthnow, *The Consciousness Reformation* (Berkeley: University of California, 1976) and *The Post-Christian Periphery* (Berkeley: University of California, 1978).

23. For references to the original research literature on these findings see T. Robbins and D. Anthony, "Deprogramming, Brainwashing and the Medicalization of Deviant Religious Groups," *Social Problems* 29 (3), 1982, 283–296.

24. Dick Anthony and Thomas Robbins, "Culture Crisis and Contemporary Religion," in T. Robbins and D. Anthony (eds.) *In Gods We Trust: New Patterns of Religious Pluralism in America* (New Brunswick, NJ: Transaction, 1981).

25. For discussion about the deprogramming controversy, see the editorial commentary following Frances Vaughan's article in Part 3.

26. See W. Adorno, *et al., The Authoritarian Personality* (New York: Norton, 1950), 480–481 for a good brief discussion of the relationship between "intolerance of ambiguity," the repression-projection dynamic, and heightened in-group/out-group boundaries.

27. Note that we are referring to *nonmainstream* groups, groups that define themselves as deviating significantly from traditional American values. Specifically, the above argument does not apply to sects such as Moral Majority, the Mormons, and the charismatic Catholics.

28. Of course, the Unification Church has been accused of "brainwashing" converts, but this accusation is based upon flimsy factual evidence and probably should be regarded more as a rhetorical social weapon employed by the anti-cult movement than as objective truth. What we have in mind in the above passage is whether the Unification Church is likely to become involved in events which would seem tragic by anyone's reckoning.

29. Nevertheless, other attributes do qualify the Unification church as a civil religion sect. It was Robbins's and Anthony's participant-observation study of the Church that originally led them to define this category of new religious movement. See Thomas L. Robbins, Dick Anthony, Madeline Doucas, and Thomas Curtis, "The Last Civil Religion: Reverend Moon and the Unification Church," *Sociological Analysis,* 27 (2), Summer 1976. See also: Dick Anthony and Thomas L. Robbins, "The Effect of Detente on the Growth of New Religions: Reverend Moon and the Unification Church," in Jacob Needleman and George Baker (eds.), *Understanding the New Religions* (New York: Seabury, 1978); and Dick Anthony and Thomas L. Robbins, "The Growth of Moral Absolutism in an Age of Anxious Relativism," in Jack Douglas (ed.), *Observations of Deviance,* second edition (Boston: Allyn and Bacon, 1982).

30. New Thought and Unity are closely related American movements that began in the nineteenth century. They involve the popularization of Transcendentalism as well as an emphasis upon success and vague references to Christianity. See "New Thought, Faith Healing and Unity" in Nelson R. Burr, *A Critical Bibliography of Religion in America* (Princeton, NJ: Princeton University Press, 1961), 342–345.

31. Werner Erhard, the creator of The *est* Training, defends this claim in the interview in Part 2.

32. Transference is a normal aspect of longterm therapy. It consists of the client unconsciously confusing the therapist with his or her parent and reenacting unresolved themes of the parent-child relationship. Both positive and negative transferences occur. The therapist must respond by enabling the client to find new ways of resolving the old themes and the emotional patterns involved in them.

33. The interview of Claudio Naranjo and the talk by Ram Dass in Part 2 give first-hand accounts of problematic experiences in the role of guru-therapist.

34. John Blofeld, *The Tantric Mysticism of Tibet* (New York: Causeway, 1974), p. 71. Blofeld, an initiated practitioner of Vajrayana, the Tantric Buddhism of Tibet, emphasizes that "the techniques for hastening Liberation by transmuting the force generated by the passions could, if misapplied, easily lead to debauchery. All sorts of evils and excesses would result, producing the very antithesis of ego-negation. Therefore it is said: 'On entering the Tantric path, you are surely bound for Buddhahood— or for the Avicci Hell!'"

35. Blofeld *(op. cit.)* describing the Vajrayana attitude states, "Though *all* things are employed as means, they must be *rightly* used and their right use is far removed from sensual gratification. . . . The danger of confounding Tantric practice with, or using it as an excuse for, libertinism cannot be stressed too strongly" (pp. 33–34). "Descent into the libertinism practiced by certain Hindu Tantrists in Bengal or by the medieval

Christian antinomianists is fraught with peril and in any case unthinkable, for it would involve a breach of the Samaya-pledge; it is taught that the Tantric adept, having set powerful forces in motion, would be destroyed by their misuse as surely as an electrician is burnt up when the current from the mains is accidentally diverted through his body" (p. 78).

36. For a detailed study of this end of the Tantric spectrum see Benjamin Walker, *Tantrism: Its Secret Principles and Practices* (Wellingborough, England: Aquarian, 1982). Practices include: cultivation of lust, malice, and hatred and violation of social and moral rules through a progression of increasingly anti-social acts culminating in murder as an advanced practice; necrophilia; cannibalism; vampirism, in particular the psychic energy vampirism of women through sexual intercourse; human sacrifice; black magic occultism of lethal potency, including voodoo forms; promiscuous and perverse sexuality such as orgiastic rites in which males have intercourse with any female, including mother, sister, or daughter; and use of intoxicants and drugs.

37. For a critique of Bhagwan Shree Rajneesh as an exponent of Tantrism, see Benjamin Walker, *op. cit.*, pp. 138–142. See also the introduction to this volume for a summary of the controversy over Rajneesh.

38. For a description of the Tantric Freudian distortion of Zen, see the editorial commentary following Steven M. Tipton's article on Zen in Part 2.

39. See for example John Heider, "Catharsis in Human Potential Encounter," *Journal of Humanistic Psychology*, 14, 27–47, Fall 1974.

40. Blofeld, *op. cit.*, states that in Vajrayana Buddhism "compassion is enjoined as an essential means for negating the ego and attaining wisdom" (p. 32). He discusses a central precept, "See all beings as Buddhas," which in practice "means that we must treat everyone with the consideration and respect due a potential Buddha, be eager to serve him and loathe to do him harm. . . . [T]he main purpose is to develop the Tantric attitude of mind which leads to actual perception of the holiness of beings. . . ." (p. 78).

41. While lust, aggression, and covetousness represent the most self-interested, primitive extremes of various urges and emotions, these urges and emotions have a spectrum of other forms less dominated by self-interest. Animal lust, for example, is the crudest aspect of sexuality or erotic feeling precisely because it lacks intersubjective awareness or empathic regard of the other, but sexuality can also of course be highly integrated with sensitive intersubjective regard. A defining feature of erotic feeling, as distinct from lust, is the urge for intimate discovery of the other; there is an impulsion beyond one's usual ego-boundaries toward the other, who is no longer an object to be used but a self to be known and to whom to make oneself known. Yet erotic feeling does not fully or automatically solve the problem because it tends to arise loaded with projections onto

the other, which obscure intersubjective perception and keep the other's significance dependent upon one's own egoic psychology. The work of removing the projections finally allows for love proper: implicit self-interest is attenuated to the point that one intensely values the other and seeks his or her best interest without wanting anything in return. The full process of removing the projections, largely freeing one's regard from egoic self-interest, can only occur through thorough mutual involvement over time, and sexual exclusivity. Peripheral sexual involvements that lack thorough mutual involvement over time re-establish and re-energize one's projections, cutting off the process. As we understand it, this whole process constitutes the potential value of marriage for promoting spiritual realization, and is the reason why many highly realized masters, past and present, emphasize restricting sex to the marriage relationship.

42. Our account paraphrases that of Blofeld, op cit., 74–82. Of course, it should be assumed that not all groups or teachers who describe themselves as Vajrayana practice authentic Vajrayana Tantrism.

43. For a discussion of Manson's assumption of the guise of a monistically enlightened master, see R. C. Zaehner, "The Wickedness of Evil," *Encounter*, 42, April 1974, 50–58.

44. The Introduction provides a review of problematic developments in Synanon. For a first person account of these developments see William Olin, *Escape From Utopia: My Ten Years in Synanon* (Santa Cruz, CA: Unity Press, 1980).

45. See John Douglas Mullen, *Kierkegaard's Philosophy: Self-Deception and Cowardice in the Present Age* (New York: New American Library (Mentor), 1981), 67.

46. See R. C. Zaehner, *Mysticism Sacred and Profane: an Inquiry into Some Varieties of Praeternatural Experience* (Oxford: Oxford University Press, 1957) and Rudolph Otto, *Mysticism East and West: A Discussion of the Nature of Mysticism, Focusing on the Similarities and Differences of Its Two Principal Types* (New York: MacMillan, 1932).

47. Aldous Huxley, *The Perennial Philosophy* (New York: Harper Colophon, 1944). Other versions of this argument include: Frithjof Schuon, *The Transcendent Unity of Religions* (New York: Harper, 1975); W.T. Stace, *Religion and the Modern Mind* (Philadelphia: J.B. Lippincott, 1960); and Huston Smith, *Forgotten Truth: The Primordial Tradition* (New York: Harper Colophon, 1976). The view that Eastern and Western mysticisms are convergent is generally part of an argument that there is an underlying unity of religion—in spite of the apparent variety of orthodox doctrines—which is constituted by its mystic central core. Ninian Smart, in *The Science of Religion and the Sociology of Knowledge: Some Methodological Questions* (Princeton, NJ: Princeton University Press, 1973, 61–62) refers to this viewpoint as "core theory" and offers criticisms of it. He concedes, however, that most phenomenologi-

cally oriented theoreticians of religion, such as Joachim Wach, Mircea Eliade, and Wilfred Cantwell Smith, describe an underlying experiential unity of religion.

George A. Lindbeck in *The Nature of Doctrine: Religion and Theology in a Post-Liberal Age* (Philadelphia: Westminster, 1984) argues that core theory is one version of the "experiential-expressive" interpretation of the nature of religious doctrines as non-discursive symbols expressing pre-cognitive inner states. He contrasts the experiential-expressive view of doctrine with the cognitivist (or propositional) and the cultural-linguistic views. According to Lindbeck the cognitivist viewpoint is now confined primarily to fundamentalist sects, the experiential-expressive viewpoint dominates in mainstream or liberal theology, and the cultural-linguistic viewpoint is influential in the history, anthropology, sociology, and philosophy of religion. He also states that the core theory version of the experiential-expressive viewpoint is increasingly influential in mainstream theology. In an interesting study, *Religion on Trial: Mircea Eliade and His Critics* (Philadelphia: Temple University Press, 1977) Guilford Dudley III interprets Eliade's version of core theory as convergent with French structuralism. Dick Anthony ("A Phenomenological-Structuralist Approach to the Scientific Study of Religion," *ReVision*, 5, 50–66, Spring 1982) more generally proposes a structuralist approach to core theory as the basic methodology for the scientific study of religion. Ken Wilber in various works—e.g., *The Atman Project* (Wheaton, IL: Theosophical, 1980) and *Eye to Eye* (Garden City, NY: Anchor/Doubleday, 1983)—develops a combination of core theory and developmental structuralism as the model for transpersonal psychology.

48. For an expanded treatment of the ideas in this paragraph, see the article by Dick Anthony cited in the previous note.

49. Some of Gurdjieff's students have stressed this dualism more starkly than others. Ouspensky in particular maintained that the consciousness, identity, and energies of an individual who ends this life without having achieved a "real I" disperse and serve as raw materials for other processes in the universe.

50. In *Glimpses of the Godman: Part III* (Myrtle Beach, SC: Sheriar, 1982), p. 256, Bal Natu, an intimate disciple of Meher Baba, writes:

Although it is rare, after coming into the Avatar's contact, unusual changes may take place in one's state of awareness. But such experiences should not be misconstrued as indicating advancement on the spiritual path, much less demonstrating one's attainment of a higher plane of consciousness. These experiences are transitory and although they have potential to aid in one's journey to Him, if not properly understood and viewed in a true spiritual perspective, they can become an obstacle in one's way.

Any unusual abilities, especially those which superficially resemble spiritual ones, can become a temptation for the one pos-

sessing them. If one succumbs, and places some intrinsic importance in the ability itself, the blessing it might have conferred
instead becomes a curse. An honest, simple life in Baba's love and
service, without any glory about it, is best. A seeker or an aspirant
wants to know more and more about God, while a lover of the God-
Man longs to lose more and more of himself in His Omnipresence.
Unadulterated love surpasses the entire range of unusual
"experiences."

51. Werner Erhard discusses this subject in Part 2.

52. Bhagwan Shree Patanjali, *Aphorisms of Yoga* (London: Faber and Faber,
1938). Theodore Roszak, in "Ethics and Ecstacy: Reflections on an
Aphorism by Patanjali" (Chapter 9 in *Unfinished Animal: The Aquarian
Frontier and the Evolution of Consciousness*; New York: Harper Colophon, 1975), enlarges upon Patanjali's assertion in a way that has implications for an understanding of the moral quality of multilevel
spirituality.

53. For an account of the moral dimension of Zen Buddhism, see Steven
Tipton's article in Part 2.

54. Consider, for example, the central importance of morality in the scheme
of liberation taught by the Buddha, as described by Wilfred Cantwell
Smith, a scholar of religion, in his book, *Faith and Belief* (Princeton, NJ:
Princeton University Press, 1979), p. 26:

> Though Nirvana was a distant reality, indescribable, not profitable
> of discussion, yet the Buddha saw and preached another absolute
> reality immediately available to every man. This is the moral law.
> The Buddha taught that in the universal flux, one thing is firm. In
> the chaos of events, one pattern is permanent. In the ebb and flow
> of human life, one form is absolute, is supreme, is reliable, is effec-
> tive for salvation. Ideas come and go; religious institutions rise and
> fall; the gods themselves have their histories; men's and women's
> goals are frustrated, and anyway are themselves historical; all
> human strivings, whether to construct something on earth, or
> through piety or asceticism to try to escape from or to dominate
> earthly ambitions, are doomed sooner or later to pass away. Yet
> through it all one thing is certain, stable, firm, enduring—and is
> always immediately to hand. That is Dharma: the truth about right
> living.

55. Wilfred Cantwell Smith, *Faith and Belief* (Princeton, NJ: Princeton University Press, 1979).

56. Smith states that as compared with belief:

> Faith is deeper, richer, more personal. It is engendered and sus-
> tained by a religious tradition, in some cases and to some degree by
> its doctrines; but it is a quality of the person, not of the system. It
> is an orientation of the personality, to oneself, to one's neighbour,

to the universe; a total response; a way of seeing whatever one sees and of handling whatever one handles; a capacity to live at a more than mundane level; to see, to feel, to act in terms of, a transcendent dimension. . . .

Faith, then, is a quality of human living. At its best it has taken the form of serenity and courage and loyalty and service: a quiet confidence and joy which enable one to feel at home in the universe, and to find meaning in the world and in one's own life, a meaning that is profound and ultimate, and is stable no matter what may happen to oneself at the level of immediate event.

Faith, being independent of "the level of immediate event," is in clear contrast to the consequentialism usually found in unilevel groups.

57. Meher Baba, *God to Man and Man to God—The Discourses of Meher Baba* (N. Myrtle Beach, SC: Sheriar, 1975), 59.

58. In Part 2, Claudio Naranjo gives a firsthand account of such experiences in a Tibetan Buddhist context and Steven Tipton describes the master-student relationship in the Zen Buddhist tradition.

59. See the interview of Dick Anthony on Meher Baba in Part 2 for a further description of multilevel monistic charismatic involvements.

60. The controversies over Baba Muktananda and Da Free John involve sexual practices. See the introduction, pp. 22–24. For our perspective on masters who involve followers in sexual acts, see pp. 88–91.

61. For a brief account of the relationship between Shams and Rumi see Reynold A. Nicholson, ed., *Rumi, Poet and Mystic* (London: George Allen and Unwin, 1970), pp. 18–22.

62. Cf. George M. Marsden, *Fundamentalism and American Culture* (Oxford: Oxford University Press, 1980).

63. In addition to the foregoing description of multilevel sensibilities, the essays in Part 3 of this volume offer many suggestions for assessing the character of a spiritual master.

64. See the Introduction, pp. 23–24.

65. Cf. John Blofeld, *The Tantric Mysticism of Tibet* (New York: Causeway, 1974), and Benjamin Walker, *Tantrism: Its Secret Principles and Practices* (Wellingborough, England: Aquarian, 1982).

66. See Janet Jacobs, "The Economy of Love in Religious Commitment: The Deconversion of Women from Non-Traditional Religious Movements," *Journal for the Scientific Study of Religion*, 23, (2), 155–171, 1984; Katy Butler, "Events Are the Teacher: Working Through the Crisis at San Francisco Zen Center," *CoEvolution Quarterly*, Winter 1983, 112–123; and William Rodarmor, "The Secret Life of Swami Muktananda," *CoEvolution Quarterly*, Winter 1983, 104–111.

Part Two

FIVE INVOLVEMENTS

The *est* Training

An Interview with Werner Erhard

This spirited interview with Werner Erhard, the creator of the *est* training, was conducted on April 23, 1981, and delves into three main areas: the meaning of enlightenment and of Erhard's claim that the training produces it; the use and misuse of authority, particularly controversial aspects of the training and of Erhard's role in the organization; and the basis of the staff's high level of commitment, energy, and willingness to work long hours. In each case Erhard identifies and attempts to refute unspoken assumptions in the ways these issues are conventionally approached, and describes his own perspective.

Erhard developed the *est* training in 1971 as a result of exploring how to share with others an inner breakthrough that suddenly occurred while driving across the Golden Gate Bridge. Previously he had worked in sales and motivation; in his personal search he had studied Dale Carnegie, Napoleon Hill, psychologists Abraham Maslow and Carl Rogers, Scientology, and Zen. In the breakthrough, "It was not a higher reality, it was the ordinary reality that I saw. I saw things for what they are rather than embedded in this story that I was given, as we are all given."[1]

Since January 1985, the training has a new format and a new

name: the Forum. While the training's confrontational tactics and prolonged periods without bathroom access have been considerably eased, the essential philosophy and pragmatics of Erhard's approach (including its two-weekend duration) have not changed. "The difference between the training and the Forum," he has explained, "is that the training brought people up to [the "domain of being"]. . . . Rather than leaving people at the brink of this opening for possibility, the Forum now takes them in. . . ."[2] Erhard's encounter with the Center for the Study of New Religious Movements seminar occurred prior to the transition to the Forum, when it was still called the *est* training.

Within Erhard's organization—which originally was named *est*, for Erhard Seminar Training, but was renamed Werner Erhard and Associates in 1981—the training and the Forum are considered to be neither a form of psychotherapy, a new religion, nor a "New Age" movement. Nevertheless Erhard's views in this interview relate directly to this volume. The *est* training has had wide influence in our present social situation, with over 425,000 American graduates as of March 1984. The value orientation and the qualities of awareness engendered by Erhard's methods have spread rapidly into psychotherapy, business management, personal life, and social action. The training plus additional workshops and seminars on personal, societal, and professional thriving are given in the United States, Canada, Western Europe, India, South America, Israel, and Australia.

John Welwood: I have questions about whether the *est* training is a quasireligious phenomenon. I've known a lot of people who've done it, and I've been impressed with the fact that it helps make their lives more workable. But then there's something else that seems a little bit suspect to me, which is that they seem to have a certain kind of . . .

Werner Erhard: Fervor?

Welwood: Fervor, yes, and also a certain arrogance, as if this were it— as if the *est* training were everything, including a substitute for any other spiritual practice or meditation, or any kind of transpersonal and transcendental path. I wonder if you could comment on that.

Erhard: It's helpful to recognize right away that the training is not the end of anything. Nor is it a substitute for another path to some end point. Interpreting it as either of those will skew your assessment of it. At most, the training is a way to examine whatever path you happen to be on; but the training doesn't tell anyone what the path is, or what it should be.

So far, it looks like it's working that way, too. People who take the training haven't reported to us that they got any kind of end or answer out of it. Also, the research done so far on the results of the training indicates very strongly that results occur over time, that whatever occurs in the training is an ongoing process, and that the only ingredients necessary to keep that process going after the training are the normal, everyday circumstances of life.

The most difficult part of this whole process for some people comes just after they complete the training. And I'll tell you what—in part, anyway—makes that so: I remember the first time I swam underwater with a mask, in water clear enough to be able to see. For three days afterwards, whenever I closed my eyes, what I saw was what I had seen underwater. I talked about that experience to everybody; it had been very moving for me. Since then, I've had one or two other experiences like that, and I've behaved the same way when they happened. Over time, I'd integrate the experience, and instead of bringing it up all the time, I'd start bringing it up only when it was appropriate. So, I think people's reactions when they first get out of the training are related to that kind of enthusiasm for the experience they've had.

Welwood: Are you saying that what people get out of the training is equivalent to some kind of enlightenment experience, that there are transcendental realizations, and that it's a substitute for what we normally would think of as religious or spiritual goals?

Erhard: No. First, I wouldn't say that it's a substitute for anything, and second, I wouldn't say that it's religious at all. I also think most religions aren't very religious. So with respect to the religion issue, let's talk first about the practices associated with religion, then let's talk about the "truth" of religion.

I don't think that the training has any of the practices of a religious exercise, at least not the way I see religion being practiced. There is no worship in the training, no theological body of knowledge, no particular dogma or code of beliefs to be propagated, and a long list of other differences which, I think, clearly distinguish the training from what we commonly think of as religious practice.

Of course, the practices of religion are not the whole story of religion. There is also the "truth" of religion, the "nature" of it, so to speak. Without getting into a long discourse on what religion provides for people, my assertion is that the training provides a fundamentally different experience from what religion is intended to provide. The training simply provides an opportunity for people to discover, or in some cases recover, their own natural ability to discriminate effectively between the different ways that you and I can *know* and can *be*.

People express a lot of things in the training, and the training is designed to deal with those expressions so that people can get a different grip on them. For example, a person might find himself or herself operating in life as if they were obliged in some way to respond to something which to them seems real. As they participate in the training, they may discover that this "something" is not a concrete reality at all but is only a memory—recent, distant, it doesn't matter, it's still just a memory. That discovery allows the person to behave appropriately to the "something" rather than inappropriately to it. We call that "completing the experience." What occurs, simply, is a shift in the epistemological domain, from a place where there's no discrimination about something to a place where there is discrimination. What is known is not altered; the way it is known is altered.

So, to answer your question, I'd say that people in the training experience some enthusiasm, which is natural; it happens to everybody—not just in the training—when they have an exciting experience. Nothing pernicious about that. Then there's something like fervor, which can have elements of perniciousness it in; and as far as we can tell, that's a phase through which many people go but in which almost no one seems to get stuck. People seem to go through it fairly quickly, but, unfortunately, with a very high profile. If we had our choice, we'd rather that phase were a little more quiet.

Welwood: What I'm trying to get at is your view of whether or not what people get from the training is somehow equivalent to what in Zen, for instance, would be called enlightenment.

Erhard: Yes, it is. Yes.

Welwood: It's equivalent. You could get that in two weekends?

Erhard: Yes, it is equivalent, and no, you can't get it in two weekends. If it takes two weekends, you didn't get enlightened. Enlightenment does not take two weekends. Enlightenment takes no time. The two weekends are a waste of time. If we could eliminate those, and just have the enlightenment, we would do that. By the way, I know that lots of people are infuriated by the suggestion that enlightenment is possible without long practice and great struggle. I consider the notion of the necessity of practice and struggle to be nothing more than a notion. It may be a notion borne out by lots of experience, but so was the notion that the earth is flat.

Welwood: Well, the Buddhists, for example, would say that your true nature is enlightened already, but nonetheless, you still have to practice because there's a long path to realization. We can act as though we're enlightened, but there's still some kind of realization that has to happen, over a long period. You can even have enlightenment experiences, but they're not particularly trusted.

Erhard: I agree with everything you've said, and I'm not simply being nice about it. What you said actually reflects my own experience and my own observations. At the same time, I know it's possible to put the end of the process at the beginning, and *then* do the process.

Welwood: So, just to get it on the record, you are saying that the training does the same thing as the spiritual traditions . . .

Erhard: You're not going to trap me into saying that, because that's nonsense. It's the same kind of nonsense that keeps people from realizing that they're already enlightened.
   Here's an observation that I know will parallel what you've seen. People are willing to give up anything to get enlightened. You and I both know people who've given up wealth, given up jobs, families, their health—people will give up anything to get enlightened. Give up talking, give up sex, give up—you name it, they will give it up. There's only one thing people will not give up to get enlightened. They will do everything they know to hold onto this thing that they will not give up no matter what. The one thing people will not give up to get enlightened is *the idea that they're not enlightened*. That's the big hold-out, not anything else.

Welwood: In the traditions there's a lot of warning about thinking that you're enlightened, that that's one of the greatest dangers of them all.

Erhard: Discussing enlightenment or thinking about enlightenment is not enlightenment. In fact, we don't talk about enlightenment in the training very much at all. We do talk about it, but not much.

Welwood: I'm wondering why you're avoiding the question of whether this is the same kind of enlightenment that's talked about in the spiritual traditions.

Erhard: Because those who know don't tell, and those who tell don't know.

Dick Anthony: I'd always heard that the training does seem to claim that it provides something that is the equivalent of enlightenment, and is just as serious an experience, just as serious or valuable a state as is provided in Zen or Hindu traditions, and I thought that that was implausible, that it must be some kind of exaggeration.

Erhard: Well, I have never said that, nor would I say it.

Anthony: But when I went through the training . . .

Erhard: Nor would I say the opposite was true.

Anthony: When I went through the training, the trainer did in fact seem to be saying that. I don't know if that was an eccentric trainer, but in fact, that was my understanding, and it was the understanding of the other people in the training whom I talked to, that that man was telling us that what was happening to us was enlightenment, and was just as genuine an enlightenment as happened in any Zen monastery or up in the Himalayas, and that there were no degrees of enlightenment; it was *enlightenment*. Now, that seems like an outrageous claim to me; much of what goes on in that training seems outrageous to me. Now, if I understand that to be what the claim is, then I don't think that I agree with it.

Erhard: As far as I know, that claim is not made. I appreciate that you were there and I wasn't. I still don't think it was made. The reason I don't think so is that I've listened to many hours of trainers doing the training, and they don't make that claim. At the same time, I do understand how you could come to that conclusion.

But none of that is the point. The point is this: I think that discussions about enlightenment are useless, and I think making enlightenment sacred is even more futile. My question is, what's all this conversation about?

What I'm trying to get across is that the structure of your questions and our conversation doesn't allow for enlightenment. We're not really talking about anything. I don't know how else to respond to you. You can't ask, "Is *this* enlightenment like *that* enlightenment?" That's counting enlightenments. That's nuts! That's truly nuts!

Welwood: Would the training then be a substitute for any other spiritual practice?

Erhard: No! That's craziness, that one thing substitutes for another. In the realm of enlightenment, there aren't substitutions. That kind of mentality can't hold enlightenment. Look, can't you hear what you're saying? You keep saying that one thing substitutes for another thing; your notions about enlightenment are all tied up with exclusivity and ideas about "one path" and "if this, then why that?" and ideas that there's someplace to get to. None of that is the way enlightenment works. You need to go back to whomever is talking to you about enlightenment and get them to talk to you about it some more. You're talking about it inaccurately. I'm not kidding. Suzuki Roshi wrote a book called *Zen Mind, Beginner's Mind.* He said if you are enlightened, then you're out doing what enlightens people. Enlightenment is not a stage you reach, and your statements seem to come from the idea that enlightenment is a place you reach. There's no such thing as enlightenment to get to.

Welwood: Where my question comes from is my perception of some people I've seen . . .

Erhard: The arrogance.

Welwood: Yes, and smugness, like: "We've done it. This is it, you don't need to do any of that other stuff. This is the whole thing."

Erhard: No, no, no, no. I can't imagine anybody saying that they don't need to do that other stuff, since people who've completed the training— we poll them every once in a while to find out what they're doing— report that they *are* doing all that other stuff.

Half the room here has taken the training. Right here in this room are those arrogant people you're talking about. I want to find the person who says to me, "This is the only thing." All I can find are people who say, "I know people who say that this is the only thing." They've got to be talking about *somebody* and I'm trying to find that person. The people in here who have completed the training don't think that it's the only thing. I certainly don't think it is.

So let me try to answer in this way. The arrogance that you perceive, I think, is there. The degree to which *you* think it's there, *I* don't think it's there. That is to say, I don't think it's something to be overly concerned about, but maybe that's because I've watched people from the time they get out of the training. I go out of my way to make sure I have interactions with people who completed the training early, in 1971, '72, '73, and '74, just to watch what's happening to those people. I had a gathering in the country to which we invited those people to come. The result was very interesting. I could remember when those people were talking about the training, and "the training" was every third word. This time nobody even mentioned it. Yes, they looked great: they talked about the things they were doing, and how wonderful things were; but nobody mentioned the training.

It's like the stink of Zen. There's the stink of *est*. The question is not whether the stink exists, but whether it's pernicious and whether it's long-lasting. As far as I can tell, the answer is no to both questions. I keep watching, because there's always the possibility for the answer to become yes.

As to the discussion about the real nature of it, is it really enlightenment—yes, it's really enlightenment. So is sitting in a room. Here. This is enlightenment. You think I'm just saying that. I actually mean it. You think that's some philosophy. It isn't. I think many enlightenment games are pointless because they're all about *getting* enlightened. *Getting* enlightened is a cheat, because the more you do of that, the more the message is that you aren't enlightened. Clearly, the practice is necessary. The practice of enlightenment is necessary, but it can be done from *being* enlightened, rather than *getting* enlightened. When you do the practice from *being* enlightened, then each one of the steps becomes a step in the *expression* of the enlightenment.

Welwood: What's the difference, in your view, between *being* enlightened and just *believing* that you're enlightened?

Erhard: Vastly different. The primary difference, technically, is that each exists in a different domain. Believing that you're enlightened exists in the epistemological domain of *belief*. It's totally different from *being* enlightened, which exists in an epistemological domain that I call *abstraction* or *context*. The language structures of belief and the epistemological domain of belief are insufficient to apprehend the domain of context or abstraction. The opposite, however, is not true; the domain of context or abstraction does include the structures of belief.

Paul Reisman: During the *est* training, the trainer frequently calls the trainees "assholes." Doesn't calling people assholes tell them that they're not enlightened, or don't you intend it that way?

Erhard: First of all, no, calling people anything doesn't necessarily make any statement about their state of enlightenment. If I call you an asshole in the context of your being enlightened, it enlightens you. If I call you an asshole to get you enlightened because you aren't enlightened, it endarkens you.

We don't understand very much about the power of context. It's useful to distinguish between believing that something is so and its actually being so, because the belief in that thing which is so is totally different from its "so-ness." As a matter of fact, the belief that something is so keeps you from *experiencing* its being so. It actually ceases to be so, because you've got a barrier between you and it; and the barrier is your belief that it's so. A belief in the truth is not the truth; yet the same thing, without the belief, is the truth.

Welwood: Maybe it's only the fervent followers who have just graduated, but it seems to me that a lot of people who have taken the training—say *some* of them—have that belief, the *belief* that they're enlightened. How does the training cut through that?

Erhard: Well, first, I'd like to leave open the possibility that some of what you have perceived as arrogance is not, in fact, arrogance. It *may* be, but I want to leave open the possibility that it isn't. Second, although you haven't said it, it is clear you have a very strong belief, *very* strong belief, that people who take the training are not enlightened.

Welwood: I don't know whether it's a belief; it's more a sense that they're on a trip about it.

Erhard: Okay. That's true, too. You have a sense of it. But preceding the sense, before you ever got to have any sense of it, you believe very powerfully and deeply that they are not enlightened, or that it's not possible to be enlightened that way, or some such belief.

Welwood: Well, if we get into the metaphysics of it, then we would have to . . .

Erhard: No, we don't have to get into the metaphysics; I'm talking about something really simple. You believe that those people are not enlightened, and your belief is a matter of fact, not a matter of metaphysics.

Welwood: In the absolute sense, we're all enlightened.

Erhard: Never mind that part of it. I'm talking about the *belief.* You believe that those people aren't enlightened. And that's a very strongly held belief for you.

Welwood: I'm wondering how *est* deals with the fact that people walk around believing that they're enlightened.

Erhard: Oh, I leave room for it, number one; because they're enlightened. It really is perfectly appropriate if enlightened people happen to *believe* they're enlightened.

Welwood: But you said that belief also keeps them from being enlightened.

Erhard: Yes. That's right; it becomes a barrier, but that's okay. Enlightened people can and do have many barriers. I have many barriers, and I'm clearly enlightened, aren't I?

Welwood: We got you to say it!

Anthony: We got it on the tape.

Erhard: I really did a better job when I was kidding about it, but to answer the question the way you want me to answer it—people who complete the training and believe they are enlightened are still enlightened. They are, in addition to being enlightened, simply moving through that specific expression of being enlightened called believing you're enlightened. Believing you're enlightened when you are enlightened is an entirely different phenomenon from believing you're enlightened when you're not. I know it might not make sense to you, but it is possible that people who have been through the training are actually enlightened, and then, from being enlightened, they may go through the steps of achieving enlightenment. I know you don't believe that. I don't want you to *believe* it. I do want you to allow that it's possible; that when people go through this silly little thing called the training, they actually come out enlightened; and that what you observe afterwards is the process of the expression of their enlightenment. I know you know it's impossible, but I just want you to keep it open as a possibility.

Welwood: They were enlightened already, right?

Erhard: No, no, no, no. They were not enlightened until they got into the training. Now remember, I didn't say that was *true,* I said I want you to entertain that possibility.

By the way, I want you to know that I think that one of the things that makes the training potent is that there are some things in it which are very accurate. If you try to practice medicine with the idea that people are sick because of spirits, you have a certain amount of success; but if you practice medicine with the idea that people are sick because there are microbes and viruses which can't be seen, you have greater success. You see, there's something workable about being accurate, and there's a lot of inaccuracy in life, some of which can actually be made accurate— even by people like you and me, unenlightened people.

Reisman: Would you say something now about what the training is, what it's supposed to do, and how it does it?

Erhard: The training is sixty hours long, done in four days of roughly fifteen hours each. Virtually all of the trainers are people with professional backgrounds, people who are already highly accomplished, in the sense in which society generally considers people highly accomplished. After a person decides he or she is going to be a trainer, it takes an average of two-and-a-half to three years to actually become one. Trainer candidates work at their training all the time—they become immersed—so, in effect, it's more like a five-year program.

I'll briefly describe a few parts of the training: The first part is designed to let people see that some of the things which they say they *know* to be true, they only *believe* to be true, and that there's a distinction between what you believe and what's true. The first day is designed to give people an opportunity to recognize that they have lots of pretense in their lives, and that they're pretending they don't; that they really are pretending a lot. They're pretending, for instance, that their marriage works; or that they want to do the work they do; or that their life works, to say it in general terms, and then on top of all that, they're pretending that they're not pretending at all.

In the first part of the second day, people see that there's a distinction between *concepts* about living and the *experience* of living, and they discover that they have not been experiencing life; they've been conceptualizing life. For instance, people begin to observe that the idea, "I love my wife," is different from the experience, "I love my wife"; that for the most part, they live with the idea of something and very infrequently have the experience of it. They also discover that the experience of something has a much different outcome than the idea of something.

The last portion of the second day is called the "danger process." About twenty-five trainees stand at the front of the room, facing the other 225, with the instruction to do nothing but just be there, just standing. While standing there, of course, they begin to notice all of the thoughts, fears, concerns, pretenses, and the like which they carry with them all the time, which have come to be even somewhat automatic, and which seriously impair their ability to be with other people. The people who are standing end up doing everything up there *except* nothing, and in the process they start to see that.

The process is very, very useful for them. It becomes clear to them that they've got an act, a mechanism, a collection of behaviors and actions and feelings and thoughts that may not be who they really are after all. They see it for themselves. It isn't something you're told by someone else. You see it yourself, and it is undeniably clear and undeniably true about you. And it opens up whole new possibilities for ways of being. It reveals a fundamental inauthenticity about our mode of living and allows for the possibility of authentic living.

After everybody has been up front and has watched everyone else being up front, they sit down and close their eyes. From previous parts of the training they're able to become quickly and accurately aware of what they're experiencing; now what they become aware of about themselves can be frightening, because they realize that what's driving their behaviors is their fear of people.

Macho men find out that they're macho because they're afraid, a discovery they make for themselves. People who are stupid or intelligent or sexy find out that they are stupid or intelligent or sexy because they are afraid of other people. You find out that you're the way you are because you're afraid.

At some point there's a breakthrough, and people get the joke. The joke is that other people look frightening to you because they're frightened. The boss is the boss because he's afraid; just like you're whatever you are because you're afraid. In the environment of the training, this becomes a major breakthrough experience for people, and it makes life profoundly different.

One of the things that I think it is very important for you to know is that the training is a mass-produced, custom service. We produce it for large groups, but the service is totally customized. If there are 250 people in the training, there are 250 different trainings. That's one of the beauties of the training. It's tailor-made for each person. If you are the kind of person who can't handle much emotion, you just don't have much emotion. It's that simple. And yet, it works for you.

Very little of the training is done at you as an individual, and if it is, it's clearly done that way to illustrate some point. In the moment you might not remember that, but after you sit down it's very clear to you that you have contributed a useful example for everyone, and the truth of the matter is, it doesn't make any difference whether you stand up or

I stand up in an interaction with the trainer; the example is useful to both of us.

The training has acquired a reputation of harshness, and in some cases crudeness. I am not going to say that trainers in the training are not straight and honest with people if they need to be, but the accusations of harshness, crudeness, authoritarianism, and the like are largely propagated by people who have not directly experienced the training, and in all these accounts, one thing is always left out: the compassion in the training.

I know—because I'm the guy who trained the people who are leading the training—that the training is done with absolute compassion, and that toughness, when and if it occurs, including calling people assholes, comes from a deep respect for people, from an intention to get straight with them, with absolutely no intention to demean them. As a matter of fact, in terms of results, people are not demeaned; they are enhanced.

The training is done with what might be called ruthless compassion, but it's done with compassion. And it's done with a real sense of the dignity of human beings—not the ordinary social grease called "respect for each other," but a really deep kind of respect, the kind of respect that lets you know you'd be willing to be in the trenches with the person alongside you. It is a really empowering thing to discover that you've been relating to the people you love out of the *concept* of love, and denying yourself the *experience* of love, and sometimes you've got to be very intrusive with people to get that up on the mat. But I tell you, that comes from a respect for them, and a commitment to them.

I want to tell you one thing that I think is kind of funny. I have a constitution that makes going to the bathroom not very important to me. I go to the bathroom about as often as anybody else does, except that if I'm doing something interesting, I just don't go. I was the only person who did the training in the beginning, so the sessions would go on forever, because I never felt like going to the bathroom. People were studying how I was doing the training, and they figured that this not going to the bathroom was a very important part of it. I mean, it's just so stupid, because it's literally that silly—people had those great theories about deprivation and whatnot. Nobody bothered to say, "Hey, Werner, what about going to the bathroom?" I'd have said, "Well, go if you've got to."

I also don't need a lot of sleep, so the trainings would go long into the night. The people in the training needed a lot of sleep, but I didn't. So we trained a lot of people who were asleep during the training, but it works just as well, whether you're asleep or awake.

Anthony: So you really don't think that those features are an essential part of the training?

Erhard: No.

Anthony: That's the window dressing that looks the most authoritarian.

Erhard: Exactly.

Welwood: Why do you maintain it then? Why not just let it go?

Erhard: Oh, in part we have let it go. There's an automatic break every four hours now. We keep doing the training an average of fifteen hours a day because if we did it in any less time per day, it would take more than the four days, which are already a problem for some people.

By the way, let me tell you something about whether the training is authoritarian. Go into a prison as an outsider who's not part of the system, and get into a room with inmates where there are no guards, and I want to see you be authoritarian. We've done the training in San Quentin Prison with no guards in a room with prisoners, 250 of them and five of us. And the training works spectacularly. It works just as well in Israel as it does in New York City. It works just as well in Davenport, Iowa, as in Los Angeles. It works every bit as well with Harvard professors as it does with—I don't know. What's the opposite of a Harvard professor?

Nevitt Sanford: A Yale professor.

Bruce Fireman: Do you think that the people on the staff of Werner Erhard and Associates have the frame of mind in which they can assess your actions, and should your actions be bad for the goals you're trying to promote, that they would get rid of you and carry on the work without you? Are there procedures in place by which . . .

Erhard: They don't need any procedures. They don't need to get rid of me. You see, I have no authority.

Fireman: But could they, if they did need to get rid of you?

Erhard: I don't wonder about it. I know that they would do that, and could do that, and as a matter of fact, since the organization's inception they've always had the wherewithal to do it, because I never held any position of authority. I had no formal authority; my power in the organization was exactly equal to my ability to be useful to the people in the organization.

The actual fact about it is that I do have a lot of authority, and I consider the authority to be counter-productive. I don't like authority—it just doesn't work. It's nowhere near potent enough for the kinds of things that I'm interested in achieving. So we've worked at the job of undermining my position of authority. When you have authority with people, they can't hear you. They can neither hear you to tell whether you're saying nonsense, nor can they hear to see whether you're saying something useful.

So that's a problem for us, as it is in any organization, and it's a problem that I think we have dealt with. We have forums for people to express themselves; the first rule as a staff member is to agree to open, honest, and complete communication. We have structures to support people when they don't feel powerful enough to make those communications. We have an ombudsman who's paid to keep whatever he or she hears in strict confidence, and whose job it is to make sure that a staff member is not damaged by any communication addressed to another staff member.

We don't think that any of those things are necessary because we don't think we operate in ways that will damage anyone. But we think that it's possible for staff members, when they're looking for an excuse not to be responsible, to say to themselves, "Hey, I can't tell the truth here, because I'll get in trouble." So we've just destroyed the opportunity to use that as an excuse. There's no way that you, as a staff member, cannot say exactly what's on your mind, because there are so many systems to protect you.

So, yes, I get called to task. I don't get called to task often, because I happen to be able to operate with a lot of accuracy. I also have one other endearing quality, and that is when I make a mistake I get off it *fast*. Maybe that's not an endearing quality.

Roger Walsh: One of the purposes of this group that's interviewing you is to try to delineate some guidelines for what constitutes beneficent versus harmful groups and teachers. You've been through myriad groups and trainings of one type or another, and have certainly met a lot of people claiming to be teachers over the last twenty years. What would you tell us, or what would you tell anyone, about how to differentiate between beneficent and harmful teachers and groups?

Erhard: This question is something that I feel a responsibility for, first off because of my own opportunities and the opportunities of my associates, and also because of the larger issue. The whole issue of leadership, authority, et cetera, seems to me to be a basic problem in our society—any society.

When the source of the authority lies outside of those with whom

the authority is exercised, you've got the beginnings of a possible problem. You're not necessarily going to definitely wind up with a problem,
but you'd damn well better be careful. See, if Dick is the leader of the
group, and is its leader because God has given Dick a mission, and God
is not directly available to the rest of us to discuss Dick's designation,
that for me is the harbinger of a problem. If Dick's authority is based on
anything that is inaccessible to the rest of the people in the group, then
I am concerned.

The times when I'm least concerned are when Dick's authority—and
then I would not call it authority—is in the hands of the people with
whom the authority or power is being exercised, when it's clear to everybody that this is the case. I think you can con people into agreeing with
your position of authority, but you can only con them if they don't know
that *they* are the source of your authority. I think that if you're attempting to avoid the evils of authoritarianism, one of the things that should
happen is that the people in the group should be very clear that there is
no natural leader; that there are people who have natural leadership qualities, but that doesn't make any of them the leader. There is no outside
authority which is unavailable to the people in the group selecting the
leader; the group is empowering the people who are being empowered.

One of the other things—and this one is a lot more subtle, so I think
a lot more dangerous—is the prevailing intellectual level or the prevailing epistemological domain, the realm of *knowing* that prevails in the
group. If that realm of knowing is conceptual—ideas, beliefs, slogans—
that for me is almost certainly going to wind up with a problem someplace. If it doesn't, somebody is going to have to be working really hard
to make sure that it doesn't become a problem. It's almost a natural
disaster.

When I see that conceptualization, though present, exists within a
larger epistemological domain that I call *experience*, I'm then a lot more
relaxed, because if somebody tries to say that Jews are bad, and in the
group it's agreed upon that we verify things in our experience, I'm not
so concerned that whoever is trying to get that one across is going to
prevail. If experience is allowed, and if experience is recognized and
respected, then I have less concern.

I begin to have almost no concern when, in addition to the domain
of concept or explanation and that of experience or process, there is the
domain of context or creation. It's a realm in which people look not only
at what they think, but at the realm in which their thinking takes place.
Attitude is certainly there in this realm, and allowed and appreciated, and
a change or process of attitudes is respected, but when the group deals
in the epistemological domain of the *context* of attitudes, then I become
even less concerned.

Fireman: One of the things that you referred to earlier was that people were too deferent to your authority. That's something that everybody notices, these charges that people are rather slavish in their adulation of you. I'd like you to talk about the specific changes that you're making that will reduce the excessive deference or adulation.

Erhard: We all know that a hundred thousand people can't love one person. If they could, nobody would be able to observe them doing it, because that isn't possible in the structure through which we'd look at the situation. If what's occurring is actually what it's concluded to be— slavish adulation—I want somebody to explain why it nurtures those people, because adulation doesn't nurture people. It only makes them right; it does not nurture them. People who are adulating don't get healthier, they don't get more self-expressive, they don't get more capable. The people who are supposed to adulate me are healthy, expressive, able, and capable. I'd like to suggest to you that the way you're looking at it is a part of the evil—that you're looking at it in a way that says: "These are the alternatives: pick one."

Fireman: I'm asking you how *you're* looking at the matter, and what you're doing about it.

Erhard: I'm going to get to that.

Fireman: We've had person after person come in here from different groups and tell us how their relationship with their leader has empowered them—people who were in fact very slavish in their adulation of that leader—they were set on fire; they were "empowered"; they went out and "dealt" with their problems. We've seen this time and time again. Now, in order to accomplish your goals for people, which is that you want them to be empowered and not slavish, you're making changes in your organization. I want to know what problems you see, and how those changes are going to contribute to the relationship between you and your underlings in the organization.

Erhard: See, but that's the whole problem.

Fireman: Well, perhaps I'm using the wrong word. But rather than make an issue of my words . . .

Erhard: I'm not making an issue of the words you use. I'm making the system from which the words are derived the problem. Given the system, I can't answer the question. You see, it's not simply the words you're using that are the problem. What I want to convey to you is this: In the assumptions from which you are asking the question, you allow for no truthful answer to the question. The words you use reflect your assumptions accurately, and given your assumptions, there's no solution to the problem. One cannot solve the problem in the system you are using. In fact, that system *is* the problem.

Now, I'm going to answer your question, because, you know, I came here and agreed to do that, but I want to tell you the truth before I answer the question. So I'm telling you that my answer will make no sense if you listen to the answer in that system from which you asked the question.

The answer is that the organization has for several years been shifting away from a structure that has a central place or a top place from which decisions are made and passed on. We always tried not to operate that way, and over the years we've become more and more successful at not operating that way. The structure of just about any ordinary organization, however, is that way. So when you're trying to go left in a structure that's going right, you can't get very far. We recognized that what needed to happen was what we called a transformation of the structure, because no matter what our intentions were, as long as they were being expressed in a structure of authority, we would not achieve our ends.

The structure we have in mind is a network of people, the center of which is wherever you are. Decisions get made locally. By contrast, if we're all operating as a hierarchical organization, you know, you might be the boss; you'd tell us what to do. We tell you what's going on; you tell us what to do. In a system which is network-like rather than pyramidal, what gets done in any given spot gets decided at the spot. The information flows to there from all over the network, and the information from there flows all over the network.

This is something that I've been studying now for two-and-a-half years, and I actually think we've come up with some breakthroughs: est came to an end this year [1981], literally went out of existence, because we're evolving into a network and we wanted to put the old organizational model to bed. So, for instance, the Master Therapist program is done by the entity called Werner Erhard and Associates and Dr. Robert Shaw, who's a psychiatrist, in a partnership. Lots of programs are done that way, and more will be done that way in the future, where our network will be affiliated with another network. Just let me cover a couple more things very quickly. We started a pilot program in 1981 in San Francisco with 1,000 people, a workshop on community in which we've been developing a program to be made available around the country and around the world, so that people in any community can work on the community—make community their business.

The Hunger Project, which was really created by graduates of the *est* training but is now much larger than *est* graduates, has 1,800,000 people who've enrolled. The Breakthrough Foundation works in international development in rural villages and urban ghettos, on the thesis that self-sufficiency is never achieved unless there's individual and societal transformation. We feel we've developed a technology that allows people to effect those transformations for themselves, independent of any outside personality. By the way, many of these organizations are wholly independent of Werner Erhard and Associates.

Anthony: That seems like a natural conclusion to that line of questioning. Another line to consider will take a minute to develop. I know people who work for your organization, or in it, and what they seem to have in common is that they work very hard and very long hours, and that they don't have much going on in their lives except *est*. Now, a certain kind of fantasy about *est* gets set off by this fact. It combines with other things I seem to have noticed about *est:* It is a very rapidly expanding organization; it has very high ambitions in terms of wanting to transform the society or perhaps the world; hopes to be able to end hunger in a certain number of years, and other things that seem implausible from a normal frame of reference; it proselytizes very forcefully, with very great energy. Putting all those things together, it's easy to view *est* as a group of people with a self-involved, very convoluted system of beliefs that achieve their plausibility by the apparent ability of *est* to grow very rapidly.

Erhard: So that growth backs up the belief, appears to back up the belief.

Anthony: Yes, so people feel that they're really somehow achieving something important with respect to their own consciousness. Now, what would happen if suddenly *est* peaked, and some of the plausibility structure started to break down? Some of the other groups that we've looked at have really only gotten into trouble when it started to look as if they weren't going to change the world after all, and as if the system that people had been devoting themselves to wholeheartedly for five or ten or fifteen years wasn't really omnipotent. The whole shared group fantasy started to break apart, and things got crazy. Could you respond to that?

Erhard: I know everybody's trying to be polite, and I appreciate your being nice about it. But, you see, it's not just trying to be polite, and it's not just trying to be nice about it; it's a flat out lie. And language carried on in lies, even if they're well-meaning lies, leads you to inaccurate conclusions.

What offends me is our willingness to carry on the conversation without getting at the truth of it. I think there's a very big possibility of missing some of the real power and value in the work that we are doing and in the whole development of that work, if you attempt to force it into the categories which you bring to it to try to understand it, because *est* is really about the very nature of your inquiry. The *est* training is aimed at grasping the categories with which one deals with the world. It's not aimed at what one puts into those categories.

You assume that the long hours and the high commitment of staff members must be brought about by some great vision. I deny that that's true. That isn't why I work long hours. I'm very committed—I say "committed" and I know the thought that goes through people's minds: "He believes in what he's doing." I don't believe in what I'm doing at all. I have absolutely no belief in what I'm doing. I already know how it's going to turn out. I know it's going to turn out exactly like it turns out. It's been doing that for eons. So you say, "But then, Werner, what's your motive, what the hell are you working all those hours for?" I'm not motivated. There isn't any motive. There's no damn vision motivating me. You know, if I stopped doing it tomorrow, it wouldn't make one bit of difference, and if I keep doing it right to the end, it won't make any difference. The only thing that's going to happen is what happens.

Now, that doesn't fit into our structure, into our categories. We know that you don't get up in the morning unless you've got a motive. That's a great explanation. Maybe you can explain people's behavior, but you can't do one thing to bring an ounce of wholeness and completeness into people's lives with that theory, because the theory is essentially a theory of explanation and doesn't get at the *cause* of things.

So I don't have a vision. I'm not selling some ideal. I don't know where I'm going. I know where I'm *coming from*. And I think that the people on the staff know where they're coming from. I think it's a great excitement to them to discover where that takes them, day by day, week by week. It's why we don't have any problem throwing things out. See, if my life is about where I'm going to get to, and you make me change, then you've upset me. If my life is about where I'm coming from, change is no problem—if I'm starting at the end, and going then through the process, instead of going through the process to get to the end.

So why do people work long hours? They work long hours because there's work to be done, and doing the work is very satisfying. I didn't say it was easy, or pleasant; I said it was satisfying. They work long hours because in that opportunity they experience the opportunity to make a difference. Not to make things different, see, but to make a difference. They experience the opportunity of being able to be useful—and they don't experience that opportunity in a lot of places in the world.

Anthony: You're saying, I think, that *est* people won't flip out and get crazy if the world isn't transformed because they don't have a certain point of view about how the world is going to be transformed; they don't have a belief structure that has to be confirmed.

Erhard: That's right.

Anthony: I think that's valid. I think that that is a difference between *est* and some of the other groups that we've seen.

Erhard: The other thing is that they don't think they're "good"; therefore, they're not made crazy by somebody saying they're bad. I don't think the *est* training is good. I don't think it's righteous. I don't think it's God's work. God is not talking to me personally any differently than She talks to everybody. You know, there's no great mission. Or, yes, there *is* a great mission, but it's the great mission everybody is on. We have no private access to the mission and no special knowledge about the mission.

By the way, before *est* I was an expert in motivation. In the realm of motivation experts, one measures expertise by income. Given my income before *est*, I was an expert in motivation. That was my business. At one time, I was fairly clear, I was one of the few people in the country who knew what motivation was. I knew it "up on the line"—my income depended on being able to teach it to people. Ultimately motivation is counterproductive, because inherent in it is the message that you're *not*. It teaches you that you're not, and it reinforces that you're not. Even achieving that towards which you were motivated just seals the fact that you're not. So, for example, if you examine intelligent people—particularly people who wear their intelligence on their coat sleeves—and you get down underneath it, you find invariably that they are intelligent to avoid being stupid. Invariably, when intelligence is not nurturing, it is a device for overcoming something, it is a motivated kind of intelligence. In my experience and in my observation, intelligence is a natural expression of self. One's self is intelligent. So I don't mean that we should throw all motivation out, because motivation is useful as an interim device, as something through which to go, something to master.

But ultimately motivation is a true exercise of authoritarianism. Our whole society is based on it, and I say that people are not freed by the values of this society, or ennobled by them; they're dominated by them. I think it's pernicious to start with; you don't need to get to Jonestown. It's already pernicious. And nobody is really teaching anybody about the science and the technology and art of *coming from*.

The thing which is really difficult—and we notice this a lot in the work that we're doing in development around the world—is that people cannot believe that there is something that moves people other than motivation. There's just no possibility of ontology being behind it. That is not held as possible. Therefore, if you see somebody moving, by God, they've got to be up to something. They've got to be moving *towards* something. It can't be that they're just moving.

Phil Zimbardo: Doesn't The Hunger Project have a vision?

Erhard: Yes. I suggest that if you read what we call the "source document" for The Hunger Project, you would see both that what I've just said is true *and* they have a vision—the vision doesn't preclude what I just said.

The Hunger Project's mission is to create a context for the end of hunger. Now, to do only that would be half-assed, if you will. Therefore, you have to face up to also creating a goal, the end of hunger; but it's the context which is The Hunger Project's job, and in the *context* "the end of hunger," what *is* is the expression of the end of hunger. Therefore you don't fail, in the context.

Zimbardo: But you could fail in that vision.

Erhard: Yes. You can fail and—no, you *know* you will fail in the objectives. One hopes not to fail ultimately, but one knows one will fail in the objectives. That's a part of the expression of a context of succeeding. In the context of succeeding, failure is contained; therefore, failure is not invalidating. Failure doesn't destroy anything. As a matter of fact, it forwards things. Errors are important. They're how you get there. Mistakes are the path.

I'll tell you the one thing that burns our people out. It's a really interesting thing. The one thing that burns our people out is when they think they got it. It's amazing. It starts to happen at exactly that moment when they figure they have it made, they have it together, they understand it now. And it's so deadly, it's really sad. They may go on to be very successful, but their success never has the quality of making a difference again.

Welwood: Do they come out of it?

Erhard: Some do. The jury's still out on some, and I think some won't. And you see, it's very clear to me that everybody will. So I'm now talking in that context. Maybe this time around, some won't, but ultimately we all will.

Notes

1. *Interview*, Vol. XIV, No. 4, April 1985, 54.
2. *Ibid.*

EDITORIAL COMMENTARY

The *est* training has for many of its graduates been so radical, liberating, and encompassing, that it would seem an injustice to describe it as anything less than transformative. Werner Erhard and his associates have described the training as producing a transformation that constitutes "enlightenment"—which, on the face of it, certainly seems to imply that the training does *something* that mystical spirituality also tries to do. Our interest here is in considering if this is indeed so, and to what extent.[1] Erhard, it should be noted, does *not* describe the training (or its subsequent expression, the Forum) as a spiritual avenue, although the allusions to enlightenment positively ring with mystical-spiritual overtones (at least of the Zen variety).

Spiritual transformation can be viewed in two basic ways: In its strict sense it involves the permanent opening of awareness to the direct experience of oneself and others as transphysical beings. The ascending stages of this radical transformation of consciousness are described by the various systems of mysticism, and culminate, according to monistic traditions, in the unbounded consciousness of ultimate being or Godhead. In its softer sense, described by Anthony and Ecker in Part 1, spiritual transformation preserves ordinary physical consciousness but reorganizes it around the multilevel orientation, which supports authenticity of relationship to one's own being, the being of others, and ultimate being.

Although we are aware of nothing indicating that the *est* training generates spiritual transformation in the strict sense, a case can be made that the training is spiritually transformative in the softer sense of Anthony and Ecker (although here Wilber dissents). For example, trainees discover experientially that their thoughts, feelings, and sensations are not their being, and that they can bring the unlimited and intrinsic intelligence, love, and creativity of their being into fuller, more direct expression in their lives. Many trainees also discover a profound regard of other human beings. There are, however, a number of problematic issues concerning the *est* training that would have to be settled before we could happily conclude that it is spiritually transformative in the multilevel sense.

First, though, let us examine the interview. At one level it contains a struggle over whose categories of meaning, whose context, will prevail. Here Erhard prevails. Repeatedly he chooses not to engage the questions that are posed to him, and responds instead with his own priorities. His rejection of his questioners' framework of inquiry is precisely the point he wants to make, but this rejection also gives him control of the interview. How then may we evaluate Erhard's views, and the *est* training?

There already exist several serious and unfavorable critiques of the *est* training, by both scholars[2] and other commentators.[3] These critiques argue that the training constitutes a sophisticated form of selling out to the narcissistic, competitive individualism that characterizes present-day materialistic society. However, all these analyses may be fundamentally biased. They assume the validity of several Christian ethical tenets, namely that the development of "virtue" (transcendence, transformation, authenticity) requires asceticism, and that both virtue and asceticism tend to be incompatible with the pursuit of self-interest (material gain, adaptation). One can pursue either virtue or self-interest, not both. The virtuous person is one who is willing to sacrifice self-interest in favor of the interest of others.[4]

Critiques of the *est* training all advance a version of this Western ethical theme, and argue that the training is able to promise both virtue and worldly attainment—both transformation and adaptation—only by cleverly rationalizing its betrayal of authentic virtue. For example, the *est* training stresses that "you are responsible for all your experience; you create it." Sociologist Donald Stone, reporting research findings on the training, notes "Critics predict that this ethic of individual responsibility will legitimize the status of the wealthy, reinforce the self-doubt and self-blame of the disadvantaged, and discourage collective organization needed to redistribute power and wealth."[5]

Yet Stone's empirical findings cast some doubt on the critics' analyses. In general his research does not find that the *est* training encourages narcissism and thereby reduces social altruism. (Werner Erhard has argued that when people become more deeply aware of their real needs, their apparent self-interest transforms into concern for others as well.) Stone also points out that in *est* parlance, "responsibility" is a term that does not have its conventional connotations of fault, blame, shame, or guilt. Evaluative moral judgments are regarded as arbitrary and dysfunctional, so that there is "no pronounced tendency for the advantaged *est* participants to blame the disadvantaged" for their own difficulties.

In the editors' view the essential issue raised by Werner Erhard and the *est* training is the possible conflict between the pursuit of transformational, transcendental interests and the pursuit of pragmatic, adaptive ones. The training promises both to produce enlightenment and to "make your life work," as *est* phraseology puts it. But whether or not the *est* training or any other orientation can always combine both types of interest remains an open question; the possibilities for self-delusion here are manifold.

The *est* training also raises the question of transformation. Transformation, in any domain, means a qualitative change of properties and of the *kind* of processes that may occur. For example, consider chess. The rules of the game define the kinds of moves that can happen during a match; so, while the specific configuration of the pieces changes greatly during play, the kinds of possible moves are invariant; there is change but not transformation. But if we change the rules of the game, thereby changing the allowed moves or the layout of the board, the game is transformed. But the type of transformation depends on context; by changing the rules we have not produced a *chemical* transformation, for example.[6]

Perhaps the *est* training can and does produce *psychological* transformation, but the central question of whether the training generates *spiritual* transformation (even in the soft sense of Anthony's multilevel orientation) remains. Not that there is any sharp dividing line between psychological and spiritual domains—but a psychological transformation does not necessarily put the individual in felt relationship to spiritual reality.

One feature of the training that diverges from a multilevel perspective is its consequentialism. The consequentialist attitude, described in Part 1 as a defining feature of the unilevel category in the Anthony typology, requires worldly effects as evidence for the value of a spiritual experience or perspective. This attitude tends to short-circuit transformative developments in consciousness. Why? A chief aspect of the mystical glimpse-experience of ultimacy is the direct intuition that one's essence or real self is not dependent on material conditions. By thus dispelling "ontological insecurity"—the root anxiety that one's being is vulnerable and could be lost—this experience deeply alleviates fear and worry in life, resulting in enhanced energy, love, comfort, judgment. For the person who regards the mystical experience as true and valuable *because* it brings material and social advantage this all runs amuck. Grasping after the consequences, even subtly, contradicts the essence of the glimpse experience and tends to cancel it. A more-or-less frantic but futile attempt to keep both the state and the desired benefits typically occurs.

Now, Werner Erhard maintains for instance (in his discussion of The Hunger Project in this interview) that to hold an empowering, life-enhancing context, and to act out of that context, has intrinsic value regardless of external consequences. On the other hand, the promotion of the *est* training (and now the Forum) has been heavily loaded with prospects of practical consequences that would delight any materialist. Perhaps the purpose is to attract consequentialist-utilitarian John and Mary Doe into an experience that will take them beyond consequentialism. But how many *est* trainees never fully get the point, and instead gain a powerful new strategy—context creation—for pursuing the materialist ends dictated by their materialist values? (Stone's data, after all, indicate only that graduates' social altruism does not *decrease*.) This resulting consequentialism, whether intended or not, would counteract the power of the training to establish trainees in an authentically multilevel orientation.

Another aspect of the training that seems inconsistent with multilevel spirituality is the issue of invariable sudden enlightenment. Some commentators perceive Erhard as claiming that the two-weekend *est* training produces enlightenment. Although he flirts with that position in the interview, only once does he seem to make the claim unambiguously, in affirming that the enlightenment produced by the *est* training is equivalent to what is regarded as enlightenment in Zen Buddhism. Wilber, a longtime student of Zen, remains unconvinced. Perhaps Erhard's enlightenment claim, even when unambiguous, might be no more than a way of shaking up rigid beliefs about enlightenment. Readers can judge for themselves. But let us assume, if only as a worthy exercise, that the claim is indeed made, and identify the issues that it raises.

The primary issue is not the possibility of attaining enlightenment in two weekends, as we see it. We agree with Erhard that enlightenment may take "no time" because we respect the mystical traditions that affirm original or sudden enlightenment. However, these traditions (such as Zen Buddhism and the Sadguru or Perfect Master tradition of Vedanta Hinduism) also affirm the utter unpredictability of the realization of original enlightenment. What is problematic about Erhard's claim is not that enlightenment takes no time, but that the *est* training produces sudden enlightenment *invariably*, in all 250 trainees of each *est* training group. To claim that the training produces this realization both suddenly and invariably—and without great effort or asceticism—has no precedent in or support from even the sudden enlightenment traditions. Within these traditions it would be viewed as a very odd and extreme claim indeed, and therefore an implausible one. Certainly the burden of proof is with Erhard and staff, and it seems to us that they have not yet made a convincing or even plausible case.

One of the apparent strengths of the est training is a capacity to reveal convincingly the relativistic or perspectivistic nature of ordinary consciousness—the arbitrariness of socially conditioned, personal "reality." Ideally, the realization of perspectivism in the est training allows one to cease identifying with any particular social or personal definition of oneself, and instead to identify with one's being as an unconditioned, timeless source of unlimited creativity, intelligence, and love. The trainee is thereby enabled to create a flexible personal "reality" that maximizes the expression of his or her creative being.

This orientation is consistent with multilevel monism. However, some graduates emerge from the training with what seems to us a distortion or misuse of the discovery of relativism. Relativism becomes for them a rationalization for not taking seriously any deeply personal, uncomfortable feedback from spouses, friends, or co-workers. What others say is only about themselves and their reality. The transcendental glimpse experience of oneself as an unconditioned being in a relativistic world is used to fortify rather than transcend the separative ego-self. A thrust of transformative development gets dispersed in translational, or horizontal, processes of adaptation.

Graduates of est who use the training in this way celebrate the discovery of relativism—it is an exhilarating, liberating discovery—by asserting their own atomistic individuality. After perhaps a lifetime of suffering the painful judgments of others, they now have a potent rationale for refusing to consider the possible truth of any unpleasant feedback. They use the training to swing from ethical absolutism to absolute ethical relativism and radical nominalism; from unilevel dualism to unilevel monism, rather than to multilevel monism, which with its ethical dialecticism would provide a synthesis of unconditional self-worth and the ability and willingness to face and acknowledge one's human weaknesses and flaws. Self-confrontation of this sort is the basis of existential authenticity, and among its most important instigators are the deeply personal forces of interpersonal relationship. Ironically, the est training sometimes gets used as a suit of armor against these forces and the essential act of self-confrontation. The tendency among est graduates towards an almost doctrinaire use of jargon seems to be an aspect of this rigid defensiveness, as well as part of the celebration of relativism. This syndrome certainly does not constitute a higher integration of the psyche; it may even be dis-integrative in certain respects. And while it may, in many cases, be a quickly passing and even necessary phase that leads to the higher integration of self-worth and self-confrontation, some *est* graduates that we have known have persisted indefinitely in this impenetrable hyper-individuality.

We have, in summary, a mixed picture: the *est* training is susceptible to a number of unilevel twists, but despite these problems, it does seem to initiate some trainees into important aspects of multilevel monism.

Notes

1. One of the editors (Anthony) has taken the training. All three editors have interviewed a number of *est* graduates whom we know personally.
2. See Steven M. Tipton, *Getting Saved from the Sixties: Moral Meaning in Conversion and Cultural Change* (Berkeley: University of California Press, 1981); also, Robert Ornstein, *The Mind Field* (London: Octagon, 1976). Ornstein's book does not name The *est* Training explicitly, but his argument is generally regarded as a thinly veiled critique of it.
3. For example, Peter Marin, "The New Narcissism," *Harpers*, Oct. 1975.
4. The opposition of virtue and material self-enhancement in the Christian ethical tradition has been regarded by some historians of ethics as an accidental rather than essential feature of an ethical system. See for example Alasdair MacIntyre, *A Short History of Ethics* (New York: MacMillan, 1966). For the early Christians, who were an oppressed minority, religious commitment brought material sacrifice; material advantage was available only by selling out one's religious position. The abstract, doctrinal generalization of this initially circumstantial split between spiritual virtue and material well-being may be a fallacy, a univocal misinterpretation of ethical meanings. It is self-centeredness, not merely a condition of material well-being or success, that stands in the way of moral and religious transcendence. The proper function of asceticism is, in our opinion, the attenuation of self-centeredness, irrespective of external material conditions.
5. Donald Stone, "Social Consciousness in the Human Potential Movement," in Thomas Robbins and Dick Anthony, eds., *In Gods We Trust* (New Brunswick, NJ: Transaction, 1981).
6. These are basic cybernetic concepts. The interested reader is referred to the seminal work of Gregory Bateson, whose thinking has had a profound effect on many fields, including psychotherapy, systems analysis, and game theory. Paul Watzlawick, John Weakland, and Richard Fisch, who

worked with Bateson, use Group Theory in their book *Change* (New York: Norton, 1974) to define "first-order change" and "second-order change," the latter being what we are calling "transformation," a change in the overarching rules or conditions that determine the set of allowed first-order changes.

A Ten-Year Perspective[1]

Ram Dass (Richard Alpert)

In 1966 Richard Alpert and colleague Timothy Leary were fired from the Harvard University psychology faculty because of their controversial experimentation with LSD and other hallucinogenic drugs. After a few years Alpert's and Leary's paths diverged when Alpert, travelling in India, met the Hindu spiritual master Neem Karoli Baba. From contact with this master and from mystical experiences he himself then had, Alpert recognized that genuine spiritual realization went beyond anything drugs could produce. He became Neem Karoli Baba's devotee, changed his name to Baba Ram Dass ("Baba," a religious title meaning "father," was later dropped), and told the story of this odyssey in *Be Here Now*, a book that widely influenced the developing counterculture. Through his talks, gatherings, writings,[2] and social projects, Ram Dass continued to have a major role in bringing Eastern spiritual alternatives to the attention of Americans seeking new value orientations. His personal spiritual journey has often mirrored and paced that of the monistic counterculture at large and transpersonal psychology in particular.

Like all true passages, this journey has had its false trails and here Ram Dass provides an inside view of his self-deception as a "phony holy," a self-exposé of psychopathology masquerading as spirituality. For Ram Dass, this experience revealed that "the doorway to the intuition is through the human heart," and that opening this doorway requires facing and accepting the distortions and weaknesses in one's emotional make-up, "because when you accept them you can transform them." Ram Dass discusses how "embracing my humanity" produced a sense of self-responsibility and an expanded, warmer sense of social bond, especially with older people. He describes the intuitive basis of his involvement in social action, contrasting this with efforts based on emotional reaction to imagined sociopolitical scenarios.

I tried to think about the last ten years, but I can hardly remember yesterday. When that first started to happen, I wondered if I was taking too many drugs, but then I noticed that when I needed something in memory it was there, and so I started to trust this state of not thinking at all—just kind of an empty mind out of which something comes and you just get to trust it. The situation is that, as you let go of personal history, each moment becomes richer and more thick with meaning. Both future and past start to lose their power. You can have plans and memories, but they don't seem to have the same pull.

A couple of years ago I found I had been moving memorabilia with me everywhere I went. It's those things one would keep in an attic or cellar. Mine were in boxes and I would pay the parcel service to move them every time I would move. When you're a wandering "Sadhu" with a whole parcel fleet behind you, it's quite a trip. I noticed that I never opened the boxes. I just kept adding to them, assuming that the time would come when I would run out of the present moment, in which case I could revel in the past. But I was getting to be able to be fulfilled in the present moment by less and less until I could just sit in an empty room and be happy. But I had old love letters and important memorabilia of the 60s and things one must hold onto—pictures of people I'd never see again, my Bar Mitzvah certificate that said I was a man. Not things to be taken lightly!

At first I decided to throw them away, but I found myself during the night going out to the garbage pail because I couldn't bear to get rid of one picture. So I decided to have a big fire and burn them all. And I did. I started out laughing, but by the second day it was really starting to get to me. My guru had said, "It's good to burn bodies because then the beings don't keep wanting to come back to them." So I thought it was good to burn that personal history. But it turned out someone was doing a movie of me those few days, so it's all on film. It's like microfilming one's history except it's his film, not mine, so now my karma is his and I'm free. I don't ever have to look at it again.

David McClelland, who was my boss at Harvard (he actually fired me and we've remained good friends over the years), is convinced I haven't changed at all. This is extremely discouraging since he's a social psychologist. I've been working all these years trying to change, and he says, "You're the same as you always were." I figure, "What does he know?" But I have changed, inside, although I'm not an enlightened being. Perhaps I am at some level, but I'm not fully consciously an enlightened being. I'm actually sort of a mouth for a process that many of us are sharing.

A year ago I was fifty years old. I've always gone to motels on my birthday because I don't like that kind of hysterical fun that people usually have at calendar celebrations. But this time was my fiftieth birthday, and I wanted to see if there was something to really enjoy and learn. So I called some people and had three parties, one on television in New York with a big birthday cake. But no matter how I milked it, I couldn't quite feel that I was any age. I have a fifty-year-old body, a 1931 model decaying perfectly lawfully, and so I was really celebrating the age of my vehicle. Yet, on one plane, I'm hundreds of thousands of years old. Or else I'm newly born. You can take your choice. It feels like all and everything.

Ten years ago I was very caught in specialness. I was what I now would call a "phony holy." I was busy trying to be high for me and everybody else. I assumed that everybody wanted me to be high all the time so I would prepare myself to be high in front of everybody. There's a certain way you are when you're high. You smile a lot, you're very benevolent—it's the holy man role. I took all the parts of me that didn't fit into that role and shoved them under the rug so that I could be who everybody wanted me to be. I wanted to be that, too. I really wanted to be Ram Dass.

You see, I had what was called vertical schizophrenia. I even had a name to go with each of my personalities. Dick Alpert and Ram Dass. Ram Dass would sit in front of a group of people and look out and maybe just love everybody and want nothing. Dick Alpert was counting the house. Worse than that, Dick Alpert was impersonating Ram Dass. Somebody would come up and say, "Oh, Ram Dass, thank you for your writings!" and I'd hear Ram Dass say, "Wouldn't you like to come up and see my holy pictures?" Well, that may seem funny to you, but what I felt was just a tremendous amount of hypocrisy, being what everybody wanted me to be. You see, what happened was that the spiritual identity played right into my hands psychologically. Psychologically there were whole parts of my being that I was afraid of and didn't accept. I had a justification for getting rid of them by becoming holy, and I was using my spiritual journey psychodynamically in order to get free of things that I couldn't acknowledge in myself. But after a while I began to feel as if I was standing on sand. I had to live with my own horror, and the predicament was that I was trying to live in the projection that other people were creating for me. But every now and then I had to be alone, and when I was alone I'd go into very deep depressions, which I hid.

My theory was that if I did my Sadhana hard enough, if I meditated deeply enough, if I opened my heart in devotional practices wide enough, all that unacknowledged stuff would go away. But it didn't, and it has taken me years to understand what the teaching was in all of this. I was busy going from the two into the one . . . from dualism into nondualism, from the multiplicity into unity. All yogic techniques are designed for that purpose: Yoga means union. I could huff and puff in pranayam, control my breath to go into a trance state, and in that trance state all of Dick Alpert would be gone completely. But I always came down again, and down had a pejorative connotation for me. I kept wanting to get high. I didn't want to come down. But I indeed did keep coming down, even with yoga techniques.

Now in the course of the years I've developed a lot of very strange friends, and one of them is a being named Emanuel. He is interesting because he doesn't have a body. He's a being on another plane and he speaks through a woman on this plane. Some might have a difficult time accepting my friend Emanuel, saying they have no prejudices about color, sex, or religion. But bodies . . . somehow if somebody doesn't have a body, you immediately don't know that you want to accept them.

But that's not a problem for me because he's my friend and the way I figure it, I'll take my teachings anywhere I can get them. Emanuel had a teaching. One of the things he said to us was, "You are here because you chose to be here because this is a learning place. Each lifetime is a wonderful opportunity to expand your consciousness and to move closer, ever closer, to your oneness with God. This happens in very small stages. First oneness with self, oneness with the human community, then oneness with God. It cannot be done in one blinding flash. It would be too incomprehensible . . . too confusing. So be patient.

"When we choose to come back, we construct an embryo to hold within us the areas of distortion that we need to work on. Then we choose our finite environment to act as a catalyst to bring out these areas. So you were where you needed to be as a very small child.

"So accept the distortions in you. Because when you accept them you can transform them. That's what life is about. You're here to find these areas of imperfection, to understand them, to love them, and to educate them into reality, which is truth, light, love. If in the transitional period you find things in yourself that are not perfect, don't blame yourself, celebrate." When I said to him, "Emanuel, what work do I have to do now?" he said, "Ram Dass, you're in a school, why don't you try taking the curriculum? You took a human birth. You're so busy being holy . . . why don't you try being human?"

Funny, I'd never thought of that. Somehow being human meant less than perfect. Even though I intellectually knew that "form is no other than formless and formless is no other than form," I knew that the manifestation was God made manifest. Everything was perfect out there except me. But original sin was going to have a last stronghold right here with me. Now I had steeped myself in a Hindu tradition of renunciation, which could produce liberated beings, but often just produces horny celibates, and it kept reinforcing my denigration of personality. So, I said, "Okay, Emanuel, here I go." I decided I'd just go and be human. Now, I'd already anticipated this. I remember being drunk with Alan Watts in a Benedictine monastery one night years ago, and at three in the morning Alan said, "You know, the trouble with you, Dick . . ." (you know you're going to get real truth at a moment like that) " . . . you're too attached to emptiness."

So with Alan and Emanuel looking over my shoulder I'd already figured out that as long as I pushed anything in the universe away I wasn't going to be free. I also saw that the game wasn't just getting high; the game was to be free, and free included the highs and the lows. Free included it all . . . "all and everything" as Gurdjieff would say. There is also that lovely line of G. Manley Hall—"he who knows not that the Prince of Darkness is but the other face of the King of Light knows not me . . . ," says God.

Emanuel said, "If you want to be free, you're going to have to embrace original sin. You're going to have to incorporate the darkness into the light." I'd been through years of psychoanalysis, and all I had done was to invest so much reality in my neuroses there wasn't a chance they were going to go away. In those days, I said, "Look at all the great saints. They're all as neurotic as anybody else; it's just that it's kind of irrelevant. And so you don't have to change your neuroses, you just stop identifying with them. You just make friends with them and they come by for tea." The analyst thought my neuroses were real because his were real, so we just kept reinforcing the reality of our identities. How could I be other than a patient? He was a doctor. There was only room for two of us in the room.

So these past few years I found myself opening up to relationship and I was like a post-pubescent. I found myself sitting in the bathtub crying with jealous rage. I couldn't believe it! I thought, "This couldn't be me." I said, "My God, Ram Dass, what are you doing? How absurd!" And there was this part of me that was giggling. And I was crying and the pain was excruciating. Now, there's something called non-attachment and there's a psychodynamic called dissociation. One often masquerades as the other. So while I was busy being non-attached, I'd say, "This depression . . . ha! ha! ha!" It looked like non-attachment, but actually, it was dissociation.

But by the time I started to open up to my personality, I had developed something inside of me that was very deep, a thing called the witness, as in Ouspensky's *In Search of the Miraculous*. The witness is just another part of your ego. It's just one part looking at the other part. Finally, however, you witness the witness, a meditative technique in which you turn in on yourself. Behind all of that there's just a place . . . you can't even call it a place. It's like sky. It just develops. It's a context, a frame of reference, of "isness." It doesn't have any quality to it. You can't say it's happy or sad or watchful. It's not looking, but it's seeing. It just is. It's the Tao. It's the Way. I was there when I opened to my personality content. I was no longer holding onto that space, but it was still there. It was there along with the pain.

At that point a friend called me—and he was somebody I'd worked with—and I said, "Gee, you sound wonderful. Why are you so wonderful?" He said, "I'm in therapy." And I said, "Is it good?" And he said, "Yes, wonderful." I asked, "What's the name of your therapist?" He told me, and I thought, "Well, I think I'll do that." I called the therapist and said, "I want some of what you sell." I hired him and we worked together. I was in Jungian analysis. People say, "You? Ram Dass in therapy?" Why not? And it was extraordinarily useful. But I did have those initial thoughts of, "Well, I'll be able to help him."

Something that is still becoming more clear to me is the movement from knowing the world through conceptual structures and knowing it "intuitively." I have felt that the problems that we kept creating with our rational minds were only going to be solved by our intuitive connection to the universe. I felt this about nuclear energy, most of the ways in which technology has taken us, the problems of the ecosphere on which we are dependent, and our human relations. I kept looking for ways to connect with that deeper and deeper part of my being that just knows. It knows because it is. In that intuitive domain everything in the universe is subject, and when I'm in my analytic conceptual mind, the universe is object, always one thought away from where the action is.

So I could see that my thinking mind was an instrument—it reinforced my sense of separateness. I didn't want to get rid of my thinking mind, but I wanted to have it around like, "Hey, you, I need you." I

wanted to change it from a master into a servant. It's very hard to rationally think through everything. It's awfully complicated.

An example of this occurred a year and a half ago in Benares, India—
the city of death. A friend and I were going to the bathing "ghats," to
the sacred bathing area in the Ganges river where you can bathe with all
of the floating dead bodies and things. Benares is a very auspicious place
to die. As we were going there we passed about 100 or 125 lepers and
they all had begging bowls and we shared our coins, my friend and I. I
had about twenty coins of different denominations and there were 125
lepers. So I started down the line. Who am I going to give coins to? Now
my rational mind thinks, that fellow is missing his arms, that's worth fifty
paisa, but that woman has her face eaten way. Do you suppose that's
worth a rupee? Can you hear how ghastly those thoughts were?—
because I only had twenty coins and there were 125 lepers. And I did this
for about three coins. I'm using a grotesque example, but life is pretty
grotesque. Finally, I just gave up. I shifted to intuitive, and went down
the line looking people in the eye and every now and then handed someone a coin. I was suddenly enjoying being with all these beings and I
didn't get into guilt and judgment which would have just destroyed the
moment. It turns out they have a union. They share all their coins. I
didn't know that, so the lesson was a great one for me.

I have been opening to my intuitive way of doing things, and I just
respond much more whimsically, without any reason for doing it,
particularly.

"Sure, I'll do this." "I won't do that"—"Why? I don't know."—
"Well, shouldn't you?"—"No." (If you can stand that original confrontation.) "I mean, you're not being rational."—"No."—"You mean you
trust?—But do you know you know?"—"No."—"And you still trust?"—
"Yes."—"Well, I don't know." This is the dialogue you have with yourself, actually. It can get extraordinarily exciting and you say, "Well, here
we go. I'm going on intuition."

But the problem that I ran into for some years was that the doorway
to the intuition is through the human heart, and I was trying to leap into
cosmic love without dealing with emotionality because emotionality was
a little too human for me. What I experienced was that I had pushed
away my humanity to embrace my divinity. When I wanted to be intuitive, the intuition, the impeccable warrior intuitive action, had to come
from a blending of humanity and divinity. Until I could accept my
humanity fully, my intuitions weren't going to be fully in harmony with
the way of things. When I went into my sixth chakra, everything looked
absolutely perfect. I could look at suffering and see the way in which it
was grace. I could see death as grace. It was a place that was clear, but
with that clarity there was no warmth. If someone fell down in front of

me I could say, "Karma." But when I come down into my human heart, it would hurt so bad because I opened to the suffering of the universe. The easiest way to handle it is to go up. It's much harder to stay down and stay open. It's excruciating.

I began to feel that my freedom was going to lie in the creative tension of being able to see simultaneously perfection and also to experience pain; to see that there was nothing to do and yet to work as hard as I could to relieve suffering; to see it was all a dream and still live within the reality of it. My present work is to get into the fullness of the human heart. People used to say, "We love you and we think you're beautiful and very clear, but we don't trust you." They would say they didn't trust me because they couldn't feel my heart, my humanness. There's an image of a Buddha statue with a tiny smile at the edge of the lips and it's known as "the smile of unbearable compassion." It's a way in which you can open to the horrible beauty of it all. You can bear it, not by deadening yourself, but by balancing.

Over the years my faith has gotten deeper . . . not the beliefs, because beliefs aren't going to keep you warm on a cold night. The faith . . . the connection to that which you are at the deepest level, to the universe, to the oneness of all things . . . as that faith gets deeper and deeper, then you can dramatically, much more freely, throw yourself into life.

As long as the faith flickers, you've got to be very tentative about the way you go into life because you're always afraid you're going to lose your connection to the spirit. But when that faith is really strong, you can say, "Here I come!" In the past few years . . . people come up and say, "You know, Ram Dass, you're really just human." It's interesting, what I have done psychodynamically. My personality felt so inadequate that I became bigger than life, so everybody would say, "Oh, look at Ram Dass. We could never be like him." And now they look and say, "Gee, he's just another guy. What do you know?" Psychologically the whole game of communication changed for me. It's a big one, embracing humanity—not embracing humanity, embracing my humanity.

Almost ten years ago I met this Tibetan rascal named Chögyam Trungpa, Rimpoche, in Brooklyn. He's a Tantrist and you never know what they're doing. For example, he just looked like a drunk, but you never know because that's what a Tantrist might want to look like. So a few days after our initial meeting he was speaking up in Vermont and I stopped by. He was speaking on Don Juan and I thought I could sneak in and sit in the back. But somebody told me, "Trungpa wants to see you." Great. So I was brought into this room with one table, one saki bottle, one glass, and one chair, and he was sitting in it. So I knelt in front of him and he looked at me and said, "Ram Dass, we have to accept responsibility." What would you do with an opening gambit like that? So I said, "What responsibility? Rimpoche, God has all of the responsibility. I don't have any responsibility. Not my but thy will, Oh Lord." He said, "You're copping out." Then we turned to other conversation, but that statement stuck in my craw.

But recently Emanuel said to me, "Ram Dass, you really have a choice of whether you want to be the victim or the creator." If you look at yourself, you have a body. You have a personality. You have senses. These are all lawful. They all work by law. Everything in form is lawful. Even thoughts are form and they are lawful. It's all working fine. It's all just flowing and unfolding and the laws of karma are working perfectly, and in that sense it's just all happening to you. And as long as you identify with forms you experience yourself as being a victim. It could be expressed as, "Poor me, look at what's happened! Look at the world I'm living in! Look at what's been foisted on me. If I didn't have this beauty mark I'd be . . . whatever."

But Emanuel said, "Ram Dass, there's a part of you that created this whole business. Why don't you accept the responsibility?" Now at the worst level that is reinterpreted as affirmation, because if I'm the creator then I can have a fine automobile. But it isn't the ego that's the creator. The ego is part of the creation. In fact, everything that you can label and point to in yourself isn't the creator and yet you are. So the first step was accepting the responsibility for the way things are. Truly. Which raised the interesting possibility that I was exactly as I should be at this moment. I wasn't three steps behind, feeling if I hurried I could catch up. Some of you must know that feeling. "I'm really schlock phony, but if I get to work, I'll clean it up and then I'll be who I really . . . ," and you keep holding these models of how you're supposed to be. So accepting responsibiity means that I accept the responsibility for the creation of what I am, and at the same time I also am the creation. I am the creator and that which is created. As long as I identify only with the creation I feel victimized. As long as I identify only with the creator I have no form.

To go back to the point where I said I started out feeling very special, I was busy holding on to a myth about myself, a scenario about myself: "Dick Alpert thrown out of Harvard, drugs, yoga, guru games . . . ," what will happen next? It's very "somebody-ish." Then I decided that really the game was to become "nobody." So I went into nobody training, giving lectures, "Nothing New by Nobody Special." But I was a little bit like the janitor in the temple. The rabbi was "davening," and he fell down on his knees crying, "Oh, God, I'm nothing, I'm nothing, I'm nothing," and so the Cantor came along and he saw the Rabbi doing that and so he fell on his knees and he said, "I'm nothing . . . I'm nothing." And the janitor came along and he saw them doing this and he knelt down and started crying, "I'm nothing, I'm nothing," and the Rabbi nudges the Cantor and says, "So look who's being nothing!" So I was going to be nobody special like the big boys. But there's a sneaky "somebodiness" in there.

I grew up at a time when the biggest thing was to be independent. One moved away from home. Visiting my father or family when I was trying to stay conscious, I used to last about twenty seconds. I'd come in as the Buddha and after a question like, "What are you doing for a living?," I'd lose my consciousness into reactivity. But I'd think, "I'm going to take on the hot fires, so I'm going to love my father." So, "Here I am, Dad, I love you." But he smelled a rat. He knew. Now it's better. I really enjoy extended family, and I really love to be with my father. We hang out, we play Yahtzee, and we watch the ball game. Does the spirit manifest only in Om mani padme hum? Isn't Yahtzee as much divine spirit as anything else? It's a way of being with another being.

When I started to open the door to the extended family, an interesting thing developed. Ten years ago I was always trying to get "juice" from young people. That's where the energy and the movements were. That's where the action was, where the spiritual change in the world was going to happen. I was sort of the uncle to a certain group of people that were going to make it happen. But even way back I began to see signs that it wasn't the way I thought it was. I kept ignoring them, even one delicious sign. At a time when everybody that came to my audience were always the same age, they all dressed a certain way: they all wore white, had smiles and had flowers and loved everybody. Now I think they were real repressed. This one night they were all there smiling and I assumed everybody had had acid, and I was talking far out talk that those "who knew" would understand. In the front row there was a woman who was about seventy. She had a hat on with strawberries and cherries and things, and she had a black patent leather bag, a print dress and responsible oxfords. I'd say outrageous things and she'd nod in knowing agreement. I'd think, "How does she know? Well, this is not an acid head." I just kept watching her as I'd say more outrageous things, and she'd nod again. At the end of the lecture she came up and said, "Oh, thank you. Everything you said just made perfect sense, and it was just so clear." I said, "How do you know all that? What do you do that gets you into the position of consciousness that you know all that?" She leaned forward very conspiratorially and she said, "I crochet."

The past few years I have begun to feel this great affinity to the elders of the society. Henry Amiel said, "To know how to grow old is a masterwork of wisdom, one of the most difficult chapters in the great art of living."

Longfellow: "For age is opportunity no less than youth itself, though in another dress, and as the evening twilight fades away, the sky is filled with stars invisible by day."

So, as I started to try to integrate the deeper parts of my inner being, I found that my inner being was acknowledging a much broader spectrum of the universe than my habitual separate self was. And I was suddenly beginning to delight in the elders as well as young people. I started to enjoy hanging out with my father, beginning to feel the way that I had cut off my own growth by pushing him away in order to get holy.

What I'm experiencing is listening more carefully to my body, to my heart, and my mind. And the more I go inside and listen, the more the inside and the outside are one. And it's interesting that the more I try to get myself together without the intellectual overlay of "I must honor my incarnation," the more I find myself involved in social action. I don't find myself involved in social action out of urgency or fear. I feel I am a member of society. I feel I must vote. There's not even a question about it. When something doesn't feel right, I must speak up about it not feeling right because that's my responsibility, and my silence is also my vote. I'm beginning to see that I am only going to be free when I'm fully involved in the world. A strange insight for me.

I've been having some interesting dialogues with various people about the motives for social action. All I experience is that the inside is the outside and the outside is the inside, and intuitively it just feels right to do certain things. And there's nothing special about it. There's no big deal about it and it's not done because I'm holding onto a scenario of what's going to happen in the universe.

People say, "Do you expect Armageddon? Or do you expect the Brave New World?" And I say, "To me these are scenarios, and I understand having a positive scenario and I will certainly move towards one, but I see them all as just scenarios." I used to listen to Walter Cronkite on television, and every night he'd say, "That's the way it is today," and I used to believe him. Then I realized it was just the way he saw it to be today. Whichever scenario we have in the universe, whether it's going to end in five minutes or five billion years, I realized that at this moment I had to do the same thing. I heard the Bhagavad Gita's injunction, "Be not attached to the fruits of the actions." I found that my social action friends had a hard time believing that I'd actually do anything useful for them or for the world if I wasn't attached to the fruits of the actions. I'd say to them, "Far out, you're here at this rally. So am I. What do you suppose I'm doing here?"

For a long time I was so busy being holy I had no time for aesthetics. So my cello just sat in the closet. Now I'm playing string quartets again and not only is it okay, but I feel like I'm in the spirit, and a group of us play harpsichord and recorder and cello. . . . We're hoping to play in old folks' homes in New Mexico.

And there is a change related to all the work I've done with dying—the dying centers and the dying project, really keeping death on my left shoulder, just opening to it by acknowledging and living with death. Now I'm learning to live with life. A new one for me. I'm also learning to honor my body. I see that I haven't really been in my body fully. And I have work to do in my body and with my heart. It's all going just fine, and I'm very patient.

Ten years ago I used to be counting, "How soon 'til I get enlightened?" Now I've developed patience. It's not despair. It's patience. It's rooted in hopelessness. My attachment to where I was going was getting in the way of being. The third Chinese patriarch says, "Even to be attached to enlightenment is to go astray."

It is said that the truth waits for eyes unclouded by longing. As you become quiet—quiet in faith and quiet in what is, quiet in the fullness of the moment—you begin to hear closer and closer to the truth. And in that hearing, or out of that hearing, comes action that happens in harmony with the way of things, and your unique manifestation expresses itself. You become a perfect statement of God made manifest through you.

No longer am I trying to imitate anyone else. I'm Dick Alpert and I'm a perfect Dick Alpert. I listen from moment to moment, and what I hear changes, and I find that I can't be afraid of being inconsistent if I'm going to listen to truth and allow my uniqueness to manifest. Now I listen, and I do what intuitively I must do. I begin to trust myself to find the unique way that I'm going to manifest this year, in this world, which has never been like this before, with this body that is totally unique, with this mind, with this childhood, with this set of experiences. The rule book isn't going to be good enough—no matter how fancy its covers and how august its authors.

Notes

1. Adapted from a talk given August 7, 1982 on the occasion of the Tenth Annual Conference of the Association for Transpersonal Psychology, held at Asilomar Conference Center, Pacific Grove, California. Reprinted from the *Journal of Transpersonal Psychology*, Vol. 14, No. 2, 1982, with modifications. Published and reprinted by permission of the author. Copyright © 1982 Hanuman Foundation (a non-profit, tax-exempt organization), P.O. Box 478, Sante Fe, NM 87501.

2. Books by Ram Dass include *Be Here Now* (1971); *The Only Dance There Is* (1974); *Grist for the Mill* (1976); *Journey of Awakening* (1977); and *Miracle of Love* (1979).

EDITORIAL COMMENTARY

Ram Dass gives us a revealing, inside view of his experience as a unilevel monistic guru. He describes how he extracted himself from a false posture of spiritual authority, and explains the neurotic functions that had been served by that posture.

The numerous correctives to his spiritual trajectory that Ram Dass describes all illustrate differences between Anthony's categories of unilevel and multilevel religion. Ram Dass cites his confusion of avoidance and transcendence, as in his use of spiritual teachings (such as karmic determinism) to avoid confronting the fact of human suffering. Dissociation and repression masqueraded as detachment. Now Ram Dass views both his earlier self-image as a spiritual "somebody" and his subsequent reversal into being a spiritual "nobody" as equal forms of mundane self-preoccupation. He came to a kind of paradoxical reconciliation of mundane and transcendent experience that allows him to be true to both rather than deny (repress) his human qualities. The years have revealed that his many genuine glimpse experiences, as valuable as they were, did not constitute transformation and did not change his psychological make-up. Ram Dass sees the spiritual transformation of the individual as a slow, vast process requiring "patience . . . rooted in hopelessness," meaning not "despair," but rather a relinquishing of self-concern, so that hope for oneself is not the guiding principle of life. He sees the ego as a pawn in the game of spiritual inner development, not vice versa. "It isn't the ego that's the creator," so that "taking responsibility" for having created one's lot does not imply that one has license to "create" whatever would satisfy egotistical desires. Ram Dass reports that for him, the deepening of spirituality has involved a decreasing sense of being part of an in-group versus some out-group (the young versus the old, in his case) and an increasing sense of identification with all humanity. He emphasizes the difference between faith and belief, and the priority of faith over belief ("beliefs aren't going to keep you warm on a cold night").

All these points correspond to Anthony's multilevel/unilevel distinctions. A possible question about this talk is whether Ram Dass means it to contain the implied message, "Now I know the right approach: I'll accept my humanity." He would, we're sure, agree that in the spiritual domain, any truth one adopts as a general strategy is distorted by the very process of doing so. A näive reader could interpret some of Ram Dass's words—"incorporating darkness into the light," "embrace original sin," "the game was to be free, and . . . free included it all," "accept the distortions in you," "my intuitive way of doing things . . . much more whimsically," plus approving references to getting drunk and using drugs—as approval of antinomian license, sensual indulgence, impulsivity, and acting out; in short, the brand of pop pseudo-mysticism that Anthony calls Tantric Freudianism. We don't think that this is actually Ram Dass's intended meaning. In context, his words make a point with which we agree: to embrace one's humanity does not mean self-indulgence, but self-honesty, a crucial quality of the authentic spiritual aspirant at every stage.

MEHER BABA

An Interview with Dick Anthony[1]

As noted in the Introduction, Dick Anthony headed the seminar group that generated most of the articles and interviews in this volume, and Anthony offered himself as the first group member who was also interviewed (on March 26, 1981). In Anthony's view the discourse among seminar members had contained unspoken secular, "reductionistic" assumptions. He chose to tell of his own experiences in relation to Meher Baba because he wished to confront directly the reductionistic viewpoints and, in the process, to explore the implicit assumptions that lay behind them.

As Research Director of the Center for the Study of New Religious Movements at the Graduate Theological Union in Berkeley and previously as a research faculty member in the Department of Psychiatry, School of Medicine, University of North Carolina at Chapel Hill, Anthony has been principal investigator of a number of research projects—funded by government agencies or philanthropic foundations—on the mental health effects of new religious movements. He is co-editor (with Thomas Robbins) of *In Gods We Trust: New Patterns of American Religious Pluralism* (1981), co-author (with Robert Bellah and Thomas Robbins) of the forthcoming volume, *Between Religion and the Human Sciences: Toward the Non-Reductionistic Study of Religion,* co-author (with Ken Wilber) of *Polarity vs. Progress: Alternative Images for the Process of Transformation* (in preparation), and has published over fifty articles on religious movements in professional journals in the fields of psychology, sociology, medicine, religion, law, and political science. He has a clinical practice in transpersonal bodywork.

A key theme in Anthony's account is the problem of integrating personal autonomy and surrender to spiritual authority. Autonomy and surrender seem irreconcilable opposites in the present cultural environment in the West, but Anthony describes how this seeming opposition was resolved transrationally through contact with Meher Baba.

He gives an inside view of a charismatic rather than technical involvement, i.e., the master's transformative influence occurs through personal relationship rather than through impersonal techniques. The seminar members question Anthony on the attitudes of Meher Baba lovers and the nature of their devotion and obedience to their master. Given Meher Baba's claim of being the Avatar, or the direct incarnation of God in human form, what keeps Meher Baba lovers from feeling the unilevel attitudes of superiority, exclusivity, and inflation? In speaking to these issues, Anthony describes how multilevel spirituality operates in relation to a master who is regarded by his followers as perfect.

Dick Anthony: I had pursued various guests for this evening, and for one reason or another everybody sort of fell through. And while I was in pursuit, I talked to various people who are involved in this seminar, including John Welwood, Mike Murphy, Frances Vaughan, Jerry Needleman, and Ken Wilber, and it started to seem like a consensus that an issue that's been latent should emerge at this point.

While we were interviewing people from groups that are generally regarded as problematic, those of us who are coming from a transpersonal perspective and those who are coming from a more secular perspective could make common cause fairly easily. Both groups of scholars tended to go towards somewhat reductionistic analyses. But now that we're starting to interview people from groups that are widely admired (by transpersonal people, at least), such as the San Francisco Zen Center or the Tibetan Buddhist groups, it seems that there is a lack of congruence between the types of analyses that are being offered by people from the transpersonal as opposed to the secular perspectives represented here.

The transpersonal participants have tended to use concepts that are intrinsically religious in commenting on interviews of people from the latter (Zen, Tibetan) groups. You secular scholars, on the other hand, have tended to explain away the religious significance of these interviews as well by reference to social scientific or psychological concepts such as "anomie" or "authoritarianism."

Since one of the two primary functions of this seminar, as I had orginally conceived of it, was to create a dialogue between people from transpersonal and secular reductionistic perspectives, I thought we might use this evening as a way of bringing those implicit models of human nature into a more active confrontation or dialogue. And, I conceived the idea of doing that by using myself as an interview subject, talking about my own relationship to a transpersonal tradition and a religious group, and to invite people to reduce my religious experience. In other words, I'll welcome reductionistic analyses, so don't be shy. In fact, I think the transpersonal people may want to do that as well, since even though I share a transpersonal orientation with the transpersonal people, it's notorious that transpersonal people don't always see each other's gurus as models of transpersonal consciousness, or each other's religious paths as exemplary of the ideal transpersonal orientation. So I'm assuming that I'll be throwing myself open to everybody, whatever your orientation, and the image just flashed before my mind of those clowns in the carnival, where you throw baseballs, and if you hit a bullseye, they get dunked in the water. I'm sure I'll get dunked a few times this evening, but I think I know how to swim, so I'm willing to chance it.

What I'd like to do is just tell my tale, and then throw it open for discussion, and I'll respond to questions. Towards the last hour or so, I have some general points that I want to make, and I'll sort of reemerge as a member of the seminar, a social scientist, and try to reflect on my own experience. That's the plan.

Michael Murphy: That was a rather alarming introduction.

Anthony: I'm trying to create some drama.

Arthur Hastings: Can we take before and after pictures, as in Rolfing?

Anthony: Sure. Take a mental snapshot and then I'll begin. I'll start with the time when I was a nineteen-year-old college sophomore in 1957, having gone to the University of Michigan from a small town in Michigan. I was well indoctrinated in the conventional middle-class framework of assumptions, from a midwestern, Protestant family, fairly ordinary from most psychological or sociological perspectives. I was more or less committed to something that I think of now as American civil religion, and my family was a good Republican one, as was every family I knew. At the university I suddenly was encountering a lot of surprising attacks on my frame of reference, religiously, politically, and philosophically. Eventually, some time during my sophomore year, I entered into a period of intense introspection. During this time I was examining the premises which seemed to structure my ego, psychologically, religiously, politically. Eventually I came to a phase where it seemed like everything was arbitrary. All the assumptions that I had made, which seemed so fundamental to my life, seemed extremely arbitrary: They were just matters of historical accident; I just happened to have been born in a particular place in a particular time. And it seemed even more that everything one could fasten onto as a set of beliefs to structure consciousness was itself arbitrary. Arbitrariness seemed the essence of existence.

I became a kind of existentialist, and in fact, I was reading a lot of existentialism at the time, and so I looked more and more closely at the assumptions that were structuring my consciousness, and eventually it started to seem as if even the use of language was extremely relative and arbitrary and that the meaning that was encoded in language was arbitrary, until finally it seemed that even the concept of personal identity, the notion of an "I" or an ego, was extremely arbitrary and built on sand. And then that came to a conclusion. My intense questioning seemed to be winding to an end. So I went through a month or two, or maybe three, where I was somewhat emotionally disoriented, but not so you could tell it by looking at me. My social adjustment was normal.

That summer, when I was working at a steel mill in Chicago, and walking down the street pondering these issues, I experienced a sudden transformation of everything. The arbitrariness of my existence disappeared and it seemed—it's hard to describe these experiences in language—but suddenly it seemed like I was part of an interconnected, harmonious, integrated world, which was transcendently valuable and meaningful, and in which my consciousness was just one aspect of the meaningful whole. It wasn't subtle; it was dramatic. One second I was in one world, and the next second I was in a transformed one. And, that sense of that harmoniously interconnected world that I was an aspect of stayed with me for a year or two.

When I thought about what the difference was, one difference was that up until that moment in Chicago I had never been *present* anyplace. I had always either been regretting the past or anticipating the future. I had never been in the present. And when I came into the present, everything seemed so rich with significance and meaning. Part of what going into the present in that way involved for me was repudiating the Protestant ethic, American civil religion, and a concern with personal success as the center of my existence. When I went into this other way of relating to the world, I lost interest in status concerns. When I went back to college, I dropped out of my college fraternity, and I was much more relaxed about getting good grades or being ambitious in a worldly sense.

Arthur Deikman: You said the experience lasted for about a year or so?

Anthony: About two years.

A. Deikman: At the same intensity?

Anthony: Yes. My ability to relate to other people empathically was incredibly improved; I was much more sensitively aware of other people's feelings and more tolerant, kind, altruistic, *et cetera*. It was quite a startling change; those who knew me were aware of it, and I was liked a lot more. All in all, it looked like a good change, from a variety of perspectives—from everybody's perspective except my father's. He was concerned that I wasn't so eager for success—he's a very success-oriented person. Anyway, after a couple of years, that state of awareness sort of faded away, much to my chagrin and surprise, because I thought it was a permanent state. I thought it was something that I had just fallen into and that it was mine; that somehow this was the truth, and the past was error, and once I saw my way through error, then why would I go back to error? But somehow, I lost the capacity to be in this state, and I switched my major and went into psychology, because I thought psychology might help me to know how to regain this state, and to keep it as a permanent state of awareness. That was my senior year, and I took all psychology courses and went off to graduate school in clinical psychology.

Well, obviously psychology let me down; it didn't help much. But, while I was there, in clinical psychology graduate school, I went into psychoanalytically oriented psychotherapy. I thought I might as well clean up whatever pathology was there, and thereby I might get to the transcendence. It didn't work out that way. I was in that therapy for about four years. It did clean up some stuff, but it didn't get me anywhere near any kind of transcendent experience. After two or three years, I got involved with human potential kinds of activities, encounter groups, and psychedelic drugs, and various kinds of meditation. I was very close at that time to a man named John Heider. The two of us were the radicals in Duke University's clinical psychology graduate program, and he and I did various experiments on consciousness. It was fun and seemed interesting, and it promised some kind of transcendence, but nothing happened. I didn't go back into that former state, although I would get hints of it when I would take LSD or take part in some of these other activities, but it really didn't accomplish much.

After I'd been there for four or five years, friends of mine started getting into various kinds of mysticism. I was a skeptic about supernatural matters. I didn't believe in reincarnation or masters; I didn't believe that there were people who could manipulate karma. It sounded crazy to me. I did have a good friend who spent a weekend at a place called the Meher Baba Center, and he seemed to be in a good space when he came back. It didn't sound particularly attractive to me, but he did *really* seem to be in a good space. So, one weekend I was working on my Ph.D. dissertation, got extremely bored, and I decided to get out of town for a weekend. The way this center was described made it seem like a good place to go for a kind of relief. It was 500 acres of virgin forest, with a fresh water lake, a few little cabins in the middle of the forest, and a mile of ocean beach, and not very many people went there. It was relatively deserted.

So, I called up to find out if I could go there for the weekend, and I could, and I went there, and I was the only person on the place. There were two elderly ladies who lived in a house on the edge of the 500 acres, who had lived in India with Meher Baba for a number of years, had come back and had started this center. In the middle of the 500 acres were all these little cabins, and they took me to a cabin, and left. Here I was in the middle of all these trees. It was great. I looked around, looked at different buildings, and decided it was a nice place. After a while I went into this one little cabin in which Meher Baba had held private interviews with his disciples when he was there; he had stayed at this center three times in the fifties, twice for two or three weeks at a time. When I went into that cabin, something started to happen. The next thing I knew, Meher Baba was present in the cabin. Now, I'll just describe this experience, talking in ordinary language, even though it seems bizarre to describe it in this way. It didn't seem bizarre to me at the time; it only seemed so afterwards.

Some presence came into the cabin, which I somehow knew was Meher Baba. I didn't see anything visually, but there was some striking presence there, which started to talk to me. And, there was a feeling of great attractiveness and peacefulness and a sort of loving quality, and the discussion was somewhat philosophical. It had to do with what it was that I was looking for, how to regain transcendence, and how it related to various social concerns. He was very persuasive and convincing. It went on for roughly twenty minutes, I'm not sure exactly.

But, no matter how persuasive the conversation seemed, it eventually occurred to me that these arguments he was using seemed to contain an implicit background assumption, which was that if you accepted them, you would also accept him as a master. That was so outlandish, compared to anything I could imagine myself doing, that I eventually thought, well, it doesn't matter how interesting these arguments are, I could never follow a master. It's crazy; I'm an existentialist.

So I said to him, "Well, this is all very well, but I could never follow an external master." I was just going to terminate the "interview" and walk out at that point, and leave the center. Then he responded to me, "I'm not outside of you; I'm inside of you." When he said that phrase, there was an uprush of consciousness from some very deep level of my being. It seemed much deeper than I had ever felt before, and at that level of consciousness, everything seemed unified. The distinction between inner reality and outer reality fell away and separative consciousness seemed illusory. At that level, he seemed, with his presence, to be the reality that made that unity the truth. That phrase, "I'm not outside of you, I'm inside of you," dissolved the distinction between myself and himself, myself and all other selves in general. The notion of an external master was no longer meaningful; he didn't seem to be separate from myself, so my objections to following him seemed ridiculous. I was swept away into a feeling of love and reverence.

So, this experience initiated another period of a kind of transformed consciousness, similar to the period which began in Chicago at age nineteen, but it seemed deeper and more real. I went back to Chapel Hill where I lived and where I was still in psychoanalytically oriented therapy. I discussed this experience with my therapist, who said it sounded crazy, and that it sounded like I was handling grandiosity. For two or three months we discussed whether it was crazy. She eventually said it was her conclusion that, whatever it was, I was in such good condition that it didn't make any sense for me to be in therapy. All of my problems and anxieties that she had regarded as neurotic weren't present anymore, and there wasn't anything to work on in the therapy. We discontinued the therapy.

I felt good, even wonderful, for some period of time. But it was only for about six months. Then various things happened which produced a challenge to this state of consciousness, and it didn't survive the challenge. It turned out to be partially dependent upon various social supports which were taken away, among which I dropped out of graduate school, and as a result my parents got up-tight again. About a year later, Meher Baba died. I still remained committed to Meher Baba as a master even after this state of consciousness left. There remained a residue of conviction that this state of consciousness existed, and that my best chance of attaining it as a permanent state involved somehow focusing my meditation on Meher Baba. During his last year I planned to see him, but he wasn't allowing people to come to India. I did write to him though, and he confirmed that the original experience had taken place, and said that he would continue to guide me as an internal master. I asked him various questions about what I should do with my life—should I be a psychologist, should I do this or that—and he said in letter reply that he wouldn't answer those questions directly in the letter, but rather he would continue to guide me as an internal master. He would answer that way.

I had felt guided since our original inner meeting, and this letter gave me even greater confidence in that sense of inner contact with him. He had refused to let people come to India to see him for about ten years before he died, and this was during that period. He was in seclusion, as it was called, with just a small number of intimate disciples; he didn't see other people at all. It was rumored that he was going to break the seclusion at any moment, and in fact he did schedule a time when people would come to meet him, called *darshan*, mass *darshan*, where his followers could come from the West.

I made plane reservations, and I was ready to go, as were various friends, when he died. This was in 1969. His disciples decided to hold the *darshan* anyway. Various cryptic things he had said made people think that he was going to make his presence available to people, even though he was no longer in the body. So, I went to India, not knowing what to expect, and not expecting anything very much.

But there was an increased sense of contact with him, and of his being present among us. It was light, and joyous, and satisfying. We were only supposed to stay for ten days, and after six or seven days, we went way out in the barren Indian countryside where Meher Baba's tomb was. There were these simple, humble buildings where he had lived most of the time. We were there just to visit, to see what it looked like. I didn't expect much from the tomb because I didn't think he was in the tomb in any real sense. People got in line, and filed into the tomb, and filed out. When it came my turn, I went into the tomb, and nothing special happened, and I came out. As I came out of the tomb and took a step or two, I suddenly fell to the ground in a very intense state of consciousness.

In this state of consciousness, there were three interconnected aspects that I was simultaneously aware of. One was a sort of divine wind that was blowing through my consciousness from the back, somehow, and it had a sense of omnipotence and benevolence, perfect benevolence, and of being capable of blowing any obstacles away—it seemed totally powerful and totally benevolent at the same time. At the front of my consciousness—these terms seem weird, but that's how it seemed—all of the physical world seemed to have become totally without substance, and to have only two dimensions. It had no real weight or substance. It was paper-thin, a mirage.

And this divine wind and the mirage of the material world were interconnected, totally, such that everything that happened in the external world was totally determined by the divine wind, even though *nothing* was really happening in the external world. It had that kind of paradoxical quality to it. Therefore, it was ridiculous to worry about anything that happened in the external world, because nothing was happening there anyway, and even the *appearance* of what was happening there was totally determined by omnipotent benevolence. This seemed true in an absolute way.

Then the third focus of my awareness was my ordinary consciousness, which is the one I'm in right now. It was thrown into such relief by the total lifting of any kind of worry, that it went into a totally spasmodic sobbing, with relief. I mean, I hadn't known I'd been worrying about anything, but it turned out that my whole normal consciousness was totally determined by worry, as it seemed, and that when it suddenly stopped worrying, it just became massive sobbing. This wasn't unhappiness at all; it was just the reverse.

So there I was, lying on the ground in the dust, outside this tomb, my body wracked with sobs. People were milling around me—and this is the oddest part: Nobody saw this happen. I was surrounded by a crowd of forty or fifty people, some of whom were walking on me and stepping on me. At one point, there was a lady standing on my hand, and I reached over and lifted her leg off, and she still didn't see me. It went on for quite some time. People were filing into the tomb, filing out of the tomb, stumbling over me as if I were a log or something, and nobody seemed to see me for ten or fifteen minutes.

One person, a close disciple of Meher Baba's, eventually did see me, came over, picked me up, and carried me over to a fountain and started washing my face with water. He started talking to me, and slowly, as I started attending to what he was saying, I came out of this state, whatever it was, and came back to some sort of normal state of consciousness, in which I was left with just the body, which had been wracked with sobs, which was very shaken, and I would not go back into that tomb, not for love nor money. I associated what had happened with going into the tomb, and I wasn't anxious to repeat such a cosmic earthquake in the foundations of my awareness, at least until I had a chance to evaluate it.

So I didn't go back into the tomb again on that visit. However, thereafter I was again in an exalted sort of transcendent state for several years, eventually lost it again, and went back to India again. When I went into the tomb again, to see if it would happen again, nothing much happened.

At that time, I'd rejected psychology, psychotherapy, and human potential interests. I thought they were not interesting to me because I was now a spiritual aspirant. I was pursuing exalted states of consciousness. I was celibate, and became ascetic and lived very simply. This continued for five years or so after the experience at the tomb. But the last two or three of those years, my consciousness began to seem rather thin and uninteresting, not exalted at all, and my inner contact with Meher Baba seemed not so very lively or real.

One weekend, on an impulse, I went to a Gestalt therapy weekend that a friend of mine was conducting. At that weekend, I was the first person to work in the "hot seat" (the person receiving the group's attention), and I popped open like a boil. Much personal, unfinished psychological business leapt into my consciousness. There were Oedipal dynamics in relation to my parents, suppressed sexuality, anger, all kinds of things that I had not dealt with throughout this period of asceticism. It now became apparent that I needed to reconnect with these feelings in order to be a real person, and not a cardboard spiritual aspirant. It seemed relatively easy to do, and shortly after that I started spending a lot of time with a woman, Louise Barrie, to whom I am now married. I got interested in psychological orientations again, and did various kinds of therapy, among which were some body-oriented therapies.

About two or three years ago, I had some further dramatic experiences in a body-oriented setting, in which I deepened my capacity to be in touch with Meher Baba on an inner level. Again, I went into a period of relative transcendence, which has now somewhat faded. Now I have gone into private practice doing a type of body-oriented therapy, a type that I think of as transpersonal. I'm managing to stay in some kind of "flirtatious" relationship with this feeling of transcendence, partially by virtue of practicing this particular kind of therapy, which helps me to keep my own body relatively open. Well, I've skipped over a lot of my spiritual autobiography very lightly, but I wanted to hit the high points, so as to give us some personal data to use as a basis for reflection.

The goal of this seminar, from my point of view, and what I'm really interested in, is to distinguish between four types of processes, or four models of human functioning, or four types of social organizations. One is conventional secular rationality, which I have talked about under the label of American civil religion. Another is a process of mystical transformation or transcendence to which esoteric religion is pointing. A third is false or inauthentic models of exoteric religiosity, or American civil religion, such as the People's Temple, or Synanon, or perhaps the Unification Church. The fourth state would be false or inauthentic models of mystical transformation or transcendence. I think we need to distinguish between these four different types of reality because an ideal of mystical consciousness may deviate from conventional consciousness in ways that may have some vague similarity to the ways that inauthentic civil religion, for instance, deviates from conventional reality.

Recently I was at a conference where anti-cult people were debating with other people who thought there was value in new religious movements, and one of the lawyers there told how he'd won a case concerning somebody who had been kidnapped and deprogrammed because the person had dropped out of medical school, and spent his time working as a janitor and meditating under the influence of involvement in a new religious movement. That served as evidence in a court of law that this young person had been brainwashed by a cult into a mentally unbalanced state. In effect the court allowed the deprogramming because the person had deviated from the norm of ordinary consciousness, and supposedly had become mentally off in some way.

But how can we distinguish between socially unconventional behavior that is determined by the inappropriate influence of an illegitimate civil religious cult on the one hand, and that associated with authentic mystical awakening on the other? I, for instance, dropped out of graduate school shortly after my first contact with Meher Baba and spent a year writing mystical poetry and supporting myself working as a clerk in a bookstore. How could the outside observer distinguish between me and the person who the court removed from a cult because he had dropped out of medical school? I don't approve of the court having done it in this case either, by the way. I think the constitutional protection of freedom of religion should be pretty nearly absolute.

I know of at least one case where a thirty-year-old woman, a follower of Meher Baba who was living and working on her own at a good job in New York City, was kidnapped by a well-known deprogrammer. He attempted to deprogram her because her small-town Christian fundamentalist parents were frantically anxious to have her return to their own more restricted way of seeing the world. The problem of distinguishing between genuine transformation and some sort of socially influenced, religiously rationalized regression to a more primitive stage of ego functioning is very complex.

Even a genuine mystical opening is usually mixed with uncompleted neurotic elements which may interact with the mystical insights and produce problems, such as ego inflation for instance. My own therapist probably detected something of the sort when she accused me of grandiosity after my original inner meeting with Meher Baba. With respect to my own experience, it seems to me it is not so simple to know what part of it is genuinely mystical and what part of it just reflects my own mental pathology. When I look at my experience, it appears that I had not become totally self-actualized, eliminating my neurotic patterns and reaching a point at which I was no longer neurotic, thus becoming somebody who was in the process of being transformed. It didn't happen in neat stages, nor has it happened yet. I'm still mundanely neurotic in various ways, but still think that I have had some contact with a form of experience which seems intrinsically valid to me and not determined by my neurosis. It occurred independently of any neurosis, and can't be explained totally by reference to it. That's my argument.

Connie Jones: When you said that in the five years after the tomb experience, your internal relationship with Meher Baba changed, became less intense, would you explain what that ongoing internal relationship was?

Anthony: At the time I originally had the experience in the cabin at the Meher Baba Center, there was an identification of Meher Baba's personality with a certain state of consciousness occurring in me. Since then I've come to identify meditation on the person of Meher Baba as continuing to evoke in me some version of that inner experience which I originally had. And I have a sense of a dialogue continuing to occur between me and this personality. Sometimes it's more vivid, sometimes less so. The way that I see myself as continuing on some kind of path, or involved in some process of transformation, is that I attempt to do things or conduct myself in such a way that this inner relationship continues to become more vivid. It feels to me that he's guiding me to go in a particular direction. I tend to think of my life as being guided by an inner awareness of this person, who is simultaneously a kind of state of consciousness for me.

But it waxes and it wanes. A year or two after I'd had that experience at the tomb, it started to wane, and then when I had the experience in the Gestalt therapy group, again it was very intense for about six months. When I started writing some very intellectual articles against deadlines, it started to wane again. For some reason, intense intellectual activity usually causes me to lose some of my contact with this state of consciousness. I might say here that it's relevant that my body had become more and more defective during that five-year period of asceticism. I developed muscular aches and pains and actually reached the point where I was almost crippled. I had extensive muscle tension in my back. My mother died of cancer during this period, and I was supposedly relating to it very spiritually. But when I went back into therapy, and particularly into the body-oriented therapy, I became conscious of this tremendous guilt, grief, and sadness about my mother's death. Then the muscular tension and pain went away. In one of the therapy sessions I reexperienced the experience at the tomb in an extremely vivid way, which ushered me into another year of relatively transcendent consciousness, during which I was very together and productive.

A. Deikman: Could you say more about the body therapy in which you are currently involved?

Anthony: Several years after I had that experience at the tomb, I went into therapy with Marion Rosen, a physical therapist who at that time was practicing in Oakland. She's in her mid-sixties and she's been doing an experiential bodywork since she was trained as a young woman in Germany by a student of Else Gindler.[2] She has modified Gindler's approach and now does a form of therapy which involves gentle hands-on manipulation of the client's muscles while the therapist talks to the client about the images, often repressed memories, that emerge. As she does that, the therapist tends to affirm states of awareness which seem transcendent. She also works with the breath.

I can't talk about it in too much detail, because it would take a long time. But anyway, it interested both me and my wife, Louise Barrie, who was already a bodywork practitioner, and we started training with her to learn how to do it. At that time, Marion offered no long-term formal training in her work, so Louise and I trained with her informally through workshops and personal contact. Louise, probably because of her previous experience in related forms of bodywork, learned the technique fairly rapidly, whereas for me it came more slowly. Then after I had that experience, reliving the experience at the tomb, it seemed that I could do it, suddenly. Both Louise and I began assisting Marion in teaching her workshops and I arranged for her to teach courses in bodywork at John F. Kennedy University where I was already teaching courses on other topics. Louise began co-teaching these courses with Marion, and I assisted them by supervising the students in their practicum work. Slowly it became apparent to me, however, that the work I was doing was somewhat different than the work Marion thinks of herself as doing. What I do seems to work because of my awareness of energy blockages and transformations, whereas Marion doesn't think of herself as working with energy. As a result I began studying and integrating various other structural or energetic approaches into my work—the Alexander Technique, Cranial Osteopathy, Eutonie, T'ai Chi Ch'uan—and began working independently of Marion. (Louise, on the other hand, has continued to work closely with her. She and Sara Webb, another of Marion's early students, now co-teach with Marion the formal certification training at the Rosen Institute in Berkeley.)

What I do is that I'm conscious of energy flowing in me in a way that I wasn't conscious of before, and when I put my hands on somebody, I can feel the energy in them flowing, and where it's blocked in muscles that are tense, and somehow by letting the energy in me flow into my hands, I can relax the character armor or blocked muscles, and the energy flows in them and then they tend to become conscious of it and to have an experience of reintegration. I also discuss with them images, memories, feelings that emerge during this process. It sounds vague, but it does work after a fashion, much of the time.

As you recall, when I originally encountered Meher Baba, I repudiated my former interests in psychotherapy and human potential techniques. The state of awareness I had glimpsed through his intervention seemed to be very far beyond any that I had experienced through such means. Therefore, I thought for a time that transpersonal or human potential approaches and following Meher Baba were probably incompatible with each other. Involvement with such techniques might sidetrack one from the process of genuine awakening by draining off energy that could be better employed in drawing closer to the master.

Subsequent events showed that, in my case at least, the situation was not so clear-cut. When I repressed my mundane emotional needs in favor of my spiritual interests, I found that my inner awareness of Meher Baba began to lack vivacity. In my case, overly ascetic suppression of mundane emotion began to block my capacity for spiritual intuition as well. Subsequently I have worked on integrating the two realms rather than suppressing one in favor of the other. If I had a toothache, Meher Baba would probably recommend that I go to a dentist to get it repaired. Similarly, I now believe, if I have physical aches and pains which are caused by emotional blockage, Meher Baba would have me go to a body therapist (or some other kind) for aid in the process of emotional reintegration.

It has become an issue not of avoiding therapy because of higher spiritual concerns, as I formerly thought, but rather of being involved in it in a way which is in conformity with those concerns. As always, I go in the direction which seems to maximize my sense of inner contact with the divine beloved. In my case that has brought me back into the world of therapy, first as a client, now as a practitioner, which I had formerly rejected.

It might be different for different people, of course. One shouldn't exclusively equate the higher spiritual concern with a particular means that is aiding in its pursuit in a concrete instance. That would involve the sin of idolatry, that is, the identification of a concrete symbol of transcendence with ineffable transcendence itself. The concrete occasions aiding transcendence are myriad, but only the Avatar himself is invariably both concrete and transcendent, finite and infinite.

In this connection it seems to me important to distinguish clearly between a transpersonal therapist and a transcendent master. I have come to believe that therapy that takes transcendence somehow into account can be more effective than secular psychotherapy even with respect to apparently mundane emotions. This is because all of the impulse-life is interconnected and at its deepest levels involves a striving for ultimacy. Emotion is more fully integrated, therefore, when this dimension is admitted into consciousness. From my point of view, the materialistic bias of secular psychotherapy involves systematic repression of this deeper level of symbolic apprehension.

This potential advantage of transpersonally oriented psychotherapy is negated, however, when the therapist who has not himself achieved transcendent realization allows his clients to identify his personality with ineffable transcendence. This usually occurs because of some unconscious ego-inflation on the therapist's part which, in turn, may be based upon episodic, spiritual experiences which themselves may be genuine enough. Such mistaken identification of the concrete personality of the therapist with transcendence itself greatly complicates the therapeutic process. One of the most valuable goals of therapy is to invite ego regression and the consequent projection of unresolved dependency needs onto the therapist so that they can be worked through and transmuted. If the therapist allows himself to be seduced by such idealization into "playing the guru," such working through of the transference cannot occur.

Unfortunately, in my view, this problem is common in transpersonal and human potential contexts. The notion that emotional development and mystical transcendence are interconnected—the "One Quest" idea—has been accompanied too often by the notion that the transpersonal therapist and the spiritual master have the same roles to play. But only the "unattached" personality of the transcendentally realized master can safely be equated with transcendence itself. Only in this case do the symbol and its object become one.

When an unrealized therapist "plays the guru," the problem of idolatry occurs and the client mistakenly equates "attached" aspects of the therapist with ultimacy itself. He has no means of ascertaining which aspects of the therapist are developed and which undeveloped, and he ends up valuing as ultimacy that which is at least partially deluded and finite. He also projects infantile delusions of grandeur onto the therapist, thus vicariously satisfying them with the therapist's covert encouragement, all the while believing that he is humbly abandoning ego-attachments thereby. He then develops ego-defenses around the relationship to the therapist, which becomes a symbiotic partnership in selfishness. That relationship which should aid in liberation from attachment to the concrete becomes itself the greatest focus of such attachment. That person who should fend off the client's attachment by rejecting it on behalf of ultimacy instead may seize onto such attachments either by not denying them or by claiming to be ultimacy personified. I have seen such nearly inextricable transference situations develop with some frequency and have seen much trauma and harm occur to even sophisticated individuals thereby—harm to guru-therapists as well as clients.

It seems to me that my relationship with Meher Baba helps me avoid this situation to some extent at least. The glimpses of transcendence which he has given me undoubtedly help me to recognize and support such openings in my clients. Yet my awareness of his perfection helps to remind me of my own imperfection and helps me to ward off the mistaken idealization of my own personality by clients. And Meher Baba's assertion that his present manifestation as Meher Baba is merely one of the Avatar's guises prevents me from placing imputations of exclusivity or uniqueness on my own relationship to him, and thus helps me to avoid subtler, pseudo-humble self-idealization as well.

At this point doing therapy is, for me, one of the best avenues of feeling close to Meher Baba, whom I believe is the Avatar and thus a perfect synthesis of a finite *symbol* of ultimacy with ultimacy itself. For this reason I am spending more and more time in my private practice and less and less time in purely academic pursuits.

Frances Vaughan: I'd like to know more about the original motivation for the period of asceticism you were involved in.

Anthony: Part of the motivation was a reaction against a former period of casual sexual experimentation. At least, my period of sexual celibacy resulted from such a reaction. After I started following Meher Baba, I was still somewhat relaxed about sexual matters, but I began to become more aware that sleeping with women casually was in neither my nor their best interests. It started to seem alienating, inappropriate, and inconsistent with a sensitive appreciation of the complexity of human experience. I didn't know anybody to whom I wanted to be married at that time. So I decided slowly, over a period of a couple of years, that it would be better not to have sex unless I met somebody I did want to be married to. Moreover, this decision conformed to Meher Baba's written statements on the issue of sex in which he recommends either monogamy or celibacy.

In looking back I can see that I was toying with the notion that I had somehow transcended sexuality and that celibacy rather than monogamy would be my path. Meher Baba had said that at a certain stage in spiritual evolution there comes a time when spontaneous renunciation of sexuality occurs and you're no longer interested in it. I thought that perhaps I'd reached that stage—erroneously, as it turned out. I was just repressing my sexuality.

The other parts of the asceticism were connected to a longstanding preference for a somewhat simple lifestyle, especially since that original experience when I was nineteen. I was making my living, during this whole period, writing grants to study new religious movements. It offered a way to live simply. I'd write a grant and receive funding for three years. I didn't have to teach any classes, and didn't have any obligatory duties other than to write a couple of papers a year, and supposedly do participant observation study of religious movements, which just amounted to wandering around and talking to people once in a while. That went on for seven or eight years. I led a rather quiet existence compared to the more socially frenetic one I had been used to during my graduate school years. I had a good income. I had plenty of spare time. About this time I began to paint very intensively. I found that painting helped to put me in touch with this state of consciousness that I was seeking, so I spent most of my time painting.

John Welwood: Were you involved in any Meher Baba groups?

Anthony: Yes. I always have been somewhat involved in Meher Baba groups. In Chapel Hill I helped to start a little group, and then in New York I went to a group when I moved up there, and recently I've been involved in the Meher Baba group in Berkeley. In fact, I'm currently the president of that group, and have been for a couple of years. These groups generally tend to be extremely egalitarian and democratically organized, and except for one group I know of, "Baba lovers" by and large don't see themselves as being spiritually advanced relative to other people, nor to each other, so there's no hierarchy. Leaders of such groups do not see themselves as having spiritual authority of any sort. Their roles are administrative only. I feel quite comfortable about that.

Jones: Are your experiences common to other members of the group?

Anthony: Not so very common. Many members have some experience of inner contact with Baba, but usually of a less dramatic type. The dramatic experiences do occasionally occur, however. Baba lovers characteristically don't talk about having had mystical experiences and in fact tend to deemphasize them, as Meher Baba did. He said that he occasionally gave people that type of experience, but that it wasn't to be regarded as indicating any type of spiritual advancement. In fact, the way he describes it is that he does it to people who are tough nuts and hard to reach in any other way. It's not something that is emphasized very much at all.

Welwood: Is there any practice involved?

Anthony: There is no formal practice that is recommended for everyone. The emphasis is on focusing on the personality of Meher Baba, who is regarded as an eruption into *maya* of pure God, somehow, such that meditation on the master is the one essential condition for spiritual progress to occur—a kind of informal, unsystematic meditation that involves your heart and mind both, and which ideally keeps going on at some level even while you're busy with practical matters. For most Meher Baba lovers this is accompanied by the practice of regarding their lives as being directly determined by Meher Baba's active intervention, without knowing what that intervention is, except possibly for an occasional glimpse of some kind. There is also the concept of shifting out of ego-oriented consciousness by relating to Meher Baba as a "provisional ego." This means that you regard everything that you do, either good or bad, as Meher Baba doing it through you. There are certain paradoxes or psychological dilemmas that result as one does that. Along with love for Meher Baba, working through these dilemmas so as to get closer to him internally seems to be what people have in common who call themselves Baba lovers.

Paul Riesman: You've been describing experiences which certainly do contradict the "secular" religions. Could you say to what extent this has been a comfort to you?

Anthony: I like that question because there is a part of me that's very attached to secular humanism and is extremely skeptical about the value of mystical experiences. For instance, after that first experience, which occurred when I was nineteen, had faded away, I became very skeptical about mysticism. After encountering Meher Baba a part of me was often saying, "This is craziness. What delusional system have you allowed yourself to be indoctrinated into?"

This tendency has faded with time and at this point is not a very prominent aspect of my awareness. My own experiences in relation to Meher Baba have been relatively private, and not socially created, so I've never thought of it as something that could be explained on the basis of brainwashing, or something like it, or even on the basis of various kinds of sociological conversion theories. After the first experience I never discussed these experiences much with people who called themselves Baba lovers. I didn't discuss the first experience at the Meher Baba Center with them for three or four years. So, if it's craziness, it's the kind of craziness that I think of as an intrapsychic eruption of some sort. And I've looked at it from every conceivable direction in the last twenty years or so. After about fourteen years of being a Baba lover, and having had that other experience eight years before that, there's about twenty-two years to talk about. What's clear to me is that the deeper I get into this kind of experience, and the more securely that I find myself established in it, the better off I am, even from a secular humanist perspective. For the last three or four years, from every direction I'm more healthy than I ever have been—I have a regular job, I'm married, I'm very productive, I'm socially responsible. I don't see anything to object to even from a secular humanist perspective.

A. Deikman: At one of our first meetings, you handed out an intro-ductory paper you had published about why people join new religions. And I commented that I was struck that in all of the factors you listed you didn't list "because there's something real out there, that has some sense in it, that these people are moving towards." I mean, you gave every kind of sociological reason. Hearing all this, now I'm wondering what kind of compartmentalization you've set up. Why would you write something like that in which the issue of a transcendent reality doesn't appear?

Anthony: A good question. For the last ten years or so, I've been laying the groundwork for talking about the notion of transcendence and the notion of the evolution of consciousness and of culture to a new stage, a stage that I would call intuitive. I want to do this in a way that will be interesting to people other than those people who have themselves already become committed to seeking some kind of transpersonal aware-ness. It interests me to attempt to talk to secular humanists about tran-scendence. I've published something like fifty articles as well as three books, that are now appearing, which all in some way establish a context for what I now want to say about contemporary possibilities for transcen-dence. I haven't said it yet, but now I'm starting to say it in what I'm writing right now. My future publications will say it very clearly, I hope.

A. Deikman: So you're establishing your credibility?

Anthony: It wasn't even primarily establishing credibility. It was think-ing through certain problems myself in a clear enough way so that I felt that I could talk about how those problems interrelated to the issue of transcendence. For instance, the introduction to my book that you read[3] talks about the decline of civil religion in its relation to an emerging interest in various types of new religious groups, including mystical groups. I believe that in my own case, various assumptions of the American civil religion were undermined in me by various intellectual and social currents, which are modernist currents, which have now become dominant in the culture. I believe that it's those currents which in fact have contributed to the interest in new religious movements, by undermining interest and commitment to that now obsolescent model of consciousness. I intend to talk about that in a lot more detail in future writings, but I don't at all regard what I've written thus far as false. Not at all. It's true.

Riesman: I think you've kind of slipped away a little bit from the question that I asked, that you were answering. You were saying how you approach certain things that the liberal humanists consider good. But, what about the underlying notion of reality? Would you say that you've really changed, or do you feel in two minds about this?

Anthony: You could say I feel in two minds. First, I think the notion of reality that underlies secular humanism is a limited one, although it has some validity, particularly relative to pathological states. But it's somewhat limited. An analogy occurs to me. Newtonian physics is an accurate model of physical reality as far as it goes. At a state of development where all that there was to physics was mechanics, Newtonian physics seemed to be an absolutely true model of reality. But as physics evolved and relativity theory and quantum mechanics emerged, Newtonian physics came to seem to be just a special case, a kind of accident. It looks true only if you don't know a whole lot about subatomic physics or relativity theory.

Similarly, the model of reality that secular humanism points to is both partially true and partially false in a way that's analogous to Newtonian mechanics. For instance, the ontological assumptions underlying contemporary secular humanism are historically relative. They result from a secularization of the Protestant ethic. Secular humanism has taken a model of human nature from the Protestant ethic which assumes that competition is inevitable, and is sort of the bottom line. The only reason that society isn't a war of all against all, to use Hobbes's terminology, is that people are socialized and learn certain restraints upon their competitive individuality. Supposedly they make a sort of grudging bargain with society so that society will give them some things they need. In return they will be less war-like and less competitive than they would by preference.

This being an uncomfortable bargain, the best that ordinary consciousness can hope for is a somewhat non-ecstatic, non-transcendent state. Freud's articulation of that particular model has been very influential, as have various sociological versions of it. Even people who think of themselves as having outgrown the supernaturalistic premises of the Protestant ethic and as having embraced a purely rational world-view from my point of view are embracing the Protestant ethic in another, more intellectually acceptable form. This more intellectual form of the Protestant ethic is also somewhat arbitrary and incomplete.

On the other hand, what becomes apparent from a transcendentally oriented frame of reference is that there's some benevolent process at work in the world. By coming into the present, one can start to live in an active relationship with it, such that one is not always trying to defer gratification because gratification is continuously available. From this perspective the model of deferring gratification as the basis of a healthy ego makes no sense, because the competition for a limited amount of gratification disappears. One can vicariously experience other people's gratification in such a way that one can be gratified with very little. Simple contact with other human beings is somehow ecstatically satisfying. The model of society which involves the competition of the many for a limited amount of material goods is seen as part of a socially conditioned illusion.

I mean, people get socialized into the illusion that the only way that they can have value is to have some status position, and have a certain amount of material goods as the evidence of that position. Then material goods seem to become essential. It looks as if there's not enough to go around, and then it becomes very rational to compete and to have to defer gratification in order to be more effectively competitive. It's all an interconnected set of illusions there, which drop away almost totally just by having a glimpse of another way of being in the world.

Etta Deikman: I'd like you to clarify something because my memory and my information doesn't seem to jibe with yours. If you would say psychology or Freud, or nineteenth-century rationalism, I would agree with you, but not Protestantism. The Protestant ethic isn't what you're describing as far as I'm concerned. I mean, what I've learned of the Protestant ethic isn't what you describe. It started out as being a direct relationship to God. That's why it was a protest. There was certainly a work ethic, but not one of "myself against the world and each person for himself," that we're basically evil, and things have to be delayed.

Anthony: The concept I refer to is the Protestant ethic as Max Weber describes it in *The Protestant Ethic and the Spirit of Capitalism.* He argues that the Protestant ethic, as articulated when the Puritans came to seventeenth-century America, was an unstable point of view. I have some other reasons besides Max Weber's reasons why I think it was an unstable point of view. I think it was the triumph of sectarianism over the medieval model of reality, and I think of it as a stage on the way towards secularization, and I have an argument about why that's so, but it would take some time to discuss it. At any rate, the Puritan ethic interacted with utilitarianism in such a way that it evolved into what could be called the spirit of capitalism, or the success ethic. That synthesis between Protestantism and capitalism is what most sociologists mean by the Protestant ethic.

Bruce Fireman: Is the idea of ecstasy or gratification from contact with people, in contrast to competition with them, a central teaching of Meher Baba?

Anthony: Yes. The notion that we are all one, that there's an underlying unity of human consciousness which one can live in relationship to, is central. It is a view of humankind as evolving towards that state of consciousness individually; also, that society is evolving towards that state of consciousness as a cultural ideal. It also assumes that there's an obsolescent model of human consciousness, which is at the present time dropping away, which is the model that I have just sketched here, which I have called the model of secular rationality. Also it anticipates that there will be a cultural ideal of this sort of transcendental unity, which will become the dominant model for a while, a few hundred years, and then it will decline.

Meher Baba has articulated a model of religious evolution in which the Avatar appears in different guises such as that of Buddha, Christ, Mohammed, or Krishna. A religion then forms around the image or symbol provided by this manifestation of transcendent reality, and the culture goes into a glorious period, where a sense of unity is experienced. Then there's a decline into a form of secular rationality in each of these civilizations, which is then eventually replaced by a new model of religious consciousness provided by an Avataric manifestation. Each Avataric appearance is accompanied by an unleashing of spiritual energy in the world such that these transcendental themes seem to have existential meaning for a period of a few hundred years. Then that spiritual energy kind of drains out of the world, and that results in the onset of a period of secular rationality. There are various degenerate religions along the way which signal the onset of such a period. I believe the Protestant ethic was such a degenerate, semi-secularized religion. As I said earlier, another central aspect of Meher Baba's teachings includes the notion of cosmic unity as an underlying metaphysical reality which is available to consciousness under certain conditions.

Welwood: In this system what's the role of a spiritual master?

Anthony: I think it's interesting to think about what distinguishes a shallow, narcissistic version of mysticism from one which supports a real maturation of consciousness and how a master contributes to that. I think one difference between groups which are narcissistic and those which are deeply mystical is the way that they distinguish between exalted consciousness and mundane consciousness. From my point of view, a spiritual master, that is, somebody who's really attained transcendent consciousness, is not like others. He or she can be judged by extremely demanding criteria of human development and survive the judgment. People in movements which center around a master who can survive that kind of judgment are forced to realize that their own consciousness is extremely fallible and mundane, even if they've had little glimpses of transcendent consciousness. This prevents sliding into narcissistic self-involvement, which is at best stagnant and doesn't involve any kind of true growth.

Nevitt Sanford: Earlier you practically urged someone to attempt a reductionistic explanation, and it probably could be done. I mean, I can make all sorts of comments about the first experience that you had in college. It was as if all of a sudden you convinced yourself that your father's authority had been overthrown, or something of that kind. But the question I have is, suppose this had never happened. You could not then have had the experience with Baba when you were in North Carolina if you hadn't had the first experience. And you couldn't have had that first experience except for what you were hinting at: this revolt against the family unit in which you were involved in a traditional way. But does that make the experience of transcendence that you achieved any less valuable or interesting?

Anthony: Well, that interpretation contradicts the felt sense of what the experience was in a way that seems to me to miss the point. I don't find it congenial to explain it by reducing it to such mundane factors. Nor do others who have had similar experiences. Such explanations seem plausible only from an external perspective, rather than from the perspective provided by the experience itself. The experience feels like a more comprehensive knowing, rather than something that can be explained in terms of some sort of lack of knowing. In other words, it feels very conscious. It feels like it includes the previous state of secular rationality as a special case, and much more as well. Explanations of it in terms of some defect of secular rationality seem confused.

Sanford: How about saying that some people have a talent for this kind of thing and others don't? I could never imagine myself having some of the experiences that you had.

Welwood: How do you regard it? Do you think of it as slightly aberrant, or. . . .

Sanford: Well, it certainly seems to be a very dramatic experience of a kind of conflict which I should think is rather common. This pattern of going from acceptance on faith of the family values, ways, and beliefs to relativism, to a very complete relativism, is kind of the norm in college, or it was in the '50s. For some, it's so much more dramatic.

Anthony: I don't think so. I know that's an explanation that might come to mind for somebody defending a secular rational viewpoint, yet experience is so tricky. It's very hard to develop criteria for evaluating it which are independent of the experience. There is a kind of notion that everything that isn't rational is mystical, that all direct experience involves the repudiation, falling away or letting go of a model of psychological reality based upon a combination of will power and rationality. Yet artists have commonly repudiated that model of human reality for two or three hundred years. Since the romantic poets, there's been a theme in literature and the other arts as well which pokes fun at a bourgeois rational model of reality, and holds out the notion that there is a transcendent state that can't be explained in secular rational terms. There has been a popularization of that point of view which expressed itself in the hippie movement in the '60s. It now has been partially absorbed by the culture as a whole, and has been expressed in many new religious movements. In one of my papers, I call it "psychedelic utopianism," and in another of my papers, I call it "one-level monism" or "uni-level monism." It's a cheap form of mysticism which may involve psychological regression rather than transcendence. Yet I don't think that what happened to me was regressive. I think it involved a degree of genuine transcendence. I also think that there's a real distinction between transcendence and regression.

Sanford: Is genuine transcendence similar to what happened to Saul on the road to Damascus?

Anthony: I would argue that something did happen to Saul, and that it wasn't simply a loss of his faculty of rationality—it was something real, it was real transcendence.

Sanford: Arthur suggested that one explanation of this is that you say it's true, you know, that that's the way things really are. But then I have the question of how alternative competing versions of transcendence get along with each other. Is there any competition among the gurus or masters? I mean, is there any argument at all as to whether my master can lick your master?

Fireman: Such as mine is the Avatar, and yours is less.

Anthony: One way to put it is to ask that if a thousand years from now all of world culture isn't centered around Meher Baba, or around his message as the central cultural influence, would I regard him as having been repudiated or proven to be a phony. Now, I have to say that the notion of Meher Baba as the Avatar, and this whole concern with cultural transformation and so on is a relatively small part of the experience for most Baba lovers. They tend not to be very interested at all in proselytizing. In fact, they do no active proselytizing whatsoever. The meetings are open; anybody can come, but people won't go out on the street and try to get you to come. And there's this notion that imperfect consciousness has no real rights, as far as affirming reality in any ultimate sense is concerned. In other words, Meher Baba says he's the Avatar, but my consciousness is very imperfect, so, what do I know? All I know is Meher Baba says he's the Avatar. I don't know he's the Avatar; if he is the Avatar, only he could know he was. What I know really is his impact upon my own consciousness. Based upon that, I have love and reverence for him and tend to accept what he says about his status as true. But I cannot really be said to know that it is true in the sense that he does. A person with unperfected consciousness cannot be said to know very much about it, really, in that objective sense.

Sanford: Isn't this outlook quite unique?

Anthony: No, there are other groups who think their leader is the Avatar, but since there is a provision that everything I know, I know imperfectly, and it always involves my interpretation of what Meher Baba has said anyway, it doesn't really bring me into confrontation with other people who think their master is the Avatar. It may bring them into a confrontation with me, and sometimes it does. But it doesn't start with me, and it doesn't produce tension in me.

Sanford: It could become a really serious question, I suppose, if Baba lovers believed he was the true master and all other masters were somehow false.

Anthony: It's not a serious question, but it's interesting why it isn't. You see, following Meher Baba does not involve belief in any serious way. There's a repudiation of the whole notion that reality is attained through having correct beliefs about reality. I mean, that's part of secular rationalism. This is a different framework. Here reality is approached through direct, felt contact with it in the person of Meher Baba and through certain experiences or glimpses of higher states of reality, and you only have that reality while you're having that glimpse anyway, and belief isn't part of that in any serious way.

A. Deikman: But the basic thing asserted to be true, as it translates into belief systems, is pretty common to almost all the systems: the notion of a channel or access to a knowledge that isn't mediated by logic or reason, and doesn't have to be; the issue of unity, of a different time and scale and frame of reference; of something that goes to the higher level of evolution—this is just the basic view that's processed out in the regular system. There is no particular conflict at that level of belief systems, either. If you get down to who's the bigger guru, that's something of a peripheral issue.

Sanford: Well, it's a really marvelous idea. I mean, you couldn't possibly say, "Those guys can't get to heaven," could you? You know, people who have a different system.

Welwood: I think one of the most horrific things to secular rationality is the idea of obedience or devotion to a spiritual master. The idea of obedience to a master contradicts the modern theme of the separative autonomy of the individual ego. Thus it flies in the face of secular rationality completely. I'm just wondering what is your experience of that, or your sense of devotion to a master.

Anthony: Most of my experience following Meher Baba has been since he died. However, when he was still in the body—while he was still alive—I asked him in my letter to tell me what to do and he refused. At least, he refused in the letter. He said he would guide me internally. And that was fairly typical of him. He didn't do a lot of externally telling people what to do. But, there was the notion that if he did, that you would be better off to do it. There's this conception that he reads your past lives and your present state of karma; he knows what would be uniquely desirable for you to do at any one point, so that if he was willing to suggest something for you, you would be a crazy fool not to do it. The people who lived with him on a day-to-day basis, the small number of people who were allowed to live with him, did obey him in that specific sense. Other followers who didn't live with him would have if they could have. So, for a certain lucky few, it came up as a daily issue. For most who followed him, it was more of a symbolic issue, such as: "I wish he would tell me what to do, because if he would, I would do it. I would accept it." And, I certainly go along with that. Of course he left discourses which express general spiritual principles, and his followers do their best to apply them in concrete situations, so this involves a kind of obedience, I suppose. Many experience some sort of inner guidance from him as I feel that I do, and this involves a sort of obedience as well.

Welwood: How do you feel about the general idea of devotion to a master?

Anthony: It's been a sticking point for me, because I've never liked doing what people told me to do. I've not gotten along well with authority figures, and it's been one of my social problems, to the extent that I've had any. But, once Meher Baba did that thing in the little cabin at Meher Spiritual Center, I felt differently. Now I try to figure out what he wants me to do. It's a constant theme in my life: What does he want me to do, what is it at every moment?

Welwood: How would you distinguish that from, say, Jim Jones's [People's Temple] followers saying the same thing. For instance, what about the man who passed the kidney stones and then found that Jim Jones knew it, and must be God, and therefore, what he told him to do must be right?

Anthony: I think that Jim Jones pretended to be some kind of Avatar, but he wasn't. It wasn't a good idea to do what he told you to, because he didn't know what was the right thing for you to do. There are more refined ways for evaluating various "masters" and distinguishing those who seem wise from those who aren't, but that's a sort of gut-level determination.

Welwood: Is it your feeling that if one has a true spiritual master, there should be no personal resistance to being devoted to that person?

Anthony: Yes, once the master has survived the initial test, which Meher Baba says that it's appropriate to make. You should initially go through a period of trying to discredit your master every way that you can figure out. Finding that you can't do it, that he survives the test, that he's a perfect master, if you think he is, then you should obey him as someone who has gone through all of his personal karma and transcended it such that he's now a perfect embodiment of love in the world. If you decide that that is true of him, at that point you would be crazy not to do anything he told you to do, because his consciousness is perfected; yours isn't. That's the whole reason to have a master. The notion is that an ordinary person's consciousness is clouded by selfishness, by incompletely worked-through karma, in a sense, by not seeing things truly. The reason to have a master is to have someone who does see things truly, and—it even goes beyond that—who *is* truly, who acts truly, who embodies truth. When everything that you see about him is truth, the notion of doing what he tells you is the least of it. Even the way he moves his hand, you know, you're learning something from that. And, the way he shakes his head, the way he laughs, the little things that he says—all of that is something that you attempt to drink in, to get the perfume of it somehow.

Murphy: Dick, have you ever worried that you might be misinterpreting his instructions to you? As in the Zen stories, where the master is scolding the disciple and says, "No, that's not what I meant."

Anthony: Yes, I worry about it. But it seems that his instructions to me are themselves a sort of *koan*, actually. He phrased them as seven things which were individually numbered, one through seven. They're short, pithy little things.

Deikman: He sent these to you in the letter?

Anthony: Yes. Among those things were that he was happy with my love for him; that he sent his love and blessings to me, and he wanted me not to worry; and "NOT" was written in big capital letters. He wrote that he was pleased with my desire to spread his message of love; that he wanted me to solve my problems on my own, and he would guide me internally; that he wanted me to remember him wholeheartedly as often as possible, and come to love him more and more; and that there were no end to questions and answers. That was the last statement. It answered the end of my letter in which I said, I accept all of this, but I don't understand it all yet, and I assume you'll fill me in in time, or something like that. All those things he said in response to me were pointed responses to my tendency to try constantly to undermine my own intuitive experience by questioning it rationally, wondering whether I'm interpreting it correctly, an obsessive-compulsive doubting pattern that is a prominent aspect of my personality. He undermines my capacity to worry that I'm not interpreting him correctly, because he told me not to worry, and he told me he would guide me internally. And if he is who he says he is, then he is guiding me internally, and not to worry about it. Around and around and around it goes, and where it stops nobody knows.

Arthur Hastings: In one sense, one might say that your allegiance to Meher Baba comes not through a devotion to him as a man, but rather because he is the focus of an experience of transcendence for you.

Anthony: There may be some truth in that.

Hastings: Does that suggest perhaps that your feeling that he's a true master may be a rationalization just so you can continue to get the experience via him? Where did the belief in him as a true master come from? Or is it simply inferred on the basis of the experience?

Anthony: It sounds a little strange to call it an inference that he's a true master, because the essence of the original experience was that he is the deepest level of my own consciousness. And since I define a true master as somebody who is the deepest level of one's own consciousness, the experience was self-validating. It was what it was. That was the experience, that he was the true master. But the notion of him as an external master or somebody different from myself is an illusion. Another way of putting it is that the deepest level of myself is a true master.

Frances Vaughan: Does your devotion to him, then, interfere with your acknowledgement of your own mastery?

Anthony: No. Not at all. I'm much more confident.

Vaughan: Does it facilitate the recognition of your own mastery? Or does it become dichotomized as being other than yourself?

Anthony: The dichotomy is that sometimes I'm at my best and sometimes I'm not. I put a gold star beside that which I think I realize when I'm at my best, and continue to affirm that perspective, even when I'm not in touch with that state of consciousness in as vivid a way. It gives a certain continuity and structure to my ego. I mean, I think one danger of a shallow mysticism is impulsivity, a tendency to act out, a lack of structure for time, and for the person in time. This approach helps me to avoid being that way.

Sanford: Does it trouble you at all, Dick, that from the point of view of secular rationality it looks as if this happened by chance? You see, that it just so happened, that you heard about this place when you were at Chapel Hill. You know, it was like luck. Or is it you were being guided by Baba already to go to that place, where you had this experience, that you were ready for it. I mean, it was a case of chance and the prepared mind.

Hastings: The first one was even more by chance. Walking on the streets, and suddenly having this breakthrough with no figure of Meher Baba or anyone. So, you didn't work for it, you didn't prepare; how do we know that it wasn't something you ate that morning?

Anthony: From the standpoint of secular rationality, the issue of contingency is an important issue. The quest for meaning within the rational framework is a quest to overcome contingency in a way, and to construct the just society and to acquire some kind of control over one's fate. It is having the interconnected controlled fate of the whole group follow some principle of justice. That is a question that would occur from that perspective. From within this other frame of reference, or this other state of consciousness, it doesn't seem terribly meaningful. Everything seems totally determined. Contingency doesn't exist. Everything seems totally determined by a benevolent and omnipotent force. The tendency to see things as contingent and requiring control to avoid arbitrariness and injustice seems like part of the state of consciousness that's transcended. This may sound callous and narcissistic. Yet the paradox is that the more nearly one's consciousness approximates the state I am describing, the more altruistic one seems to become, even by secular rationalist criteria.

Sanford: I don't understand that, but I assume everybody else does.

Murphy: Because so many people are concerned with the issue of contingency and fate-control, they've worked out these elaborate philosophies to decide how people at different stages of awareness should act in the world. Because they've had those moments of awareness of unity, the neo-Platonic philosophers worked on these hierarchies, which extended between the realm of complete unity on the one hand and the sensible realm on the other, and where you might be located. That was their solution—and there are many other solutions. But it is a big problem.

Anthony: Weber pointed out, for instance, that most religions seek to solve that problem. Such solutions are called "theodicies." A theodicy is a way of explaining God's ways to man so that the problem of evil is dispensed with. The classic one in Eastern religions is the karma and reincarnation theodicy, which does explain it rationally, and which I agree with. For instance, my encounter with Meher Baba in this life may have been prepared for by former lifetimes of seeking such contact. And this explanation is supplemented, of course, by the notion of God's grace which descends as it will and can't be completely accounted for by rational principles.

Hastings: In the transpersonal realm one would say that your first experience was a natural experience, one that didn't necessarily connect with Meher Baba or anybody. There's a dimension or domain in which people have those kinds of experiences. It probably related to your earlier introspection and concern, which prepared you for letting go of a lot of material that would otherwise load your system and keep you enmeshed in this reality. It's a loading factor. But then, after one experience, you are in a sense more available, or more accessible. So that any channel then is more open for you—you're more drawn to it or you're more open to it, whether it's Meher Baba or possibly some other form. And you don't have to work for those experiences, necessarily. That probably relates to the concept of God's grace, as you say, which is part of a very long tradition. You know, you just had it. The experience was a transcendent one, so it transcends rational explanation also. So, whether it is the grace of God or not, that may just be another way of explaining it in some system. The only thing you can say is, yes, it grows, just like trees and plants grow.

Vaughan: Not only does it grow, but there may be negative consequences from not allowing it to grow. In other words, if you attempt to shut it off and pathologize it, or deal with it in the way that you experienced in your original therapy, the possibility of its evolving further into a genuine transpersonal experience could be thwarted.

Anthony: Yes, I think that therapy was harmful to me from that point of view.

Sanford: Which therapy?

Anthony: The psychoanalytically oriented therapy.
      I want to come back to the use of the term "asceticism," because taking it in an extreme form, it might mean living in a cave or something. As Weber uses the term, and in Freud, too, there's the notion that the capacity to have control and to structure the ego in time involves the sublimation of sensuous appetites, in a partial form. It's important to submit yourself voluntarily to frustration because according to Weber, this is how the modern ego evolves. It didn't exist in the Middle Ages. And according to other scholars, people were much more impulsive in the Middle Ages and had to have their behavior controlled by social constraints much more. The Protestant ethic involved a self-imposed asceticism which developed an ego which was capable of structuring itself in time. It seems to me that there is some kind of asceticism, a moderate form of asceticism, which is supported in many of the mystical groups that I admire.

A. Deikman: Could the term "self-control" substitute for asceticism?

Anthony: Perhaps. Take my example of evolving out of a stage of casual sexual experimentation. It was an important transition, and one that was supported by everything that I could learn that Meher Baba said about sex and the role of sex in human consciousness. I took it further than was appropriate for me, given my state of development. I took it all the way to celibacy. But, Meher Baba has written discourses which say that chastity or the appropriate expression of committed sexuality is preferable from a mystical point of view to impulsive sexuality. We have several chapters in Meher Baba's discourses about why that is so, and it has to do with the development of consciousness. It's an argument for a form of asceticism as being essential to a mystical aspirant.

Riesman: You've asked people to reduce what's happening to you to some other explanation. It might be helpful to turn it around and say, could a lot of people like you make a society?

Anthony: That's a good test.

Riesman: Is there a conflict between the requirements imposed by the fact of living in society and the kind of self-realization which you were talking about? Most people are simply not going to be able to do this. Not because they may lack the inner capacities, but because in order to make society work, they must refrain from doing it.

Anthony: I don't agree with that at all. I don't even see where you get that idea. For instance, Meher Baba almost always completely discouraged his followers from withdrawing from normal social commitments. Only the few people who actually lived with him were allowed to withdraw from conventional social roles. Yet they and Meher Baba himself spent a great deal of their time in charitable activities with the poor, lepers, the mentally ill, and so on. Everybody else had to go out and get a job and earn a living and satisfy the requirements of citizenship in a normally satisfactory way, and they all do it. I don't see the problem from that point of view.

Riesman: But in those religious groups where the people do not depend upon one another economically, there is less likely to be corruption.

Anthony: Perhaps. But of course, most Baba lovers, although not dependent on one another economically, are involved with each other in other ways. Most of my friends are Baba lovers; I have relationships that are rather intimate with them. You might say that the sharing of a framework of spiritual assumptions helps to promote intimacy and understanding. I'm not a loner. Yet there is the distinction of having a consciousness that's not totally dependent on social confirmation. That does seem to be a desirable tendency in a religious group—a certain balance between social involvement and individual autonomy. I'm quite comfortable with most Meher Baba groups from that point of view. I don't think most Meher Baba lovers are either dependent on each other or independent of conventional social confirmation in a way that makes them poor citizens of society. I think that it would be a better society, not a worse one, if everybody were involved in a genuine mystical quest.

Notes

1. Reprinted, with minor modifications, from the *Journal of Transpersonal Psychology*, *14*(1), 1982.

2. Else Gindler, a pioneer in the field of mind-body education or bodywork, was active in Berlin during the first third of this century. She developed techniques which demonstrated that greater sensory awareness of inner kinesthetic and proprioceptive feedback predisposes the muscular system to adjust itself to more efficient functioning. She trained many pupils who have since spread her work throughout the world.

Among the better known of Gindler's students is Charlotte Selver, who emigrated to the United States in the 1930s and whose "Sensory Awareness" technique has deeply influenced the thought of Erich Fromm, Fritz Perls' Gestalt psychology, and Wilhelm Reich's attitude toward the breath. Authorities on Zen such as Alan Watts and Richard Baker, former *roshi* of the San Francisco Zen Center, have argued that the Gindler-Selver techniques for mind/body integration produce states of awareness similar to those produced by Zen meditation (cf. Thomas Hanna, *The Body of Life* [New York: Knopf, 1980], 157–162 for a fuller discussion of the work and influence of Gindler and Selver).

Marion Rosen and her associates (most prominently Sara Webb and Louise Barrie) have significantly extended Gindler's mind/body techniques by integrating them with the verbal processing of emotional and transpersonal material. Until recently Rosen worked in relative obscurity and there are to our knowledge no previously published discussions of her work. However, the Rosen Institute in Berkeley has for the last few years been offering formal certification training in the Rosen Method as well as public lectures, workshops, and demonstrations. These activities are resulting in greater public awareness of the merits of this approach, which will presumably in time include published accounts.

3. Thomas Robbins and Dick Anthony (eds.), *In Gods We Trust: Changing Patterns of American Religious Pluralism* (New Brunswick, NJ: Transaction, 1981).

EDITORIAL COMMENTARY

Dick Anthony's involvement with Meher Baba exemplifies the multilevel charismatic monism category of the Anthony typology. He accepted Meher Baba on the basis of a mystical experience of Meher Baba's conscious, transcendent immanence, and this occurred in relative isolation with no expectations from a group that it would or should take place. Indeed, Anthony had had no contact with any Meher Baba group at that point. This contrasts sharply with unilevel settings, where unusual experiences largely occur as a result of intense group indoctrination and pressuring—what anti-cult critics have called brainwashing—and are used to "prove" the group's meaning system.

Followers of Meher Baba perceive him as the visible personification of the ultimate spiritual reality that links superficially separate individuals. Meher Baba is everyone's secret self, whether or not they consciously accept him. Therefore, Meher Baba lovers feel a positive basis for relatedness with all members of the pluralistically diverse larger society, and this sense of relatedness is independent of that society's attitude toward Baba followers and their spiritual orientation. Meher Baba groups generally have little if any sense of formal membership criteria separating them from the surrounding social world. The absence of elitist separatism is a characteristic of multilevel groups.

Participation in a Meher Baba group is not in itself considered transformative or even necessary, but is simply one way of celebrating a personal relationship with Meher Baba and focusing attention on him. The heads of Meher Baba groups, like the close disciples who lived with him for decades, do not regard themselves as spiritually advanced or as having spiritual authority. The inner development that is sought here is greater love for Meher Baba as the Divine Beloved, and the reduction of egotism to allow a closer inner communion with him. But as Meher Baba stressed, this is a very private matter of the heart, so there is no real basis for a hierarchy of spiritual authority.

All of these conditions help minimize ego-inflation, safeguarding against the unilevel tendency to see spiritual advancement or transformation where it is not. Meher Baba's descriptions of the state of ultimate spiritual realization also reflect a multilevel view, emphasizing that the God-realized state infinitely transcends all other states of spiritual development, no matter how advanced. In affirming God's immanence and each person's eventual realization of God as the real self in everyone, Meher Baba excludes no one. However, the attainment of this awesome spiritual goal of God-consciousness is so far beyond one's conscious control, and the process so vast and complex over so many lifetimes, that it becomes useless to try to gauge one's own or anyone else's spiritual development univocally or consequentially. For spiritual orientation the aspirant instead must develop his or her own intuitive sense of intrinsic spiritual values, and above all must maximize inner, felt contact with Meher Baba as the guiding, indwelling divinity.

As in multilevel involvements in general, belief is not the basis of spiritual commitment here; commitment is based rather on what Meher Baba terms the intuition of the heart. He describes the optimal relationship between rationality and intuition in spiritual life:

"True faith is grounded in the deeper experiences of the spirit and purified intuition. It is not to be regarded as the antithesis of critical reason, but as its guide. . . . True faith, grounded on pure intuition, is an imperative which cannot be made subject to reason; for it transcends the limits of the mind and is fundamental and primary. . . . Beliefs and opinions exist in a superficial layer of the psyche; they do not have an integral relation with the deeper psychic forces. . . . Living faith has a vital relation with all the deeper forces and purposes of the psyche. . . . Such fruitful and living faith in the Master is always born of some deep experience which the Master imparts to the disciple."[1]

While Meher Baba downplays spiritual experiences as essentially meaningless in regard to one's degree of spiritual advancement—which again counteracts inflation in Meher Baba lovers—these experiences nevertheless are a foundation for spiritual conviction and faith. Even when momentary, they tend to entail for Meher Baba lovers a heightened awareness of his internal presence and intimate interaction with them, and so are highly valued while simultaneously appreciated as only small glimpses of a transcendent spiritual reality.

The term "glimpse experience," which we are introducing in this volume, is intended specifically to be a counter-inflationary term, emphasizing that the great majority of mystical or transpersonal experiences are only temporary glimpses beyond mundane ego-consciousness and do not involve true transformation to a more transcendent, encompassing state. True transformation is always permanent and requires far more than a peak or plateau (extended) experience and a change in values. Peak and plateau experiences involve immersion in an exalted state and can seem to mimic actual transformation; the exalted state is independent of social confirmation, and so subjectivity becomes highly valued as the domain in which such experiences exist. Anthony describes how he felt permanently transformed and enlightened for nearly two years after his initial plateau experience while walking along in Chicago, only to experience "chagrin and surprise" when it faded away. (See the Claudio Naranjo interview for a similar episode.)

Glimpse experience describes the transrational experiences most relevant to spiritual aspirants. While not constituting transformation, it can be pro-transformative and can foster spiritual development in many ways, provided there is an awareness that the glimpse is relative and not absolute, initiatory and not conclusive, temporary and not permanent. The editors consider nearly all mystical experiences, including peak and plateau experiences, to be no more than glimpse experiences; actual transformation to a transcendent state beyond identification with the physical body and psychological ego is very rare; and far rarer still is ultimate enlightenment or God-realization.[2]

Glimpse experiences in multilevel charismatic involvements such as Meher Baba tend to involve the master as both the trigger and the content of the experience. Anthony's inner encounter with Meher Baba in the retreat cabin is a striking example. In the multilevel charismatic view the personality of a God-realized master functions as a direct link with ultimate being, and so transrational glimpses of the master are actually glimpses of the ultimate being. Wholehearted relationship to such a master thus represents a way of opening oneself to a transformative influence of unlimited potency.

Meher Baba emphasizes the disciple's love for the master as the crucial bond of inner contact. This relational or charismatic path has received little recognition in Western transpersonal studies and differs significantly from technique-oriented approaches and apprenticeship types of involvement. One important difference is the degree of appropriate acceptance of the master's authority. In our view, technical and apprenticeship orientations should involve a limited, conditional acceptance of the master's authority and preserve the kind of autonomy that American culture strongly favors at present. In contrast, multilevel charismatic orientations regard the master's authority as worthy of unconditional acceptance; but as Anthony describes, this unconditional acceptance is of a fundamentally different order than submission to external, paternalistic authority.

Anthony's initial, transrational opening on the Chicago sidewalk led him to reject paternalistic, hierarchical authority and to affirm individual autonomy, subjectivism, and pluralism, a transition that mirrored the large-scale change in American cultural values in the 1960s, from a social framework of externalized, paternalistic authority to one of internalized, autonomous authority. Relinquishing autonomy to accept the all-embracing, external authority of a master seemed entirely contrary to his values—so much so that he was prepared literally to walk out of involvement with Meher Baba even in the midst of the extraordinary and profound experience of contact with him in the retreat cabin. But the apparent opposition of autonomy versus external authority dissolved when Meher Baba said, "I'm not outside of you, I'm inside of you," and Anthony experienced an "uprush of consciousness" that made "the notion of an external master . . . no longer meaningful; he didn't seem to be separate from myself, so my objections to following him seemed ridiculous."

Anthony's subsequent acceptance of Meher Baba's authority was not a reversion to paternalism, but rather a transrational resolution of the split between paternalistic and autonomous schemes of authority. That split is a dilemma in ordinary ego-consciousness, which tends toward one extreme or the other (paternalism in unilevel dualistic groups, autonomy in unilevel technical monistic groups). At the unitive level of awareness that Meher Baba apparently imparted to Anthony, the split between one's own autonomy and the master's authority does not and cannot exist, and the culturally determined mindset falls away. The key was the transrational glimpse of the master's immanence or indwelling presence. This glimpse gave Anthony an enduring conviction and intuitive faith that the external form and personality of Meher Baba is a direct and stable expression, on the material plane, of the real Self that he glimpsed internally.

Anthony's case illustrates the spiritual potency of multilevel charismatic involvements, but a spiritual seeker should always remember that charismatic orientations are also potentially more dangerous than technical involvements. One should accept a charismatic master's authority only when wholeheartedly convinced that he or she is *completely* plausible as a living embodiment of ultimate spiritual truth, love, being, and therefore is worthy of unconditional obedience and surrender. If after stringent testing of the master's character the prospective devotee cannot unreservedly regard the master as such an embodiment, he should not accept the master's authority at all. Test above all to see whether the master's character leaves no doubt that he or she is worthy of one's total, unguarded commitment. If not, go elsewhere. Charismatic spiritual discipleship is the deepest and most penetrating of all forms of human relationship. The greatest danger is to whitewash one's image of the master by ignoring or rationalizing distressing indications of something amiss.

To say that Meher Baba represents a multilevel involvement is not just to say that his teachings encourage multilevel spirituality, but also that his followers actually practice multilevel attitudes. However, multilevel spiritual practices of any kind includes an ongoing process of recognizing and revising the unilevel or pseudo-transformational attitudes that one brings (often unconsciously) to the involvement—a process of continual refinement of discrimination. Meher Baba lovers face two important unilevel "temptations": (1) The ideal of profound reliance on Meher Baba's inner guidance and outer orchestration can be used to rationalize passivity and the avoidance of appropriate struggles with oneself and life. (2) To please Meher Baba—in the sense that a lover naturally wants to please the beloved—a devotee may repress what he thinks are bad emotions and thoughts, despite Meher Baba's emphasis that neither repression not indulgence of egotism and worldly passions, such as anger and sexual desire, promote spiritual development. Celibacy, for example, was in Anthony's experience merely a form of repressed sexuality. Spiritually rationalized repression is a false substitute for the arduous process of facing and reconstituting oneself. According to Meher Baba, this process of self-exploration and conscious struggle with oneself is necessary in order to develop the love and the true detachment needed for genuine spiritual transformation.

Notes

1. Meher Baba, *God to Man and Man to God* (North Myrtle Beach, N.C.: Sheriar Press, 1975), 59–61.
2. Our contrast of glimpse versus transformation versus God-realization corresponds to the Vedantic contrast of *bhav* versus *sthan* versus *Satyan-ubhuti,* and the Sufi contrast of *hal* versus *muqam* versus *Marefat-e-haqiqat.*

Many Inner Lands

An Interview with Claudio Naranjo

Claudio Naranjo, M.D., combines backgrounds in psychiatry, psychoanalysis, Gestalt therapy, medicine, music, and a variety of spiritual disciplines. A Fulbright scholar and Guggenheim Fellow, he has conducted research on the psychology of values and in psychopharmacology, was on the staff of Esalen Institute in the 1960s, and is the founder of SAT Institute in Berkeley, California, which addresses a wide range of psychospiritual concerns. He has taught and lectured widely and is the author of *The One Quest, The Healing Journey, On the Psychology of Meditation,* and *Techniques of Gestalt Therapy.* In this interview Naranjo offers an intimate account of a psychospiritual journey that has brought him to "many inner lands" as both seeker and guide. Roughly half of the interview focuses on Naranjo's experience of discipleship with Tarthang Tulku, Rinpoche, the well-known Tibetan Buddhist master who "has been my guru more than anybody else."

Naranjo, who trained as a psychotherapist before his spiritual interests arose, also candidly tells of his own misuse of authority as a self-styled, charismatic guru-therapist. The eventual collapse of his guru persona revealed to him a narcissistic dimension of his spiritual aspiration and ushered in a purgative "dark night" of psychological death/rebirth. As a result of these experiences, Naranjo sees narcissism, grandiosity, and ego inflation as inevitable, natural accompaniments of genuine spiritual development, along with the tribulations of "dark nights" in which these pathologies are purified.

Naranjo, like Anthony, was one of the members of the Center for the Study of New Religious Movements seminar who was interviewed by the seminar, on April 9, 1983.

Dick Anthony: Claudio Naranjo is with us to talk about his experiences in relation to Tibetan Buddhism, and in particular his relationship to Tarthang Tulku.

Claudio Naranjo: For some reason I have the feeling this may be difficult. It should be the easiest thing in the world, because Tarthang Tulku, Rinpoche has been my guru more than anybody else. But I have been the very opposite of Carlos Castaneda as he depicts himself in his books[1]—I've rarely taken notes, even in my mind, and I think that's fairly typical of people who are around him. I remember hearing somebody who is in the circle of those people closest to him say, "I have no idea what's happening; I don't know at all what he's doing to us," implying that it was an expression of understanding, and not at all an undesirable attitude, to accept this lack of orientation with regard to the process, this lack of an ordinary frame of reference.

I met Tarthang Tulku very soon after his arrival in the United States from India. It must have been '68 or '69. He came with John Bleibtreu, who was involved in Esalen, and Dick Price;[2] they came to my house in Berkeley, California, thinking that I might be able to help in terms of connections or future publication projects. Joel Sheflin, who had served as a link for his coming to this country, came too. I don't remember much of that meeting; scarcely more than his complimenting my wife for the mushroom soup that she had prepared, and what he said when I took from the shelves the recently published translation of Gampopa, by Herbert Gunther: "I'm not a scholar, but I appreciate scholars."

Months later—perhaps a year—I saw him for the second time, now at Newman Hall in Berkeley. It was his first public appearance in Berkeley and his English was dreadful. What I remember most from this occasion was his comment in response to someone's question: "But I'm just learning." I had been always waiting to connect with a teacher of the Tibetan tradition. Here was an opportunity that came to *me*—Rinpoche's first visit to my little house—and I wondered if this visit were an omen that I would be involved with him. Later, I figured that in some sense he had come to "fetch" me—but also very typical was my lack of reaction. I came away from the Newman Hall meeting disappointed. His answer seemed to be that of a "mere seeker." Could he be a Lama? An "Enlightened One?" I thought, "He doesn't seem to know very much. No, this is not for me right now."

Instead, I went to Chile to work with Oscar Ichazo, who, friends there had written me, was a very remarkable Sufi master. In those days I was involved with Idries Shah, and I knew of the existence of something called "the rapidness," a legendary technique of the Sufi tradition that you can read about but are bound to find inaccessible. Yet here was someone who was offering this *Shattari* or "rapidness" technique. In my greed I decided that this was what I needed, so off I went.

This was a very important episode in my life. I made two successive visits to Chile. On the first one I met Ichazo, learned many things, had very remarkable experiences, and decided that I would come for more. Then came the "Arica experience," when a group of us went to Arica, the northernmost city of Chile. Ichazo sent me into the desert, to a retreat that was for me a definite, new beginning. It was a dramatic spiritual opening, which at the time I thought was definitive, but it lasted only about three years. Actually, even within the first year—which was when I again came into contact with Tarthang Tulku—it was beginning to fade away. I was by then a little past the peak of my expanded state, and beginning to worry that I was losing it. This made me receptive once more to having a spiritual teacher. At the time I was a charismatic group leader. I was feeling very confident that I had a "higher connection"; that is, I felt guided from within or from above. And it was not much more than curiosity that now prompted me when I saw a poster in the street announcing a seminar of Tarthang Tulku, Rinpoche, at the Nyingma Meditation Center.

I went to the seminar and found Rinpoche sitting, very relaxed, on a sofa, with a crewcut and a very lazy look directed at the sky beyond the trees, and seeming not to pay any attention to those in the room as we settled in for about forty-five minutes. It seemed never to end, just sitting there, and he, silent, looking at the sky. Then he started to talk. He talked about samsara[3] and about sound and visualization as ways out of samsara. I understood very little. I didn't know whether this was due to his broken English or his highly non-linear style. (Later, when I felt that I could understand his English, I still had trouble following the meaning.)

At some point in the workshop, which was attended by about nine people—a very small group—he took us into the *puja* room, a meditation hall with a very impressive altar. He took the high seat, as is traditional in Tibetan ritual, and took us through a chanting of the Padmasambhava mantra. Padmasambhava is the Tibetan Buddha *par excellence*. He brought Tantric Buddhism to Tibet in the eighth century and is revered by Tibetans as earlier Buddhism reveres the Buddha, for he is regarded as a later expression of enlightenment particularly guided to our "dark age." The Nyingmapa order is the oldest in Tibet, the line of descent of Padmasambhava. I had never heard of Padmasambhava. I don't remember what, if anything, Tarthang Tulku said about him. He just said, "There are many ways of doing mantra, but right now, just say it."

I was in a very ordinary state of consciousness when we started. I don't remember whether my eyes were open or closed. I just said the mantra, but I felt, while we were doing it, something that I had never experienced in my life. I had had all kinds of experiences before, I had travelled many inner lands, but this particular experience I'd never had before: I felt that he, Tarthang Tulku, was inside my body, working on my *chakras*[4] like a switch operator or a plumber. I felt activations through the different *chakras*; something definite was happening, and it was linked to his presence; it was not that I was visualizing him, but clearly felt that he, a person, was inside my body, adjusting something, performing a kind of tune-up. It was not something impressive, but strange, and very definite.

When we came out of the *puja* room there was a time of sharing. He responded to people's accounts in a way that was frequently humorous and a bit challenging—as I later came to know was his style. For instance, I remember that a well-known T'ai Chi teacher who was present spoke about how, during the chanting, he'd had an experience in which "I was not there; the chanting was doing itself." Tarthang Tulku kept asking him, "And, who knows that nobody was there?" When it came to my turn, I just said, "It was very strange, but I felt that you were in my body." He immediately replied, "You got Guru Rinpoche's blessing." Later, he remarked that in America some people had experiences in a very short time that it would usually take a Tibetan eight years or so to have.

There were several highlights for me in that first workshop at what was to become Nyingma Institute. Some of the things that stand out in my memory might seem irrelevant detail, and yet they strike me as significant and very characteristic of Rinpoche's teaching. To give an example: There was a grand piano in the meditation room. I came again a little later and the piano was gone. I never saw it again. I am a pianist and a musician at heart, and I later wondered whether there might have been an intention and not mere synchronicity in the "meaningful coincidence." I don't think I would have suspected any deliberateness if this had not been one among many such coincidences, so that in the face of each of these details I began to wonder: "Can it be that the Lama can read our minds—and signals to us through such signs?" Whenever I asked, however, in the course of the months following, he only indicated that "it happened so."

After the conversation period that followed our experience in the *puja* room, Tarthang Tulku guided us on a meditation involving the visualization of green light. This experience turned out to be, if not so strange as the one with the *mantram*, a more impressive one, and one related to experiences that were at the core of what I had undergone in my apprenticeship with my earlier teacher. For this meditation, he did something that seemed to me very un-Tibetan. He asked somebody to go through a collection of records and suggest some appropriate music. After a number of Oriental and Western classical pieces were named, he finally pointed out Grieg's Piano Concerto, the kind of music that I had always put down as sentimental. But after a few minutes of this meditation on green with the background of the Grieg concerto, I had tears running down my cheeks. I was in a state of gratefulness and abundance, which stayed with me during the following hours, while the sharing and conversation resumed.

The last day was devoted to personal interviews. "Personal interview" is a very light way of saying what it was. I sat opposite him. His presence didn't invite a conversational mode; it was one of those pregnant silences, and I felt something was happening in that silence that would be irreverent to break with words. I felt that a sharing of consciousness was happening, such as I had known from my experience with Ichazo; it was what had hooked me to him. Ichazo formally said one day, "Now we will do a transmission of consciousness," and zap! I was taken into a state of mind which I couldn't compare with anything, in spite of having had a variety of psychedelic experiences in the past. This was a different quality, but as dramatic. With Rinpoche it was very clear again. It was not dramatic in the same way—it had another quality—but it was, for me, another conviction that he was doing something to my mind— *in* my mind—he could do that. He was the first person I met after Ichazo who could.

So, I decided that he was somebody I would like to explore working with. I asked him, "Do you recommend I become your disciple?" He said, "You will liberate yourself," which I have understood in different ways in the course of time. I certainly have been a disciple; I have related to him as a guru, more in an inner than in an outer sense. But he has treated me differently than most of his students. He hasn't taken me through the typical Tibetan path, through the culture-bound path, let's say. In retrospect, I see that much of what I have learned from him corresponds to the Dzogchen teachings, which are usually given after a long preparation and which are very amorphous. The essence of these teachings is precisely to become unconditioned; they are described as a way of "self-liberation." But it was years before I heard or read about Dzogchen (or Ati yoga) or received explicit teachings of this kind from other lamas. With Tarthang Tulku it's always been very implicit; he never talks theory, never refers to this or that book or what this or that Tibetan master said or where his indications and formulations come from. My experience of Tarthang Tulku has been one of working under another Sufi master—a Sufi master teaching through the *form* of Tibetan Buddhism. By "Sufi," of course, I mean something transcending Moslem or any cultural vehicles, a continuous creation and re-creation out of a timeless understanding, according to what he perceives as appropriate to America today.

After that initial contact I attended many workshops with him, learning meditation techniques and visualizations, breathing practices, and so forth, and hearing him speak—one never knew what it would be about. I would occasionally see him individually. These individual contacts have been more and more infrequent, and lately I've been seeing him about once a year. This has been surprising to me. At first it was surprising that, while he had become the most important person in my life, I didn't ask to see him more. To want to see him, I needed to feel that I had "done my homework," or to have a clearcut question—an honest ground before I allowed myself to ask to see him. Later, I started getting the message that it was not for me to ask to see him anymore, but rather, to wait for his initiative to see me. The last two times he has called me—when I least expected it—were also at very appropriate moments, such as the day before I was leaving for a work tour in Europe for several months and had an important decision to make.

At the beginning these individual meetings had more of an initiatory tone, more ceremonial; like taking me into a dark room and whispering some instructions for spiritual practice—something that would "smell" Tibetan, so to speak, such as visualization. But more and more the content became what from the outside would seem an ordinary conversation. I say "would seem" because even though the earlier, initiatory style was not there, a transmission of consciousness continued to be present as a background to the conversation. On the earlier occasions special paraphernalia seemed to signal the non-ordinary nature of the event. He would have a special object in his hands, for instance. I especially remember a time when I hadn't seen him in several months and he called me, and something I never saw before or after was there: the reception room was completely surrounded by Tibetan manuscripts, wrapped in saffron, saffron packages piled all over, and for the first time I saw (very high on top of a bookcase) the picture of Dudjom, Rinpoche, the head of the

Nyingmapa order. All this gave me a feeling that this was a special occasion, yet the content of that meeting was that of an ordinary conversation. He kept asking me, "What's happening?" "What do you mean, in me or in the world?" "You, the world. . . . What do you see happening?" He kept pulling and pulling, about an hour of my answering to this, "What's happening?" That was all. No teaching, but a definite state of mind—it was as if the whole room were filled with something thick, watery, and heavy. The most typical aspect of the occasion was that context; not the words but the quality of his silent presence. The apparent content and the setting have been getting more and more ordinary, but always his interventions are very enigmatic, and usually he asks me those questions—seemingly very ordinary questions—that I need to address myself to, such as, "What's this theater business?" when I forgot how much I wanted to ask his opinion about my joining a performing company for a season, so as to get some experience in theater; or, "So you sold your house"—very concrete, but as useful as the best psychotherapy because somehow his question is precisely connected with something pending or something I need to look at better or be more honest about. Many times I thought I was giving straightforward answers and even felt proud of myself, and after leaving I would think, "What a bunch of lies I've said." My ready-made answers, after being directed at him, became apparent for what they were, without his ever confronting me or acting critical, but just playing naïve.

What this involvement has meant to me is very hard to describe: just plain growth or plain development. And, it's also hard to say just what has been his specific influence, among the many other influences in my life. To begin with, my involvement with him led me to an involvement with other Tibetan teachers. I became formally a disciple of Karmapa, for instance. I took vows with him, received many important initiations, travelled with him—all significant enough that Karmapa eventually told me, "You are of the Kargyu lineage." Tarthang Tulku's influence, in contrast, has been from the side, so to speak, and always supportive of my "doing my thing," never objecting to my involvement with other teachers of various traditions.

There was a time when I was about to drop out of teaching. I was encouraged to continue, first by Trungpa, while visiting him, then implicitly by Tarthang Tulku, who also made me feel that I could be useful, and that I didn't have to be completely enlightened for that. He cornered me into doing it by asking me to teach at Nyingma. That was a very important part of my experience, at a time when I was tempted to drop out of the role after being "guru" for a season and coming to realize the extent of narcissistic involvement that I had in it. I was embarrassed by what I had seen myself doing, and my temptation was to plead guilty and drop out. Rinpoche's request that I teach at Nyingma Institute obligated me. It was a gruelling period, being back in the teaching role but not being able to assume the style I had elaborated around a now dying persona. I had lived out fully a "great teacher" style, and this didn't hold water anymore, so I had to find a support different from my earlier self-image.

The single most important thing for me during the time of my apprenticeship to Tarthang Tulku has been a deepening progress and understanding of meditation. This meditation has meant an increasing understanding of emptiness and an ability to become empty or to accept emptiness—which was exactly what I needed after the "big bang." I had "found it" and was becoming desperate about losing it. The whole process was one of learning to be empty-handed again, and comfortable with not having it, with just being. It was definitely a death process—of course, a death of the ego, but with overtones of death in a literal sense, because the death of the motivations that had animated me throughout my life had something to do, I think, with the onset of a serious illness (that was now over). I had no more energy, and it was a time of pulling back to a very intense contemplative life, and yet a very dry contemplative life in comparison with my earlier period in Arica and the time that followed, which was rich in visionary experience, full of grace, and useful to others. Now I was longing for something I had lost. I felt very dry, but at the same time, compulsive about meditating, meditating all day long.

Now I can see in retrospect that it's been a great purification. I can see the shape of the pattern. I went through a period of great expansion followed by one of profound contraction; or I could say enthusiasm followed by depression, or grace and then feeling removed from any sense of the holy; feeling a great man and feeling a fool. About two years ago I started feeling that I was moving toward a synthesis for the first time, and longing to "get it" again—a desperate longing, because I felt it was a miracle that I had been up that holy mountain, and thought that the epiphany of that time, which I had invited through a tremendous effort, was something that I could never get again. Yet I never lost faith completely, but despaired and hoped in equal measure. And then that began to change, and I was increasingly reassured that I am on a path, on the way, in some sense "getting there," though what or where I'm getting, I can't spell out.

Years ago I was exchanging notes with a friend with whom I had a similar background, first in psychoanalysis and then with Oscar Ichazo, and looking back, we were saying things like, "Well, do I suffer less?" "No, really not, no. It's just a different attitude, but I don't suffer less than before." "And what about virtue? Do you feel more virtuous than you were?" "Oh no, definitely not." "No, I don't either." "And would you say that you function better in life?" "No, maybe a little worse. I'm more concerned with myself and the growth process, and somehow I got involved with something that takes energy. No, I wouldn't say I function better." "And what about the quality of your experiences? Do you have richer, more profound experiences?" "No, I would rather say the opposite. In the beginning, my experiences seemed to be much deeper." There was nothing we could name that we were doing better at, but we ended up saying, "But I think I've come a long way." We were in agreement that we were evolving, but we couldn't point at anything in particular. It was more a sense of evolving through the awareness of what we've left behind.

The most important thing in my life for the last five years or so was triggered by a practice that was given to me by Tarthang Tulku, a traditional Tibetan practice called *Tummo*, or inner heat yoga. Something very concrete happened when I was doing this: Something seemed to pop in my head, and my skull bones started making little noises. When I meditated, there was a tick, tick, tick, tick, which was audible to others for several years. Once at a retreat a companion said, "Won't you please take off your watch?" There was this constant pulsation and a feeling as if a fluid was passing through tiny vessels. People talk about "energies"— there was definitely a sense of *something* going through, and there seemed to be a sort of switch over the palate, at the base of the cranium. This ticking has since become my main occupation, so much so that I don't know whether to call it meditation any longer—it's so much focused on a physical process. When it first started it was associated with a numinous aura, or there were insights and all kinds of feelings with them.

This ticking has been going down from my head throughout the years, and now is coming to the base of my trunk and *finally* to my hands and feet, and for the last several years I have felt as if I don't have hands and feet, due to the keen awareness of a blockage there. I'm very hopeful. I have the impression that something will be completed, because where will the flow go after the hands and feet? I have the sense that I am getting ready for another quantum leap, a second crossing, and that this will be the coming to rest of an intense process that has been like the sacrifice of the mother who is giving her blood to the child in her womb. I feel like I've been going through a long incubation, I call it the "black hole," and I feel that I am coming out of it—with vestiges of it still—and I am totally hopeful, as if the river could smell the ocean into which it is going.

Arthur Deikman: When you say that you function no better, I find that hard to believe in any complete sense, if you've left behind a lot of the patterns and egocentric thinking that constitute narcissism.

Naranjo: I should qualify that, yes. Let me put it this way. I was once a healthy animal, not at the beginning of my seeking, but after the first stage of it, in which I was Gestalt therapized, psychedelicized, and made bodily aware. I came to a sense of feeling great, having graduated as a patient and as a psychotherapist. I felt finally healed. And then, on entering the spiritual path proper, there was a loss of that, a fall from psychological well-being. It was a breaking-through to another domain at the expense of a loss in the psychological domain. Finally, I had to go through what I regard as a purification: I came out of the "fall" into messianic grandiosity. As a consequence of working through that grandiosity, I feel very much like I'm coming to the point of departure—by which I don't mean the "healthy animal" state before the spiritual pilgrimage, but my state before psychotherapy. For instance, I feel very much in touch with the insecurity and shyness of when I was a teenager. One of the transactional analysis experts said that my "T-shirt motto" is, "What have I done wrong?" Whenever I give a talk, for instance, I tend to feel that somebody has become bored, and I think, "What could I have done wrong?" I notice that somebody wears such-and-such an expression and I think, "That must have been because I was being devious, or maybe I was not such-and-such." I even went through a phase of feeling a complete idiot in the presence of others, so intense was that feeling of "What am I doing wrong?" Also, I don't feel the "umph" of the healthy animal, though I'm coming to it.

Now, this insecurity is skin-deep. At the deep level, I feel peaceful, I feel in accord with myself. I have found a level of self-acceptance which I didn't have before—though I may have felt more self-assured. Yet, my reactions in the immediate situation are another matter. I think of how, after acupuncture treatments, when you vent a latent disease, you get eruptions or full of boils, or have an explosion of symptoms for a few days. I feel I am going through a healing period in which I am visited by old sicknesses.

A. Deikman: What about interpersonally?

Naranjo: Well, I think it's a two-sided thing. I know I'm more genuine; my motivations are more sound or more truly kind, less narcissistic; at least, I administer my self-interest in a better way. There's a fairer judge—I handle my passions better. But in some sense, that makes me less "successful" in some situations. For instance, about two years ago I taught at the University of California at Santa Cruz. It was a return to academia after a long absence. I definitely didn't want any more to play the bright professor who has read every detail of the latest papers published, and I didn't want to act the guru, as I felt the kids might have loved—and expected in coming to my class. I was teaching things that I know very well, such as systems of psychotherapy, psychoanalytic ideas, humanistic psychology, or encounter groups, after years of experiencing and distilling the essence of these things, and having arrived at a perspective. I felt like an older man, an older person talking to kids out of his experience. I had never felt the generation gap before. People got bored. It was the first time I had the experience of relative failure. Many didn't like my class. Now, I believe I had then the same abilities as in years before, but I was not interested in doing the things that are conducive to "success," so in some sense, whatever it is that I had "attained" made me less successful.

Bruce Fireman: You also said before that you don't feel any more virtuous, yet I also hear you saying that you feel more genuine and kinder in your motivations.

Naranjo: Well, it was years ago that that conversation took place. I think I'm a little more virtuous today—but my opinion about it may depend on the day when you ask me. The process is such that for every step you take, you seem to become a little bit more virtuous, and at the same time you become more aware of what a pig you are.

Fireman: I was trying to come at it from another angle. You've emphasized that you recognized each new stage in this evolution process by an awareness of what you were leaving behind, or by seeing through old patterns, plus feeling more at peace with what you see as your deeper self. When you're leaving behind some stage, what are the criteria by which you see through it, if you're not seeing through it as being less virtuous, or less successful, or less wise in some way? Is the real thing, then, sensing somehow that you're not really being yourself? Is that fundamentally what starts you toward each higher stage in your evolution? Are there other things you can say about what it is to be more deeply in touch with yourself?

Naranjo: I suppose it is a sign of coming to myself, in some measure, that I am beginning to truly understand things. I am spontaneously understanding things at another level, lately—not only spiritual teachings, but also history and other things—and I suppose that this is a sign that I am coming closer to myself. And at the emotional level I am feeling less need to be loved and therefore a little bit more available to giving a few drops of love; or at least, handling my need for love more ethically. It has to do with being clean of the subtle forms of exploitation that are, I think, part of the omnipresent human wish to be loved. I am much less dependent, in a very complete sense, because I live by myself. I've become virtually chaste, also. I rather prefer not to have sex, though I can enjoy it very much. I think that I would not enjoy it if I were not engaged in a meaningful relationship with a younger woman. I manage to live for many months without orgasms. I think something psychological is involved in being able to give sexual satisfaction without needing an orgasm or being greedy for intensity; something akin to the loss of spiritual greed. I am not looking for more "experiences."

Arthur Hastings: Claudio, something you've touched on relates to certain problems that occur in spiritual groups. People have psychological needs that lead them into certain roles. You're distinguishing between psychological needs or psychological work, and spiritual work. Can you say what you see is the difference there, if I'm correct in assuming that you make that distinction?

Naranjo: I think we are one piece. We have different levels, but these levels are in a complex interaction or interrelationship. However, I think it is possible to say that you can have spiritual experiences and at the same time undergo a psychological regression. This is the condition that Oscar [Ichazo] in his system called the state of "Saint Ego." I think it's very much a part of all the kinds of people that we want to study in this group, people who really have a breakthrough that involves experiences which are very hard to label anything other than spiritual, but they have not sufficiently transcended their ego, and their spiritual experiences are concomitant with an intensification of their narcissism. I think this is not exceptional, not an aberrant development. It would seem, on the contrary, that this is a common pattern, and I feel an identification with it and with people who experienced ecstatic states before losing them. I tend to believe that all ecstatic religion is contaminated by the ego; that even in the best mystic, the ecstatic experiences are the reflection of true spirituality upon the imperfect mirror of the ego; that it's the ego's excitement that causes the ecstasy, where the deeper experience, though numinous, is not ecstatic any longer. It is as if the spiritual breakthrough or the dawn of spirituality must always get interpreted by a personality that has not matured, as in the Christian metaphor: When a new man is born, the old man receives his death blow, but it takes a time between the blow and the death of the old man, so the two live side by side in us for some time. I think it's part of the natural process to be inflated, because if we are novices and have contact with something much beyond us, we will, necessarily, have a novice's interpretation of it. And yet there seem to be degrees to which people get stuck in the grandiosity; some live on it for the rest of their lives. Spiritual capital gives the ego credit. The ego then, more than ever, lives on the strength of the real being.

Anthony: I want to push you a little bit to talk about Tarthang Tulku's authority. With regard to authority, how does your relationship with Tarthang Tulku differ from the relationships that the people we've interviewed have had with Jim Jones, or with Chuck Dederich of Synanon, or with the man who was the leader of the San Francisco Psychosynthesis people?

Naranjo: It's very hard to say.

Anthony: How do you know that Tarthang Tulku is not taking you off on some weird ego trip of his own?

Naranjo: Well, I perceive him as a friend. Very early in our contact he said to me, in one of those apparently in-passing moments while coming out to the door with me, "You know I love you." It was both a question and a statement. It was very meaningful to hear. I have believed him, and I do believe him. He has acted as a friend. I was sick some years ago with a pulmonary abscess, and my doctor thought I should go into surgery. I had neither insurance nor money at that time, and he heard about this and offered to help me. So I trust his caring, and I couldn't prove it, but I just feel it's genuine.

On the other hand, I do relate to him as an authority. It's as if I give him authority, but he doesn't impose authority. Sometimes I have gone to him with a question, such as, "Should I go to Mexico for such-and-such experience?" "What do you feel like doing?" he says. "I really don't feel very much like going." "Well, do what you feel." Or, in another case, "Whatever you decide will be best."

And yet, from the very beginning I felt like I'm in the palm of his hand. He sees through me, his mind encompasses mine. I am in a position of spontaneously being willing to listen, in a true sense. If I come to a difference of opinion with somebody else, I will always pick my opinion as the best. It's a very rare phenomenon to think that the other person's opinion will be the better one. In that sense, I give him authority.

Paul Reisman: I gather that you are a guru yourself or have acted as a guru yourself. Could you say anything about what it's like to be on both sides of the fence, so to speak? Does having that experience make some difference to you?

Naranjo: There are different sides to being in the position of a guru. One is instructional, which is not the specific guru activity. Then, there's another domain, that of giving tasks. It's prescriptive, such as: "You two people move into the same house and deal with your conflicts." I was once at a point of having evoked in people enough of that willingness to hear or to follow that I used such authority. I used it well at the beginning, and then not so well. My authority was very invited at the beginning, and very lightly used. The first things that I did prescribe were very right-on. For instance, I remember saying to a certain person, "You should write the story of your life, and publish it." He eventually wrote an autobiography and it was a very fulfilling experience. Then, I started to abuse that authority and to demand of myself that I have something to prescribe for everybody; I overdid it, and started to force things. I asked for things that were harder and harder to do.

A. Deikman: Why?

Naranjo: I was feeling more insecure, more challenged, and I started to put down people who implicitly challenged me, and to invalidate them by pointing to their pathology, such as, "You need to work more on that." It may have been appropriate to some extent, and I think I did a lot of good, but there was a bad motive. The worse the motive got, the less that my prescriptions were good, until I put an end to the whole thing. I didn't feel I was doing such a clear job as at the beginning, and I didn't feel the internal authority to be in that position.

Anthony: You broke it off yourself? You weren't overthrown?

Naranjo: First, I delegated. I created for myself the job of "process designer," which meant that I decided what would happen in each particular session, but I didn't attend the meetings—a form of avoidance. I didn't feel comfortable there, so I had a team of assistants and somebody through whom I communicated instructions, and whom I supervised in turn. I had more and more groups. I was at any point involved with about five hundred people in different cities, and getting communications and homework from all of them, so I had teams to process it all, with me "at the end of the line." I was establishing a teaching bureaucracy like Scientology. I did do something creative through that; it was certainly another way of using myself, between involvement and disengagement.

Then I had my chief assistant, who had become my girlfriend, run the Berkeley groups, and I assisted her more and more sporadically. I progressively did less and less until finally I didn't want the responsibility of having my name connected with what other people were doing, people who by now had developed their own skills and were standing on their own. A factor in this was that people came for me, and instead of getting me they were getting work with other people who were supervised very indirectly by me; and so they hoped that they would be getting me at the end of the line. I now was seeing it as more and more remote that I wanted to be involved, so I pulled out.

Notes

1. Castaneda's well-known books chronicle his apprenticeship with the Yaqui shaman, Don Juan.
2. Co-founder of Esalen Institute.
3. *Samsara* is an important Buddhist term which, like the Hindu term *maya*, denotes the cosmic illusion, particularly the apparent but illusory existence of separate beings and things.
4. Many mystical traditions describe the existence in the human body of important energy centers associated with various mental, emotional, and physiological functions. These centers are termed *chakras* in the Hindu traditions.

EDITORIAL COMMENTARY

Claudio Naranjo's overlapping roles of disciple, guru, and therapist bring up a number of issues. His discipleship with Tarthang Tulku and Karmapa appears to be, in terms of Anthony's typology, a multilevel, monistic, technical orientation, authentically transformational. Yet his role of guru to some five hundred people, which drew heavily on his skills as a psychotherapist, illustrates how a psychologically sophisticated and highly trained person having genuine spiritual experiences can still be genuinely mistaken about his or her own spiritual stature.

Several features of Naranjo's account indicate the multilevel nature of his Tibetan Buddhist involvement. Clearly it is based on the direct experience of states and events in consciousness which simultaneously transcend and include ordinary rationality, and do not repudiate it. The overarching, nonrational frame of reference remains stable; it does not degenerate into prerational indulgences. While Tarthang Tulku's spiritual influence is not authoritarian, neither is it merely a narrowly defined, technical-instructional one. He intervenes directly in his disciple's consciousness in a profound and very intimate way. So, while the master-disciple relationship here could be viewed as one of apprenticeship, it is not the popular, trivialized form of apprenticeship in which the master is wholly externalized as a teacher-instructor-expert, from whom the disciple "learns" consciousness skills through rationally communicated procedures.

Another distinctively multilevel element of Naranjo's perspective is his sense of what constitutes spiritual "progress." He sees it in terms of what he has "left behind" and unlearned —the removing of layers of ignorance—not in terms of gain or dramatic experiences. He cites the increased capacity to give love as a key expression of spiritual growth; and also a parallel, paradoxical increase of awareness of "what a pig you are" (meaning himself or any individual seeker) in a way that engenders humility, not inferiority. And several times Naranjo makes the point that spiritual inner development cannot be gauged by conventional (mundane) standards of psychological health. In all these ways, Naranjo affirms that authentic spiritual development does not cater to the disciple's ego.

Naranjo sees the ego persisting during spiritual development, and we agree, based on our acquaintance with the literature of the mystical traditions. However, Naranjo apparently envisions an egoic component of consciousness even at the ultimate level of mystical realization: "I tend to believe . . . that even in the best mystic . . . it's the ego excitement that causes the ecstasy. . . ." Here we differ with him. Our understanding is that in ultimate enlightenment, no trace of a separate ego-self remains. Naranjo's assumption that *all* masters still have egos may explain why he seems to take apprenticeship for granted as the appropriate general form of master-disciple relationships: He has the good sense not to engage in profound surrender and obedience to another ego, which apprenticeship respectfully avoids.

Claudio Naranjo's premature evolution from transpersonal therapist to guru illustrates a general temptation transpersonal psychotherapists face. Competent therapy that takes the transpersonal or spiritual dimension of the person into account is, in our view, more effective than competent therapy that does not, even as judged by pragmatic, secular criteria. However, the heightened effectiveness of transpersonal therapy is almost always a result of achieving a more thorough personality *integration* (an improved relationship among ordinary psychological elements) not transformation to a transpersonal state of awareness. But the transpersonal therapist values transformative spiritual development, and through enthusiasm for that goal is tempted to regard his or her work as transformational—and one who brings about *that* sort of growth in others is a guru.

Zen Practice and Moral Meaning

Steven M. Tipton

Zen Buddhism was one of the first forms of Eastern mysticism to become popular in America, largely through the beat movement of the 1950s. Here Steven M. Tipton describes the authentic practice and ethic of Zen and shows how they resolve the conflict between mainstream and countercultural values that erupted across America during the 1960s.

Tipton is Associate Professor of Sociology and Ethics at Emory University and its Candler School of Theology. He is the author of *Getting Saved from the Sixties* (1982), co-editor of *Religion and America* (1983), and co-author of *Habits of the Heart* (1985), the highly acclaimed study of individualism and commitment in contemporary American life. His knowledge of Zen Buddhism is both personal (he has practiced *zazen*, or Zen meditation, since the late 1960s) and scholarly (*Getting Saved from the Sixties* includes a detailed ethnographic account of American Zen, the most comprehensive social and ethical study of American Zen to date).

Tipton notes that the danger of misconstruing Zen as "yet

another license for the individual to 'do his own thing' . . . is particularly real for those 'interested' in Zen but not engaged in its practice." He discusses at length the nature of authority in the Zen master-student relationship and examines the Zen master's exemplary role as a kind of moral mirror for students.

The past two decades have seen striking changes in the moral outlook of Americans. What we loosely label "liberalism," that synthesis of rational religion, humanist principle, and individualist common sense that has long held sway over our moral middle ground, has now begun to loosen, if not give way. The diminished size and vigor of the mainstream liberal religious denominations—and their political counterparts—suggests that this loosening has undermined our sense of social commitment, particularly among those young adults who came of age during the cultural conflict of the 1960s.

No new, encompassing vision of a good life in a good society has coalesced yet to renew our major religious and political institutions. Instead we find ourselves surrounded by unmistakable signs of a widening moral pluralism. Polarized on issues such as abortion, this pluralism stretches from the resurgent religious right to the withered political left, running through single-issue political ideologies no less than the middle-class privatism taught by therapies of self-fulfillment. Against this backdrop of cultural change without closure, a sense of shared social commitment cannot be renewed apart from efforts to ground the meaning of our own lives more deeply in practical experience. Within the course of such efforts, alternative religious movements take on their enduring importance for us. They are experiments in meaning, in moral and social coherence, that can be lived out as well as thought out. They are part of a quest for character that can be practiced day by day.

Powerful ritual experiences such as tongue-speaking, healing, and prayer have accompanied the recent resurgence of conservative Christian morals, for example—in ways not unlike the impact of psychotherapeutic and human potential experience on the attitudes of much of the urban middle class.

The growing interest in meditation plays a part in this effort to make moral sense of ourselves, a part still small in numbers but already significant in its cultural influence. To weigh this influence, let us look at one form of meditation in America—that transmitted by Zen Buddhism. It is the upper middle-class youth of the 1960s who now compose the core of its following here. We find no narcissistic escape here from the larger society, but the experiential groundwork of a renewed moral order in the making. However, to reach such conclusions about any religion, we must first discern the patterns of meaning that link its specific rites, beliefs, and organization to the general process of cultural change.

STYLES OF MORAL MEANING IN AMERICAN CULTURE

The conflict of values between mainstream and counterculture during the 1960s framed problems that ideological movements of the 1970s and 1980s have sought to resolve by mediating the conflict's two sides and transforming their divergent moral meanings.[1] Contrasting styles of ethical evaluation have shaped this conflict and its mediation. These styles mark the various moral traditions that underpin our culture: biblical religion, classical humanism, and two forms of modern individualism, one utilitarian and bourgeois, the other Romantic and bohemian.

Let us take Athens and Jerusalem first, as moral traditions passed on to us from Socrates and Moses through such all-American hands as Thomas Jefferson and John Winthrop. The revealed tradition of biblical religion (Jerusalem) embodies an "authoritative" style of ethical evaluation. It poses the moral question, "What should I do?" by asking, "What does God command?" An act is right because divinely revealed authority commands it. A person is good because he or she obeys this authority.

Classical humanism (Athens) shares with the rationalist tradition of biblical religion a rule-governed, or "regular," style of evaluation. It poses the question, "What should I do?" by asking, "What is the relevant rule or principle?" An act is right not only because of its consequences, but because it conforms both to principles of conduct defined by dialectical reason and to the regularity of nature conceived as a cosmos and entailing a *telos*, an ultimate purpose, to human existence. To do the right act, therefore, is a matter of rationality defined by canons of consistency and generalization that stretch back to Socrates; and by a substantive, natural-law-like ideal of justice that recalls the Greeks' *dikaiosune*. Thus the cardinal virtue of the regular ethic is Aristotle's "practical reason," as distinct from the purely technical reason that utilizes strategic means to achieve subjective ends.

From Athens and Jerusalem we move to the early modern city, for example, Adam Smith's Glasgow or Ben Franklin's Philadelphia. Here we find utilitarian individualism, which uses a "consequential" style of ethical evaluation. It begins with each person asking first, "What do I want?" and then, "Which act will yield the most of what I want?" Wants are taken as given, in a way that points to states like happiness, pleasure, or self-preservation as the basic good. Good consequences are those that most satisfy wants. Right acts are those that produce the most good consequences, as reckoned by a cost-benefit calculus. A person is good because he or she is efficient in satisfying wants.

The Romantic tradition scorns Athens, Jerusalem, and the industrializing city for the grassy countryside of the poets Wadsworth and Whitman. It views the individual not as an agent efficiently pursuing self-interest but as an experiencing and expressing personality. Neither a logic of following rules nor of maximizing consequences guides this ethic, but rather the idea that everyone ought to act in any given situation so as to fully express inner feelings and the empathic experience of the situation. This situational and "expressive" style of evaluation poses the question, "What should I do?" by asking, "What's happening?" An act is right because "It feels right." It expresses one's self and responds to the situation most appropriately. A person is good because he or she is sensitive, in touch with himself or herself and with the moment.

Echoing its Romantic predecessors, the 1960s counterculture rejected money, power, and technical knowledge as ends good in themselves. Instead it identified these mainstays of the utilitarian culture's "good life" as means that do not, after all, enable one to experience what is intrinsically good—love, self-awareness, intimacy with others and nature. Utilitarian culture grew away from biblical and classical morality in a modernizing America, but it could not generate autonomous moral rules by itself. This created a moral vacuum in which the counterculture emerged. But because it relied on unregulated feelings, the counterculture could not stably institutionalize its values. Further, utilitarian culture fits the structural conditions of modern society: technological production, bureaucratic organization, and empirical science. This institutional fit blocked the counterculture's growth and doomed its revolutionary impulse to failure. But in the process, utilitarian culture was stripped of moral authority, especially in the eyes of the young, many of whom have since sought out alternative religious and therapeutic movements. In the most coherent of these movements they have found a way both to cope with the instrumental demands of adulthood in conventional society and to sustain the counterculture's expressive values by recombining them with moralities of authority, rules, and utility. Changes in the ethical outlook of 1960s youth today practicing Zen Buddhism exemplify one aspect of this larger transformation.

ZEN BUDDHISM AS ORTHOPRAXY

The Zen Buddhist tradition plays down doctrinal understanding in favor of actually experiencing meditation, encountering a master, and liv-

 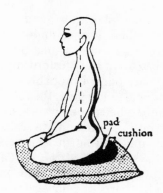

ing monastically. Through these avenues it claims a "special transmission outside the scriptures" of Buddhist orthodoxy. To do Zen-style meditation, called zazen, the students are instructed to sit upright and cross-legged, with their buttocks on a low, firm cushion and both their knees on the floor. This tilts the pelvis forward and straightens the back, which sets the spine in a gentle curve and allows the muscles above the waist to relax. It lowers the chest cage and pushes the lower abdomen forward, where the body's gravity becomes centered. These conditions give the posture great stability and, more importantly, they encourage diaphragmatic or abdominal breathing. Students place their hands together in their laps, palms upward and thumbs lightly touching (see illustration).[2] The head is held erect along the line of the spine, leaving the face tilted downward slightly and the chin in. The eyes are half-opened and unfocused about a yard forward on a bare wall or floor. The mouth is closed, the tongue lightly touching the palate just behind the front teeth. Beginning students are told to count silently "one" as they inhale naturally through their noses, and "two" as they exhale slowly and fully. They count up to ten and then begin over again. Students are told not to follow out or push away any thought that might come to mind or a sensation they might feel, but to let them come and go without moving or losing count of the breathing. Eventually students may simply "follow" their breathing without counting, work on a koan (a contextually meaningful question without an answer reasonable in itself),[3] or "just sit."[4] Thus students meditate without meditating on any conceptually defined object.

Buddhism traditionally obliges its adherents to follow moral rules that to Western eyes resemble natural laws or the Ten Commandments. A set of general "precepts" forbids killing, stealing, lying, sexual misconduct, anger, and intoxication. They also forbid "abusing the Three Treasures" of "Buddha, Dharma, and Sangha"—the personal embodiment, lawful teaching, and practicing community of Buddhism's truth. Numerous "Rules of Order" and *ad hoc* regulations govern monastic life. Despite their formal importance to the Buddhist tradition, however, these precepts and regulations are hardly mentioned in Western literature on Zen or by Western students of it. "I don't think much about that stuff," says one. "I probably couldn't even tell you what all the precepts are offhand."[5] In effect, the rules offer an *ex post facto* description of compassionate behavior flowing spontaneously from the "nonattached" yet all-accepting state of mind realized by the ideal meditator. Consequently, moral rules and norms can be seen as formal manifestations of meditation. Says a priest, "It's just as accurate not to talk about the form of the precepts, and just say, 'The precepts are *zazen*.' It's not necessary to name the parts of a flower for it to bloom. It just blooms."

Zen's ethic apparently follows the self-expressive and situationally responsive style favored along much of America's new moral frontier. It posits unfailing intuition and spontaneous performance of whatever act fits a given situation at a given moment, here and now. It invites us to practice *zazen*, and then to act however we will—on the premise that the ideally sensitized and all-accepting consciousness bred by meditation will lead us to harmonize with the situation and respond appropriately to it. This seems to reverse the usual notion of rule-based morality which argues that a good state of consciousness or a praiseworthy character results from the commission of right acts and omission of wrong ones, as defined by the rules. But the practices by which the Zen student develops the ideal state of consciousness are already, in their own way, "right" acts defined by rules, standards of excellence, and intrinsic values, which in Zen make up an orthopraxy—"right practice"—more clearly than they do an orthodoxy—"right doctrine." Thus a regular and reliable moral order guides an intuitive and self-expressive ethic of immediate experience. It does so through the precisely exemplified practice of Zen meditation, focused in the relationship between Zen master and student, and framed by the daily regimen of monastic life. In Zen you express "your original nature" as revealed through these institutional forms instead of simply "doing your own thing" as given by individual impulse.

HOW *ZAZEN* ALTERS SELFHOOD

How does the experience of *zazen* generate the "non-attached" state of mind and the compassionate character that generate right action in Zen's ethic? "*Zazen* is not so logical," responds a student. "It's more *physio*-logical. It's like there's a big heart beating everywhere through Zen. Practice is something you work on for a long time, fifteen or twenty years, say, because there has to be an organic, physical penetration of the teaching." As this suggests, zazen seems to be a psychosomatic (de)conditioning process that alters the student's thoughts, feelings, and behavior by influencing the causal links between his physical and mental states and the external situation in which he finds himself. How does zazen do this?

Immobility is the most obvious characteristic of zazen posture. Put simply, stillness of body stills the mind.[6] Zazen posture is unmoving, upright, with eyes unfocused and limbs pulled in. This posture and the abdominal breathing it induces serve to diminish stimuli reaching the brain and the cortical activity processing them. In particular, this posture and breathing result in a loss of the body's conceptual image, position, and location, without causing the subject to fall asleep or to go numb.[7] These neurophysiological effects correspond closely to the philosophical teachings of Zen Buddhism, especially its interpretation of the individual ego not as an enduring entity but as a succession of physical and mental events that momentarily appear and pass away. "Because each existence is in constant change, there is no abiding self," a master states. "In fact, the self-nature of each existence is nothing but change itself, the self-nature of all existence."[8] Zazen alters the meditator's body-sense accordingly. The discrete self at once dissolves into "no-self" and joins with everything else. "Instead of your skin being the barrier between yourself and the world," attests a priest, "it becomes the connective tissue that joins them." In zazen, then, posture changes breathing, which changes state of mind. So a master can say, "To take this posture itself is the purpose of our practice. When you have this posture, you have the right state of mind."[9]

Like immobile posture, quiet breathing quiets the mind. In breathing during zazen, only the muscles of the abdomen and the diaphragm are active. Other muscles, notably those of the chest, are either relaxed or in a state of constant, moderate tension. Continually retensing the abdominal respiratory muscles in opposition to the diaphragm, without moving any other parts of the body, inhibits thinking yet sustains wakefulness.[10] As when staring fixedly while holding one's breath for a minute, the subject can continue to sense things without having ideas or associations about these sensations. Immediate sensations occur, but emotion and thought fall off. This "falling off of body and mind" discussed in Zen teaching seems to correspond to behaviorally induced changes in neurological activity,[11] and makes itself felt first with the easing of circumstantial stimuli, then of reflective self-consciousness, and finally of space, time and causation, the categories of consciousness itself. A student testifies:

Before I started sitting I had some idea of who I was, and I took that seriously. Drugs gave me more ideas, only now they weren't reasonable ones, whereas Zen has freed me from my ideas more than anything else. Zen practice is a mystery to me. I don't *know* anything about it or about myself from doing it. We're here and we're not. We are and we aren't. The mind, which is the normal tool we know things with, is really a sixth sense. Impressions come in and go out. All we can do actually is let them come and go.

In sitting you can *feel* your breathing. It feels like any other phenomenon you experience. The quality of the experience is the same. My breathing is as close as I can get to the "core of my being," right? So what is it that's experiencing the breathing? I don't know. Some kind of nothing. And this breathing *is*. It's breathing me. I don't have to wonder about it anymore. The doubt of "What's this? What's that? Who am I?": that doubt explodes. It's all one absolutely continuous fabric of existence. You can't separate out anything.

The functionally rational self of utilitarian culture is reenchanted by psychedelic drugs and set shimmering. The irrational self that problematically ensues is resolved radically into Zen's "no-self." This resolution takes place through the experience that one's own breathing establishes neither the identity of a subject nor that of any object distinct from a subject.[12]

This sort of condition, traditionally called *samadhi*, is retrospectively reported as a kind of "emptiness" or "pure awareness" or "big mind" that transforms conscious activity in its wake.[13] Observes a master:

When we sit we are nothing, we do not even realize what we are; we just sit. But when we stand up, we are there! That is the first step in creation. When you are there, everything else is there; everything is created all at once. When we emerge from nothing, when everything emerges from nothing, we see it all as fresh new creation. This is nonattachment.[14]

Experiencing "nothing" in *zazen* introduces the experience of everything being created fresh and new, undulled by association or distraction. Interrupting ordinary perception in this way "dehabituates" it and thus renews it.[15]

RITUAL PRACTICE AND MORAL VIRTUE

What does such experience in *zazen* imply for moral behavior? Relatively undistracted by background stimuli and uncompelled by thoughts and preconceptions, desires and fantasies, the ideal Zen student can be fully "there" in the situation at hand, and so can see it truly and respond to it appropriately. Zazen demands continuous, active attention of a peculiar sort in order to count and follow one's breath, and "just sit." Because it is non-evaluative, such attention may seem to have little moral relevance. But repeatedly performing such activities, detached from the immediate payoffs of both utilitarian and psychic self-maintenance, requires attention not based on thinking, feeling, or judging in relation to the self. Because it is, in such a radical sense, not self-interested, such attention appears to provide an ethic that is both expressive and trustworthy.

Unlike the Romantic or hip counterculture, Zen holds that one's capacity for unselfish attention can be realized only through disciplined practice. In zazen it offers the forms to develop this capacity, forms which can be mastered and yield results only with persistent effort of will by the subject. Indeed, their results include convoluting and changing the will through this effort. How does this occur? As we have seen, while focused on breath-counting, working on a koan, or just sitting, the meditator is not to follow out or suppress other objects of attention. When thoughts, feelings, and images enter the mind, the meditator is instructed to "let them come and go. Hold on to nothing." But this turns out to be difficult to do, and in a baffling way. "You start out trying to do zazen like you do other things," remarks a student. "But then you find out you can't. You can't make it happen. You can't make yourself do it. The harder you try, the more frustrated you get. You have to be it to do it, but how do you do that? How do you give up trying to do it, and keep on doing it?" The conscious mind cannot by itself diminish its own activity of perception and cognition and actually seems instead to resist this. But it can choose to persist in a posture and a mode of breathing that gradually cause such diminution.

Physically, even ideal zazen posture exerts ongoing pressure on the muscles and joints of the legs, which eventually brings pain even to experienced students. Discouraged from moving or abandoning the posture, the beginning student tends to squirm, to quicken or force breathing by using the chest muscles, and to tense these muscles against the leg pain. But the student discovers that these responses intensify the pain, and through practice learns to maintain posture, continue breathing abdominally, and relax the muscles "through" the pain. By thus "relaxing into" the pain and "becoming one with it," the student feels it lessen. The student thereby demonstrates to himself or herself the practical truth of Zen's monistic teaching. As long as the student "holds onto" and struggles against the leg pain as if it were a separable object, the pain intensifies to the point of numbness. Once the student accepts and monistically merges with it, leg pain comes and goes with a bearable, wave-like constancy. While "just sitting" and doing nothing else, the pain seems to disappear utterly.

This physical dynamic operates along with a mental one. Denied physical movement, social interaction, or any directed mental activity save breath-counting, the student becomes acutely aware of his or her own undirected mental activity in *zazen*. A captive audience of one, he or she can freely observe but not manipulate otherwise unconscious, repressed, or rationalized associations, thoughts, desires, and fears as they come up and go through the mind. If a student begins to follow them out or fight them off, he or she is distracted from the correct posture, breathing, and muscle relaxation, thereby inviting the leg pains to intensify. This occurs even when the associations seem pleasurable. The student discovers that mental events in themselves, unaccompanied by their external causes or conditions, trigger physical discomfort marked by quickened breathing, increased muscle tension, and leg pains. A master draws the monist moral of this discovery:

> Many sensations come, many thoughts or images arise, but they are just waves of your own mind. Nothing comes from outside your mind. . . . You yourself make the waves in your mind. If you leave your mind as it is, it will become calm. This mind is called big mind.[16]

The student learns to "leave the mind as it is" by continually returning attention from its "waves" of thought and feeling to breathing, *koan*, or just sitting. By repeating this effort the ideal student gradually becomes more able: (1) to focus conscious attention without reference to any particular object, notably himself or herself; (2) to see and accept otherwise unconscious associations passing through the mind without being distracted from the present situation or biasing responses to it; (3) to maintain a relaxed, wakeful physiological state relatively uninfluenced by the passage of unsettling external stimuli or internal associations. The student comes to experience and exercise these three abilities as one and the same.

Insofar as these abilities generate motives, knowledge, and choice that are not self-interested, they produce moral awareness and right action. The counterculture usually claimed that knowledge of what is right is a sufficient condition of doing what is right. This recalls Plato's position, although for the counterculture, moral knowledge is by nature intuitive and affective, not rational. Some Zen students hold this view, but others attribute right action at least in part to what we usually call strength of will, a category developed in Aristotle's moral philosophy.

Zen practice itself appears quite Aristotelian if it is considered as a form of moral education: Regularized repeated enactment of right acts, even when performed without the appropriate emotions, breeds a virtuous character that subsequently feels such emotions and naturally does the right act. Practicing zazen with a regularly prescribed posture, breathing, and mental focus ideally leads to intuitive moral knowledge, feelings, and choice free of "self-clinging" and ambivalence toward others.[17] In effect zazen breeds virtue.[18]

Strength or weakness of will is not a category in the discourse of American Zen students, but "willingness" is. Zazen involves massive doses of frustration and convolutes individual volition. It calls at once for the individual to surrender willfulness and exercise willingness in persistently "doing nothing" in the face of discomfort and doubt. The transformation of moral viewpoint that Zen practice involves is not exclusively gnostic. It also includes a transformation of the will and thus a change of heart.

Zen's conception of the moral agent stresses willingness and the strength to be vulnerable. This sense of self seems continuous with the counterculture and its receptive, all-accepting, even passive quality— being rather than doing. But Zen holds these characteristics as a ground or medium of action, not simply a state of being. It does not stress being instead of doing, but being as a continuous doing. The focal question of koan practice, for example, is not, "What's the answer to the koan?" but "How do I express the answer to my teacher?"

The continuously attentive self practicing Zen differs sharply from the bohemian or psychedelic self immersed in its own visions and separated by them from the world around it. Psychedelic ecstasies, soaring to heights outside of ordinary experience, distort perception and impair judgment. Zen meditation comes down to a sort of ground-level experience, or "enstacy," which includes ordinary experience and focuses its nature. Zazen reportedly strips perception of its associations, ideas, and interests, clarifying instead of distorting it. Concludes a student, "Like roshi says, 'The world is its own magic.' Your life feels totally different than before, but it's totally ordinary. It's the way it's actually always been."

MASTER, STUDENT, AND AUTHORITY

The student takes on Zen's moral viewpoint not only by meditating but also by engaging a master. What is the nature of this relationship, and how does it combine with meditation to yield a sense of social order and moral authority? A long-time student writes in tribute to her master:

> A *roshi* is a person who has actualized that perfect freedom which is the potentiality for all human beings. He exists freely in the fullness of his whole being. The flow of his consciousness is not the fixed repetitive patterns of our usual self-centered consciousness, but rather arises spontaneously and naturally from the actual circumstances of the present. The results of this in terms of the quality of his life are extraordinary— buoyancy, vigor, straightforwardness, simplicity, humility, serenity, joyousness, uncanny perspicacity, and unfathomable compassion. His whole being testifies to what it means to live in the reality of the present. Without anything said or done, just the impact of meeting a personality so developed can be enough to change another's whole way of life. But in the end it is not the extraordinariness of the teacher which perplexes, intrigues, and deepens the student, it is the teacher's utter ordinariness. Because he is just himself, he is a mirror for his students. When we are with him we feel our own strengths and shortcomings without any sense of praise or criticism from him. In his presence we see our original face, and the extraordinariness we see is only our own true nature. When we learn to let our nature free, the boundaries between master and student disappear in a deep flow of being and joy in the unfolding of Buddha mind.[19]

In this description something very like the cardinal virtue of the expressive ethic—a flow of consciousness that "arises spontaneously and naturally from the actual circumstances of the present"—catalyzes all the other characteristics that make up the master's exemplary personality. Simply by being who and how he is, the master transforms what is possible in the student's life. To do so, he need do nothing in particular, let alone hold any ritual or bureaucratic office. His extraordinary yet utterly ordinary identity as a human being, realized and enacted in some absolute sense, mirrors the "original face" of the student's own identity.

A master stresses the relational rather than exemplary character of the master's identity:

> A teacher is a spiritual friend who's entirely willing to be there for you and put up with you the way you are. He doesn't have to be a good person, although if he is, all the better. In one sense a *roshi* is someone whose teacher has acknowledged him as having received the teacher's understanding. Because of that ability to understand someone else thoroughly the *roshi* is a fully realized person. But anybody can be your teacher. You make him your teacher by choosing him. The point is that he understands you thoroughly and you come to understand him, not

that he be perfect. The emphasis is not so much on the teacher being a perfect person as being a perfect mirror. This makes the Zen master different from the guru.

This encounter, significantly enough, opens up an evaluative insight for students in to their own "strengths and shortcomings" without transmitting "any sense of praise or criticism" from the master. The moral character of the agent is illuminated without being colored by any subjective approval or disapproval. Here emerges the inner experience that at once frames Zen's formal ethic of natural laws and makes it vanish into "the empty mirror" of awareness shining in the unbound consciousness of the non-attached meditator. As the ideal student's meditation practice deepens, he or she enters more deeply into the master's state of mind, until it becomes identical with an absolute and universal consciousness ("Buddha mind") that fuses with his or her own. "What the teacher really offers the student," writes a master, "is literally the living proof that all this talk and seemingly impossible goals can be realized in this lifetime."[20] Adds a student, "If you ask someone why they practice, maybe the simplest answer is, 'Well, I want to be like *roshi*.'" The master embodies Zen's ideal person and the promise of its practice.

As the picture above suggests, Zen students do not perceive their master primarily in ethical terms comparable to those describing the prescriptive moral authority of the biblical tradition. But the master's gnostic status as a fully realized human being able to see and reflect life as it truly is makes him an ideal observer of moral phenomena and thus a perfect moral judge. A student makes this point:

Does your relationship to *roshi* have a moral side to it?

Yes, but that's not the main part of it. I know, though, he's gonna be right on moral questions, because he doesn't have any particular bias. Just about everybody I've known looks at things in terms of what's gonna be the best for them. *Roshi*'s different. He's an enlightener, you know. He's there to open your eyes, wise you up. That's not like telling you the right thing to do, but the right thing comes out of it.

In this view, from true moral intuition, however nonprescriptive, comes right action. Impartially at one with the situation, the master unerringly acts in appropriate response to it. His relationship with the student helps him or her to do likewise.

Students usually object to interpreting this relationship in terms of ideas of "authority" and its acceptance. Counters one, "To me the word 'authority' means that power and inequality is being expressed. *Roshi* isn't an authority figure. He acts authoritatively. He goes out and does it, that's all." Another adds:

> Most of our generation have a problem with authority, being against it. *Roshi*'s a perfect teacher, because with him there's nothing to push against. He keeps returning your projection of authority back to you, until you see it's just yourself.
>
> When I first really met him it was in *dokusan* [a formal interview preceded by the student's ritual bowing]. I didn't know how to bow, so I just stood there. So he gets up and does a full prostration, with his forehead down on the floor in front of me, to show me how to bow. It was so moving. That kind of sincerity expressing itself cuts through all the lies in your life.

In the drama of this relationship, the student has the experience of transcending the dualistic, submit-or-rebel problem of authority. Instead, through paradox and reversal, he or she comes to respect and identify with the master: "He is you, but you are not him." This relationship is actually just two persons engaging each other with a "Hi, how are you?" explains a master, but it uses monastic rules "to give us some distance beween teacher and student. So because of the distance, student may have some freedom in his activity and teacher will find out how to help him."[21] Monastic rules, such as those defining bowing, free the student to experience his or her own needs and to recognize the master's response to them as so fitting as to be exemplary.

The charismatic authority enacted by the master in his *zazen*, teaching, and interaction with students is accompanied by ritual and bureaucratic forms of authority, renewing their value for practitioners who repudiated them as 1960s youth. Each master is the "*dharma* heir" of his master, a status based on the realization of his own enlightenment and teaching power but formally recognized by rites of "*dharma* transmission." Successive generations of *dharma* heirs form a "lineage" traced back for centuries in historical fact and for eons in Buddhist liturgy to Gautama Buddha himself. A Zen master is also the abbot and chief priest of the community in which his students live, joining his personal authority to the institutional demands and resources of a monastic organization. The master's personal authority is typically seen to generate and legitimate the institution's authority. "This whole institution grew up around *roshi*," says a student. "It's an offshoot of the quality he's continually manifesting in his life." Adds a priest, "Zen is not a church. It's a person-church. It's an institution that should have one person's stamp." As such it can call for the surrender of individual discretion to social authority— a familiar object of countercultural complaint—as no conventional bureaucracy can.

Practitioners who were youths of the 1960s have accepted bureaucracy in Zen communities not only because it has benefited them
(enabling them to live more cheaply, stably and securely under conditions tailored to meditation practice, while devoting less time to outside
work), but also because its forms have been re-merged with those of charismatic and traditional authority, and so have been made more humane.
A priest points out some personal and communal characteristics of one
such community:

> We haven't let ourselves get any bigger than where all the students
> know one another and each one knows the teacher. That's the upper
> limit, the number that can know the master. In fact, that's one way they
> know each other, through all knowing one person and being known by
> one person. The community itself becomes an expression of the mas-
> ter's life. He becomes accessible through it.
> We come to trust each other in the form of committees for the same
> reason we accept the *roshi*: we trust that they both really care for us
> and our practice, even when it runs counter to the organization's wel-
> fare. Again and again you'll see someone get taken off a job that needs
> to be done so he can sit [*zazen*] or so he can do something else that he
> needs to do.

A scale that still permits face-to-face relations, a permeable leadership
that makes decisions by consensus, and a policy that gives religious goals
priority over organizational ones: such characteristics help humanize a
relatively large and bureaucratic institution, headed by a central authority, enabling it to function in ways that resemble the expressive dynamic
of a smaller group.

The ritual omnipresence of rules in a monastic Zen community
embodies Zen's natural law-like assumption that human beings continually face obligatory moral choices. "There's always something you
should be doing," observes a student, "even when you're trying to ignore
it or get out of it. When the bell rings in the morning, just say Yes! and
get up. Don't even think about it. Wanting to do it or not wanting to
doesn't make any difference. Practice means just doing what you have to
do." Neither authority nor individual want-satisfactions in their usual
form justify Zen's practical rules. The beginning student may believe, on
the master's authority, that following the rules will facilitate that state of
enlightened awareness he seeks. The older student comes to feel that
doing so expresses that awareness in itself.

The committed Zen student has voluntarily entered and remained
in a semi-monastic community. Engaging this situation by following the
example of its older members, the student appropriates the community's
rules. They become almost invisibly the student's own, and through

them he or she develops an intuitive familiarity with the monastic situation itself and the smoothly meshing interaction of its participants. Zen's monastic social control rehearses its meditational self-control. The meditator lets mental images come and go without approving or rejecting them, instead concentrating on posture and breathing, the orthopractical forms of zazen. One thereby develops an intuitive familiarity with zazen as the situation of one's own life. Reportedly the student does not stop his or her thinking, but lets it stop by itself. In this way the student obtains a characteristic calmness of mind, but not by rejecting certain mental activity and adopting rules to calm his or her mind directly. Self-control or concentration is not the purpose of zazen, observes a master: "The true purpose is to see things as they are, to observe things as they are, and to let everything go as it goes. This is to put everything under control in its widest sense."[22]

Social control operates similarly in a Zen community through its rule-governed monastic situation. The master offers a metaphor:

> Even though you try to put people under some control, it is impossible. You cannot do it. The best way to control people is to encourage them to be mischievous. Then they will be in control in its wider sense. To give your sheep or cow a large, spacious meadow is the way to control him. So it is with people: first let them do what they want and watch them. This is the best policy.[23]

In the institutionally enclosed "meadow" of monastic communities those who were free-roaming youths in the 1960s come to experience Zen's daily regimen and meditational orthopraxy as the basis of their own positive liberty to express the truth of their maturing lives and their society in the 1980s. "We're remaking society by sitting zazen," says a priest, "because we're formed by social ideas. In practice we're asking ourselves, 'Who forms a form?'" If social ideas both originate within our consciousness and form it, according to this insight, then society can be transformed by transforming consciousness. The community of persons practicing Zen can reach outward through others, extending its sense of our interdependence to include the whole of society.

Beyond the Monastery

What does Zen practice mean for Americans outside the monastery's walls? The full impact of its insight and ethic requires a monastic organization built around daily meditation and relationship to a master. As such it will remain the province of small numbers of monks, now little more than a thousand nationwide. But larger numbers meditate regularly in non-residential groups or by themselves. They may meet with a master or hear a lecture on occasion, and they are usually familiar with Zen literature in English. The institutional location of these persons (in the arts, education, ecology, psychotherapy and the human potential movement, liberal denominations, and Catholic religious orders) gives them an important part in spreading Zen's ethic. To whom? To a larger and looser circle made up mostly of well-off and well-educated urbanites at work in precisely the sort of professional and white-collar settings characteristic of the fastest-growing segments of our society.

In these wider social circles an ideal of character I will call "the monk in the world" has taken root. Drawn from Zen monastic and lay traditions in tandem with countercultural motifs, this ideal represents a person who works diligently and carefully to serve others, nurture the environment, and express the "original nature" he shares with them. Self-awareness and compassion make up the touchstone of his moral motives, not self-preservation and advancement. He works to deepen his practice, integrating meditation and daily life, as an expression of all life's unity; not to achieve success as a sign of heavenly salvation or worldly accomplishment, or as a means to consumption and leisure. Care in work is a mode of self-expression and sensitive relationship more than success in work is a measure of self-worth. Uninsulated by the celibacy or cloister of the classic Christian contemplative, this figure echoes the Reformation ideal that everyone should be a monk in the world of ordinary work and householding. Yet his attitude toward the world in which he moves is mystically undriven. He is less "attached" and more accepting than the ascetic Puritan striving toward salvation across the entrepreneurial threshold of early capitalism, or his secularized successor striving to build his kingdom entirely on earth.[24]

As pure ideal, technique, or inner attitude, Zen's "this-worldly mysticism" fits smoothly into the bureaucratic and individualistic order of the contemporary middle-class world. Its cool self-discipline meshes with both the educational and professional discipline that marks the upper social strata of this world at work, and with the regimens of athletic and sexual skill, physical fitness, and emotional fluency that mark their leisure. Indeed, various therapeutic and behavioral training organizations are now promoting technologies of meditation to control stress and tension symptoms and to increase ego-performance in bureaucratic work, education, and interpersonal relations. More importantly, mystical and monist views of reality are now making significant headway in middle-class American culture, though here they are peculiarly vulnerable to pop psychological, sectarian, and cultic bastardization. This is because American culture, unlike that of pre-modern Japan, for example, is so deeply individualistic.[25] Here personhood is commonsensically authenticated by immediate individual experience instead of by membership in an organic social group and dutiful conformity within a cultural web that joins us together. In this context the monist axiom that "All is One," which overrides subject-object and self-other distinctions and identifies one's own true self with all existence, translates much too easily into conventional practice as the illusion that "All is I," which overrides the objectivity of duty and virtue, and identifies one's own wants with universal needs and rights—unless checked and repeatedly reordered by unselfish practices, relationships, and institutional structures like those of Zen.

The idea of Zen in American popular culture can be convoluted into yet another license for the unencumbered individual to "do his own thing" (as long as he does his job) at the center of an instrumentally arranged universe empty of binding love, justice, or community. This danger is particularly real for those "interested" in Zen but not engaged in its practice. For it is through actually doing *zazen*, side by side with others in relationship to a master, that students can come to accept the world without selling out to it, and then re-create the world by taking care of it. Zen practice replaces the psychological goal of individual self-realization with the experiential ground of religious enlightenment. It enables its students to grasp that they practice for the sake of all beings (for "Buddha, *Dharma*, and *Sangha*"), not for their own sake. They come to enlightenment through the goodness of all existence, not through their own efforts.

For those of us outside the daily rhythm of this community, the ethic of Zen stands as a personal ideal more thought about than socially practiced. But we, too, are searching not so much for new ideas to fill our heads as for ways of life and forms of relationship to renew the habits of our hearts. On such mores, as Tocqueville saw, our society finally rests.[26] Zen practice dramatizes that these moral moods, motives, and ideals of character cannot be bred apart from the social and ritual practices that elicit and exercise them.

Notes

1. For elaboration of the following thesis, see Steven M. Tipton, *Getting Saved from the Sixties: Moral Meaning in Conversion and Cultural Change* (Berkeley: University of California Press, 1982), especially chapters 1 and 3.
2. Katsuki Sekida, *Zen Training* (New York: Weatherhill, 1975), 41, 43.

3. The student recites and "works on" a *koan* with his mind, breathing, and respiratory muscles during meditation. For discussions of *koan* practice see Sekida, *Zen Training*, chapter 9, and Phillip Kapleau, *Three Pillars of Zen* (New York: Harper and Row, 1966).

4. "Just sitting" describes the relatively formless meditation known as *shikantaza*, in which there is no particular point of mental focus like breath-counting or a *koan*. It is characteristically associated with the Soto School of Japanese Zen Buddhism, while the *kanna* Zen ("seeing into the topic") of *koan* practice is associated with the Rinzai School.

5. These data and quotations come from formal interviews averaging four hours each with ten Zen students, done in the San Fransisco Bay Area from 1976 to 1979, and from earlier informal interviews with twenty or so others done over several years of participant-observation. The average age of formal interviewees is representative of 1960s youth practicing Zen, as is their sex ratio, marital status, social class, religious-ethnic background, and employment. All come from upper-middle-class backgrounds. Three are Protestant, five are Jewish, and two are Catholic. Five do unskilled blue collar work (gardener, housecleaner), two do skilled blue collar work (carpenter, mechanic), two are teachers, and one is a lawyer. All but one had used marijuana and psychedelic drugs, several of them steadily. Compared to other Zen students of this age group, these interviewees are among the most highly educated, verbally articulate, and politically active. Six had been active in political protest. Four hold advanced degrees (three M.A.s, one J.D.), another three B.A.s, and three had two or more years in prestigious colleges. For a related sample of students see David Wise, "Dharma West," University of California, Berkeley: unpublished Ph.D. thesis, 1971, chapter 3.

6. See Sekida, *Zen Training*, chaps. 1–3, especially 31, 47.

7. See Sekida, *Zen Training*. chap. 3; also Albert Stunkard, "Some Interpersonal Aspects of an Oriental Religion," *Psychiatry* 14 (1951):422.

8. Shunryu Suzuki, *Zen Mind, Beginner's Mind* (Tokyo: Weatherhill, 1970), 98.

9. Suzuki, *Zen Mind*, 22.

10. See Sekida, *Zen Training*, 49–59.

11. Akira Kasamatsu and Tomio Hirai, "An Electroencephalographic Study on the Zen Meditation," in Charles Tart, ed., *Altered States of Consciousness* (New York: Wiley, 1969), 493.

    Electroencephalographic indicators of these changes show the appearance of alpha waves, their increasing amplitude and then decreasing frequency, and finally the development of a theta rhythm.

12. Youths of the 1960s experienced with psychedelic drugs often found easier entry to Zen meditation than those who were not. But a tendency to model their *zazen* experience according to psychedelic patterns later made special problems for drug veterans, since Zen meditation did diverge from the psychedelic pattern.

13. *Samadhi* is also described as a "fullness" or "totality of which there is no outside," a meaning that shares with emptiness the "nondiscriminating" quality of a monist reality indivisible into constituent elements.

14. Suzuki, *Zen Mind*, 63.

15. The neurophysiological response of monks in *zazen* to repeated sound stimuli consists of sensation without association that does not become habituated. Electroencephalographic (EEG) comparisons between Zen and yoga indicate how closely such response corresponds to Zen teaching:

    "The adept practitioners of both forms of meditation show almost continuous alpha waves (normally associated with a state of relaxed alertness in ordinary subjects) during meditation. This is particularly startling in the case of the Zen monks because their eyes are open: one almost never sees alpha rhythm in the eyes-open condition in ordinary subjects. The Zen monks also show normal blocking of the alpha rhythm in response to stimulation which does not adapt with repeated trials as it does in ordinary subjects. The Yogins, on the other hand, show no response to stimulation at all. . . . These differences may be quite consistent with the differing philosophical outlooks of Zen and Yoga. The Zen monks are striving to exist in the here-and-now of immediate sensory experience. Yoga philosophy, on the other hand, has a strong world-denying quality, a belief that the phenomenal world is all illusion and ensnarement (*maya*), which the Yogin must learn to transcend. Thus it makes sense that they show no EEG response to stimulation and also report being unaware of the stimulation when questioned after the meditative state is terminated." (Charles Tart, *Altered States*, 485–86.)

    For a discussion of the implication of such responses as a class see Arthur Deikman, "Deautomatization and the Mystic Experience," in Tart, *Altered States*, 23–43.

16. Suzuki, *Zen Mind*, 30–31.

17. Albert Stunkard, "Some Interpersonal Aspects of an Oriental Religion," *Psychiatry*, 14 (1951): 419–431, esp. 430.

18. See Alasdair MacIntyre, *After Virtue* (Notre Dame: Notre Dame University Press, 1981), especially chapter 14, for a general account of how moral virtues entail and arise from specific social practices possessed of their own "internal goods" and standards of excellence, and established within cooperative relationships and institutional structures ordered to pursue these practices.

19. Suzuki, *Zen Mind*, 14.

20. Ibid.

21. Zen Mountain Center Library, "Warm-hearted Practice," Xerox, February 23, 1971.

22. Suzuki, *Zen Mind*, 29.

23. Ibid., 28.

24. See Max Weber, *The Protestant Ethic and the Spirit of Capitalism* (New York: Scribners, 1958); also his *The Sociology of Religion* (Boston: Beacon, 1963), ch. 4.

25. Here and in the following paragraph I draw on Robert N. Bellah, "The Meaning of Dogen Today," in William R. LaFleur, ed., *Dogen Studies: The Tassajara Conference* (Honolulu: University of Hawaii, 1984); and on my *Getting Saved from the Sixties*, especially 111–120.

26. See Alexis de Tocqueville, *Democracy in America*, J. P. Mayer, ed. (Garden City, NY: Anchor Books, 1969), vol. I, part II, chapter 9; also see vol. II, part II on individualism.

Editorial Commentary

In terms of the Anthony typology, authentic Zen practice is a multilevel, monistic, technical engagement—the category least likely to produce harmfully problematic involvements. This hardly means, though, that Zen is distortion-proof. No psychospiritual systems are, and as Tipton mentions, Western popular culture has indeed distorted Zen. This pseudo-Zen results largely from the American cultural bias that the Anthony typology terms "Tantric Freudianism," which, as we have seen, is the view that transcendence of mundane rationality occurs by admitting into awareness the emotions, desires, thoughts, and images we ordinarily repress because they seem dark and dangerous. It suspends the moral rules and social restraints that help maintain the state of repression. Tantric Freudianism strips Zen of its moral dimension, transforming its meditative practice of choiceless awareness into a generalized "anything goes, all is one" attitude toward life. The potential for this misinterpretation is apparent, for instance, in Tipton's statement that "Zen's ethic . . . invites us to practice *zazen*, and then to act however we will"—the Tantric Freudian reading stops here, but Tipton continues—"on the premise that the ideally sensitized and all-accepting consciousness bred by meditation will lead us to harmonize with the situation and respond appropriately to it" through unerring moral intuition.[1]

The American counterculture of the 1940s, 1950s, and 1960s had had its fill of the mainstream's rigid, unilevel-dualistic moralism and was eager to repudiate it. It is no wonder, then, that countercultural circles would misperceive Zen's transrational, multilevel morality as unilevel amorality, thereby rationalizing a bohemian-antinomian lifestyle.[2] However, to swing from the unilevel dualism of American civil religion, in which religious virtue is equated with obedience to fixed rules, to a uni-level monism in which moral rules are repudiated, is to chase a false image of freedom—false because it amounts to choosing indulgence over repression, which brings not freedom but a whole new set of psychosocial problems.[3] What is needed is to resolve the polarity of indulgence versus repression by achieving a true synthesis of them in consciousness, as mul-tilevel morality manages to approximate, e.g., in authentic Zen.

Tipton's article touches upon many features of transrational moral-ity. Its nonjudgmental character, which Anthony and Ecker discuss in Part 1, is worth commenting on in relation to Zen. The Zen master, Tipton explains, produces "insight for students into their own 'strengths and shortcomings' without transmitting 'any sense of praise or criti-cism'. . . . The moral character of the agent is illuminated without being colored by any subjective approval or disapproval." The student's dis-covery of his or her own moral condition occurs not through univocal rules or criteria applied to oneself (or that one could apply to others), but through contact with the transrational consciousness of the master. The student is in no position to take the moral measure of anyone else until he or she becomes, like the master, a "shining mirror" of purified moral intuition.

Moral intuition, which is central to Tipton's treatment of Zen prac-tice, is in various mystical traditions associated with a domain of intrinsic values that exist transcendentally and are knowable in consciousness. For example, in Advaita Vedanta Hinduism the operation of karma and rein-carnation is wholly governed by cause and effect in the realm of values, through the medium of man's causal body or *karan sharir*, the most tran-scendent of man's three bodies (physical body, energy body and causal body). In Mahayana Buddhism, Buddha's concept of the *dharma* repre-sents the intrinsic, eternal moral order, which is the only stable pattern in a universe of forms ever in flux. It is only through attunement to the *dharma* that man can approach and attain the ineffable transcendence of Nirvana. To experience true moral intuition, then—to be guided by direct, transrational awareness of the value nature of a situation—is to access a highly transcendent level of being. Experientially, moral intui-tion has a unique quality of unified seeing-knowing-feeling.[4] It is not a conceptual knowing-about. The illumination of intrinsic values seems to be the distinguishing feature of intuition proper, as distinct from other kinds of direct, nonrational knowing, of which there are many types, including sensory, instinctual, emotional, and psychic. In popular idiom, of course, "intuition" covers all kinds of nonrational knowing, but their differences are an important area of spiritual discrimination. True intui-tion inherently brings a transcendental awareness of intrinsic values or *dharma*, and so has a lasting impact on one's "heart" or deeper feelings;

whereas, for example, psychic knowing in itself lacks the value dimension and is either purely informational or involves also the awareness of subtle energies.

Tipton's description of the "ideal meditator" raises some interesting questions. He argues that technically correct meditation practice plus "persistent effort of the will" result in transcendent awareness, unself-interested attention, moral intuition. This could be interpreted univocally as saying that if you do *zazen* meditation, then your behavior will conform spontaneously to Zen's ethical precepts—a rather extreme claim, a univocal orthopraxy, and seemingly an American variation of Zen (a reflection of the American utilitarian-technical ethos). On the other hand, it might be argued that if one can perform the specifics of intensive Zen practice, then the precepts will spontaneously emerge *because* they are the implicit precondition of the practice and the hidden cause of their own manifestation in practice (a view argued by Wilber). It is perhaps for this reason that Tipton seems to deemphasize formal obedience to precepts and study of scriptures in Zen practice, relying mainly on meditation to bring the precepts to life spontaneously.

Precepts and textual teachings serve a major purpose in multilevel spiritual orientations, guiding the unenlightened in the highly complex, dialectical process of balancing the opposites of experience so as to make inner transformation a possibility. In multilevel groups precepts and texts are not applied as univocal rules, but are appreciated as having levels of meaning that the student apprehends only as he or she develops subtler levels of intuitive knowing-seeing-feeling. Take, for example, the Zen precept, "Do not take what is not given" (which is often oversimplified as "Do not steal"). The student takes this precept to heart at face value, with whatever level of understanding he or she has of it, knowing that this is but a point of departure for further realization of what the precept points toward. Living with the precept over time, one begins to recognize the act of taking what is not given in very subtle forms. A very sensitive awareness of the operation of the separate-self mentality with which one approaches each successive moment of experience may dawn. And so on. In this kind of working relationship to precepts, one takes them at face value, but not in the univocal manner, *i.e.*, without presuming to understand what they mean in any final or exhaustive sense.

Zen Buddhism is an important example of the very real problem of relating to a mystical avenue through the distorting lens of cultural sensibilities—in this case a double lens of Japanese and American sensibilities. Historically, Zen developed its forms in a cultural situation that is quite foreign to the Western mind. A question that arises among American students of Zen is, therefore, "To what degree are we practicing Japanese culture and to what degree are we practicing Zen Buddhism?"

The faithful transmission of Zen into the American milieu would seem to require teachers who possess a sensitive understanding of both cultures.

Finally, although Tipton says little about the ultimate nature of things here, his few references seem to have a pantheistic slant in which ultimacy is equated with the unified totality of the natural world-process, and ultimate enlightenment is viewed as full, direct awareness of, and participation in, the naturic unity. A pantheistic interpretation of Zen would be a unilevel divergence from traditional Zen Buddhism, which views ultimacy as radically transcending the world-process, yet one with it as its true nature. Whether or not Tipton makes this unilevel error is not really the issue, since he is not a Zen master offering instruction to others. But the pantheistic distortion of Zen is one indicator of unilevel sensibilities that a prospective member of an American Zen group should have in mind.

Notes

1. We are reminded of St. Augustine: "Love God and do what you will." To love God in Augustine's sense brings about both the transcendence of self-interest and the attainment of moral intuition, so that to then "do what you will" is inevitably and unselfconsciously to act morally.
2. For a short, lively critique of the counterculture's misappropriation of Zen, see "Beat Zen, Square Zen, Zen" by Alan Watts in *This Is It* (New York: Vintage, 1973). This essay was first published in the summer of 1958. One passage (found on pages 98 and 99) is particularly relevant here: "The realization of the unswerving 'rightness' of whatever happens is no more manifested by utter lawlessness in social conduct than by sheer caprice in art. As Zen has been used as a pretext for the latter in our times, its use as a pretext for the former is ancient history. Many a rogue has justified himself with the Buddhist formula, 'Birth-and-death (*samsara*) is Nirvana; worldly passions are Enlightenment.' This danger is implicit in Zen because it is implicit in freedom. Power and freedom can never be safe. They are dangerous in the same way that fire and electricity are dangerous. But it is quite pitiful to see Zen used as a pretext for license when the Zen in question is no more than an idea in the head, a simple rationalization." See also Ken Wilber's critique of the 1960s, "Dharma Bum" variety of Zen in *Up From Eden* (New York: Doubleday/Anchor, 1981), 323–4.
3. See C. Trungpa, *The Myth of Freedom* (Berkeley: Shambhala, 1976).
4. H. Benoit, *The Supreme Doctrine* (New York: Viking, 1955).

Part Three

TRANSPERSONAL PERSPECTIVES ON GROUPS, GURUS, AND GRANDIOSITY

The Spectrum Model

Ken Wilber

Since the late 1970s Ken Wilber's prolific writings articulating the transpersonal dimensions of psychology, sociology, and anthropology have made him the transpersonal school's foremost theorist. In a period of nine years, ten volumes have emerged bearing his name as author or editor.* Concurrently he was for several years Editor-in-Chief of the journal *ReVision* and is now (1985) General Editor of New Science Library/ Random House, as well as Consulting Editor for both the *Journal of Transpersonal Psychology* and the *Journal of Humanistic Psychology*. Wilber holds a graduate degree in biochemistry.

In the following article, adapted from his 1983 work *Eye to Eye*, Wilber reviews his "spectrum" model of stages of human development and then derives from it criteria for assessing spiritual and consciousness groups. He also examines the relationship between his framework and that of the Anthony typology, and offers an explanation of their agreement in identifying helpful vs. harmful groups.

---

* Ken Wilber is author of *The Spectrum of Consciousness* (1977), *No Boundary* (1979), *The Atman Project* (1980), *Up From Eden* (1981), *A Sociable God* (1983), *Eye to Eye* (1983) and *Quantum Questions: The Mystical Writings of the World's Great Physicists* (1984); co-author of *Transformations of Consciousness: Conventional and Contemplative Perspectives on Development* (1985); editor of *The Holographic Paradigm and Other Paradoxes* (1982); and co-editor of the present volume.

A DEVELOPMENTAL-STRUCTURAL APPROACH

The new religious movements in America are, on the whole, singularly problematic. On the one hand, some of them are obviously—at least in hindsight—disastrous, Jonestown being paradigmatic. On the other, some of them seem—at least in theory— genuinely beneficial, even enlightening. Heidegger, for instance, stated: "If I understand [Zen scholar Suzuki] correctly, this is what I have been trying to say in all my writings,"[1] which at least suggests that not all the new religions are merely sophomoric platitudes and mind-numbing cultisms.

The great problem is devising any sort of believable grid or criteria for differentiating the more valid movements from the less valid (or even harmful) ones. In such a terribly complex and problematic field, even a very general and somewhat imprecise grid would be better than none.

Several such general grids exist. I myself have attempted to present one, based explicitly on the modern disciplines of developmentalism and structuralism (primarily) and phenomenological hermeneutics and functionalism (secondarily). The result is a scale or "ladder" of the structure-stages of psychosocial growth, from birth to the "higher" or "highest" levels of development. The lower half of the scale is based on the works of such developmental psychologists as Piaget, Werner, Arieti, Kohlberg, Loevinger, Erikson; the upper half is based on a hermeneutical reading of the world's esoteric spiritual texts (for example, Zen, Vedanta, Vajrayana, Kabalah, Sufism), with the proviso that these higher structure-stages of growth can be verified using essentially the same techniques (developmental-structural) that established and verified the lower levels. This external verifiability—should it indeed prove sound—is what confers upon this type of model its potentially believable status, and thus allows it, within broad limits, to act as a potential scale for the adjudication of the relative validity or authenticity of a particular psychosocial engagement, including, most notably, religious involvement.

What does it mean in this context to "adjudicate?" Kohlberg, for example, has postulated six stages of ascending moral development. In this scheme we have no difficulty in saying that stage-5 is higher than stage-2. There is real and verifiable meaning in that statement. Just so, with a general overview model of psychosocial development on the whole, one that would include not only Kohlberg but Piaget, Loevinger, Erikson, as well as the hypothetical "higher" stages of development (for example, yogic *chakras*, Vedanta *kosas*, Mahayana *vijnanas*), we would be better able to judge—adjudicate—the relative degree of maturity or authenticity of any given psychosocial production (moral, cognitive, egoic, religious, etc.). That is basically the aim of the general overview model I have presented elsewhere.[2]

Space prevents even a simple summary of the model I have developed—its sources, methodologies, verification procedures, and actual
stages. (For these, the reader is referred to endnote 2.) For the purposes
of this paper, however, such detail is not necessary. Rather, I will distill
its twenty or so stages into seven general ones—and I will then further
distill those into three major realms of development, and it will be with
this simplified model that we can make most of our points.

The seven general stages of development are:

1. *Archaic:* This includes material body, sensations, perceptions, and
   emotions. This is roughly equivalent to Piaget's sensorimotor intelligence, Maslow's physiological needs, Loevinger's autistic and symbiotic stages, the first and second *chakras*, the *annamayakosa* (food,
   oral) and *pranamayakosa* (sex, genital) in Vedanta, etc.
2. *Magic:* This includes simple images, symbols, and the first rudimen-
   tary concepts, or the first and lowest mental productions, which are
   "magical" in the sense that they display condensation, displacement,
   "omnipotence of thought," etc. This is Freud's primary process,
   Arieti's paleologic, Piaget's preoperational thinking, the third *chakra*.
   It is correlated with Kohlberg's pre-conventional morality, Loevinger's impulsive and self-protective stages, Maslow's safety needs, etc.
   (The archaic realm is basically *matter* and *body*; the magic realm is
   the beginning of *mind*.)
3. *Mythic:* This stage is more advanced than magic, but not yet capable
   of clear rationality or hypothetico-deductive reasoning, a stage Geb-
   ser explicitly termed "mythic." This is essentially Piaget's concrete
   operational thinking; it is correlated with Loevinger's conformist and
   conscientious-conformist stages, Maslow's belongingness needs, the
   fourth *chakra*, the beginning of *manomayakosa* (Vedanta) and *manovijnana* (Mahayana), etc.
4. *Rational:* This is Piaget's formal operational thinking, propositional
   or hypothetico-deductive reasoning. It is correlated with Loevinger's
   conscientious and individualistic stages, Kohlberg's post-conven-
   tional morality, Maslow's self-esteem needs, the fifth *chakra*, the culmination of *manomayakosa* and *manovijnana*, etc.
5. *Psychic:* This does not mean "paranormal," although some esoteric
   texts suggest paranormal events may more likely occur here. Rather,
   it refers to "psyche" as a higher level of development than the mind
   per se (e.g., Aurobindo, Free John). Its cognitive structure has been
   called "vision logic," or integrative logic; it is correlated with Loevinger's integrated and autonomous stages, Maslow's self-actualiza-

tion needs, Broughton's integrated stage, the sixth *chakra*, the beginning of *manas* (Mahayana) and *vijnanamayakosa* (Vedanta), etc.

6. *Subtle:* This is, basically, the archetypal level, the level of the "illumined mind" (Aurobindo); the culmination of *manas* and *vijnanamayakosa*; a truly transrational structure (not pre-rational and not anti-rational); intuition in its highest and most sober sense (gnosis, *jnana, prajna*); not emotionalism or merely bodily felt meaning; home of Platonic forms or ideas; *bijamantra, vasanas*; beginning of seventh *chakra*; start of Maslow's self-transcendence needs, etc.

7. *Causal:* Or the unmanifest ground and suchness of all levels; the unbounded end-state of growth and development; "spirit" in the highest sense, not as a Big Person but as the "Ground of Being" (Tillich), "Eternal Substance" (Spinoza), "Geist" (Hegel); at and beyond the seventh *chakra*; the *anandamayakosa* (Vedanta), *alayavijnana* (Mahayana), *kether* (Kabbalah), etc.

As I said, those seven general structure-stages of development can be further reduced to three general realms. Since a large part of the problem of the new religions concerns whether or not they are rational, we can divide this overall "great chain of being" into those structures that are pre-rational (subconscious) and those that are transrational (superconscious), with rationality (self-conscious) as the great divide:

archaic	magic	mythic	rational	psychic	subtle	causal
●	●	●	●	●	●	●
PRE-RATIONAL (subconscious)			RATIONAL (self-conscious)		TRANS-RATIONAL (superconscious)	

THE PRE/TRANS FALLACY

As I have tried to suggest elsewhere,[3] one of the great problems with discovering an overall model of development is that although the rational, self-conscious realms are almost universally agreed upon, the other two realms are almost as universally confused. Because the pre-rational and transrational realms are, in their own ways, non-rational, they appear similar or even identical to the untutored eye. Put simply, pre-rational and transrational are often, even usually, confused. This confusion generally leads to one of two opposite mistakes: either the transrational is reduced to the pre-rational (Freud), or the pre-rational is elevated to the transrational (Jung). Some examples follow: on the one hand, causal identity (the Supreme Identity of subject and object, soul and Godhead) is reduced to neonatal narcissism, or subtle archetype is reduced to childish mythic displays, or psychic vision is reduced to infantile magic animism. On the other hand, neonatal fusion is elevated to spiritual wholeness, or infantile magic is thought to "really" be psychic paranormality, or childish myth is elevated to subtle archetype. Now I am not using a "straw-man" argument here; I can, and have, given concrete and historically significant examples of each of those six confusions; I believe those confusions have been as pandemic as they have been theoretically calamitous.[3]

I call any of those confusions "the pre/trans fallacy," and it is the pre/trans fallacy that, in my opinion, rests precisely at the center of the controversy over the new religions because about half of the new religions are pre-rational, and about half are transrational. That is the strange mixture of trick and treat that has made this whole issue so extraordinarily difficult to unravel.

But whatever we decide on that particular issue, I would like to remind the reader that this general model—which I have simplified as pre-rational, rational, and transrational, or pre-personal, personal, and transpersonal, or subconscious, self-conscious, and superconscious—is based on developmental and structural criteria that are potentially open to external and experimental confirmation. This model is offered not dogmatically and conclusively, but as an hypothesis requiring verification. *If* it proves sound, then we will be able to draw certain conclusions on the nature of the new religions, not to mention the old.

LEGITIMACY VS. AUTHENTICITY

We need one more bit of technical information before we look specifically at some of the new religious movements. This concerns differentiating between what goes on *within* a particular level-stage of development, and what goes on *between* levels. We can approach this distinction from several angles.

Using our seven-level model, we say that the basic defining form of each level is its deep structure, whereas a particular element or component of each level is a surface structure. A change in deep structure we call transformation; a change in surface structure, translation. It's like a seven-story building: moving furniture (surface structures) around on one floor is translation; moving to a different floor (deep structure) is transformation. Finally, any psychosocial institution that validates or facilitates translation we call legitimate; any that validates or facilitates transformation we call authentic.[4]

Legitimacy, so defined, is a horizontal scale. It is a measure of the degree of integration, meaning, coherence, stability, organization, of or within a given level of structural adaptation. One of the greatest needs of individuals—an over-arching need—is to find legitimacy at their present level of development or structural adaptation. For example, people at the magic-safety level are seeking legitimacy, or sanctified existence, via the safety or self-protective (preconventional) needs of their animistic and narcissistic world-view. People at the mythic-membership (conventional) level seek legitimacy through conformist-belongingness, trying to be sanctified by the group. People at the rational (postconventional) level seek legitimacy via conscientious or self-esteem needs: they can legitimate their existence only by following their own conscience and by interacting with similarly structured social institutions; and so on. One of the great tasks of any society is to provide its members with a legitimate and legitimizing world-view, one that is believably capable of sanctifying existence on the average expectable level of structural adaptation reached by its members (in our society, the average expectable level is approximately mythic-rational).

Authenticity is a vertical scale. It is a measure of the *degree of transformation* offered by any particular psychosocial institution. Every society has to act as a pacer of transformation (development) up to its average expectable level of structural adaptation, and thus it must provide authentic modes of transformation up to and including that level (generally, this task falls to family, educational, and occasionally religious systems). In our society, for example, we attempt to move or develop individuals up to the rational level, or at least the mythic-rational. Those at the archaic level have to be institutionalized, and those at the magic level are labeled psychotic and subsequently isolated. But somewhere around the mythic-rational stage, our society's force as a pacer of authentic transformation (or vertical growth) ends, and any higher growth or authenticity has to occur either on one's own initiative or in micro-communities of the higher- and like-minded. But this power and degree of transformation we call authenticity.

Any given religion, like any other psychosocial production, can be judged on the basis of both its legitimacy and its authenticity. That is, does it seek merely to confirm, validate, and sanctify a person at his or her present stage of adaptation, or does it seek to transform a person to genuinely higher levels of growth and development? Not merely help a person translate better, but transform significantly? Now both of these scales are important—even authentic religions (ones that explicitly engage transrational, transpersonal, superconscious realms) have to be legitimate on their own levels, and even a legitimate but not very authentic religion can serve several useful purposes. Like the categories of pre-rational and transrational, legitimacy and authenticity are often, even usually, confused. In the Graduate Theological Union seminar series, Dick Anthony, responding to these distinctions, made the following very succinct and important summary:

> This is a theme that has come up over and over again. We need to distinguish between transpersonal criteria, in other words, groups that are authentically spiritual in some transpersonal sense, versus groups which aren't, and then another dimension, which is groups which are in some sense or other legitimate, such as civil religious sects, or conventional religious groups, or whatever; and groups can deviate in a negative way along either one of those dimensions. And the dimensions interact, so you get a kind of four-cell table. And when we try to make everything fit along some unidimensional criterion of value, then everything falls apart.[5]

We might summarize the relevance of the last two sections in one sentence: It is these two confusions—pre and trans, and legitimate and authentic—that have so helped to muddle the study of the new religions. We can now attempt to study the new religions without these confusions.

THE BREAKDOWN OF CIVIL RELIGION AND THE NEED FOR LEGITIMACY

American civil religion—sociologist Robert N. Bellah's term for a mixture of American nationalism and biblical mythology—apparently served as a legitimizing world-view for a great majority of Americans up until the 1960s, when, according to most scholars, the civil religion finally and fatally hemorrhaged. Now whether one laments the decline of the civil religion or rejoices in its passing, the individuals so affected—and that means virtually all Americans—were faced with a legitimation crisis: where and how to find a new and legitimate world-view. That is, Americans had to look elsewhere for legitimation.[6]

In my opinion, the very structure of American civil religion's world-view, belief systems, and cognitive maps basically embodied and expressed a mythic level of development. Thus, when the civil religion "broke" it left in its wake four general populations, all in search of legitimacy (I am simplifying drastically): (1) those who more-or-less surrendered their mythic world-views and developed to, or at least embraced, the rational level of structural adaptation, for example, secular humanism; (2) those who were attempting desperately to resurrect and relegitimate the old civil religion, for example, the Moral Majority; (3) those who, under the strain of a collapsing legitimacy, began to regress to more blatantly mythical or even magical and archaic structures—a slide into pre-rationality (over and above that which would be expected under more "normal" conditions); and (4) those who began to develop beyond rational realms into higher structures, self-actualizing and self-transcending—a move toward trans-rationality in an authentic sense (again, over and above that which would be expected under more "normal" conditions. See endnote 4).

It is the last two movements, especially, that will concern us. In the next section I propose certain criteria based on developmental-structuralism that might be helpful in distinguishing possibly beneficial and useful new religious movements from those that are possibly detrimental or even disastrous.

THE CRITERIA

Our methodology is simple: We take the particular socioreligious movement in question, examine its statements and actions, and subject these to (1) a developmental structural analysis, in order to determine its degree of authenticity, or vertical range and maturity; and (2) a hermeneutical-functional analysis, in order to determine its type and degree of legitimacy. (See endnote 4.)

First, we consider its authenticity. Which stage along the developmental-structural scale does the group foster? Is it archaic, with moments of self-other indissociation, primary narcissism, primitive fusion, oral needs, perhaps even cannibalistic or murderous (homicidal or suicidal) impulses? Or is it magical, with "omnipotence-of-thought" rituals (for example, voodoo), emotional-sexual (Oedipal) impulses, magic beliefs, self-clan confusion (totemism)? Or is it mythical, with intense conformity needs, a cosmic parent world-view, authoritarian figure "representative" of the parent, mythic ritual, emphasis upon in-group (saved) and out-group (damned), lack of rational justification? Or does the group seem to promote truly transcendental aspirations? Is it psychic, subtle, or even causal—these being characterized, as I will soon suggest, by genuine study and discipline aimed at affecting authentic transformation, and in ways that can be impartially determined by strict developmental-structural analysis?

In short, with regard to authenticity, is the group in question pre-rational (archaic, magic, mythic) or transrational (psychic, subtle, causal)?

Second, we analyze the psychosocial productions of the movement in order to determine their degree and type of legitimacy. This is a particularly intricate and complex analysis. Odd as it sounds, it is much more difficult to perform legitimacy analyses than authenticity analyses; the latter is a vertical scale which admits of little variation; the former is a horizontal scale, and there are numerous and equally valid horizontal scales that intersect the single vertical scale at right angles, much as numerous spokes surround one axle. Put differently, each deep structure can sustain a multitude of different but equally legitimate surface structures; this makes it very easy to adjudicate deep structures and arrange them hierarchically (as in our seven-level hierarchy), but it makes it very difficult to adjudicate the legitimacy of various surface structures within each deep structure.

I have therefore selected two legitimacy criteria as being at least as important as any others: one is more-or-less subjective, and deals with the degree of moral-intention, meaning, interpretation—the hermeneutical scale (for example, Gadamer). The other is more-or-less objective, and deals with the degree of integration, functional stability, pattern maintenance, both within and across the group's boundary, as determined empirically—such as the functional or systems theory scale (for example, Parsons).

Without going into details, suffice it to say that once we determine the group's level of authenticity, or its vertical degree of structural adaptation, we then try to determine its type and degree of legitimacy, or its horizontal scale of integrative meaning. How and why, within that level, does it earn its legitimacy—how does it validate its existence? What sanctions are used? How coherent and organized are they? Most importantly, is legitimacy conferred by a whole society? by a tradition? by a single person? That is, within the given level of structural adaptation, who or what has the final power to tell you that you're OK?

While it is always difficult to say what constitutes a "good" religious movement, it is somewhat easier to suggest certain factors that, if present, strongly indicate the religious movement in question is (or soon will be) deeply problematic. In the following sections I shall point out some of those factors, based upon the structural analysis of authenticity and the functional analysis of legitimacy. Before we do so, however, we need to discuss the nature of authority.

AUTHORITY

Let us discuss not what constitutes "bad" authority—authoritarian personalities, fascist dynamics, group ego subservience to superego projections, transference hypnosis—but what constitutes "good" authority—

that is, under what circumstances would most people agree that an authority is necessary? What is a benign, useful, nonproblematic authority?

One type of benign authority is "functional authority," conferred to the person who, by special training, is authorized to perform certain tasks and functions, for example, plumbers, doctors, lawyers. That type of authority is nonproblematic because subjection to it is voluntary. There are certain types of involuntary subjection to authority that are also generally thought to be nonproblematic—law enforcement, for example; but the best example is compulsory education because its existence is based upon a developmental argument and upon society's need to act as a pacer of development up to at least a certain average-expectable level of adaptation. The benign authority in this situation is, of course, the teacher. The teacher has a peculiar form of authority. If, for example, a student says, with regard to a particular task, "But why do I have to do it that way?" the teacher's final authority is, "Because I say so. Once you have learned to do it that way—once you have graduated—you can do it any way you wish. But experience has shown us that that is the best way to learn that task, and that is how you are going to do it in my class if you want to pass."

Even though the teacher exercises compulsory authority, it is viewed as benign, nonproblematic, and necessary, because: (1) it is effecting development, and (2) it is phase-temporary or phase-specific. That is, the teacher's authority over the pupil is temporary; it effectively evaporates once the pupil's degree of understanding approaches that of the teacher (supposedly symbolized by graduation). At that point, the pupil can become a teacher—and even disagree with his or her previous teachers.

Phase-specific authority is inescapable in any process of education (development). Even in higher or non-compulsory education, the gap between the teacher's and pupil's understanding of a topic confers on the teacher a phase-specific authority that is only annulled when and if that gap is sufficiently closed. At that point, teacher and pupil become more-or-less equals; prior to that point, the teacher's phase-specific authority role is inescapable.

Now we cannot conclude from these examples that all functional and phase-specific authority is benign and nonproblematic. But we can conclude that authority which is not functional and phase-specific might very likely be problematic, because then the only major reasons left for its existence are often those that fall into the category of "bad" authority—authority that does not serve a necessary (objective) function or phase-specific (subjective) growth, but rather rests on certain psychological dynamics of "master-slave" (Hegel), "power-over" (Fromm), "superego projection" (Freud), "transference hypnosis" (Ferenczi), "herd mentality" (Hegel/Berdyaev), "emotional plague" (Reich), etc.

For our present purposes I have chosen the short-cut of not attempting to explain the nature of all those various conceptions of "bad" authority; rather, I have simply suggested two major characteristics of "good" authority (functional and/or phase-specific), and then added this condition: If the authority in question displays neither of those characteristics, odds are that that authority is or will be problematic. (The reader can fill in the nature of the "problem" using whatever theory he or she wishes.)

Using the ideas of pre/trans, authenticity, legitimacy and authority, we can now examine some of the new religious movements.

PROBLEMATIC GROUPS: AN ABSTRACT OUTLINE

As I said, it is easier to suggest what constitutes a "bad" group than a "good" one; accordingly, if we take each of the dimensions we have discussed—authenticity, legitimacy, and authority—and look at their "bad" manifestations, we arrive at a tentative list of problematic factors, the more of which any group contains, the more problematic the group probably is (or will become). These are not the only factors involved; they are simply those most directly related to developmental, functional, and authoritarian considerations. Let us first discuss these in abstract form, and then give some concrete examples.

Problematic groups tend to be characterized by one or more of the following:

1. *Engagement of a pre-rational realm:* In my opinion this is probably the single most significant problematic factor. Fortunately, it can be adjudicated fairly precisely and easily using standards already accepted by most developmental psychologists: The pre-rational realm consists of those stages *below* rationality, e.g., below Piaget's formal operational thinking, Kohlberg's postconventional morality, Loevinger's conscientious stages, Maslow's self-esteem. There are, of course, degrees to this "belowness," or degrees of pre-rational engagement (for example, archaic, magic, mythic), degrees it is important to determine; but I think the overall idea is evident enough.

   While these pre-rational levels are phase-specifically necessary and appropriate enough for infant and child development, they tend to become increasingly problematic for adolescents and adults. For, when engaged by otherwise mature individuals, they are phase-specifically "out of sync," anachronistic, inappropriate; in fact: regressive. For example, exclusively oral needs and magical cognitions are appropriate enough for the infant and young child, but when fostered in an older child, adolescent, or adult, they are evidence of, or actually inculcate, regressive/fixated trends, the results of which, for *structural* reasons, are almost always problematic or pathological. Likewise, mythic-membership cognition, with its Oedipal overtones (cosmic parent) and intense conformist or peer-pressure needs, is phase-specifically appropriate enough for the older child and young adolescent, but beyond that its persistence is evidence of either arrest, fixation, or regression—again, problematic or pathological.

With regard to religious movements, the easiest way to gain a first approximation as to their level of development is simply to note their relation to formal rational thinking. Specifically:

a. Does the group allow free and rational inquiry into its teachings? Or does it discourage or even prevent critical analysis of its own tenets? Does it allow or encourage comparison and assessment of its methods and teachings with those of other paths, not as propaganda but as free inquiry? A transrational group will usually insist on this; a pre-rational group will avoid it.

b. If the group claims a knowledge that is supposedly "outside" or "beyond" reason, does it nonetheless retain access to reason? In developmentalism, a higher level is defined as one that transcends but includes its predecessors. For example, formal operational thinking (the capacity to think about thinking) transcends but includes concrete operational thinking (the capacity to think about the concrete world). Just so, a truly transrational group transcends but includes all manner of rational inquiry. Thus, a transrational group will usually claim reason is necessary but insufficient; reason is accorded a necessary and honored function, but it is supplemented by other modes of awareness thought to be higher in capacity (gnosis, *prajna, jnana*).[7] On the other hand, a pre-rational group neither transcends nor includes reason; accordingly, it will usually claim reason is insufficient and unnecessary—reason tends simply to be dismissed. Pre-rationality, in other words, always betrays itself by an anti-rational stance no amount of propaganda can disguise. And it is that anti-rational stance that contributes to, or helps instigate, the regressive catastrophe.

2. *Engagement of a permanent authority figure:* This is perhaps the

most visible of the problematic factors, and the one that has gained most notoriety. We saw that, whatever the nature of a "bad" authority, a "good" or benign authority is usually phase-temporary. Many, perhaps most, new religious movements are headed by an authority figure: master, *roshi*, guru, swami, or simply leader.

The teachings of the non-problematic groups are usually very explicit regarding the function and status of the guru: The guru possesses a temporary authority, an authority generated by the fact that the guru is developmentally (or educationally) more aware of his or her own higher structural potentials. The authority of the guru is said to disappear once the student awakens to a similar understanding. It rests not in the guru himself, but in the sleep of enlightenment in the student; it is exactly like the teacher in an educational system. Thus, once the student awakens to his or her own equally higher status as Buddha-Brahman, the function of the guru is ended and the authority of the guru evaporates. In Zen for instance, once a person achieves major *satori* (causal insight), the relationship between *roshi* and disciple changes from master and student to brother and brother (or sister–brother, or sister–sister)—and this is explicitly so stated. The guru, as authority, is phase-temporary.

Problematic groups, on the other hand, tend to be headed by a permanent authority figure, one whose authority is anything but phase-temporary. The aim of this authority is not eventually to render himself unnecessary, but to install himself permanently as power bearer. All of the theoretical analyses on "bad" authority swing into play here, regarding both master and slave. The master needs to dominate as much as the slave needs to be dominated, and this is the secret key that binds the oppressed to their oppressors.

The paradigm of the benign or phase-temporary authority is the physician (or teacher); the paradigm of the permanent or problematic authority is the preacher. The former considers himself effective the quicker he can get rid of you as a client; the latter considers himself effective the longer he can hold on to you.

3. *Engagement of an isolated legitimacy:* This brings us to our scale of legitimacy, which, as we said, is harder to state in a generally agreed-upon fashion. I will therefore limit myself to one factor among many: not the nature, type, or degree of legitimacy, but the source of legitimacy. For this ties in directly with our discussion on both authority and civil religion. It is this: the civil religion had a legitimacy implicitly offered, more or less, by an entire society to individuals. As that legitimacy began to crumble, individuals were forced to look elsewhere for validation, and that search was part of the impetus for the

rise of various new religions. Now these new religions, aside from whatever authenticity they might or might not offer, have anyway to deliver various types of legitimation for the searching self. Since this legitimacy is no longer offered by a society at large, the question becomes: is the new legitimacy offered by a tradition or by a single individual?

Legitimacy offered by a tradition—say, Hinduism, Buddhism, Sufism, Christian mysticism—tends to be less problematic than legitimacy offered by a single person (leader), simply because it is less open to permanent, isolated, single-authority-figure domination and distortion. If, for example, you are a Buddhist *roshi*, it is infinitely more difficult to proclaim yourself permanent authority and sole arbiter of legitimacy, because there lies behind you, as ballast, 2,500 years of corrective teaching. Lineage, in other words, is one of the greatest safeguards against fraudulent legitimacy.

On the other hand, if you are the sole legitimate leader, without historical ballast, then the validation of every member in the group rests upon your whim. What society or tradition once conferred upon individuals now revolves to one person. And—it's rarely pointed out—this places a vicious strain, not just on the slaves, but upon the master. The leader himself might begin to deteriorate under the stress, a deterioration that is then passed on to all followers in one form or another.

This does not mean that all groups headed by sole legitimate authorities are problematic. After all, we must allow for new and creative teachings and teachers. Who enlightened Buddha? Who psychoanalyzed Freud? New truths, and therefore new and nonprecedented authorities, arise everywhere. But such true heroes are, I suspect, much rarer than the number of new religious authorities claiming such status. Therefore, isolated legitimacy must be viewed as probably problematic. And that factor seems crucial, because if the source of legitimacy falls on one person, and if that person is psychodynamically problematic, then the results tend to be both pre-rational and non-phase-temporary. An entire nexus of problematic and pathological factors couple and conspire to spell probable disaster.

THE CULT-CLAN AND TOTEM MASTER

Having presented some abstract criteria for recognizing problematic groups, we can now examine some concrete examples.

In the seminar series of the Center for the Study of New Religious Movements, Graduate Theological Union,[8] out of some dozen or so new religious movements examined, probably three out of four were deemed—by orthodox and transpersonal scholars alike—to be problematic, or at least to have degenerated into problematic status. These included such movements as Jonestown, Synanon, an unfortunate twist on Psychosynthesis, and the Unification Church.

What emerges from those transcripts is a general pattern of problematic groups, and that pattern unmistakably correlates with the "bad" criteria we suggested in the previous section. So ubiquitous is this general pattern that we can refer to it with a generic heading: the problematic group is more often than not a *cult-clan with a totem master*, a phrase that I shall define after a look at specific cases of groups whose degeneration is well documented.

The paradigm for this, of course, was Jonestown. It was pre-rational, eventually sinking past mythic-belongingness needs to magical-sexual ritual to archaic sacrifice; it was headed by a permanent authority, "the father" Jim Jones, who was even so addressed; and its legitimacy—the very "OKness" of every member—rested upon a sole person, Jones. The dynamic of Jonestown was textbook in the way it followed almost exactly our three "bad" criteria.

But a similar pattern could be observed in most other problematic groups, even those existing in entirely different circumstances (although none degenerated to the final degree of Jonestown). An unfortunate example is the atypical situation that arose in one particular school of Psychosynthesis.[9] I say "atypical" because Psychosynthesis itself is a rather sophisticated and authentic teaching, and what happened to one of its schools is simply not indicative of its theoretical potential.

This particular group began as a concerned community of individuals—virtually all of whom were at or near a rational level of structural adaptation—interested in pursuing an authentic transrational growth and development. Through a series of events that can only be conveyed by the original (and quite terrifying) transcripts, the upward transformation began to go sour. What followed was classic group regression into pre-rational realms, a regression that almost, *almost*, ended in a "Jonestown."

We can follow this regression using virtually any of the developmental scales we have discussed; the individuals started out at the self-esteem (conscientious) stages, interested in the higher realms of self-actualization and self-transcendence. As that upward development began to falter, individuals not only failed their own self-esteem needs, they apparently began to regress to conformist-belongingness-conventional modes. Individuality was shunned; the "group ego" began to demand allegiance. In place of rational individuality and logical inquiry there arose mythic-membership and the "wall of terror" that demanded group allegiance. Conformity to the particular world-view was now the measure of legitimacy: to leave the group was "to die." This is all the more extraordinary because the people so caught up were extremely well educated—doctors, lawyers, professionals. The move towards and into pre-rational realms was well under way; nobody was encouraged, or even allowed, to question the teachings rationally. Criterion number one—pre-rationality—was already in evidence.

Worse, *one* individual soon became the sole arbiter of "the teaching," a situation that represented a regression from a still potentially phase-temporary authority to an authority that was, for all practical purposes, permanent (criterion number two). This person—I shall call him Smith in view of the consensus among those close to the situation not to stigmatize him permanently—was looked upon as the sole and permanent leader of the organization. This eventually led to Smith being perceived (by himself and all others) as the sole and individual bearer of legitimacy: Smith, and Smith alone, had the final power to tell you if your actions were OK or not OK (criterion number three). So blatant was this power that Smith would spend hours—literally hours—"processing" individuals, either directly or by phone, telling them exactly what they had to think, feel, and do in order to be OK, to be legitimate, to be validated. And, given the group regression to intense conformity needs, virtually no one objected.

The situation soon worsened, both on the part of the master and the slave. Mythic belongingness and group conformity gave way in further regression to the magical stage of primary process cognition and delusional reference systems. Invisible forces—graphically described—were "out to get them"; both master and slave became, literally and clinically, paranoid (as was Jim Jones). Had not extraneous circumstances such as chance contacts with friends or relatives outside the group interrupted this pattern, it might indeed have ended in archaic, masochistic, and literal sacrifice: "Since the world doesn't understand us, since, in fact, they are all out to get us, let us get ourselves first," as a heroic statement.

Although not all problematic groups follow that overall pattern exactly, or at least do not follow it to such extremes, I believe the pattern itself is general enough to be considered essentially paradigmatic—and that pattern I call "the cult-clan and totem master."

Cult-clan refers to the general absence of self-esteem or conscientious or postconventional needs (our overall rational level). For, prior to the general rational level, the opinions of others are equal to, or more important than, the opinions of self. For example, at the conventional (mythic) level of morality an individual accepts the norms of the group in an absolute sense: there are no exceptions, no alternatives—what has been called the "law and order" stage.[10] At the postconventional (rational) level, on the other hand, a person can judge the validity of society's norms for himself; he might find them acceptable and end up embracing them, or he might find them ignoble and end up rejecting them. But in either case he does so not out of blind conformity, but out of rational and conscientious considerations. Prior to that point the individual basically has little considered choice. As such, pre-rational engagements tend to center on intensely conformist modes; in that sense they are cultic, clannish. Legitimacy tends to revolve around what the group says: "What we want is what you want."

But there is a catch: What the group wants is often, even usually, decided by what the leader of the group wants. Since group members are other-directed, a strong other (leader) usually and easily dominates the group. Specifically, the magical and mythic stages tend to be dominated by patriarchal and authoritarian overtones. In addition to the structural reasons, there are psychodynamic causes for this: The cognitive transition from magic to mythic modes generally occurs around ages five to seven, or, as Freud would have it, during the Oedipal phase, and that means that both magic and mythic modes tend to be dominated by a patriarchal authority figure. We can say that legitimacy at these levels tends to be conferred in the group but via a permanent authority figure, and that figure—almost always patriarchal—I call the "totem master."

"Totem" emphasizes the magical-mythical connotations given to this father figure, and "master" emphasizes the extraordinary power of validation rested in this individual (expressly for psychodynamic reasons). Thus, Jim Jones was the totem master or temporal father of his entire community. He was not representative of the "eternal self" of each individual, as is an authentic guru. Rather, he was viewed as the temporal and even biological father of the group—a belief supported by apparently bizarre sexual fertility (magical) rituals. When a member of the seminar exclaimed, after hearing the Psychosynthesis interviews, "Thank God for the incest taboo" (see endnote 9), he must have had exactly that worry in mind—the group was one jot away from being "sexually fathered" by the "leader," the totem master, the temporal father of the entire group. Not "Our Father who art in heaven," but "our father who art next door." Regardless of actual sexual practices (they are rare), the totem master is viewed as somehow being the temporal father of the entire group, literally or figuratively. He is totemically "in" the group and the group is "in" him. I think it no accident that Jones, and others are often referred to as "father" (not meaning priest), and that more than one totem master has found Fuhrer and Vater synonymous.

So the general pattern of especially problematic groups seems to be a pre-rational cult-clan headed by a totem master. However much the specifics vary—and they vary immensely—I believe that is the single simplest generalization that can adequately summarize the especially problematic aspects of the new religions.

A CORROBORATIVE SCHEME

I would like very briefly to mention how the empirical categories in the new religions typology of Dick Anthony tangentially support the criteria that I have suggested here. Anthony's categories define three (non-developmental) dimensions: (1) charismatic/technical, (2) unilevel/multilevel, and (3) monism/dualism.[11]

The monism/dualism dimension refers to whether a group believes that all individuals are ultimately one with Godhead, or whether only a select "in-group" can achieve exalted status. Unilevel religion tends to look at the manifest or *presently* available level (usually material) as the arena of salvation, whereas multilevel religion tends to see liberation as occurring in actual transformation to a transcendental realm. Charismatic religion tends to center on the personality of the group leader, whereas technical religion tends to center on certain impersonal techniques and practices (or traditions). These three bipolar dimensions form a typology of eight cells (see diagrams in Part 1).

Anthony has found that correlations exist between individual cells and problematic movements. Negative or problematic groups tended to be unilevel, while positive groups tended to be multilevel. Further, charismatic groups tended to be more problematic than technical groups. Finally, dualistic groups tended to be more problematic than monistic groups.

What I am suggesting is that the developmental-structural criteria outlined earlier form the implicit substructure of the categories in the Anthony typology, and thus the conclusions regarding groups that seemed problematic are not arbitrary but rather are grounded in the inherent structure of development itself. Thus:

Dualistic groups tend to be more problematic than monistic groups because they foster the pseudo-structural notion that only some people are qualified for (or can evolve to) the highest estate. This leads to an extreme emphasis on the in-group vs. the out-group, the sheep vs. the goats, which itself invites pre-rational regression to exclusively conformist needs. Monistic religions, on the other hand, acknowledge temporary differences in development, but emphasize potential equality or unity in divine essence—a drastically different (developmental) stance.

Unilevel religions tend to be more problematic than multilevel because they disregard vertical growth and development (*i.e.*, authenticity), and instead pitch their salutary desires forward in an everlasting horizontal or temporal fashion, attempting thereby to secure in time that which can only be conferred by timeless eternity. Because unilevel religions deny necessary vertical development or growth, they are always open to reinterpreting their own level of structural adaptation, however mediocre, as *the* highest level (as long as one merely adopts its legitimacy criteria), and this level—should it be magical or mythical—then acts as a seed crystal of regression, not transcendence. Multilevel religion, on the other hand, *is* multilevel because it refuses to equate the present level with the ultimate level, and thereby holds open the possibility, indeed the necessity, of higher growth and development.

Charismatic religion generally tends to be more problematic than technical (or traditional) religion because it necessarily relies on the authority of a sole person. Should this person prove to be less than a Christ, Buddha, or Krishna—and guess how often that happens—then charismatic religions degenerate into sole authority and isolated legitimacy—with all the problems therein. Technical religion, on the other hand, takes as ballast either an impersonal technique or an historical tradition, thereby counterbalancing the possibly idiosyncratic whims of any potentially totem master.

Of course there are exceptions; for example, in multilevel charismatic groups a fully enlightened master is appropriately the focus of disciples' devotion and meditation. It is the unilevel charismatic groups that give rise to perhaps the most severe problems because, while resting *legitimacy* on a sole person, they deny *authentic* development.

Anthony's scheme is very detailed, and I do not wish to slur over these important distinctions; but our general points remain unchanged by them.

THE NON-PROBLEMATIC GROUP

Given the above criteria of "bad" religious movements, can we state any criteria, however nebulous, for "good" religious movements? I believe we can; if nothing else, we can state the converse of the above. But more specifically, we can say much in terms of general guidelines.

According to Anthony, for instance, we can *probably* point to monistic, multilevel, technical religions as being the most likely to foster vertical development non-problematically. Or, more realistically, we can empirically recommend combinations of any two of those three categories: if the movement is charismatic, hope it is monistic and multilevel; if dualistic, hope it is technical and multilevel. In terms of developmental-structural criteria, however, we can suggest the following. A positive, authentic group will likely:

1. *Be transrational, not pre-rational:* Specifically, it will utilize teachings and disciplines that engage psychic, subtle, and/or causal levels of structural adaptation. I have outlined the nature of these levels and their respective disciplines elsewhere (see endnote 2). Suffice it to say here that these disciplines generally involve sustained practice, concentration, and will; they explicitly rest on a moral foundation, which usually includes appropriate dietary and sexual regulations; and they are at least as difficult to master significantly as is, say, a rigorous doctorate.

Most orthodox sociologists, unfortunately, seem intent upon seeing the new religions as nothing but a search for a new legitimacy prompted by the breakdown of traditional or civil religion, and fail to consider that some of the new religions—the expressly transrational ones—are also in search of a higher authenticity, an authenticity never offered by the old religions (see endnote 4). Civil religion never offered authentic, mystical, transcendental, superconscient experience; it offered, at best, a sturdy legitimacy. Some of the new religions are explicitly and structurally in search of that authentic, not merely legitimate, dimension: for example, Zen, Vedanta, Raja yoga, Vajrayana.

On the other hand, these authentic disciplines ought not be confused with the plethora of "pop mystical" movements. The laid-back, blissed-out, Marin County high is exactly what these authentic disciplines are not; the beat Zen, *Dharma* bum, go with the here/now—that, too, is exactly what these disciplines are not. In fact, virtually all of such "beat Zen" approaches are based on the pre/trans fallacy (see endnote 3). As the book, *Serial,* a parody of "laid-back" Marin County life, so whimsically put it, "Everybody knew, in these days of heightened consciousness, that the rational mind was a screw-up; the really authentic thing to do was to act on your impulses." That, of course, is exactly the pre-rational mood that has so distorted the current Western view of mystical and Eastern teachings, and, alas, that pre-rational approach is behind perhaps half of humanistic, transpersonal, and human potential movements—not to mention the new religions so dubiously allied with them. Even worse, this pop mysticism, all-is-one, beat Zen attitude has been used by more than one religious cult to rationalize their monstrosities. ("Since all is one," said Charles Manson, "nothing is wrong.")

2. *Anchor legitimacy in a tradition:* I have already explained this factor. The point is simply that a religious movement tends to be less problematic if it rests its legitimacy in a long line of previous teachers and teachings. Otherwise, the individual teacher becomes the sole source of legitimizing power. Since individuals must have legitimacy (on whatever level of structural adaptation they presently exist), they will do or be whatever the legitimizing authority says—an invitation to problematic occasions.

3. *Have a phase-specific authority:* It is common knowledge that virtually all authentic Eastern or mystical traditions maintain that the guru is representative of one's own highest nature, and once that nature is realized, the guru's formal authority and function is ended. The guru is guide, living exemplar, teacher, or physician, not king, president, or totem master.

Buyer beware, then, of any religious movement headed by a permanent authority. Or—it comes to the same thing—any authority that cannot, at least in principle, be replaced. Even Dalai Lamas and Popes can be replaced by their successors; but there was, and could be, no replacement for Jim Jones or Charles Manson—when they die, the movement ends or fizzles. Either a religious teacher is there to bring you up to his level of understanding—in which case his authority is phase-temporary—or he is there to keep you in your place, which by definition is somewhere below or under him. The list of disastrous cult leaders is a list of permanent "authorities," not replaceable and not phase-specific ones.

As for the relation between the "good" guru authority and his or her disciples, I have been a participant-observer in almost a dozen non-problematic new religious movements, Buddhist, Hindu, Taoist, Christian mystical. In none of those groups was I ever subjected to any harsh degree of authoritarian pressure. In fact, the authoritarian pressure in these groups never even equalled that which I experienced in graduate school. The masters in these groups were looked upon as great teachers, not big daddies, and their authority was always that of a concerned physician, not totem boss.

There is another way to state what a nonproblematic authority looks like. A positive group:

1. *Is NOT headed by a Perfect Master:* Perfection exists only in transcendental essence, not in manifest existence, and yet many devotees
consider their master "perfect" in all ways, the ultimate guru. This
is almost always a problematic sign, although it is rarely disastrous.
It is problematic for the devotee because, in confusing essence with
concrete existence, the devotee is invited to project his or her own
archaic, narcissistic, omnipotent fantasies onto the "perfect" guru.
All sorts of archaic and magical primary process cognitions are thus
reactivated: The guru can do anything; how great the guru is; in fact,
how great I must be to be among the chosen. It is an extremely narcissistic position.

   Of course, the guru eventually displays his or her human side,
but the devotee is devastated, disillusioned, crushed. The devotee
then either leaves because the guru can no longer support the devotee's narcissistic glamor or spends his time trying to rationalize the
guru's actions. "Drunk? The master got drunk? Well, you know, he
was just emphasizing the evils of intoxicants by example."

   A good master might indeed be fully enlightened and divine, but
he or she is also human. Even Christ was said to be one person (Jesus)
with two natures (human and divine). Further, the fact that a guru
has been thoroughly educated in soul and spirit does not mean he or
she has been thoroughly educated in body and mind. I have yet to
see a guru run a four-minute mile with his "perfect body" or explain
Einstein's special theory of relativity with his "perfect mind." The
Perfect Master cannot manifest worldly perfection until the humanity in which he or she is grounded—until, indeed, all manifestation—
has evolved to its own highest and perfect estate. Until that time,
perfection lies only in conscious transcendence, not in concrete manifestation, so beware the concretely "perfect" master.

   There is a corollary to this: A positive group:

2. *Is NOT out to save the world:* A very high percentage of those in
problematic groups initially enter with apparently very altruistic and
idealistic impulses, a desire to help people, to better the world. But
that "idealism" actually has a structure very similar to that of the
"perfect master"—archaic and narcissistic. The underlying impulse
is, "I and the group are going to change the world," emphasis on "I."
Further, its narcissistic core is evidenced in the arrogance of the
stance itself: "We have the only way, and we will change the world,
by imposing our ideas on the poor ignorant folks out there." Now,
they may not state it that way (I put it rather harshly) but they must

in fact more or less feel that way—how can you possibly presume to help someone, especially without being asked, unless you assume they are in need of help (*i.e.*, inferior) and you are capable of providing it?

This narcissistic "altruism" usually shows up in a missionary zeal and proselytizing fury that no amount of high-sounding "idealism" can disguise. Such obsessive drivenness is always open to problematic occasions, not the least of which is that if you have *the* way, then that end will justify virtually any means, up to and including holy war. And holy war, in this sensibility, is not a sin, it is not murder, because the people you are killing in order to save are not really people—they are infidels.

On a smaller scale, in new religious groups the psychological dynamic is the same, if toned down. But any group "out to save the world" is potentially problematic, because it rests on an archaically narcissistic base which looks "altruistic" or "idealistic" but in fact is very egocentric, very primitive, and very capable of coming to primitive ends by primitive means.

Notes

1. In William Barrett, ed., *Zen Buddhism: Selected Writings of D. T. Suzuki* (Garden City, NY: Anchor, 1956).
2. Ken Wilber, *The Atman Project* (Wheaton: Quest, 1980).
   ———, *Up From Eden* (New York: Doubleday/Anchor, 1981).
   ———, *Eye to Eye* (New York: Doubleday/Anchor, 1983).
   ———, *A Sociable God* (New York: McGraw-Hill, 1983).
3. Ken Wilber, "The Pre/Trans Fallacy," *ReVision*, vol. 3, no. 2, 1980; reprinted in *Eye to Eye*.
4. Ken Wilber, *A Sociable God (New York: McGraw-Hill, 1982).*
5. Center for the Study of New Religious Movements seminar series, 1980–1981; transcript, May 7, 1981.
6. Bellah first defined his notion of civil religion in his article, "Civil Religion in America," *Daedalus*, Winter 1967; reprinted in Robert N. Bellah, *Beyond Belief: Essays on Religion in a Post-Traditional World* (New York: Harper and Row, 1970). Later, in *The Broken Covenant* (New York: Seabury, 1975), Bellah argued that contemporary civil religion is an "empty and broken shell." In his last chapter of that work (Chapter VI: "The Birth of New American Myths," 139–163) and in his essay, "New Religious Consciousness and the Crisis in Modernity," in Charles Y. Glock and Robert N. Bellah, (eds.), *The New Religious Consciousness* (Berkeley: University of California, 1976), Bellah spelled out the impli-

cations of the decline in civil religion for the growth in popularity of the new religions. The view that the decline of civil religion has provided the motivating context for the current popularity of the new religions has been elaborated further by various scholars: cf. Steven M. Tipton, *Getting Saved From the Sixties: Moral Meaning in Conversion and Cultural Change* (Berkeley: University of California, 1982); Thomas Robbins and Dick Anthony, eds., *In Gods We Trust: New Patterns of Religious Pluralism in America* (New Brunswick, NJ: Transaction, 1981); Dick Anthony and Thomas Robbins, "Spiritual Innovation and the Crisis of American Civil Religion," *Daedalus*, Winter 1982.

7. Ken Wilber, "Eye to Eye," *ReVision*, vol. 2, no. 1, 1974; reprinted in *Eye to Eye*.

8. The Introduction to this volume describes the seminar series.

9. Center for the Study of New Religious Movements transcript, February 12, 1981.

10. Cf. H. Gruber and J. Voneche, eds., *The Essential Piaget* (New York: Basic, 1977); L. Kohlberg, *The Philosophy of Moral Development* (San Francisco: Harper and Row, 1981); and C. Gilligan, *In A Different Voice* (Cambridge, MA: Harvard University Press, 1982).

11. See Part 1 of this volume for a full explication of the Anthony typology. The summary here is highly simplified and represents my own understanding of the typology categories.

EDITORIAL COMMENTARY

Ken Wilber's framework for assessing mystical-spiritual involvements has strong correspondences with the Anthony typology. Anthony and Wilber recognized the implicit convergence of their projects when they became familiar with each other's work during the middle 1970s, and since that time they have frequently consulted with each other. More recently they have been working on various collaborative projects, of which *Spiritual Choices* is the first to be presented to the public.[1] The implicit convergence of Wilber's framework with the Anthony typology has been taken for granted within the editorial perspective of this volume; in this commentary we will sketch the major areas of agreement as well as possible divergences and the questions that they raise.

Wilber's view of groups is based on his three major stages of human development: pre-rational, rational, and transrational. The table indicates how these three categories correspond to those of Anthony's typology, and also to the categories of an earlier framework developed by Anthony in collaboration with the sociologist Thomas Robbins.[2] In that frame-

CORRESPONDENCES OF ASSESSMENT SCHEMES FOR CONSCIOUSNESS GROUPS

Wilber	Robbins & Anthony	Anthony Typology
Pre-rational	Disintegrative	Unilevel charismatic
Rational	Integrative	Unilevel technical
Transrational	Transformative	Multilevel

work, Robbins and Anthony attempted to assess the impact of the contemporary upsurge of new religious movements upon the structural integrity of the larger society. They found that this impact was complex and had been categorized as either disintegrative, integrative, or transformative by various commentators, depending upon whether they thought the new religions were helping to make society fall apart, stay the same, or move closer to the ideal. Robbins and Anthony also found that new religions could be classified into these three categories. The scheme of disintegrative, integrative, or transformative consequences of different types of groups was later elaborated by Anthony and various collaborators into the eight-cell typology presented in this book. The link of the Anthony typology to Wilber's three-fold scheme of pre-rational, rational, and transrational stages becomes obvious when the relationship of the Anthony typology to the earlier scheme of Robbins and Anthony is taken into account.[3] Contemporary Western society is—as the sociologist Max Weber noted—primarily structured according to the tenets of instrumental rationality. Religious movements are integrative, then (i.e., they enhance people's adjustment to the existing social order), to the extent that they embody such "rationality." For all intents and purposes, then, Robbins and Anthony's "integrative" movements are equivalent to Wilber's "rational" movements. In addition, Wilber's term "pre-rational" corresponds to Robbins and Anthony's term "disintegrative" and the meaning of "transformative" is essentially the same in both frameworks. Therefore, the threefold scheme of Robbins and Anthony is essentially equivalent to the threefold scheme of Wilber with respect to its articulation of the consequences of involvement in different types of movement. Since the Anthony typology preserves the Robbins and Anthony scheme (as implicit, dependent variables, with the new, explicit dimensions as independent variables), it is not surprising that the typology and Wilber's scheme tend to agree regarding the effects of particular religious or consciousness movements.

Wilber's stage of rationality corresponds to groups that are "integrative" because, obviously enough, rationality is the working basis of contemporary culture and is a necessary (though perhaps not sufficient) condition for a group to be regarded by the culture as legitimate. Anthony's sociocultural view adds another dimension to what rationality connotes here: In rational culture, the precise calculability of the world is a key motif. Discursive reason provides a way of maximizing calculability and so makes broadly available a practical mastery of the world, without which individualism could not flourish. Rationality and individualism are closely linked as cultural trends. One could argue that in present-day American culture, rationality functions essentially as a means of systematic self-interest that supports hyper-individualism and utilitarianism. Practices such as meditation, when used to optimize personal efficacy in rational-individualist-utilitarian culture, are serving not a mystical but a rational, integrative function. In general, mystical teachings can be used to contribute to personal efficacy and to the mundane calculability of the world, and this is just the slant given them in groups that Anthony classifies as unilevel technical, as indicated in the table. The tendency to co-opt mysticism in this way reflects the predominant cultural bias toward utilitarian rationality.[4]

Pre-rational groups are those which repudiate rationality and hence are disintegrative with respect to society at large. These are the unilevel charismatic groups, in Anthony's terms. They react against rationality by asserting a primitive emotionality as their key value motif, which actually intensifies conflicts and polarities rather than resolving them, and promotes narcissism, impulsive acting-out, and the roller-coaster of so-called borderline character problems in monistic groups, and authoritarian submission in dualistic groups.

Transrational or multilevel groups retain rationality even while pursuing transcendence. Whereas rationality in itself breeds a separative state of hyper-individualism and isolation, transrationality involves experience of connectedness and participation in a holy unity of beings. Wilber defines the attainment of transrationality in terms of the profound transformations of consciousness described by the mystics. Anthony includes also the case of ordinary physical consciousness when it is imbued with a felt sense of relationship to ultimate being and is accompanied by the constellation of attitudes he terms multilevel.

In his article, Wilber discusses the predictive agreement between his and Anthony's frameworks and gives his interpretation of why the two schemes concur. Wilber sees his developmental-structural concepts as being the hidden variables, as it were, within Anthony's non-developmental system of classification. He interprets the agreement of his intrapsychic model with Anthony's sociocultural analysis as corroborating his scheme of individual development.

Anthony agrees with a threefold description of human consciousness along lines corresponding to Wilber's pre-rational, rational, and transrational categories, but he does not see these categories as separate structural stages that trace out a linear sequence of development. In Anthony's view world cultures are cyclically reimbued with living faith and experiential relatedness to spiritual ultimacy by the impact of an Avataric advent such as Zoroaster, Ram, Krishna, Buddha, Jesus, and Mohammed. After several centuries, this transrational, multilevel atmosphere is gradually lost as culture increasingly rationalizes its spiritual orientation. This process of cultural rationalization, which was identified and studied by Max Weber,[5] has its own kind of flowering, but nevertheless takes the cultural climate further and further from sacred resonance and eventually produces a condition of extreme materialism, as we now experience. (Weber's analysis is widely accepted among sociologists, theologians, historians, and anthropologists.)

Thus, from Anthony's viewpoint, contemporary univocal, rationalized culture has degenerated from an earlier multilevel condition, whereas Wilber sees contemporary culture as an advance over previous eras. Wilber does not see such cultural development as rigidly linear but does adopt a developmental evolutionary stance in a normative, critical fashion. Anthony's and Wilber's differences on this central issue are the subject of a separate volume.[6]

Interestingly, Wilber derives his key problematic factors—the engagement of pre-rationality, isolated legitimacy, and dysfunctional authority—from his developmental model, yet they all retain their significance as major indicators of trouble in groups when viewed from Anthony's perspective on development. That is, Wilber's problematic factors are also fully consistent with Anthony's picture of human development. (For example, Anthony accepts the "engagement of pre-rationality" as a criterion that is fully meaningful psychodynamically, but he questions its interpretation in terms of developmental-structural stages.) Since Wilber's assessment of groups is achieved on the basis of problematic factors that are consistent with Anthony's view of development, the predictive agreement of the two schemes does not in itself constitute corroboration of Wilber's developmental-structural model. Other tests of the underlying developmental process are necessary. However, the substantial agreement between these two schemes, despite being developed independently from very different sources, at least suggests that the possibility of a genuinely critical-normative analysis of religious engagements is not an idle hope.

Notes

1. Wilber functioned as a consultant for Anthony in shaping the seminar out of which this volume emerged. He made suggestions with respect to the composition of the seminar and, as the only member not in attendance (he was residing in Lincoln, Nebraska at the time), received transcripts of all meetings and frequently discussed the ongoing development of the seminar with Anthony. At the conclusion of the seminar, Anthony invited Wilber and Bruce Ecker to co-edit this volume.

2. Thomas L. Robbins and Dick Anthony, "New Religious Movements and the Social System: Integration, Transformation or Disintegration?," Annual Review of the Social Sciences of Religion, Vol. II, 1978.

3. The disintegrative, integrative, and transformative categories are implicit in the Anthony typology and refer to the consequences of different types of movements for the individual or for society. They thus constitute the dependent variables of the typology. On the other hand, the explicit dimensions of the typology (monism/dualism, unilevel/multilevel, technical/charismatic) refer to characteristics of a group's meaning system that we can, at least in principle, assess independently of their consequences. These explicit dimensions are assumed to account for, or in a sense cause, the consequences of involvement in a particular group and they thus constitute the independent variables of the typology.

4. The large-scale shift of values that occurred in the United States in the 1960s, from a culture of role and status to a culture of self and satisfaction, still leaves a highly rational culture. Of six themes that defined pre-1960s rational culture—consequentialism, the idea of progress, voluntarism/ autonomy/free will, utilitarian individualism, asceticism, and philosophical monism (or technical rationality)—only the last two have changed; asceticism, or the strategy of disciplined postponement of satisfaction to achieve success, has been replaced by the attitude that fun and leisure are beneficial; and technical rationality, or the view that a single, objective, unified body of rational explanations can describe the world, has been replaced by a relativistic, pragmatic rationality. Integrative or unilevel-technical groups take into account the collapse of the objectivist worldview and still find a way to be rational and motivate personal efficacy.

5. Max Weber, The Protestant Ethic and the Spirit of Capitalism (London: Unwin, 1930); and Sociology of Religion (London: Methuen, 1965).

6. Dick Anthony and Ken Wilber, Polarity Versus Progress: Alternative Images for the Process of Transformation; in preparation.

A Question of Balance:

Health and Pathology in New Religious Movements[1]

Frances Vaughan

The risk of a regrettable involvement in a spiritual group depends in large part on the prospective member's capacity for self-deception. Frances Vaughan's article provides ways of inquiring into oneself and into the group and leader one may be considering. A psychotherapist in private practice and professor of psychology at the California Institute of Transpersonal Psychology, Frances Vaughan, Ph.D., is a past president of the Association for Transpersonal Psychology, the author of *Awakening Intuition* (1979), and a co-editor of *Beyond Ego: Transpersonal Dimensions in Psychology* (1980). In the following paper she surveys a wide range of motives for joining a group, only some of which reflect genuine spiritual aspiration. The psychological effects of membership may surpass or fall short of the member's original motives, and Dr. Vaughan discusses these possible effects in terms of two basic types of ego attenuation, regressive and transcendent. To distinguish between these is a task which apparently eludes conventional ego psychology, especially as "the principles of healthy development beyond ego-identification may appear to be reversed relative to those of sound ego development."

The author reviews pathological group styles and structures, and in a section on "masters and mastery," provides practical points "to facilitate making the distinction between mastery at the ego level and mastery at authentically spiritual levels," or between genuine masters and their imitators. Vaughan then formulates a program of penetrating self-questioning for individuals considering involvement with a particular group or teacher.

Our society is currently in the midst of a cultural-spiritual crisis.[2] The decline of American civil religion—those traditional religious observances that combine Christianity with patriotism and social altruism[3]—and the failure of orthodox religious practices to provide genuine experiences of transcendence have created a climate of spiritual deprivation and an intensified search for transcendental answers. Today, it seems, popular demand is for experience rather than theology or dogma, and for the direct inner knowing of mystical states.[4]

While societal unrest and the disintegration of traditional institutions pose a serious threat to existing social structures, the popularity of spiritual groups offering a variety of pathways to transcendence calls for a new perspective on the part of observers attempting to formulate practical guidelines for healthy psychological and spiritual development throughout life. The challenge is to evaluate groups that claim to offer pathways to transcendence in terms that make sense to people who want to weigh the potential benefits of joining such groups against hazards of indoctrination, coercion, and authoritarian control.

Popular new religious movements in America include those groups that follow a particular personality, such as Meher Baba, Bhagwan Shree Rajneesh, or Reverend Moon; those that derive from Eastern disciplines, such as Zen, Vajrayana or Theravadin Buddhism; those that focus on esoteric teachings, such as those of Gurdjieff, Alice Bailey, or the Kabbalah; and those that are oriented toward personal growth and social change rather than explicitly religious training, such as The *est* training and Synanon.

Evidence of abusive authoritarianism has drawn public attention to such groups as the People's Temple and Synanon, but authoritarianism and abuses of power are certainly not unique to those groups. Cultic tyranny can issue from many sources. It may be a condition in the culture at large, where it is more difficult to identify (for example, scientism), and it may also occur in the behavior of individuals or group leaders unaffiliated with any of the new movements.

The problem of evaluating groups that combine psychology with religious idealism has plagued both psychologists and sociologists for over a decade. Certainly the growth of new religions must be viewed in the context of a broader challenge facing American society, and the breakdown of traditional institutions can be considered both as cause and effect in the proliferation of religious groups and spiritual psychotherapies (see endnote 3).

In addition to having popular appeal, many of these groups operate with a high degree of psychological sophistication, offering perspectives on human behavior that could be useful to social and behavioral scientists who are now beginning to consider spiritual growth as an integral aspect of healthy human development. Buddhism, for example, offers a variety of perspectives on consciousness and the mind. When Buddhism spread across Asia from India to Tibet, China, and Japan, it was absorbed by the culture of each area, so that specific indigenous practices evolved. Today we have many culturally transplanted forms of Buddhism in America.[5] Tibetan, Theravadin, and Zen Buddhism are popular sects, but each retains, to a large extent, the trappings of the culture from which it has been imported. A truly indigenous American Buddhism has yet to evolve; it may well be that Buddhism will be absorbed into this culture as a psychology rather than as a religion.[6]

The problem to consider here, however, is not the relative merit of alternative spiritual practices, but the psychological consequences of joining a group that purportedly offers spiritual self-realization. Freedom and autonomy are accorded value in terms of psychological health, but the thirst for spiritual nourishment apparently leads large numbers of individuals to surrender self-determination willingly in order to gain a sense of purpose in a world perceived to be meaningless. The desire to relieve suffering in ourselves and others can also be an incentive to relinquish autonomy and surrender to someone who is presumably better qualified to prescribe behavior for optimum well-being. While the psychological consequences of participating in a group are not necessarily contingent on motivation for joining, the variety of individual motives should not be overlooked.

MOTIVATION FOR JOINING GROUPS

Part of the motivation for joining a group may be either a temporary alliance for the purpose of satisfying felt needs and fulfilling idealistic aspirations, or a lifetime commitment that provides a viable alternative to the existential anxiety and alienation that seem to be inherent in a materialistic world-view. Indeed, the desire to be part of something larger than oneself seems to be intrinsic to healthy human development on the level of self-actualization,[7] the stage at which fulfillment of one's higher psychological potential is a felt priority. But spiritual seekers are not necessarily healthy self-actualizers. Those who are looking for someone to whom they can turn over responsibility for their lives are easy prey to idealistic as well as cynical manipulators of the human condition.[8]

Some spiritual groups actively recruit members, either on college campuses or in public places such as airports, where people who are feeling alienated, lonely, and lacking in some religious or philosophical support system may be susceptible to the attraction of belonging to a community of people who appear to share common values, a sense of purpose, and definitive answers to the perennial search for meaning. From a psychological perspective, motivation for joining spiritual groups may span a broad spectrum of needs. Individuals may join a group because they are unable to support themselves adequately; because they feel lonely and isolated and welcome the sense of belonging to a community; because they are looking for a teacher or substitute parent figure to mitigate the awesome uncertainties of existence;[9] because they are personally attracted to the leader or someone else in the group; because they feel empowered to be more effective in the world as a result of group support; because they genuinely want to make a contribution to the well-being of others; because they want to improve social conditions and relieve suffering; because they feel they are actualizing their potential and progressing along a path of spiritual development; or because of a desire to become spiritually enlightened and attain personal liberation from the conflicts of life.

The process of deciding to join a group, like many of life's major decisions, is likely to be subjective (either impulsive or intuitive) rather than objective (rational and analytical). The process seems more analogous to falling in love than to careful strategic planning. When intuition is well developed as a way of knowing, it can provide reliable guidance for decision-making.[10] For most people, however, reliability only develops after considerable training of intuitive awareness, and even then intuition should not, in my view, be considered a substitute for reason and discrimination. Wholeness implies balanced, appropriate use of all faculties.

Whatever motives or combination of motives predominate among spiritual seekers, groups should not be evaluated solely on the basis of whether or not they satisfy these demands. While the *legitimacy* of a particular religion may be determined by how well it meets the psychological needs of a given population, Wilber[11] has pointed out that its *authenticity* depends on the degree to which it actually facilitates transcendence. Almost any religious group can satisfy the desire to surrender to something larger than the separate self, but an authentic, viable belief system must also accommodate psychological needs for continuing integration and transcendence.

CRITERIA FOR EVALUATING SPIRITUAL GROUPS

From a transpersonal perspective, health and growth at each stage of development can be viewed as a matter of balance, as one self-identification is transcended and a new, more encompassing one is assumed. Some spiritual groups evidently enable people to grow and develop their potential in this manner, while others appear to be detrimental in that they support a regressive tendency to relinquish awareness and responsibility in favor of unquestioning obedience to a charismatic leader or dogmatically enforced world-view. Reductionist approaches to the study of new religious movements add to the confusion by failing to make the crucial distinction between regression to pre-rational states and the attainment of transrational qualities that contribute to authentic transpersonal development. The common tendency to interpret transpersonal experience as pre-personal narcissism[12] is a key element in this confusion and leads to the mistaken assumption that all states not dominated by the rational-verbal ego are pathological and consequently detrimental. Transpersonal development may begin at any age, but it is growth beyond ego, not regression and not a substitute for the state of ego development.

Ken Wilber suggests that since society at large is currently undergoing significant transformations, it is incumbent upon social scientists to determine the direction of these transformations (see endnote 12). Is the search for ego-transcendence likely to devolve into pre-rational chaos? Do spiritual groups contribute to either or both of these possible directions? Clearly, no definitive answers can be given for all spiritual groups. Each group would have to be examined as a unique case.

In attempting to evaluate a particular group, it would be useful to determine whether participation in the group promotes pathological regression to pre-personal states or healthy, authentic transcendence of ego. Attempting to determine this from the standpoint of ego psychology is virtually impossible, since the assumptions of that school of thought preclude recognition of the transcendent. The task requires recognition of ego formation not as an end state but as an intermediate stage of evolutionary development. Even then, investigators are faced with differentiating transpersonal from pre-personal states in order to avoid pathologizing genuine transpersonal awareness or mistaking regressive ego loss for mystical experience.

Philosophy teacher Michael Washburn[13] has delineated specific distinctions between pre-personal and transpersonal states. In his view ego transcendence is characterized by: (1) integrated, articulate wholeness in contrast to undifferentiated oneness; (2) consciously cognized intuition in contrast to trance or passive, unconscious perception; (3) faith and grace in contrast to infantile dependence; (4) insight in contrast to undifferentiated perception; (5) spontaneity in contrast to reactivity and impulsiveness; (6) altruism in contrast to narcissism; and (7) purity of heart in contrast to ignorance. Ego development in this framework is viewed as a transition that inevitably involves both alienation and evolution of consciousness. It is at the ego level that conscious, effective action becomes possible.

The manner in which the group or its leader handles the loyalty or disloyalty of members is often very revealing of group pathology. Some leaders overtly threaten potential defectors with physical violence; others threaten ideological or eternal damnation. Others simply withhold love, approval, and recognition. Although we may judge some methods as more reprehensible than others, the effects seem similar. When loyalty is coerced, the person's integrity and sense of worth are undermined. Only when participation in group activities is clearly the result of free choice can it be expected to contribute to healthy self-esteem and development.

Discipline in some spiritual groups seems reminiscent of the familiar Puritan ethic that equates suffering with purification. The belief that if something hurts, it must be good for one, while pleasure must be bad, sustains earnest members' endurance of leaders' abuses. Also, puritanical self-condemnation can, like self-aggrandizement, be an indication of pathology on the spiritual path.

To the extent that social controls are exercised by manipulation of fear, guilt, or greed for power or bliss, a group may be regarded as pathogenic. To the extent that a group empowers individuals to accept, love, and forgive themselves and others, to appreciate both unity and diversity, and to be capable of detachment and self-transcendence, it may be expected to provide a healthy environment that fosters authentic spiritual growth.

SELF-CONCEPT, BOUNDARIES
AND STRUCTURE IN GROUPS

Underlying the teachings of every spiritual group are specific beliefs about the nature of the self. It might be assumed that a group which defines the self as loving and growth-oriented is likely to be less authoritarian than a group which defines human nature as evil and aggressive. Actually, inconsistencies abound. It is generally true, however, that individuals within a spiritual group tend to subscribe to the group belief or definition of the self. Joined together through this shared orientation, minds in a group seem to behave like a coherent living system that harbors certain attitudes—in many cases hostile—toward the larger social structure in which it exists. Spiritual groups, characteristically idealistic if not utopian, typically find fault with the culture at large, thereby legitimizing their more or less marked tendencies to separate from the larger whole.

An examination of the boundaries established by the group between itself and the surrounding society can provide an indication of tactics used by the group for control of members. Since healthy living systems engage in a continuous exchange with the environment, rigid boundaries coercively maintained can be an indication of pathogenic tendencies within the group. It could be argued that a group that isolates its members and discourages contact with non-members is potentially dangerous not only to the existing social structure, but more specifically to its own members. On the other hand, the freely chosen monastic life can be conducive to healthy transpersonal development at certain stages. When group members are humiliated and prevented from leaving the group by intimidation, however, it is evident that the emotional climate within the group is more likely to be fostering repression than healthy human development.

The self-sense of an individual who joins a spiritual group may become completely identified with the group. The structuring of knowledge, normally managed by the individual ego, can be taken over by a pathogenic group, just as it is preempted in totalitarian states for purposes of information control.[14] The structure of the group may reflect the developmental stage of the leader, or it may represent disowned, unconsciously projected aspects of the leader's psyche. The responsibility of individual members for pathogenic group behavior should not be overlooked, however. Attributing negative group characteristics to the leader alone can be misleading. The intrinsically dynamic nature of groups precludes a definitive analysis of separate parts as if they existed independently of each other. Assuming that the group has a leader, an evaluation of the group cannot be divorced, in my opinion, from an assessment of the leader's own level of development and an examination of the master-disciple relationship as practiced in the group.

MASTERS AND MASTERY

Mastery implies power in any field, but spiritual mastery has unique characteristics. Whereas mastery at the level of ego consists largely of self-determination and expertise, mastery at the level of transpersonal realization is a matter of integration and self-transcendence. "Masters of the world," says Sufi master Inayat Khan,[15] "are those who have mastered themselves, and mastery lies in control of the mind. If the mind becomes your obedient servant, the whole world is at your service."

In common usage the noun "master" generally refers either to a male having another person subject to his will, or to one who uses or controls at will that which is mastered. As a verb, to master means to subdue, to become adept at a particular skill, or to rule or direct. Whereas ego mastery implies superiority and control of the external world, spiritual mastery implies self-mastery and mastery of the mind. For example, this type of mastery may be developed through the practice of concentration meditation and the strengthening of the will, or by various types of insight meditation that aim at detachment from egoic mental productions. The power of penetrating insight is an aspect of mastery that becomes available when control of the mind has been attained.

Practicing consciousness disciplines that aim at control of the mind can also contribute to the development of psychic powers, those powers of the mind commonly called "extra-sensory." These tend to become available at transpersonal levels of development. However, the attainment of psychic powers does not ensure either ethics or spiritual understanding, and such powers may be abused by someone who has not yet transcended egoic identification. In many spiritual disciplines extra-sensory powers are considered by-products of spiritual work and are traditionally eschewed as traps that can lead a spiritual aspirant to ego entanglements in the domain of occult energies, or subtle realm. While healthy transpersonal development demands eventual transcendence of ego, the actual process of growth to higher, more subtle and complex levels of development does not necessarily ensure immediate transcendence of lower levels. In attempting to assess levels of mastery, then, the display of psychic powers by one who has mastered them should not be considered an indication of spiritual mastery. On the contrary, the use of such abilities in the service of ego goals, such as attracting or intimidating followers, should automatically be suspect. A spiritual master who has truly transcended ego could be expected to disdain the use of special powers for purposes of manipulation and control.

To facilitate making the distinction between mastery at the ego level and mastery at authentically spiritual levels, let us review some of the characteristics of each. At the ego level a person is said to be a master of destiny when he or she is self-determining, rather than being subject to control by others. In personal growth, self-determination is often equated with mental health. Clients in psychotherapy improve as they learn to take responsibility for initiating change and designing their lives in accordance with a realistic appraisal of their potentials. Psychological health, however, is not just a function of increasing self-control, but rather a function of learning to maintain an appropriate, dynamic balance between effort and surrender, control and relaxation, assertiveness and receptivity.

In contrast, the principles of healthy development beyond ego-identification may appear to be reversed relative to those of sound ego development. Where self-determination, self-regulation, and appropriate self-concept were essential to developing a cohesive sense of ego-identity, attachment to an independent sense of self can impede progress at higher levels. For example, a display of psychic powers is considered hazardous to anyone using them for ego goals. Just as the spiritually enlightened human being is said to be in the world but not of it, the powers of spiritual mastery are said to be in the master but not of him or her. This attitude can be a safeguard against the risk of ego inflation which transpersonal experience may stimulate, but does not necessarily preclude such risk. One may see oneself as a vehicle of spirit, or identified with spirit, but any personal claims to manipulation or control indicate egoic attachment rather than authentic transpersonal mastery.

The transcendence of ego goals and desires is manifested in the quality of non-attachment. For example, the path of the warrior as described by Don Juan to Carlos Castaneda,[16] demands that everything in life be perceived as a challenge rather than as blessing or misfortune. The warrior chooses to act in the world *as if* actions mattered, despite perceiving their lack of absolute meaning. A warrior's actions are called "controlled folly," and the warrior has no personal stake in their outcome. Ego attachment to power becomes an obstacle to further development, as does attachment to recognition, success, or any form of personal achievement. In traditions where the master is also a trickster (Gurdjieff, Don Juan), invisibility rather than fame is considered a desirable attribute. The person who wishes to advance on the path of spiritual development is invariably instructed to practice detachment, for to be attached to mastery is to be ruled by that which one seeks to master. According to the teachings of the ancient Chinese sage, Lao Tsu,[17] a master's leadership based on love and respect is better than leadership based on fear and coercion, but leadership is best when the people say, "We have done this ourselves."

Spiritual masters can use everything as an opportunity for inner development. They do not assign credit or blame, either to themselves or others. Authentic spiritual masters, unlike the mass leader who seeks an appearance of infallibility and cannot admit error,[18] are not concerned with winning or losing. They have already won. There is nowhere to go because they have already arrived. By contrast, a leader whose mastery is only at the ego level may actively seek disciples in large numbers. In master/slave relationships that develop at this level, the master is apt to become the slave of his own passions. Genuine spiritual masters, on the other hand, do not hold power as if it belonged to them personally. They know that they do not own (in the egoic sense) the wisdom and power manifested through them.

In the Buddhist tradition the spiritual master knows himself to be nothing. This realization of no-self, the recognition of the illusory nature of ego identifications, is the basis of liberation. The Buddhist practice of mindfulness meditation, which trains awareness of the body, of feelings, of consciousness and truth, is described as a path of spiritual purification for the seeker. Qualities cultivated in the practice of mindfulness meditation are investigation, energy, rapture, generosity, renunciation, patience, loving-kindness, truthfulness, calm, concentration, and equanimity. A master of this discipline is expected to manifest these qualities, being totally free of "defilements" and negative emotions.[19]

Similarly, the Christian mystical teaching of A Course in Miracles[20] describes "teachers of God" as manifesting the following characteristics: trust (in the power that is in them but not of them), honesty, tolerance, gentleness, joy, defenselessness, generosity, patience, faithfulness, and open-mindedness. Attributes such as love, perfection, knowledge and eternal truth are not on the list because they are held to be inherent in everyone. The task of the teacher in this system is to remove the obstacles to this realization. Mastery in this context would be defined as corrected perception.

The paradox is that spiritual mastery is attained through surrender of ego. Ego-motivated striving, therefore, is counterproductive, and the person who would attain mastery must be willing to renounce even the desire for mastery. The Third Zen Patriarch says, " ... even to be attached to the idea of enlightenment is to go astray ... [W]hen thought is in bondage the truth is hidden."[21]

Although different meditation practices lead to different levels of consciousness, many aim at mastery of the mind and evidently culminate in the awakened state of unchanging awareness of reality as it is, as distinct from transient flashes of insight. When flashes of insight have been stabilized into the abiding light of the awakened state, spiritual mastery has been attained. There are many different approaches to this goal,[22] and every mystical tradition has its own name for the awakened state, but all describe the diffusion of the effects of spiritual practice into waking, dreaming, and sleeping states. Moreover, what requires arduous effort at the outset becomes effortless as the seeker learns to maintain awareness in the midst of other activities. Since an awakened being transcends cultural origins, the enlightened master can be recognized by a person of any faith who has developed the capacity for such perception.

Despite these distinct characteristics of spiritual mastery as defined in religious traditions, it is difficult for the untrained observer to distinguish a genuine spiritual master from a fraudulent one. Of course, anyone wishing to develop the necessary discernment through spiritual practice is free to do so, but the novice who has no training in this area cannot be expected to make accurate evaluations of spiritual mastery, much as anyone who is not trained in science cannot adequately evaluate a scientific experiment.

CHOOSING A TEACHER

Nevertheless, in the absence of trained observation, we are called on to make subjective evaluations in choosing a spiritual teacher. Ram Dass[23] has observed that the best protection against being misled on the spiritual path by false teachers is the purity of the seeking. Unfortunately, good intentions do not preclude gullibility. Furthermore, it may well be that our spiritual seeking is motivated by the range of desires described earlier, so that "pure" and "impure" motives are interlaced and operating at once. Self-awareness, therefore, is a valuable asset to the seeker who wants to avoid the pitfalls of spiritual tyranny.

In order to choose a teacher or group with some degree of self-awareness, one could begin by asking oneself some questions. In considering involvement with a self-proclaimed master, for example, one might ask: What attracts me to this person? Am I attracted to his or her power, showmanship, cleverness, achievements, glamour, ideas? Am I motivated by fear or love? Is my response primarily physical excitement, emotional activation, intellectual stimulation, or intuitive resonance? What would persuade me to trust him/her (or anyone) more than myself? Am I looking for a parent figure to relieve me of the responsibility for my life? Am I looking for a group where I feel I can belong and be taken care of in return for doing what I am told? What am I giving up? Am I moving towards something I am drawn to, or am I running away from my life as it is?

Regarding the master, one might reflect on whether his or her presence conveys a feeling of inner peace. The presence of a spiritual master is said to have a soothing and healing effect on others without any intentional manipulation on the part of the master. On the other hand, a charismatic leader who is not a genuine spiritual master can have a hypnotic effect on a group, so as to induce a sense of peace and well-being by intentional manipulation. A particular seeker may or may not be sensitive to the difference. Furthermore, if one is absorbed in a subjective state such as anxiety or despair, the presence of a true master could go unnoticed. Being in the presence of a master might actually be anxiety-provoking to someone experiencing conflict about surrendering to a spiritual relationship or discipline. Whatever form egoic resistance may take, as long as an individual is afraid or unwilling to be honest with oneself and look directly at the truth of one's own make-up and beliefs about reality, it is not possible to perceive another clearly, particularly someone who has attained more advanced levels of development. When a particular leader appears to agree with personal biases and preconceptions, one may be willing to trust him or her without asking any questions. It is easy to question apparently irrational, funny or bizarre beliefs of others, but one's own are usually assumed to be true.[24]

Finally, another important question to ask regarding a purported master is: Does the master manifest compassion, generosity, loving kindness, honesty, calm, and open-mindedness? These questions will not provide definitive guidelines for action, but they can provide a basis of self-awareness and thereby reduce the likelihood of making regrettable choices. Just as parents cannot prevent sons or daughters from falling in love with partners of whom they do not approve, scholarly cautions based on research are not likely to be particularly effective in preventing fraudulent masters from gathering disciples. Individuals who leave groups after being disillusioned characteristically claim that they originally joined with pure intentions, wanting to ally with others for the purpose of making a positive contribution to society. It appears that neither self-awareness nor good intentions are sufficient to prevent errors in judgment. The purity of the seeking, then, may provide some protection, but it may also contribute to naïve, unquestioning acceptance of corrupt leadership.

In addition to questions pertaining to self-awareness, anyone who is considering joining a group might be advised to consider the following:[25] Does the group keep secrets about its organization and the leader? How do members of the group respond to embarrassing questions? (For example, does the leader have a Swiss bank account or indulge in sexual relations with group members?) Do members display stereotypic behavior that emulates the leader? Does the group have a party line that does not permit members to express how they really feel? Do members see themselves as having found the only true way? Are members free to leave? Are members asked to violate personal ethics to prove their loyalty? Does the group's public image misrepresent its true nature? Are humor and irreverence permitted?

In many instances recovery from disillusionment with a fraudulent master or pathogenic group is marked by the decision to trust oneself more than powerful leader figures. Denouncing shortcomings and maintaining a noncommittal stance can serve to prevent problematic involvements, but can also stall spiritual development and obscure feelings of vulnerability to deception in an area where we are inadequately trained to make informed judgments. Just as a fearful parent might try to dissuade a child from risking intimacy and thereby cripple the child's emotional development, excessive skepticism can stifle healthy spiritual development. Of course reasonable caution and investigation of group practices certainly are appropriate for anyone considering joining. Yet, if one is capable of taking the warrior stance (see endnote 16) and accepting all experiences in life as challenges, then even a difficult experience in a group can contribute to wisdom and maturity. Many persons who have joined a spiritual group and then left have reported feeling the experience was valuable despite considerable hardship. When an individual leaves a group, an empowering sense of having met the challenge of the experience may be gained in its retelling. This process has been described as a task of psychological growth through restoration of integrity.[26]

CONCLUSION

Current interest in new religious movements points not only to the dearth of spiritual nourishment in the culture at large, but also to the universality of religious impulses and the desire for genuine transcendence. The vacuum created by the decline of traditional American civil religion is being filled by both exploitative charlatans at one extreme and true spiritual masters at the other. Social scientists can best view the new movements as participant observers, with awareness that observations invariably reflect the level of inquiry. While we are working on expanding our perceptual framework, it behooves us to be aware of the limitations of our ability to pass judgment on teachers and teachings we have not been trained to evaluate.

Despite these limitations, we must somehow learn to discriminate between genuine and counterfeit spiritual teachers. In doing so we can bear in mind that transpersonal development beyond the conventional ego-identity is never a justification for the violation of basic human rights or individual dignity. In genuine transcendence the intrinsic value of individuality is affirmed and integrated in a larger context.

In attempting to evaluate spiritual groups, individuals must honestly consider their personal limitations. We must be willing to free our own minds from dishonesty and self-deception if we are to do more than cling to uninformed opinions. In certain instances it may seem appropriate to suspend judgment about a group when different individuals report different reactions to participation. Certainly individual differences make some groups appropriate for some people, and not others, at certain times. Some groups may be clearly detrimental to healthy human development, but many are ambiguous, and others apparently have contributed to healthy psychological and spiritual growth for at least some individuals who have made a commitment to participation.

Groups could be considered as being stage specific, insofar as any one group contributes to certain areas of development and not others. For example, one who has a highly developed intellect or logical-analytic function might choose to subject himself or herself to rigorous meditation discipline in order to achieve balance by developing contemplative awareness, which is not based on the intellect. On the other hand, the same form of practice might not be beneficial for someone who has failed to develop integrity at an ego level.

Most orthodox religious institutions in the West have failed to provide training in contemplation in any disciplined way. Yet healthy human development calls for a balanced integration of physical, emotional, mental, and spiritual aspects of well-being. The transpersonal dimension of human consciousness cannot be ignored, and there is no value-free stance. Continuing human development demands further investigation and exploration. Each of us must choose, despite our limitations, where to look for guidance in this domain.

In the final analysis, efforts at evaluation might best be guided by the words of Buddha:

> Do not believe in what you have heard; do not believe in traditions because they have been handed down for many generations; do not believe anything because it is rumored and spoken of by many; do not believe merely because the written statement of some old sage is produced; do not believe conjectures; do not believe merely in the authority of your teachers and elders. After observation and analysis, when it

agrees with reason and it is conducive to the good and benefit of one and all, then accept it and live up to it.[27]

Notes

1. This article has appeared in modified form in the *Journal of Humanistic Psychology*, Vol. 23, No. 3, 1983.

2. M. Ferguson, *The Aquarian Conspiracy* (Los Angeles: J. P. Tarcher, 1980).

3. D. Anthony and T. Robbins, *In Gods We Trust: New Patterns in American Religious Pluralism* (New Brunswick, NJ: Transaction, 1981).

4. J. Needleman, *The New Religions* (New York: Pocket Books, 1972).

5. R. Fields, *How the Swans Came to the Lake* (Boulder: Shambhala, 1981).

6. W. Anderson, *Open Secrets: A Western Guide to Tibetan Buddhism* (New York: Viking, 1979).

7. A. Maslow, *The Farther Reaches of Human Nature* (New York: Viking, 1971).

8. S. Keen, "Spiritual Tyranny," *Co-Evolution Quarterly*, Spring, 1974, 84–94.

9. E. Becker, *The Denial of Death* (New York: Macmillan, 1973).

10. F. Vaughan, *Awakening Intuition* (New York: Doubleday/Anchor, 1979).

11. K. Wilber, *A Sociable God* (New York: McGraw-Hill, 1983).

12. K. Wilber, "The pre/trans fallacy," *Journal of Humanistic Psychology*, 22 (2), Spring, 1982 (a).

13. M. Washburn, "The bimodal and tri-phasic structures of human experience," *ReVision*, 3 (2), Fall, 1980.

14. A. G. Greenwald, "The totalitarian ego," *American Psychologist*, 35 (7), July, 1980, 603–618.

15. Hazrat Inayat Khan, *Spiritual Dimensions of Psychology* (Lebanon Springs: Sufi Order Publications, 1981).

16. C. Castaneda, *The Teachings of Don Juan* (New York: Ballantine, 1968).

17. Lao Tsu, *The Way of Life*, translated by W. Brynner (New York: Perigee Books, 1980).

18. H. Arendt, *The Origins of Totalitarianism* (New York: Harcourt, Brace and World, 1966).

19. J. Goldstein, *The Experience of Insight* (Santa Cruz, CA: Unity Press, 1976).

20. Anonymous, *A Course in Miracles* (New York: Foundation for Inner Peace, 1975).

21. Third Zen Patriarch, Sengstan, *Hsin Hsin Ming: Verses on the Faith Mind,* translated by Richard Clark (Sharon Springs, Zen Center, New York: 1976).
22. D. Goleman, *The Varieties of Meditative Experience* (New York: Dutton, 1977).
23. Ram Dass, Personal communication, 1980.
24. T. Hersch, "The phenomenology of belief systems," *Journal of Humanistic Psychology,* 29 (2), Spring, 1980.
25. D. Goleman, "Early warning signs for the detection of spiritual blight," *Association for Transpersonal Psychology Newsletter,* Summer, 1981.
26. R. Lifton, *Thought Reform and the Psychology of Totalism* (New York: W. W. Norton, 1969).
27. Kalamas Sutra, cited in Boorstein, ed., *Transpersonal Psychotherapy* (Palo Alto, CA: Science and Behavior Books, 1981).

EDITORIAL COMMENTARY

Frances Vaughan's distinctions between healthy and pathological religious groups correspond well with Anthony's multilevel/unilevel distinction. It would be overly repetitious here to cite these numerous correspondences; instead, we will consider some less obvious but important points that are not addressed elsewhere in this volume.

In terms of the general types of spiritual master described in the Introduction, Vaughan's section on Masters and Mastery coaches the reader in distinguishing between masters who are still under the sway of their own egotism and highly advanced masters in whom self-interest is no longer a distorting factor. Obviously, awareness of this "great divide" in the levels of mastery is an important asset for the seeker, and in this regard Vaughan's discussion is most helpful. She points out, for example, that occult abilities and phenomena are in themselves no indication of spiritual realization.

She argues too that group members, as well as leaders, are responsible for pathological developments. This goes to the heart of the deprogramming/brainwashing controversy involving the more sharply authoritarian groups. The anti-cult movement maintains that members of ardent, unconventional, authoritarian religious groups have no pre-existing motives for joining, but are "captured" by cultist techniques that are so potent as to constitute brainwashing or mind control. Members therefore are not responsible for what they think, feel, and do during membership, since they are psychologically enslaved and incapable of critical reason. Coercive deprogramming is thereby justified as a necessary ther-

apeutic intervention desperately needed by the supposedly helpless converts. However, an extensive body of social scientific research has refuted
these anti-cult tenets and has shown that while the leader's and group's
influence can be quite strong, the individual member is not enslaved but
in effect allows his or her psychological seduction to occur.[1] For example,
studies document a large voluntary turnover in supposedly mind-con-
trolled groups, showing that members are not incapable of individual
judgment and initiative without outside intervention. In short, the bulk
of this research supports Frances Vaughan's point that individual members are co-responsible for participation in group pathology. Thus anything that enhances the psychological self-awareness of prospective
members should reduce their propensity for involvement in a pathological situation.

The qualities of genuine, non-exploitative masters that Vaughan
describes seem entirely valid to editors, but we are struck also by the fact
that a number of group leaders who evolved into dangerous, authoritarian tyrants seemed truly to have some of those special qualities in the
early years of their leadership—loving kindness, generosity, selflessness.
These leaders were extremely dangerous precisely because they did combine such an unlikely mix of extreme beneficence and extreme abusive-
ness within them. The beneficence was prominent first, attracted a large,
devoted following, and then gradually gave way to a "dark side" that
came increasingly into expression over ten or twenty years, impercepti-
bly turning heaven into hell for the followers. It is the test of time that
seems to reveal the true caliber of a spiritual leader or master, but it is
difficult to make practical use of this important point. One might be able
to document certain trends in the master's past; one might affiliate loosely
for an extended time to see any trends for oneself. It is an ancient tradition in the East that a prospective disciple is entitled to test the master
until there develops a deep conviction in the master's capacity to guide.

Notes

1. For extensive references to this research literature, see T. Robbins and S.
   Anthony, "Deprogramming, Brainwashing and the Medicalization of
   Deviant Religious Groups," *Social Problems* (Feb. 1982), 29, 283–297; and
   D. Anthony, "The Fact Pattern Behind the Deprogramming Controversy:
   an Analysis and an Alternative," *Review of Law and Social Change*
   (1980), 9, 73–90.

On Spiritual Authority:

Genuine and Counterfeit[1]

John Welwood

If authentic and inauthentic spiritual masters differ so greatly in their consciousnesses and their effects on followers, why is it so difficult to tell them apart? It is because, according to John Welwood, "the counterfeit and the genuine master both undermine the habitual patterns of self. Yet one does this in a way that creates bondage, while the other does it in a way that promotes liberation."

John Welwood, Ph.D., is a clinical psychologist in private practice and Director of the East/West Psychology Program at the California Institute of Integral Studies in San Francisco. He has taught at the University of Chicago, The University of California, Antioch University, and the California School of Professional Psychology. He is Associate Editor of the *Journal of Transpersonal Psychology*, author of many articles on transpersonal subjects, and editor of *The Meeting of the Ways: Explorations in East/West Psychology* (1979) and *Awakening the Heart: East/West Approaches to Psychotherapy and the Healing Relationship* (1983).

Welwood begins his article with a review of five major patterns of bondage used by pathological spiritual groups and leaders. He then notes that while such characterizations may help alert people to potential dangers, they nevertheless "fall short of clarifying the larger question of what constitutes genuine spiritual authority," to which he devotes the rest of the paper. As a practical focus for assessing spiritual authority, Welwood emphasizes the teacher-student relationship rather than the teacher's isolated behaviors. Welwood sees personal devotion to a master as a natural part of the process of "turning one's allegiance away from the tyranny of ego-centricity and toward the deeper source of wisdom in oneself, which the teacher exemplifies. . . ." He makes a sharp distinction between mindless *submission* and mindful *surrender*, defining submission as a condition of weakness that leads to enslavement, while surrender to genuine spiritual authority is a condition of strength that leads beyond egocentricity. The article concludes with a survey of criteria that can help in recognizing an authentic teacher.

Just as a goldsmith gets his gold
First testing by melting, cutting, and rubbing,
Sages accept my teachings after full examination
And not just out of devotion to me.—*Sakyamuni Buddha*

Counterfeiters exist because there is such a thing as real gold.—*Rumi*

The hunger for ultimate values increases in an era such as ours, marked by the decline of agreed-upon mores and meanings, as evidenced by the revival of interest in religion and spirituality during the past fifteen years in America. At the same time most Americans do not have a high level of spiritual sophistication and seem to prefer their religion simple. The intense search for ultimate values combined with a certain naïveté in matters spiritual has set the stage on which charlatans and false prophets have appeared, strutting and fretting, pouring out words full of sound and fury, but signifying very little. Ours is an age in which spiritual deceit and counterfeiting seem rampant. Yet within the contemporary religious revival one can also find spiritual masters who appear to be authentic, who represent genuine wisdom traditions that may contain important guidance for people in these troubled times.

However, in the wake of Jonestown, which enacted everyone's worst fears of what could happen when a self-styled religious leader gains control over the lives of his followers, there has been widespread debunking of all spiritual teachers who fall outside mainstream Judeo-Christian contexts, and a simplistic dismissal of their communities as mere "cults."[2] How then can we distinguish intelligently between false prophets and genuine spiritual masters, between misguided cults and wholesome spiritual communities?

CHARACTERISTICS OF SPIRITUAL
GROUP PATHOLOGY

From the interviews conducted in the Center for the Study of New Religious Movements[3] seminar, as well as from personal observations of spiritual seekers and communities over many years, I have assembled the following list of characteristics peculiar to groups with the greatest potential for pathological or destructive behavior. However, I would like to emphasize that any such criteria can never fully distinguish between healthy and unhealthy groups. We naïvely assume that a spiritual group should have transcended human failings and neuroses, but this is rarely the case. On the contrary, a spiritual community may uncover and work with basic neurosis (greed, envy, hatred, delusion, fear) more intensely than any secular community. And in the process, members of the group may take on some of the characteristics described below. Therefore, in the second part of this paper, I will propose an additional, complementary approach for distinguishing a genuine spiritual teacher: personal discernment, based on an awareness discipline. In short, the following criteria cannot be applied in any absolute way; it is more a question of how fully a given group manifests them.

1. *The leader has total power to validate or negate the self-worth of the devotees, and uses this power extensively:* The leader in such groups is a magnetic, charismatic person who exudes, in the words of psychiatrist Eric Hoffer, "boundless self-confidence. What counts is the arrogant gesture, the complete disregard of the opinion of others, the single-handed defiance of the world."[4] Something about this unflappable self-assertiveness appeals especially to those who lack self-esteem; the recruits of such cults seem to be primarily those with little faith in themselves. As Hoffer points out, "Faith in a holy cause is ... a substitute for lost faith in ourselves." So it seems that those especially lacking in self-confidence are attracted and mesmerized by the grandiose displays of the self-proclaimed cult leader. The false prophet and the true believer are made for each other. Through their mutual collusion, the leader gains power and control, while the followers gain not only reassurance and security from his approval, but also vicarious power through identification with him.

The cult leader seems to prey deliberately on the followers' sense of personal inadequacy in order to gain control over them. For example, meetings at the People's Temple often included degradation rituals where members' flaws and failings were paraded before the group and ridiculed in front of everyone. After thoroughly degrading a follower in this way, Jim Jones would often build the person back up, as one survivor of Jonestown describes:

> First you become nobody. They first tear you down and strip your mind, you don't know anything. And after that, whatever he do, then you have to thank him for what he did. And then you'd become totally dependent on him, because you don't have anything else yourself. Everything you had was bad. I mean, he said, "You will listen to me and I will instruct you of things that was good," and most people actually believed that ... He made everybody think like they was somebody.

Chuck Dederich of Synanon had a similar way of operating, according to one former member's description:

> You get a group of people around you, and you say to them, "I am very happy. My life is wonderful. I have done an enormous number of good things, and I love it. How are you? Now you ain't so good. Now who would you rather be, you or me?" Now we have just established that *you* feel lousy, *I* feel fantastic. So that you say, "You."

Dederich at first impressed this member with his "boundless self-confidence": "He was charismatic, he was funny, he was bright, he was involved, his instincts were unbelievable. And I really fell in love." In admitting he would rather be Dederich than himself, he gave Dederich power over him. Dederich then increased his control by telling the follower that he too was fantastic:

> And because Chuck Dederich said that I was fantastic, now it's wonderful. Because he said it, I believed it. And it changed my life, no question about it. And I would say to people, "Who would you rather be, you or me?" And they would say, "You." And I would think that was just fine.

In this way leaders such as Jones and Dederich take away the old (already crumbling) ego supports and replace them with their own affection and approval, which makes their followers feel important and special—"like you was somebody." The person's new identity is defined in terms of being a follower in the group. Instead of an adult, eye-to-eye relationship built on a respect for human dignity, the relations between cultic leader and follower are like parent and child. (The members of Jonestown even called Jones "Dad.") The more the followers give the leader power to validate the worth of their existence, the more he can "up the ante" and force them to do anything he wants in order to maintain his approval. As one ex-member put it:

> If you have that experience of love [from the leader], and then you're cut off from it, it's like being put in quarantine—there's a tremendous motivation to get back to it, tremendous desire to reconnect with that love. And you'll do anything to get back to that love. Because it makes you feel good and makes you feel like you're a good person.

2. *The group is held together by allegiance to a cause, a mission, an ideology:* Cultic groups often attract people by appealing to their altruistic ideals, their desire to do good, to be of value, even to save the world. The leader in such groups defines the cause and the ideology, while the followers repeat unquestioningly the beliefs handed down to them. Furthermore, the leader often maintains a favored position by claiming to have special access to God or to a source of wisdom or authority that is not accessible to the followers. This increases their dependence on the leader for "the Word," for telling them what to do and interpreting events for them. Since they must always go through their leader to determine what is true and real, their own intelligence further atrophies.

The ideology is treated with deadly seriousness, so that the members cannot stand back from it or have any humor about themselves or their leader. They are caught in what one ex-member called "an airtight world-view, an intellectual maze." Eric Hoffer (see endnote 4) describes this:

> All active mass movements strive ... to interpose a fact-proof screen between the faithful and the realities of the world. They do this by claiming that the ultimate and absolute truth is already embodied in their doctrine and that there is no truth or certitude outside it. The facts on which the true believer bases his conclusions must not be derived from his experience or observation but from holy writ ... It is startling to realize how much unbelief is necessary to make belief possible.

The effectiveness of such an ideology derives from its apparent certitude, not its meaning or its inherent truth. It must be the one and only "Truth." For a doctrine to have such absolute certitude, it must be "believed in" rather than understood or tested out. For in trying to understand it or test it out, a person would have to trust in the validity and meaning of his own experience; but insofar as the person joins the group out of low self-esteem to begin with, there is little or no inclination for him to appeal to the truth of his own experience.

Furthermore, any independent frame of reference is interpreted as heresy, disloyalty, or betrayal of the group's mission. There is a great deal of suspicion among the members, lest any of them betray the "Cause." Hoffer points out, "Strict orthodoxy is as much the result of mutual suspicion as of ardent faith." Despite the seeming solidarity of the group, spy networks may exist to report members who dissent from the leadership. The more of their own intelligence and autonomy that members have had to give up for the sake of their new identity, the more they resent and are threatened by independent thinking from other members, and so the more they become willing informers. As one ex-member described this,

> If you were in a group with me, I couldn't say to you, "Boy, that was really an awful meeting," because I couldn't be sure that you wouldn't call [the leader] as soon as you left and say, "Betty just said that was an awful meeting." And these were good friends. But you couldn't be sure, even between husbands and wives, that you wouldn't get turned in. That was a really important dynamic of control. For good friends, we did some terrible things to each other, I would say.

In a group where self-esteem depends on the Cause, doubt becomes a deadly sin.

And because allegiance to the Cause is based primarily on belief, as well as on emotional needs for belonging and approval, rather than on a genuine search for truth or a discipline of self-knowledge, the ideology can easily be used to justify morally questionable behavior. Eventually the Cause may take precedence over common decency or respect for human dignity.

3. *The leader keeps his followers in line by manipulating emotions of hope and fear:* The coin of the realm governed by the cultic leader is the promise. The leader promises his followers they will reach salvation or attain a special status above the rest of the world if they remain true to the Cause. This "carrot approach" often appeals to the greed, vanity, and impoverished self-esteem of the followers rather than to their basic intelligence or inherent sense of well-being. The Cause takes precedence over any appreciation or enjoyment of present experience, which is deferred in favor of future rewards. To insure that the flock stays in line, moreover, the cultic leader also uses the "stick method," intimidating members with threats of doom, ven-

geance, or damnation if they stray from the Cause. A "wall of terror" surrounds the group: If a member decides to leave, he may be threatened with persecution or death. A survivor of Jonestown describes this tactic of Jim Jones: "He'd say, if you leave the Temple, he had connections with the Mafia, he had connections with the CIA. He said, 'If you leave, forget it, 'cause they'll find you in a hole somewhere.'"

An ex-member of another group that became pathological observes:

> The "transpersonal carrot in the sky" was: this is the way to salvation. If you deviate in any way, you're going toward your evil part, you're making it bigger. So that became very frightening. And another thing that became frightening was that if you thought about leaving the group, you had to face the fact that in the system you'd be spiritually damned.

Absurd as these fears may seem, we must remember that cult members have already given up their autonomy and critical thinking for the sake of approval and belonging, and so become prey to having the leader control them through stirring up and channeling intense emotion. As Hoffer (see endnote 4) puts it:

> The estrangement from the self, which is a precondition for both plasticity and conversion, almost always proceeds in an atmosphere of intense passion. . . . Once the harmony with the self is upset . . . a man . . . hungers to combine with whatever comes within his reach. He cannot stand apart, poised and self-sufficient, but has to attach himself wholeheartedly to one side or another.

4. *"Groupthink" is used to knit followers together:* Like-mindedness within the group takes precedence over individual common sense and independent judgment. Members of the group are often discouraged from spending much time alone or with their families. Pair-bonding between couples may also be deliberately undermined to foster greater dependence on the leader, as happened at Synanon. The more that self-trust and self-confidence are broken down, the more the follower must look to others for his example. He models himself after what he considers to be the ideal group member, and imitates the actions, mannerisms, and thought of the leadership.

Moreover, the boundary between being inside and outside the group is very strictly drawn. Such a group may even maintain a notion of "absolute evil," defined in terms of the world outside its boundaries. Hoffer points out, "Usually the strength of a mass movement is proportionate to the vividness and tangibility of its devil."

5. *Cult leaders are often self-styled prophets who have not studied with great teachers or undergone lengthy training or discipline themselves:* Many of the world's great religious traditions have lines of spiritual transmission. A person's realization is tested by his teachers before he is allowed to represent himself as a master. This is especially true in all Buddhist lineages as well as in other Asian traditions. The process of testing and transmission serves as a kind of "quality control" to insure that a given teacher does not distort the teachings for his own personal gain. But many of the most dangerous cultic figures of our times have no such stabilizing context of tradition, lineage or transmission; they are self-proclaimed gurus who sway their followers through their charismatic talents. Other cult leaders spuriously claim transmission, more to inflate their image than to acknowledge genuine spiritual lineage.

SOME BASIC ASSUMPTIONS

Spelling out the characteristics of problematic groups is important in helping alert the public to causes of cultic fanaticism. However, such characterizations fall short of clarifying the larger question of what constitutes genuine spiritual authority. The methods and assumptions of social science are generally much more useful in analyzing what pathological groups do wrong than in telling us what sane spiritual communities may be doing right. In fact, Western psychology and sociology as a whole have been much more concerned with diagnosing sickness than in specifying health, and this is nowhere more true than in the realm of spiritual development, which has been viewed reductionistically by the social sciences. Insofar as the perspective of traditional social science attempts to be value-free, while limiting itself to purely rational, secular criteria, it has difficulty grasping the fundamental meaning and purpose of spiritual practices or religious ideas, much less prescribing guidelines for judging spiritual authority. At the very least, those who set out to study this issue should spell out their own assumptions and attitudes regarding spiritual endeavors. What follows are my own philosophical assumptions, which help me understand the role of genuine spiritual teachers in the world.

Simplifying greatly, there seem to be two major kinds of awareness available to human beings who have passed through the pre-egoic stages of development and have developed a relatively healthy sense of self. One of these is an open, awake, expansive kind of awareness through which we experience most fully our *being* level, and which allows us to feel the basic quality of our aliveness. Human consciousness, as described by Western phenomenonologists such as Sartre and Heidegger and Eastern traditions such as Buddhism, is characterized by a basic receptivity, openness, and "no-thingness" that allows us to let the world come into us and to appreciate the world for what it is.

Precisely because we are so open and sensitive, however, a counteracting tendency to contract, shut down, and defend ourselves against the unconditional openness of our basic awareness seems to arise as a protective defense. In this other basic mode of awareness, we try to defend and maintain a fixed, familiar identity, to achieve "some-thingness" by grasping onto anything that appears to support us. The chronic contraction involved in protecting and defending a fixed image of ourselves not only consumes a great deal of life energy, but also makes us habitually egocentric, with an attendant existential anxiety toward anything that threatens to negate us.[5,6]

The differences between these two qualities of human existence can be summarized as follows:

Egocentricity	*Being*
Concern with maintaining appearances	Concern with discovering truth
Concern with maintaining and validating a self-image	Interest in, appreciation of the world, independently of how it affirms or negates any self-images
Contraction around "I-ness"	Expansion outward toward life and the phenomenal world
Sense of insecurity and inadequacy	Basic sense of wholeness, well-being, aliveness, intelligence

All the great spiritual traditions have spoken of these two modes of awareness in different ways. However they are conceived, the purpose of spiritual practice is to overcome exclusive identification with one's separate self-fashioned identity—egocentricity—and to expand awareness to include and realize the deeper, larger qualities of one's being.

It is particularly difficult to judge the validity of a given spiritual community solely through secular social science criteria because conventional logic and reason often serve to support the ego-centered approach to life. The logic of undermining exclusive identification with ego often appears quite scandalous to reason. In Kierkegaard's words, "The self must be broken in order to become a self." Or as Goethe expressed this scandalous logic:

> I praise what is truly alive,
> What longs to be burned to death . . .
> And so long as you haven't experienced
> This: to die and so to grow,
> You are only a troubled guest
> On the dark earth.[7]

And here precisely lies one of the subtle ambiguities involved in recognizing a true spiritual master: The counterfeit and the genuine master both undermine the habitual patterns of self. Yet one does this in a way that creates bondage, while the other does it in a way that promotes liberation. What is this important difference?

AUTHORITY AND RELATIONSHIP

We cannot rely on descriptions of external behaviors alone to distinguish between genuine and problematic spiritual teachers. Developing criteria for judging a teacher's genuineness by examining external behavior alone would, for one thing, neglect the context—both interpersonal and intrapersonal—from which the behavior draws its meaning; and for another, it would tend to identify one particular model of a spiritual teacher as being ideal or exclusively valid, which would be as great a fallacy as elevating a single mode of psychotherapy to a similar position. There are many different therapeutic styles and approaches that can be effective, but we would be hard pressed to say what the therapy of Carl Rogers, Fritz Perls, and Milton Erikson had in common that achieved therapeutic results. Each of these men had a different personality type, a different style of working, and perhaps even a different type of client with whom he would be most effective. Similarly, the specific chemistry between a student and a spiritual master is quite important in determining whether there will be a meeting of two minds. And since genuine spiritual teachers come in many different shapes and forms, we will no doubt fail if we try to spell out how a good guru should behave.

Instead, we need a more subtle analysis which looks at the quality of the relationship or process that goes on between teacher and student. This involves examining the nature of spiritual authority in at least two different respects: (1) how it is defined in the relationship between teacher and student; and (2) the source from which a teacher ultimately derives that authority.

The first aspect of spiritual authority is relative or relational; that is, a given teacher has this kind of authority only for those who respond to his or her presence and teachings. A disciple (Latin for "learner") is one who recognizes that he or she has something essential to learn from a given teacher. In this regard, the function of a spiritual teacher is like that of other kinds of teachers. For example, we would expect someone who wanted to play the piano to learn and accomplish more by studying with a master pianist than just by reading "how-to" books or studying with a musicologist. Just as one would turn to an acknowledged master in any field one wants to pursue in depth, so a person who feels a longing to overcome the limitations of egocentricity would feel drawn to someone who has actually mastered how to do that. The role of an effective teacher is to instruct, encourage, provide feedback, and inspire through the example of his or her own accomplishment. Moreover, the more effective teachers tap and nurture the inherent potential of students, rather than imposing their own style and agenda.

This relational aspect of spiritual authority could also be compared in certain ways with a similar type of authority that occurs in a healthy therapeutic relationship. As a therapist I generally feel uneasy with the authority role many clients grant me, yet I often have to accept this special position, especially in the early stages of the work. Clients can often let themselves proceed with the changes they need to make more readily if they grant me some authority to guide their process. Initially my authority stems merely from the social role of therapist and from the technical knowledge and procedures I may have at my disposal, but soon another kind of authority comes into play, a more truly relational authority. I prefer not to explain this authority solely as a "transference" of needs from the parent-child relationship. What also seems to give me a special authority in this relationship is my allegiance to clients' inherent sanity and well-being, as well as my willingness to hear and accept their most intimate feelings and thoughts. In giving clients a special quality of attention and acceptance, a therapist may provide a model of how the clients could relate to their own experience. To the extent that the therapist helps clients connect with their own basic well-being, they accord him a natural authority, beyond the formal, conventional authority of his social position as a professional expert. This is an important step on the way toward recognizing their own authority—that they are indeed the "authors" of their own experience, rather than a passive victim of circumstance. When a client finally realizes that the therapist is not responsible for the changes he has made, but has rather been helping him connect with his own inherent positive life directions, he can begin to move forward on his own.

In a parallel, though far deeper and more complete way, a genuine spiritual master's presence may serve as a mirror that reflects back qualities of the student's own greater being: openness, generosity, discernment, humor, gentleness, acceptance, compassion, straightforwardness, strength, and courage.

Beyond the relative authority he takes on in relation to the student, the true master is also in touch with an unconditional source of authority—awakened being—inside himself. This is the same source of wisdom all people may tap into, and the genuine teacher is more than willing to help others to do so, if they are ready. Usually such a master has spent many years developing a direct awareness of the deeper nature of human consciousness beyond egocentricity through self-knowledge disciplines, such as meditation and contemplation. Having fully witnessed and understood the many neurotic twists and turns of the mind, all the tendencies toward self-deception and self-aggrandizement, great teachers have mastered the way to tap into a deeper source of aliveness and power in themselves and others beyond these ego entanglements. Sharing this source of their own realization means encouraging students to engage in a self-knowledge discipline.

An awareness discipline such as meditation sharpens the students' perceptions so that they can discern more clearly whether the teacher's words are true. Without such a practice, students are totally dependent on the teacher to tell them what is so. The students' increased discrimination and discernment may also lead to a greater appreciation of the teacher's mastery, in the same way that when we begin to study and practice any art, we soon deeply appreciate the dedication and skillfulness of an accomplished master much more than we could before. This appreciation may also give rise to natural feelings of respect and devotion.

From a secular perspective, it may be difficult to understand such devotion as anything but slavishness. Yet the real point of honoring the teacher's mastery is not to aggrandize the teacher by placing him or her in a superior position above or apart from the student. Rather, genuine devotion can be a practice of turning one's allegiance away from the tyranny of egocentricity and toward the deeper source of wisdom in oneself, which the teacher exemplifies in a fully developed form. Insofar as we are ordinarily devoted to enhancing our own self-image, we are enslaved by thoughts and emotions revolving around greed, envy, pride, aggression, and fear. Devotion to a teacher whose presence exemplifies freedom from this inner tyranny can be an important part of the process of switching allegiance from egocentric compulsions to a path of awakening. However, it should be emphasized that, particularly in our culture, the practice of devotion to a master can be quite dangerous and lead to many of the perils of the path unless it is preceded by a thorough training and grounding in an awareness that sharpens the student's discernment and cuts self-deception.

Yet, lest we imagine that the authority and the function of a spiritual mentor only has meaning in the Eastern traditions, we might consider the following words of the Trappist monk Thomas Merton, emphasizing the importance of spiritual instruction from a qualified guide:

> The work of getting rid of the "I" is, in fact, so difficult and so subtle as to be completely impossible without the help of others. The disciple must submit unconditionally to the most rigorous obedience and discipline. He must take without question and without murmur every possible difficulty and hardship. He must bear insult, weariness, labor, opprobrium.[8]

Although such words, so boldly stated, may rub against certain egalitarian and democratic sensibilities, they do point to an inescapable fact: If we seek out a teaching designed to help us overcome the compulsion of egocentricity, then we cannot insist on having everything our own way along this path, which is inevitably laced with many opportunities for self-deception. In this subtle and difficult process one sometimes imagines ego is being shed while in fact it is solidifying in a new guise. This is how charlatans and false prophets lay their traps, promising spiritual rewards and using the language of transcendence in the service of further dependency on themselves. The genuine master's work of dislodging entrenched patterns of ego-identification yields no such security.

SURRENDER VS. SUBMISSION

To understand the value of commitment to a genuine master, we need to distinguish between mindful surrender, which can be enlivening, and mindless submission, which is a deadening flight from freedom. The notion of surrendering is widely misunderstood in our culture. It often conjures up images of "come out with your hands up"—waving a white flag, admitting defeat, being humiliated. For many people today, the idea of surrender implies losing intelligence or individuality to another person and taking a weak, submissive, "one-down" position. True surrender, however, is never enslaving, but rather is a step toward empowerment, the discovery of one's own most genuine power.

Submission means giving up our own power to someone who appears to be more powerful. We are most likely to do this when we feel unworthy and in need of something in return from the other person in order to feel well about ourselves. Yet depending on another for validation forces us to act in ways that compromise our integrity just to win approval. The more we compromise our integrity, the less we trust ourselves and the more dependent on the leader we may become. Such submission is also narcissistic, because in submissively identifying with the leader and the group, followers subtly inflate their own self-importance.

The recent critics of narcissism in our society tend to see all involvements with spiritual masters in this light, failing to distinguish between submission as a developmentally regressive retreat from maturity, and genuine surrender, which allows people to move beyond egocentricity to a fuller realization of their being.

We could also define surrender here as the act of giving ourselves fully to life, without trying to control the outcome. True surrender may be purposeful, yet it does not have a finite object; that is, it does not consist in giving ourselves to a limited personality or ideology. One simply surrenders for the sake of giving oneself. If we give ourselves to something finite, such as the teacher's personality, that is, in my view, submission. To be able to give ourselves fully to life, we first have to appreciate our own fullness of being; otherwise the "giving" is liable to be submission— "I give myself to my guru because he is so great and I am so small." True surrender can only happen out of inner strength, while submission happens out of inner weakness. What is surrendered is egocentricity, not intelligence, not discrimination, not strength. When we are in touch with our own fullness, we do not lose anything by giving our being to others, because there is always more where that came from—more life, more energy, more love. In submission, however, we do lose by giving away our power to another and becoming dependent on the other to make us feel well, valid, adequate. The value of an awareness discipline in this regard lies in helping us develop inner strength and confidence, so that we can give ourselves more fully to what life asks of us.

With a genuine spiritual master, surrendering means presenting oneself in a completely honest, naked way, without trying to hold anything back or maintain any facade. How rarely are we able to let anyone see us as we are, without donning a mask of some kind. Being in the presence of a true master is a rare opportunity to let down all one's pretenses, to unmask and simply be as one is, acknowledging both one's egocentric tendencies as well as one's larger being. This is quite different from submissively trying to live up to an external prescription, to be "good" or "devoted," to please someone in order to feel worthy.

The spiritually authentic teacher-student relationship transcends narcissism because it also promotes the student's larger task of surrendering to everyday life itself as one's ultimate teacher. The real test of the students is not how well they please the master, but how fully they can face the demands of life at each moment, instead of holding themselves back or apart from life. Everyday situations then begin to present themselves as opportunities to be as responsive, transparent, and open as one is with one's teacher. Thus genuine surrender does not enslave one to the limited perspectives of an "in-group," but rather helps one open toward all people. Working with others in a compassionate way based on surrender means being sensitive and responsive to what every situation calls for from us, without aggrandizing ourselves through our altruism. Those who criticize the path of self-knowledge as narcissistic fail to appreciate these all-important subleties and difficulties of the inner work necessary to make oneself truly available to all beings. The Zen master Dogen's famous words describe this path:

To study the self is to forget the self.
To forget the self is to be illumined by all things.

IN SEARCH OF A GENUINE TEACHER

How, then, can a person recognize a teacher he or she can trust? Certainly no one master or teaching could be expected to appeal to all people, any more than any one psychotherapist or school of therapy would prove effective for all potential clients. The ultimate criterion for judging masters is whether they wake their students up from self-preoccupation to experience their larger, universal being. Different masters work in different ways, but genuine teachers will not condone or indulge in any of the characteristics of pathological groups mentioned earlier. For instance, they will have a deep respect for human dignity, rather than appealing to personal inadequacies and insecurities. Whereas the charlatan will undermine self-respect in order to capitalize on regressive tendencies, genuine teachers will encourage self-respect as the basis for self-transcendence. They will be willing to share the source of their authority and wisdom with students, so that their relationship will be based on real experiential understanding rather than on ideology or belief. They will allow tolerance for ambiguity and paradox, rather than insisting on absolute certitude in the "One and Only Truth." Their concern will be directed toward all people, rather than elevating a group of followers to a privileged status above their fellow humans. They will not manipulate the emotions of their students, but will appeal to their natural intelligence. They will encourage people on the path of self-knowledge through example, rather than mainly through promises of future salvation and reward. Instead of encouraging herd behavior, they will recognize the importance of people's time alone with themselves to discover what is true in a fresh and alive way. And they will themselves have undergone extensive training and practice.

These characteristics are far more important than whether we approve of the teacher's lifestyle, appearance, or tendency to engage in puzzling or unconventional behavior. The annals of all the great spiritual traditions include many examples of masters who outraged conventional morality with behavior designed to awaken people to a deeper truth. (In Christianity, there is no greater example than Jesus; Francis of Assisi is another.) Genuine teachers often do not live up to ordinary preconceptions of a "pure and holy" lifestyle, and may at times act with a ferocity that aims at cutting through a student's thick shell of arrogance and egotism. Nor are great teachers necessarily lacking in their share of human imperfections. Spiritual teachers themselves usually emphasize the importance of judging the quality of teaching by the effect it has upon one, rather than by the personality traits of the teacher. For instance, one Hindu teacher, Nisargadatta Maharaj, once replied to a questioner who asked him whether a master should be "a man of self-control who lives a righteous life":

> Such you will find many of—and no use to you. A guru can show the way back home to your real self. What has this to do with the character or temperament of the person he appears to be? The only way you can judge is by the change in yourself when you are in his company. ... If you understand yourself with more than usual clarity and depth, it means you have met the right man.[9]

The Buddha once responded in a similar vein when approached by a group of villagers, the Kalamas, who had been visited by various monks and brahmins expounding their different doctrines. They asked the Buddha, "Venerable sir, there is doubt, there is uncertainty in us concerning them. Which of these reverend monks and brahmins spoke the truth and which falsehood?" The Buddha replied:

It is proper for you to doubt, to be uncertain . . . . Do not go upon what has been acquired by repeated hearing; nor upon tradition; nor upon rumor; nor upon what is in a scripture; nor upon surmise; nor upon an axiom; nor upon specious reasoning; nor upon a bias towards a notion that has been pondered over; nor upon another's seeming ability; nor upon the consideration, "The monk is our teacher." Kalamas, when you yourselves know: "These things are good, these things are not blamable; these things are praised by the wise; undertaken and observed, these things lead to benefit and happiness," enter on and abide in them.

The Buddha proceeded in the rest of this *sutra* to point out that one can recognize a worthy teaching if it helps to reduce the three poisons of greed, hatred, and delusion in one's own life.

In sum, assessment of a master's authenticity may be made through both the character of the master's influence on followers, viewed objectively, and the character of the master's influence on oneself, experienced subjectively. I have described several important criteria in each of these two areas, but the question of spiritual authority is a most subtle and difficult matter, which permits of no easy answers or hasty conclusions. Although I have stressed the distinction between true and false teachers here, these are probably but two ends of a broader spectrum of teachers with varying degrees of spiritual realization. Some teachers may have had a genuine realization, but have not fully processed or integrated it, so that their teaching is not as ripe or complete as it could be. Some start with good intentions, but are not sufficiently developed to avoid leading their followers astray. Other teachers may be quite wise, but lacking in the skillful means necessary to communicate or manifest their wisdom and help others discover it for themselves.

Certain masters seem to be models of perfection, while other great teachers are most effective precisely because they are so human, because they are so fully in touch with the limitations all people share. In the archetype of the wounded healer, the healer can help others only because of directly experiencing the nature of sickness in himself or herself. For example, the great Buddhist sage, Vimalakirti, to whom many *bodhi-sattvas* came for teachings, was always sick, and when asked about this, said: "I am sick because all beings are sick." If the spiritual path is about transforming the basic "sickness" of ego-clinging, then we can hardly expect spiritual teachers and communities to be completely spotless and pure.

To discount all spiritual masters because of the behavior of charlatans or misguided teachers is as unprofitable as refusing to use money because there are counterfeit bills in circulation. The abuse of authority is hardly any reason to reject authority where it is appropriate, useful, and legitimate. It is possible that in the present age of cultural upheaval, declining morality, family instability, and global chaos, the world's great spiritual masters may be among humanity's most precious assets. Glossing over important distinctions between genuine and counterfeit masters may only contribute further to the confusion of our age, and retard the growth and transformation that may be necessary for humanity to survive and prosper.

Notes

1. This article has appeared in modified form in the *Journal of Humanistic Psychology*, Vol. 23, No. 3, 1983.
2. The term "cult" has both the neutral meaning of "a religious sect" and a pejorative meaning. I will use the term in its pejorative sense here, to distinguish fervid or fanatical groups, which rigidly adhere to a fixed ideology under the leadership of a charismatic figure, from genuine spiritual communities.
3. The term "new religious movements" should not obscure the fact that though these approaches may be new to America, some of them continue traditions and lineages of spiritual transmission that are thousands of years old.
4. Eric Hoffer, *The True Believer* (New York: Harper & Row, 1951).
5. M. Washburn and M. Stark, "Ego, Egocentricity, and Self-transcendence: A Western Interpretation of Eastern Teaching," in J. Welwood, ed., *The Meeting of the Ways: Exploration in East-West Psychology* (New York: Schocken, 1979).
6. John Welwood and Ken Wilber, "On Ego Strength and Egolessness," in J. Welwood, ed., *The Meeting of the Ways: Exploration in East-West Psychology* (New York: Schocken, 1979).
7. Robert Bly, ed. and transl., *News of the Universe* (San Francisco: Sierra Club, 1980).
8. Thomas Merton, *Mystics and Zen Masters* (New York: Farrar, Straus & Giroux, 1970).
9. M. Nisargadatta, *I Am That*, Vol. 2 (Bombay: Chetana, 1973).

EDITORIAL COMMENTARY

Regarding "healthy" groups, Welwood makes a wide range of points that correspond to Anthony's multilevel category of genuinely transformational orientations. He places the overcoming of egoic self-preoccu-

pation and self-interest at the center of spiritual development and recognizes the constant possibility of self-deception in this task; he describes
healthy surrender to spiritual authority as drawing the student out of religious exclusivity and judgmental attitudes; he recognizes the incapacity
of secular, univocal rationality, as in the social sciences, to encompass and
assess matters of transformational spiritual development; he sees belief
as subordinate to experience; he affirms the need for awareness of one's
own assumptions in any spiritual dialectic; he acknowledges a spectrum
of many degrees of spiritual realization; and he regards it a fallacy to view
any one model of master-disciple relationships as exclusively valid.

Welwood's metaphysics are monistic; and while he does acknowledge important elements of the charismatic orientation (he ascribes special value and efficacy to devotion and surrender), his major emphasis
regarding practice is plainly technical.

In addition to the abundant multilevel content of Welwood's paper,
there are some questionable elements. These are chiefly some ambiguities
between non-transformational and transformational attainments, possible
flirtation with antinomianism and absolute relativism, and overgeneral-
ization of the apprenticeship style of relationship to a master. The
remainder of this commentary addresses these issues, which frequently
crop up in the discourse of transpersonal psychology.

Welwood emphasizes that it is undesirable to identify any one type
of teacher-student relationship as being the sole valid approach, yet he
does center his perspective implicitly on the apprenticeship model,
which is far from general. For example, he says, " . . . great teachers have
mastered the way to tap into a deeper source . . . beyond these ego entanglements. Sharing this source of their own realization means encouraging
students to engage in a self-knowledge discipline. An awareness discipline such as meditation sharpens the student's perceptions so that they
can discern more clearly whether the teacher's words are true." This
statement takes for granted the apprenticeship model's assumptions
about the teacher's fallibility, the student's capacity to judge the teacher,
and the need for techniques. Also, using the therapist-client interaction
and the value perspective of humanistic psychology to illuminate spiritual teacher-student relationships might do justice to apprenticeship situations, but it does not fit many important historical masters who are
highly regarded and whose relationship with disciples is more aptly
described by Anthony's multilevel charismatic category.

In describing a genuine teacher's inner state, Welwood no doubt has
authentic mystical realization in mind, although his key descriptive
words—open, responsive, receptive, alive, sensitive, deeper, larger—
while certainly true of transcendent states, are also true of psychological

states attainable in ordinary consciousness, such as in going from rigid rationality to spontaneous feeling in psychotherapy. The seeker has to discern whether a master having the qualities emphasized by Welwood is actually in a transcendent state carrying genuine spiritual authority, and to this end Welwood gives many important guidelines.

Welwood's discussion of the master's state makes no explicit reference to spiritual ultimacy, such as Buddha-nature or Nirvana. He does speak relatively of "consciousness beyond egocentricity," "fuller realization of being," "awakened being," "deeper source of wisdom." The absence of an unmistakably transcendent reference point in Welwood's picture also adds a degree of ambiguity regarding the authentic master's state of consciousness. These aspects of his paper have, for us, something of the flavor of absolute relativism or radical nominalism, a view in which the final truth is that no absolute truth, reality or being exists; therefore, freedom and transcendence reside in being uncommitted to all fixed forms and assumptions. In this view, ultimate enlightenment involves not the conscious realization of absolute being, but total freedom from all fixed identifications. The master's behaviors, whether socially acceptable or scandalous, are expressions of this rule-transcending freedom; therefore one can never tell a genuine teacher from a fraud based on behavior alone. Absolute relativism is a unilevel monistic perspective.

Welwood's rejection of behavioral criteria for masters and his broad tolerance of imperfection in masters make his formulation seem close to antinomianism, the unilevel view that transcendence and freedom involve non-adherence to moral and ethical codes. A distinction between ethics and etiquette is helpful here. Historically, some masters' behaviors have indeed seemed outrageous, but usually because of disobeying an encrusted idolatry of etiquette—relatively superficial codes of social and religious legitimization. Much more rarely, we would argue, have authentic masters violated ethics or morality, the deeper principles that uphold the intrinsic worth and sacredness of human beings.

If Welwood's framework gives possible scope for antinomianism, his concluding review of specific criteria for recognizing trustworthy teachers is a good safeguard. These criteria help identify problematic psychological postures such as exploitative antinomianism and authoritarianism, although they are not actually tests of spiritual realization and true spiritual authority. Welwood's use of these criteria as tests of a master's genuineness could again be viewed as an ambiguity between transcendental and psychological domains. All of his criteria are met by a good humanistic or transpersonal psychotherapist.

A characteristic of spiritual charlatans not found in genuine masters, according to Welwood, is the way the charlatan "often maintains a favored position by claiming to have special access to God or to a source of wisdom or authority that is not accessible to the followers." This claim can of course be part of an exploitative deception, but is it necessarily so? Ultimate enlightenment or God-realization is described in several major traditions as involving a consciousness of ultimate reality that the disciple is intrinsically capable of having, but is in fact very far from having. There is no pretense at parity between master and disciple in these and other respects. Buddha, Prophet Mohammed, Al Hallaj, Jesus, and recently Meher Baba all plainly maintained they had a special, direct access to ultimate reality or God. Clearly, a God-realized master has to be viewed as a "bad" psychotherapist according to humanistic criteria. Welwood does not speak to the case of masters who have attained spiritual ultimacy, just as he does not refer to ultimacy itself, as mentioned earlier. He regards "perfection" as a necessarily false posture of being free of humanness and human frailties. There can be no arguing that such pretenders exist. But charlatans aside, we regard as important the distinction between the "humanness" of untranscended imperfections, and the divine "humanness" of conscious submission to the human condition by one who has radically, perfectly transcended it.

Inflated by the Spirit

Gary Rosenthal

Gary Rosenthal, a former Buddhist monastic, is a psychotherapist in private practice who holds graduate degrees in clinical psychology and transpersonal counseling. He received his early training at the C. G. Jung Institute in Zurich, Switzerland. Here he
discusses "the ubiquitousness of ego inflation in human experience"
and provides a cyclical model of "inflation as part of the natural
process of transpersonal development."

Inflation, Rosenthal reminds us, is clearly apparent as a recur-
rent theme in ancient mythology, and in sociopolitical history it has
been all too common a condition, spawning harmful extremes of all
sorts. Rosenthal argues that everyday psychological life is also constantly subject to cycles of inflation-deflation, and he discusses some
psychotherapeutic perspectives on ego inflations associated with
transpersonal experience. The therapist's first task is to recognize a
transpersonal inflation, which requires distinguishing the nonrational character of transpersonal experience from the nonrational
character of regressive, prerational experience. Rosenthal describes
Jungian, Zen Buddhist, and pre-literate tribal approaches as examples of transpersonally oriented treatments of inflation.

The second half of the paper presents the author's model of the "crystallization" and "decrystallization" of transpersonal inflation. Rosenthal describes the formation of an inflation in terms of five contributing conditions: characterological predispositions; psychological disruption by spiritual experience; egoic appropriation of spiritual experience; external reinforcement of grandiosity by group or leader; and absence or dismissal of disconfirming feedback. Recovery from inflation, or its decrystallization, is described as a three-phase process: penetration of the inflated self-sense by disconfirming feedback; realization of distortion; and "work on what's been spoiled," enabling a return to "beginner's mind." In his concluding remarks, Rosenthal views transpersonal inflation as ultimately a mechanism serving the spiritual maturation of consciousness.

---

in·fla·ted: "Blown up, distended with air, unrealistically large and important, beyond the limits of one's proper size; hence to be vain, pompous, proud, presumptuous."—Webster's New International Dictionary, Second Edition

Historical perspectives tend to smack of inflation—the god's-eye-view above time and space. Nonetheless, I shall begin by briefly tracing the recognition of inflation in history, which will indicate the ubiquitousness of ego inflation in human experience. I will then discuss my main theme of inflation as part of the natural process of transpersonal development.

Scholars have equated the Greek concept of *hubris* with inflation, and have noted that it was the typical sin committed by the early Greeks. *Hubris* in its original usage meant wanton violence or passion arising from pride—the human arrogance that appropriates that which belongs to the gods, a transgression of proper human limits.

Many Greek myths, such as the stories of Icarus, Phaeton, and Bellerophon, depict the state of inflation, of going too high, acts of *hubris* that led to crashing falls. So, too, does the Judeo-Christian myth of the Garden of Eden, significantly called the "fall of man."

Much of the suffering throughout human history has been an outgrowth of the wanton violence of *hubris*/inflation. The institution of slavery, for example, and the belief that one's own race is superior to another, is a culturally induced inflation. Genocide, too, is the product of an inflation. The United States was at least partially settled through inflation-motivat-ed acts of wanton violence perpetrated upon the "heathen savages" native to the land. Any such "master race" mentality seems to be a manifestation of inflation.

We inflate when we fall in love; when we create, we tend to inflate. Our successes are breeding grounds for inflation; conversely, our failures can be "negative inflations," wind taken out of our sails as we fall short of an exalted ideal. Inflations would seem to be a significant, perhaps unavoidable component of human experience, applying not only to the sense of self and our professional and interpersonal relations, but also to our inter-*species* relations—what we have done to the earth and the other species we share it with.

There are many other examples of the inflations of everyday life. Jungian psychologist E. Edinger mentions that spells of anger, attempts to force or coerce the environment, and vengeance and power motivations of all kinds are symptomatic of inflation[1]—as is an intellectual rigidity that attempts to equate its own opinion with universal truth, a stance behind which lurks the assumption of omniscience. Lust, greed, and anger all produce inflation insofar as these and other passions tend to feel as if their fulfillment were the central imperative in the universe. Nuclear arsenals, which threaten not only rival governments, civilian populations, and wildlife, but also *life itself* with extinction, are certainly a transgressing of proper human limits. It is dangerous for human beings to appropriate to themselves the powers of a Shiva, Kali or Pluto-nium. To amass the capacity for such wanton violence is a colossal arrogance that reaches the very height of *hubris*/inflation.

Even too much guilt, humility, love, or altruism can support inflation when these feelings intensify self-importance. In fact, *too much of anything* tends to swell the ego-self beyond proper human limits. The arbitrary pronouncements of an animus-possession are a "deity" talking, as are the sullen resentments of the anima-possessed man who says in effect, "Be what I tell you to be, or I will withdraw from you; and without my acceptance you will die" (Edinger, pp. 14–15).

Inflation seems to be an occupational hazard of practically all social roles and professions, from parenting fathers who know best, to doctors with their supposed "God complex," or movie stars, politicians, athletes, even the foreman on the job. But since our topic is to be *transpersonal* inflations—inflations by the spirit—perhaps no "occupation" can offer us as much insight into the problem as spiritual teachers, or those who claim to be such, for they are the "professionals" who profess to know, to be able to guide. The very calling contains the scent of inflation—or as it is called in Zen, the "stink of enlightenment."

Jesus claimed to be the Way, the Truth, and the Light of this world; the Reverend Sun Myung Moon, the youthful Maharaj Ji and Jim Jones all have laid claim to be the new Christ. The current spiritual scene may at times resemble the insane asylum with several patients saying they are the real Napoleon. Some of the claims we hear may be truth, and clearly some delusive. What are we to make of them? How are we to separate the wheat from the chaff without ourselves becoming presumptuous, inflated?

One aspect of this complex problem is the ability to recognize inflation-inspired behaviors, in oneself as well as others. A sharpened sensitivity to the dynamics of inflation, the conditions that support it and the conditions that disperse it, is one antidote to the problem of egoic distortion in spiritual guides, who not only may be inflated themselves, but may "hook" their followers at least partly through feeding their inflation as well.

SOME PSYCHOTHERAPEUTIC PERSPECTIVES

Edinger asserts that "We are born in a state of inflation" (p. 7), but it is basically only the Jungian school that tends to see the original, unitary consciousness of early infancy as transpersonal inflation. I agree, however, with Ken Wilber in seeing early infancy as a pre-personal rather than transpersonal state, and consequently question the validity of speaking of ego inflation during a developmental phase wherein the personal ego has yet to emerge fully.

Part of the confusion may lie in mistaking certain qualities of transpersonal states (diminished subject/object separation, altered time/ space, choiceless awareness) for apparently similar qualities of pre-personal states, and vice versa, as Wilber has pointed out.[2] Although we may need to become like little children in order to "enter the Kingdom of Heaven," there is a big difference between a spiritually evolved adult who has achieved ego-consciousness (or "object constancy") and then learned to transcend it, and an infant who has yet to achieve it.

Assagioli, who formulated the transpersonal psychology known as psychosynthesis, observed that although transpersonal disturbances— including inflation—may have the same symptoms and appearance as ordinary neuroses, they in fact have different etiologies, and so may require different treatment methods. He argued that while transpersonal disturbances are increasing nowadays, they are also easier to cure than ordinary neurotic disturbances.

Jones, Freud's biographer, gave a detailed study of an inflated character style—people who have a "God complex."[3] Yet he failed to account adequately for the fact that the very characteristics he finds in his "neurotic" and "psychotic" subjects (non-separation between God and self, foreknowledge, infusion of humility and altruism, impulse to help others, conviction of one's own immortality, spiritual idealism, deep interest in religion and psychology, sense of power and confidence, curiosity, the capacity for public speaking and preaching), are also to be found in practically all the great spiritual figures throughout history. Quite possibly, many of the subjects of Jones's study had intimations of the transpersonal self, yet their glimpse of this higher perspective would have taken place in a turn-of-the-century, European, scientific-rational cultural context that could not really offer adequate means for understanding, grounding, or integrating the experience. The legacy of religious ambivalence, scientific rationalism, and ascending materialism of the late nineteenth century was perhaps nowhere more evident for twentieth-century thought and modern psychology than in Freud's enthronement of the ego as the final arbiter of reality and the administrator of the reality principle. Part of this legacy—voiced by Nietzsche, who was one of the most influential thinkers of the time and whose death in 1900 ushered in our century— was that "God is dead." Actually, Nietzsche's intended meaning in that famous phrase is widely misunderstood; but at any rate, God was no longer to be given admission into the reality principle.

In such a context, were a person not only to believe in the reality of God, but also to have an experience of God (no matter how distorted), then such a person would be demonstrating an "impairment of reality-testing"—which is, a priori, a definition of psychosis. The prevailing winds of the time and of Jones's psychoanalytic school in particular, may have tended to pathologize what had been essentially experiences of transpersonal awakening. This view is supported by one transpersonal psychologist, Bryan Wittine, who wryly notes, "There are no [such things as] 'transpersonal disturbances' in Chagrin Falls, Ohio." For there (or in turn-of-the-century Vienna), one is simply presumed crazy.

Other transpersonal psychologists make the point that the failure to recognize the emergence of transpersonal energies can lead to their becoming perverted. Somehow, the crux of the therapeutic task seems to be first that of recognizing when an inflation is, in fact, associated with the "up-lifting" pull of transpersonal energies, and second, treating the "disturbance" in such a fashion that one does not sever what Edinger has termed the "ego-Self axis." In other words, how do we stay in relationship to the "transpersonal" while overhauling the psychological distortions (in particular, inflation) which have fed upon our "divine connection"?

THE TREATMENT OF INFLATION

Jungians see the transpersonal self as an a priori inner determinant, "inevitably experienced initially in projection on to the parents" (Edinger, p. 39), whereas Freudians reductionistically interpret God as being merely a "magnified, idealized, and projected form of the personal father" (Jones, p. 204). These are radically divergent theoretical perspectives, and one might expect considerable difference in the treatment of inflation between schools of thought which recognize and validate the transpersonal factor and those that do not. The latter tend to view inflation in terms of reaction-formation, narcissistic omnipotence, grandiose-exhibitionistic regression, or as compensation for "organ inferiority," and thus the need for ego-reducing techniques (hence the term "head shrinker"). But while schools of thought which do recognize the presence of transpersonal factors have a different theoretical map, they, too, utilize ego-reducing strategies, which may appear similar to interventions generated from a non-transpersonal framework.

The Jungian psychologist Hillman examines the inflated approach to life found in *puer* character styles,[4] which involve interminable adolescent qualities, avoidance of commitment to persons or situations (they are never good enough), and flight from ordinary life. Hillman notes that *puer* figures in mythology are typically wounded in the lower extremities (Achilles's heel, Oedipus's feet, Ulysses's leg, Bellerophon's limping). He observes that in these mythic figures, the higher (transpersonal) energies, the energies of the spirit with which such figures are associated, are not fully brought down to earth, or grounded. "It's as if the transcendent seems unable to posit itself as fully human."

Von Franz, another noted Jungian psychologist who has written on the *puer*,[5] stresses that hard work and perseverance in it even when one is not inspired are the sure means to bring the *puer* down to earth and have him give up his mother-bound inflation. *Puers* must learn to face the developmental task of committing themselves towards becoming real as a fragment of their unlimited potential, rather than holding out for being an unreal whole. They must be willing to ground themselves in a concrete form and acknowledge the limiting, structuring principle of the Father archetype, which is difficult for them, usually to the extent that they are enmeshed in a negative reaction to the personal father. This dynamic alerts us to the ways in which the experience of our personal conditioning may color our relationship to the transpersonal, and vice versa.

Edinger maintains that though the Self archetype (through which one realizes one's ultimate spiritual identity, in this view) is an *a priori* inner determinant, it cannot emerge without a concrete parent-child relationship; this is what Neumann refers to as the "personal evocation of the archetype." Thus, alienation or rejection by the personal parents may injure the ego's relation to the Self. Similarly, disturbances in a disciple's or patient's relationship with a guru or transpersonal therapist can distort or damage the "transpersonal connection." Rejection by someone perceived as a spiritual authority may be experienced as a divine rejection. Conversely, receiving affirmation from a spiritual authority may result in either a healing blessing or the potential for ego-inflation.

In terms of therapeutic strategies, one may choose to work along the "fault lines" of the personal conditioning in treating an ego which needs to deflate. In such cases there may be little if any difference in treatment strategy between practitioners having a transpersonal perspective and those who do not. But in other cases it can prove extremely valuable to have the added option of a transpersonal intervention. For example, individual considerations may suggest it would prove advantageous to first establish a positive, loving relation to the "Heavenly Father," and to "anchor" this experience before proceeding to work through the unresolved and perhaps highly defended relationship with the personal father and mother.

A contemporary Zen teacher, Richard Clarke, whom I interviewed in researching this paper, mentions that the way his inflation or "Zen sickness" was treated by his master was "to be fundamentally ignored, allowed to stew in my own juices, or ridiculed." This echoes the treatment of the young Hui Neng (who was to become the Sixth Patriarch of Zen) at the hands of the Fifth Patriarch. Hui Neng had had a spontaneous enlightenment experience (kensho) as a youth, while overhearing someone recite the Diamond Sutra. When later he went to interview the Fifth Patriarch for the purpose of studying under him, it was evident to the Fifth Patriarch both that Hui Neng had had an enlightenment and that he suffered from the "Zen sickness" so common following kensho. When Hui Neng asked, "How do I become a [full] Buddha?" the Patriarch in part tested him, in part ridiculed him by asking in return, "How can you, a barbarian from the south, hope to become a Buddha?" Hui Neng gave quite a good account of himself in replying, "Although there are northern men and southern men, north and south make no difference to their Buddha-nature." But the Fifth Patriarch replied, "This barbarian is too bright," and he then ordered Hui Neng to go to work in the stable and speak no more. More than eight months passed, months spent at hard labor pounding rice, before Hui Neng received any positive acknowledgement from the Fifth Patriarch. We see from this example that the Zen tradition, which shows an awareness, certainly, of both the transpersonal factor and of the egoic disturbance following kensho, treats such disturbances with ego-reducing interventions as might a psychoanalyst, as well as by hard work, as might a Jungian therapist in treating a puer.

The Zen treatment of ignoring an inflated (though advanced) practitioner also corresponds to practices in certain pre-literate tribes, where a warrior's great exploit in the hunt or on the battleground is followed by his being sent away to live on the outskirts of the village or settlement, until he "returned to normal." By virtue of his kill, the warrior had become like the Great Spirit, the giver and taker of life, and so was in need of a "coming down" period. He had become like an immortal, stepping beyond "the proper human limits," and thus needed time to "mortalize," time for his ego to reconstellate along less inflated lines.

CRYSTALLIZATION AND DECRYSTALLIZATION PROCESSES OF TRANSPERSONAL INFLATIONS

Inflations do not occur in a vacuum. Just as there are certain conditions that enable a plant to grow (air, water, soil, sunlight), there are certain conditions that, in their collective impact, form an ideal "culture medium" for breeding transpersonal inflations. In particular, transpersonal inflation tends to crystallize around the following factors:

1. A characterological predisposition (which we might liken to the "seed" of an inflation);
2. An actual transpersonal experience (the seed sprouts, comes to life);
3. Identification of the ego-personality with the infusion of transpersonal energies ("I am this blossoming");
4. The impact of a teacher or group that helps instigate, validate, or perpetuate egoic identification with "higher states" (like the soil that holds and feeds the roots of the seedling);
5. The absence or active avoidance of disconfirming feedback; this may be coupled with the ignoring or ignorance of one's character-fixations (all of which serve as a "fence" to protect the seedling from being trampled by deflating forces).

The crystallization of transpersonal inflation may be followed by a process of decrystallization. The latter consists of:

1. Disconfirmations—either from within or without—which manage to break in and poke holes in one's inflated system;
2. The stage of transmuting the personality-inflating distortions, obstructions or beliefs, which can now be seen as such;
3. Return to "beginner's mind."

The notion of a cyclic progression through stages of inflation/deflation/inflation has also been put forth by Edinger (see Fig. 1).

Figure 1.

The Psychic Life Cycle. (Reprinted by permission from Edward F. Edinger, *Ego and Archetype*, Baltimore: Penguin, 1973.)

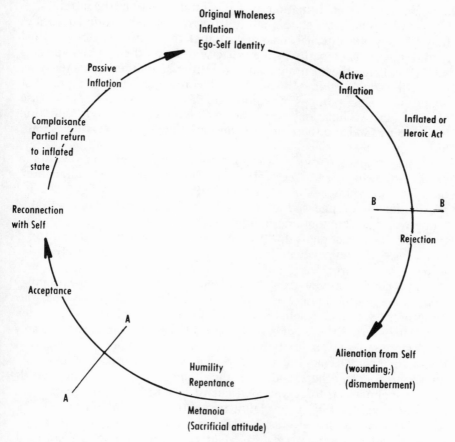

Edinger's cycle shows how consciousness evolves during early stages of development. Yet Edinger points out that the model depicted in the figure "leaves out of account the later stage of development when the cycle is superseded," to be "replaced by a more or less conscious dialogue between ego and Self" (p. 42).

Let us consider the inflation-deflation factors and processes in greater detail, beginning with the characterological predispositions to inflate. Differing character styles seem to be predisposed to inflate around differing issues. For example, one character style may be especially prone to inflate in regard to its accomplishments and productions, what one has done, rather than who one *is*. A person with such a style would typically have a split between his or her work-identity and private self, with the tendency toward inflated self-importance arising from the former, and a tendency to resist disconfirmation by a general disregard of the latter.

Another character style might, in this regard, tend to inflate pridefully (largely via internal dialogue) around the cultivation of personal qualities, such as empathy or the capacity to help others. This type also tends to inflate others through flattery. With yet another character type, the attribution of value is outside the self completely. They long for that which is missing, perhaps pining for the distant beloved. A special case of this "negative inflation" is that of the "divine victim" whose suffering is caused by God and therefore has supreme significance, making the sufferer supremely special.

Other characterological predispositions to inflate may involve some of the following issues: perfectionism and self-righteous indignation; hero-ism, the counter-phobic "undoing" of fear and paranoid grandiosity; avarice for knowledge and an "ivory tower" withdrawal from a frightening world; seeking/joining/merging/falling in love; revenge and punitiveness; idealistic plans for the future, charlatanism, and gluttony, including overindulgence in drugs which "lift" the user "above" the anxiety that would otherwise be felt.

This cursory survey of characterological predispositions toward inflation is based rather loosely upon the schema of personality known as the enneagram, which originated in certain Sufi mystical schools. The reader could draw up a list of predilections toward inflation using practically any other system of personality typing. I should add that a person having one dominant characterological predisposition will also usually experience affinity to several others; and *all* of the predispositions could be considered as incliniations to pervert particular transcendental attributes.

The next factor in the crystallization of transpersonal inflations is the actual transpersonal experience, perhaps brought on by meditation or other spiritual practice. Like the clutch in an automobile, spiritual practices enable one to disengage attention from the "gears and machinations" of the personality and shift into transpersonal states. Disengagement (or disidentification) with the ego-constrictedness of the personality makes one available for a more expansive sense of self. Such practices can help the ego establish, as Edinger might say, an "axis" (as well as access) to the Self.

In such states where the ego is drawn into relation with transpersonal energies, all manner of phenomena may occur. Assagioli mentions that "the opening of the channel between conscious and superconscious" may lead either to a healing or to an incapacity of the mind to stand the illumination. He notes that the sudden influx of spiritual energies can lead to emotional upheaval and outbursts, to playing the role of prophet, and to "spectacular proselytism." Parapsychological perceptions, visions, voices, and messages may ensue. In such cases it is important for the individual not to give validity to orders or commands "received," especially those tending to exalt the personality.

The third factor in the crystallization of transpersonal inflations is that of the ego-personality becoming identified with the infusion of higher knowledge or more subtle energies. This is where the ego steps in and interprets what has happened during its relative absence from the scene. The experience may be wrongly interpreted, leading to a "confusion of levels." One might think that one is the higher level that has just been contacted—and in a sense one is, but not as the ego. Ego's taking credit for transpersonal faculties is at the heart of transpersonal inflation.

The ego's identification with spiritual "contents" (insights, beliefs, experiences of all kinds) need not come solely from actual transpersonal experience. "Spiritual contents" of a lower order can be appropriated from the environment—such as taking on the beliefs of a group or guru, or subscribing to some doctrine such as a "revealed" book. This leads us to the fourth factor in the crystallization process of transpersonal inflations: spiritual groups and teachers.

Spiritual communities and/or their leaders may play an active role in instigating, validating, and/or perpetuating false identification with "higher states." Like an infectious disease, one might become inflated through another's thought-process. For example, a leader may promote the idea that group members are not ordinary people, but extraordinary, elect—perhaps the incarnations of spiritual heroes of the past. Or, by one's very membership in the group one is a "chosen" person—with a mission in the world. Such inflated beliefs and assumptions are remarkably common in religious and quasi-religious groups. A most poignant example is given by Mills[6] (pp. 80–81), who spent six years in Jim Jones's People's Temple.

[Jones] began to hint broadly that he was none other than "God Almighty." In a secret meeting he told us that he knew his previous incarnations. He bragged that he had been Buddha, the Bab, Jesus Christ, and, most recently, Lenin. "Of course," he warned them, "this is highly confidential and you aren't to tell anyone else. The members might not understand, especially about that last incarnation."

When he realized that his staff members were awed by this revelation, he decided that the rest of his members would probably be impressed too. In the next Sunday service he announced that he was going to tell those who were present one of his greatest secrets. With a great deal of ceremony he announced, "I have lived on this earth before. I have come for a special mission and you who are following me are my chosen people. Most of you have been with me during some of my previous incarnations. I lived thousands of years ago as Buddha. Then I spent a short incarnation as the Bab, the person who founded the Baha'i faith. I have lived on earth as Jesus the Christ, and my last incarnation was in Russia as Vladimir Lenin." *He spoke with such authority and sincerity that we all believed him* (italics mine).

Thus, regarding spiritual communities and teachers, though the ideas and beliefs being circulated may have transpersonal themes and content (such as the "perfect master" or "chosen people" fantasies), the dynamic may actually be, as Wilber has pointed out, not transcendent but regressive, or concerned more with "legitimacy" than with "authenticity." (I refer the reader to Wilber's essay in this volume.)

In many spiritual groups there is a tendency toward group exclusivity, whereby group members find themselves—either for logistical reasons, such as living in an isolated commune, or for reasons of choice—spending most of their social life with other members of the group. Such a state of affairs does not allow much opportunity for alternative, potentially disconfirming feedback to whatever inflationary tendencies may be present in the group's belief system. In some religious cults isolation from alternative sources of feedback seems quite calculated for purposes of conversion and allegiance-maintenance of recruits. Both the absence of alternative feedback and the unwillingness to take seriously what alternative feedback is available tend to create a "fence" (defense) around inflation, sustaining it.

One may also either be too close to (identified with) the system that is upholding one's inflation, or too invested to be willing to see it. If inflated beliefs include thoughts such as "I am (or, we are) the highest person (or group) on the planet"—which is quite common—then any disconfirming feedback from outside the system may be readily dismissed: "They just don't understand," "They're just deluded (or in league with the devil)." Another potential "fencing operation" is that of pointing out the reactivity of the person challenging the inflation. For example, if the challenger is against all groups or religions in general, then the reactivity or one-sidedness of the "disconfirmer" may be used to justify a blanket rejection of the challenge, including that which is valid in it.

It should be clear that one might suffer a transpersonal inflation and even pass it on to others without being aware that all this is occurring. Transpersonal inflations often tend to occur in people who are in many ways mature, accomplished, successful—and perhaps gifted with intuitive insight, creativity, and charisma. Yet it is the very giftedness or persuasiveness which may blind such people to their remaining distortions (such as inflation), just as it is their giftedness which often leads others to treat them as "special"—which can blind an individual all the more to an inflated identity or belief system.

Unfortunately, the capacity for giving or receiving even genuine spiritual insight does not rule out the danger that one might also be inflated—in fact, the two often go hand in hand. There is, therefore, the ever-present risk of psychological exploitation by such a guide, in the sense that inflation may involve the manipulation of others in service of one's own grandiosity. This "unholy union" of the giftedness and the inflatedness, which can result from having access to transpersonal states, is a critical pitfall both for those who follow and those who guide others on the spiritual path.

DECRYSTALLIZATION

At a certain point the inflated system may begin to break down. The wandering elephants of reality may begin to knock over the fences. This process of "bumping against reality" may eventually become so uncomfortable and unavoidable that one begins to deflate, come down, and/or take another look at one's predicament.

Any number of factors may be involved in the deflation process, including simply a reversal of the factors which first contributed to inflation. For example, a rapid succession of external disconfirmation may lead to a shocking self-insight. Suddenly it may seem, as one interviewee put it, "like the universe was blowing its whistle at me." Or the meditations or practices which once got one "high" (and relieved doubt or anxiety) no longer work. The group leader or the behavior of group members may become so distorted that one can no longer fail to notice that something weird is going on. Assagioli mentions that one may come to see that the personal self was only temporarily overriden, not permanently transformed. Rocks and rubbish concealed at high tide emerge once again.

Circumstances sooner or later may leave no choice but to come to terms with the distortions of the personality. This may be a rather shocking jolt to a previously inflated sense of self, and may lead to the false belief of having "fallen" lower than before. Lower dormant drives in the personality may suddenly become reactivated. There is also the danger of becoming so disillusioned as to repudiate former ideals and beliefs, perhaps becoming embittered and cynical toward matters spiritual. The decrystallization of inflation can be excruciating, truly a dark night of the soul.

The disconfirming of the inflated system leads to the phases of transmuting the distortions of the personality—which now may be seen—and coming to terms with what happened. Assagioli has employed the image of a caterpillar to suggest the dilemma of passing out of an old stage without yet having arrived at the new—and as he notes, there may be a temporary impairment of ability to manage ordinary tasks of life. This may be in part due to the fact that much psychic energy is now mobilized in the effort to come to terms with what has taken place and to "work on what's been spoiled."

During the process of decrystallization, therapeutic strategies (in addition to the "reductionistic" approaches outlined earlier) may include humor and the use of personal sharing as part of the effort to educate the client as to what is happening and to assist in finding what is for him or her the right attitude to meet it. Assagioli describes using the will to master (without suppressing) the emerging awareness of unconscious drives, and suggests techniques for transmuting aggressive energies which might otherwise persist or turn against the self.[7] The point, of course, is to become able to assimilate transpersonal dimensions of experience without activating the ego into inflation.

This phase of "cleaning off the barnacles" should signal the "death" of the old, inflated identity and a return to "beginner's mind." To the extent that the decrystallizing wipes the slate clean and creates again a sense of openness, one may begin again to follow transpersonal aspirations, this time, one hopes, with fewer and less blatant distortions that now may be more readily apprehended and transformed.

CONCLUSION

In later stages of development, inflatedness is consciously suffered as a distortion and disruption of not only our "divine connection," but also our relatedness to other people and things. Richard Clarke observes that by continuously working on oneself, this suffering becomes a teaching that sensitizes or inoculates against repeating the indulgence of inflation in the future.

And yet, inflations are natural and at times needed phases in our growth, as in the myth of the Garden of Eden, where an inflated act or stance is needed in order to give birth to a new orientation of consciousness. Of the Garden of Eden, Edinger writes, "An old state of affairs is being lost, and a new conscious insight is being born. What is a crime at one stage of development is lawful at another, and one can't develop to a new stage without daring to challenge the code of the old stage" (p. 21). He points out that inflated acts may be "crimes that beget," rather than impede, consciousness. Many people arrest their growth just at the point of the necessary "crime" (against parents, church, state, guru, therapist) that would constitute a crucial step in their individuation. In fact, the phenomenon of the negative transference in psychotherapy can be interpreted in this light. Thus, if at some stages of development, as in the Garden of Eden, inflations help us to individuate by leading to an expulsion from a pre-personal paradise, in other instances (as with *puers*, for example) the inflation may keep one bound in a pre-personal, relatively undifferentiated state.

Transpersonal inflation can be an attempt to maintain or stabilize a newly gained expansion in consciousness. The danger is the tendency to cling to and worship the expansion gained more than the Source out of which all expansions and contractions occur. In short, inflations seem to be a necessary dynamic in the maturation of consciousness, though they become an impediment in later stages where the ego must finally be dissolved and superseded by the higher imperative which is God.

Notes

1. Edward Edinger, *Ego and Archetype* (New York: Penguin, 1972).
2. Ken Wilber, "The Pre/Trans Fallacy," in *Eye to Eye* (Garden City, NY: Anchor/Doubleday, 1983).
3. E. Jones, "The God Complex: The belief that one is God and the resulting character traits," *Essays in Applied Psychoanalysis* (London and Vienna: International Psychoanalytic Press, 1923).
4. James Hillman, "Puer Wounds and Ulysses's Scar," in James Hillman, ed., *Puer Papers* (Irving, Texas: Spring, 1979).
5. Marie-Louise von Franz, *Puer Aeternus*, 2nd Ed. (Santa Monica, CA: Sigo, 1981).
6. J. Mills, *Six Years with God: Life Inside Rev. Jim Jones's People's Temple* (New York: A & W Publishers, 1979).
7. Roberto Assagioli, *Psychosynthesis: A Manual of Principles and Techniques*, 6th Ed. (New York: Penguin, 1976).

EDITORIAL COMMENTARY

Gary Rosenthal's article informally surveys the interrelated psychology and sociology of ego inflations that occur in spiritual involvements. His view of spiritual inflation is highly convergent with Anthony's unilevel category of religious attitudes. Let us first consider Rosenthal's initial point, the ubiquity of inflation in human affairs. Ken Wilber's concept of the "Atman project," which synthesizes Western psychological and Eastern mystical descriptions of human development, puts this in an interesting light. Atman is ultimate, transcendent being or Godhead, the true nature of all beings and things on all planes. The Atman project is each individual's striving to realize and enjoy the Atman-state consciously. This great process is largely unconscious in most people, yet, like a river winding its way across a continent to the sea, it includes every wayward meander of one's consciousness.

> Every individual—every sentient being—constantly intuits that his prior Nature *is* the infinite and eternal, All and Whole—he is possessed, that is, with a true Atman-intuition. . . . Every individual *correctly* intuits that he is of one nature with Atman, but he *distorts* that intuition by applying it to his separate self. He feels his separate self is immortal, all-embracing, central to the cosmos, all-significant. That is, he *substitutes* his ego for Atman. Then, instead of finding actual and timeless wholeness, he merely substitutes the wish to live forever; instead of being one with the cosmos, he substitutes the desire to possess the cosmos; instead of being one with God, he tries himself to play God.[1]

Inflation, in this view, is ubiquitous because the Atman project is ubiquitous, although, of course, the specific degrees and types of this inflation may vary considerably.

We referred above to a convergence of Rosenthal's view of spiritual inflation and Anthony's concept of unilevel spirituality. The "confusion of levels" and the "false identification with higher states" that mark spiritual inflation, according to Rosenthal, are also the quintessential flaws of unilevel mysticism. Rosenthal cites the confusion of a temporary mystical glimpse-experience with a radical, permanent transformation of consciousness as a factor in spiritual inflations. The confusion of glimpse and permanent transcendence is a common unilevel error—and one that is serious because it involves a failure to appreciate the enormous difference between the consciousness of the disciple or devotee and that of the authentic, truth-conscious master.[2] In general, a spiritual aspirant's easy presumption of mastery involves a confusion of the state of true masters with the state of aspirants. In such a climate of reduced standards, "masters" get away with all types of personal weaknesses and abuses of authority.

Anthony defines unilevel spirituality in terms of univocality and consequentialism, both of which figure heavily in Rosenthal's view of inflation. To take one's beliefs, one's understanding, as truth—which Rosenthal sees as an important ingredient of inflation—is the essence of univocality. Likewise, he names explicitly consequentialist modes of inflation, most obviously those based on one's accomplishments and productions. On close consideration, virtually all of the spiritually inflationary motifs named by Rosethal have both univocal and consequentialist underpinnings. (Note that univocality and consequentialism are intimately linked as religious attitudes: Univocality is consequentialism in relation to words and ideas. The ideas are idolized as veritable crystallizations of truth, and their truth is proven by the power they give to control what happens, both in one's consciousness and one's circumstances. The truth-value of the ideas comes from the desirable effects that they enable one to produce—consequentialism.)

Rosenthal describes various ways in which inflation is institutionalized on the group level, with one form or another of exclusivity and isolation serving as "fencing operations" that shield against disconfirming feedback. The institutionalized inflation of a group seems to involve an interconnected pattern of univocality, consequentialism, exclusivity, and isolation. Univocality gives the group a stable, clear way to define ingroup versus out-group: Those who believe unquestioningly are in, those who do not are out. Thus univocality generates a sharp group boundary, which brings all sorts of possibilities into the picture: Exclusivity and social isolation become extremely tempting, easy ways of heightening the univocal solidarity of the group and creating a group self-image that emphasizes its uniqueness, superiority and importance (consequentialist mystique). The inflated group self-image generates ardency and inspiration in members, reinforcing solidarity, while exclusivity and isolation minimize the chances that conversations with outsiders will reveal flaws and inconsistencies in the group's univocal orientation.

The four interrelated factors of univocality, consequentialism, exclusivity, and isolation are no doubt mutually and circularly self-reinforcing in the inflated group, yet it seems that univocality might be the prior condition—the "soil" in Rosenthal's metaphor—that supports and sustains the development of the inflated system as a whole. The inflated unilevel group's point of vulnerability, the weak link in the system that can finally rupture, is usually its consequentiality: The group's meaning system fails to give the group the expected potency in the world, or it fails over time to enable individual members to control their own circumstances or inner states.

In summary, unilevel groups, by the very attributes that make them unilevel, maximize inflation. Multilevel groups, by the attributes that make them multilevel, minimize it. The members of a multilevel group regard the group's meaning system as inherently surpassing any of their attempts at definitive, rational understanding, and as pointing toward a truth that can be glimpsed only transrationally and fully known only in ultimate enlightenment. There is little if any "soil" for the roots of exclusivity to take hold of, and an attitude of superiority based on privileged, authoritative knowledge does not develop. Multilevel group members are more impressed by how little they know than by how much they know of spiritual truth. The atmosphere of the multilevel group fosters a natural humility rather than inflation. The enormity of the difference between the consciousness of aspirants and that of a true master is keenly appreciated.

Rosenthal's article should be of considerable help to readers who are assessing a possible group involvement. He provides a wide range of observable clues to the operation of inflation. Although the article lacks the coherence needed in an adequate theoretical description—"inflation" here becomes so broad a term as to mean almost anything—it works nicely as an informal look at the phenomenology of inflation in individuals and groups.

Rosenthal's article speaks to the chemistry that occurs between egotism and genuine transcendent experience. We get the impression that in Rosenthal's view, a deep involvement in a group or a profound commitment to a master is generally undesirable because it tends in itself to produce inflation and narrowness. Whether or not this is actually Rosenthal's view, it warrants comment as an attitude that often forms part of the apprenticeship model of spiritual practice. In our view, deep commitment to an authentically transformative, multilevel path and/or to a genuinely transcendent master prevents inflation and broadens the aspirant's relationship to life, as we saw in Part 1.

Notes

1. Ken Wilber, *The Atman Project* (Wheaton, IL: Theosophical Publishing House, 1980); 102–103.

2. In fact, the difference in consciousness is *infinite* according to the teachings of Persian Sufism, Mahayana Buddhism, and Vedanta Hinduism. This is so because the ultimate reality is not only the true nature of all levels of matter, energy, and mind, it also infinitely transcends them all. The state of the reality-conscious master is therefore infinitely "far" from (*and* infinitely "close" to) *any* point on the path of spiritual development. Notions of "progress" are relative at best, and are irrelevant in general— one is never truly "closer" until the moment of ultimate realization.

Part Four

OVERVIEW

When Is Religion Transformative?

A Conversation with Jacob Needleman

Jacob Needleman's *The New Religions,* published in 1970, was a groundbreaker in calling attention to the new religions and the emergence of a new religious consciousness in America. As a professor of philosophy and scholar of religion, Needleman has contributed as much through the style of his writings as through their substance: The eleven volumes that he has authored and edited on the new religions and the quest for self-knowledge are themselves exemplary of the new, pluralistic, nonreductionistic sensibilities that are emerging. Titles include *Lost Christianity* (1980), *Consciousness and Tradition* (1982), and *The Heart of Philosophy* (1982). In the conversation that follows, Needleman approaches the task of recognizing authentic mystical spirituality, *transformative* spirituality, not as an outside scholar-analyst, but as one who is himself deeply engaged with these issues.

Needleman was the director of the Center for the Study of New Religious Movements, which sponsored the series of seminars that generated most of the interviews and essays in this book. Because the following conversation, conducted January 5, 1983, explores virtually all of the key themes that run through this volume, it serves as a fitting concluding interview.

Ken Wilber: You in many ways spearheaded the theoretical understanding of the new religious movements in America. Particularly through the 1970s a sense of enthusiasm and a great deal of euphoria surrounded many of these movements—the idea of the new age, the greening of America, and so on. I think that for a large portion of the population, during this period, the critical intellect was out to lunch. People got involved with groups, some of which were very beneficial, some of which, in hindsight, were quite catastrophic. We're now out of the 1970s and into the 1980s and I think people are starting to assume a more critical stance, in the sense of being more discriminating. Do some involvements really lead to transcendence? Do some lead to herd mentality or regressive phenomena, Jonestown being paradigmatic? The volume for which we're interviewing you is an attempt to draw together a wide spectrum of articles, interviews, and examples of different types of new religious movements in order to come up with some initial guidelines for distinguishing non-problematic groups from groups that are in some sense problematic.

Jacob Needleman: Yes, it's a very, very useful thing to do, I think, and needed. The only problem is, it's fundamentally an unanswerable question—as you might know. Why is it unanswerable? It's the same type of question as, what are the guidelines for selecting a wife? What are the guidelines for selecting a god? There's got to be an answer, and yet it's unanswerable. In a culture like ours, where tradition is not believed in and is not really part of people's psyche, we need to begin from zero. There's no sense that this is the way it was done of old, and therefore we will do it this way now. The American mind simply cannot manage with that anymore, for better or worse. So we have to begin our discussion from zero.

Dick Anthony: Well, I don't know if I believe that you really think that. Are we really beginning from zero? I think a certain strategy that you've taken in your public pronouncements—and it's not merely a strategy, I realize it has a truth to it—is that you're a philosopher by training and background, and so in a sense you play a Carlos Castaneda role in relation to Don Juan. You're always the person who starts from scratch and is looking at things with fresh eyes, and seeing just what a rational man could see, looking at things with an eye on subjectivity. In each situation, you find yourself in a dialogue with people who are committed to something, people who aren't seeing something from scratch. In the dialogue that emerges between the persona of Jacob Needleman, the philosopher, and these other wise figures, a certain kind of communication or illumination occurs. You're the representative of modern man, and these are people who are committed to something that might be called a perennial wisdom or a tradition, something really quite ancient. My hunch is that somehow you're articulating both positions, and there must be a sense in which you believe in something that isn't starting from scratch.

Needleman: Oh yes, I believe in the truth of the great traditions. But I can't say I started by believing it. Thirty years ago I had tremendous— well, I wouldn't even call it doubt, I simply ignored them. I did my doctoral work in the field of existential thought and existentialism in psychiatry. I had dabbled in some things, including Zen. I had a very, very powerful experience meeting D. T. Suzuki, and I'd come across great ideas, but I never really felt that I was a believer in spiritual tradition as such. And when I came out to San Francisco, I taught a course in the history of Western religious thought and started to see things in the Old Testament and New Testament that I hadn't seen before. It was something they never told me about in my Harvard and Yale training. I began, gradually, to have more interest in religion than in philosophy as such.

You mentioned my writings. So much of my writing—I'm thinking particularly of *Lost Christianity*—is an intentional attempt to create a form where the feeling appropriate to the idea that I'm speaking about is manifested and can be touched in the reader. Just to communicate ideas abstractly or discursively is not as effective, in certain cases, as to communicate them with a literary form. You said that I present myself publicly as this Castaneda-like figure, and that's partly true of me, personally, but also partly a question of the form of the writing. I've never said this in public about my writing. One of the principal means of communicating great ideas is in the form of myth. Abstract, discursive communication is very good, in its way, but we also need something that touches the feeling of the higher, which myth does. In our twentieth century we have the myth of the "fact." The fact is our myth. Partly this is a good thing: The modern mind wants unvarnished truth, "just the facts." The impulse toward that ideal is wonderful, but it's much harder to do than is commonly thought. The aim is to communicate the meaning of facts through the mythic form of a factual account.

Anthony: This is what I wanted to explore with you. It seems to me that the common element in your various interests—a philosopher who is interested in existentialism, a novelist, a student of religion—all of these interests have in common a certain concern with man in his actual situation or predicament. This differs from a certain prevailing temper, a positivist spirit that assumes that the world is essentially fact and is objectively knowable, that is, describable in a way that is true independently of the knower. All of your interests seem to reject that positivist spirit, which has dominated Western philosophy and the analytic tradition.

Needleman: As a world-view, logical positivism in all its forms is, I think, simply childish. But mystical positivism, if you want to call it that, is eminently sensible. Logical positivism simply bases all its understanding on a very narrow part of the mind and external senses, which is the way children understand things. But most of us are not that childish; that's why logical positivism never worked. Science, or free inquiry, is one thing; scientism is another. Science is a wonderful ideal. On the other hand, scientism we all agree is foolishness. But science, as an ideal, has the power to cut away conditioning, to cut away suggestibility—my telling you what to think, and your being a passive recipient of my and other people's opinions and views. That's why science was such a wonderful thrust. But it degenerated into scientism, as we all know. Still, you could have a mystical positivism, just inventing a term, which would uphold the ideal of science and would freely inquire into matters of spirit, of the mind, of the self, and so on.

Wilber: That's interesting to me, and I would agree. You're saying that the scientific enterprise, in a sense, can extend to subtler ontologies than merely physical data and sensory impressions. That being the case, we might have a science, in the large sense, of religion, or a mystical positivism. Wouldn't that science be able to make some sort of adjudicating statements about the truth claims of various religions . . .

Needleman: Yes, of course it would.

Wilber: OK, so the question is not totally unanswerable.

Needleman: No, it's not unanswerable in that sense. It's answerable, but in order to answer it—well, let me give an example: the marks of the Buddha described in Buddhist scripture. Now, you can reel off the list . . .

Wilber: Thirty-two rather strange . . .

Needleman: Rather strange marks. Then you begin to realize, if you become a student of the spiritual, that every one of these marks is a communication that is meant to touch you in a different way, that they can't be grasped literally, in the sense of, "Well, now, I'm going to go look for somebody who has arms that look like an elephant's trunk." They can only be understood in a more sensitive way. They have what you could say is symbolic meaning—and that term, too, needs to be opened up.

Wilber: Subtler perception.

Needleman: A subtler perception, and more feeling; a more intuitive way, which is not imprecise, it's just not the kind of precision we are accustomed to. So, the thirty-two marks of the Buddha themselves require that you have already understood enough to begin to feel what's at stake, so that you're not out there looking in some external way. In other words, you can't have spiritual standards be spelled out by somebody who's non-involved spiritually. Now, I don't think there are *no* things you can say if you're non-involved. I think there are certain common sense things you can say, things that any reasonable person would, more or less, agree upon. But when you get to the fine points of what the real standards of a good religion and a bad religion are, I don't think you can answer that based on common sense.

Anthony: Well, let me try to push you on that, because it seems to me that everything you have said points toward a general standard of distinguishing between movements dominated by a literalistic, univocal, discursive rationality, or cultural positivism, versus movements that somehow appeal to a higher symbolic faculty in man. In terms of the typology that I've been working on for some years, unilevel religious groups understand religious ideas in a very literal, positivist way, and define their value in terms of material consequences in the world. Unilevel groups that draw upon Eastern mystical ideas, such as Scientology and various kinds of American popularized mysticism, generally claim to produce enlightenment in so many hours of training at so many dollars per hour, and the proof that you've achieved enlightenment is that you can then go out and get a better job and better relationships and achieve happiness. Unilevel groups based on Western, dualistic ideas, I argue, are groups like Jonestown, Synanon, and the Unification Church that claim to be able to create a utopian, godly society very quickly by reinterpreting traditional Western religious ideas in terms of some social ethic. What the unilevel Eastern and Western groups have in common is the idea that you can translate religious ideas into empirical consequences in a very straightforward way, in the same way that you can turn science into technology.

It seems to me implicit in what you're saying that that kind of approach to religious ideas is inherently problematic, and that religious ideas, insofar as they are going to enable a person to experience spiritual truth directly, have to be understood in some more refined or subtler or symbolic way—what I call multilevel. Multilevel groups take it for granted that religious ideas and symbols cannot be definitively understood by everybody in the same way. There's an existential component to one's understanding of religious ideas, such that the understanding essentially occurs in experience and cannot be definitively translated or paraphrased into general ideas.

One of the chief consequences of this multilevel sensibility is the attitude that you yourself don't know what level of understanding you've achieved, let alone what others have achieved, so you don't see a sharp boundary between your group and the rest of humanity in terms of spiritual attainment or virtue. Another multilevel attitude is that moral norms are valuable. The acceptance of moral limitations on personal selfishness as appropriate for seekers, the lack of exclusivity, and the experiential rather than cognitive-conceptual character of religious knowledge, those themes in concert seem to describe the groups that I generally admire in contemporary situations, and classify as multilevel.

Needleman: Well, I think the unilevel-multilevel distinction is useful, but it's limited, like every conceptual distinction. In the East and West, as I see it, there are very great, authentic teachings that are what you would call unilevel—some of the *bhakti* or devotional traditions, for example, in the Middle East and in the West, where you have to take things literally and simply in the beginning. It's a different spiritual strategy. It doesn't mean it's inauthentic. It means it starts from a different place on the circle. Some people who have a certain kind of emotional life can be reached by certain statements and commands and strictures, which the more intellectual person would find simplistic or univocal. So a tradition sometimes opens and expresses itself in different ways. By the unilevel standard, you could say a lot of very untrue things, I think, about Christianity and about Hinduism in certain of its forms. Millions of Hindus go to worship gods in a temple, and if somebody said, "This is just a symbolic aspect of the great Self," they wouldn't know what you're talking about. And yet, they're being led to refine their feelings in an important way, spiritually. You can't just sweep that away and say it's just unilevel.

I don't mean to criticize your distinction as it applies to the American new religions. I think that's an interesting and useful distinction, but in terms of the sweep of the history of religion, somebody who is bowing down at a temple idol with all his heart and everything he's got, even though he's taking it literally, may be moving closer than some very sharp, sophisticated person who's saying, "Oh, it's symbolic."

Anthony: Well, I agree that intellectual sophistication can itself be an obstacle. It's not intellectual sophistication I mean, though, when I talk about the symbolic sensibility in multilevel groups, and it's not unsophisticated naïveté that I mean by the term unilevel. Unilevel groups can and do have a high degree of intellectual sophistication. I'm not sure that we mean the same things by "symbolic" and "literal."

Needleman: It's a funny thing—somebody can say something which is sophisticated, interesting, all-encompassing, and yet it doesn't have the ring of truth. You have to say that you can smell a rat there—you can smell when a teacher doesn't understand what he's talking about. What Trungpa calls spiritual materialism would enter here, too. It's also what I spoke about in my writings on psychiatry and sacred tradition—that, strictly speaking, some of the ideas of spiritual traditions are being used for non-spiritual purposes—which is not to say they don't do people good, but they sometimes are what you call adaptive rather than transformative. I think that's a useful distinction. It's hard to refine more, but it's a useful distinction.

Anthony: So, in this cultural context, can we understand you as agreeing that movements that appear to appeal primarily to a kind of material self-interest are probably not helpful, in terms of transformation and raising people to a higher level of consciousness?

Needleman: Yes, but it gets subtler. Frankly I would prefer a religion that out-and-out says, "You're going to get a lot of money and sex from this religion" to one that says, "You're going to get transformation" and is really trying to get money and sex out of it, without even knowing it themselves. We're talking about a perennial, eternal human problem. Your typology reflects the internal human situation itself: In every human being, there is this impulse to aggrandise through the ego, or in Ken's terms, to take all spiritual or transformational communications and turn them into adaptive or selfish or egoistic implements. This is a fact of human nature. This is why man is what he is. Every great spiritual teacher understands this about human nature and has to take it into account. Anyone who doesn't understand that is underestimating the human problem. And that produces very bad religion.

Wilber: I can see why you like Kierkegaard, because one of the things that he talked about so much was that human beings are an intersection between the infinite and the finite, and it's that paradox, that tension, that agonizing struggle, that is the human condition; and that if people don't understand that, they're going to err to one side or the other, with bad infinity or bad faith.

Needleman: That's right. I think that's well put. And when that is not taken into account, it's the job of the science of religion to take it into account, exactly, in people—for mankind, and for this or that individual.

Anthony: I want to return to a point that you made earlier. You said that in a way you would like movements better that helped people to get more money and sex, if they just said that right out and didn't say what they were helping people to do was gain enlightenment. It seems to me that some kinds of movements are about a different kind of self-aggrandising or craving than money and sex. There's a distinction I see among contemporary literalistic movements, unilevel movements: The ones that pull their ideas from the East tend to be more individualistic and to be more about individual achievement—including money and sex—and the ones that pull their ideas from the West tend to be more about sacrificing individuality in favor of a collective identity, authoritarian submission, and the construction of a utopian society—for example, Synanon, the Unification Church and the People's Temple. It seems to me that when Eastern and Western religious positions go wrong, they go wrong in different ways. I'm interested in whether you see any intrinsic difference between Eastern and Western religion, both at the consequentialist level of what I call the unilevel groups, and also at a more esoteric or mystical level, in multilevel groups.

Needleman: It's hard to generalize that the East is one thing and the West is another. Everything that's great in the East you can find in the West, and vice versa. You can find very activist orientations in the East, and socially oriented movements and so forth. We don't know the East very well at all. But, on the whole, I suppose you could say the East has been more concerned with inner life and the West more with outward action. That's a very simplistic generalization, but on the whole, you could say that, with lots of qualification. The crime of the West has been to be too much outward, and the crime of the East has been to be too much inward.

Anthony: So, if you apply that to the contemporary spiritual scene in America, you might say that when Western religion goes bad, it goes bad in the direction of loss of personal authenticity in favor of sacrificing the self in submission to a group, and when Eastern religion goes bad, it goes bad in the direction of narcissistic indifference to others.

Needleman: Yes, you could put it that way, but all these are very provisional ideas.

There is a very interesting essay in a book I edited called *Sacred Tradition and Present Need.* It's called "The Two Vedantas—The Best and the Worst of India," and it makes the distinction between the yogi and the brahmin. The yogi is concerned with his own inner development and says to hell with society, and the brahmin is very much involved with the transformation of the social order, a theocracy in the deepest sense of the term. The article says that the brahmin, in that sense, is the great spiritual force of ancient India, and that it's all gotten twisted up now, but the yogi is the danger.

So I think it's a good distinction to make if it's taken to be provisional and also metaphorical of all of us. Transformation means everything in man is transformed, is put into a new order, and for that, you have to be sensitive to the total environment of man, the inner as well as the outer. I think it's true that people go wrong in both ways, and maybe the East has tended to go wrong more into the inward way, and the West, more in the outward way, but ultimately, I see them more as metaphors.

Anthony: The point you just made brings us to the issue of whether the Eastern-Western distinction is more valid among unilevel, literalistic-consequentialistic religious groups than among multilevel, mystical-esoteric ones. Viewed through unilevel sensibilities, Eastern and Western religious imagery and ideas seem to be talking about quite different things and tend to pull you in different directions. But as you go to the more esoteric, inner level the Western and Eastern ideas seem to be more about the same kind of thing, and we even have religious scholars— for instance, Schuon and other writers associated with the British journal *Studies in Comparative Religion,* and Huston Smith and Aldous Huxley, and so on—who argue that there's a perennial wisdom common to all of the traditions, that they are really essentially the same. You've had some association with these writers. What is your position on that? Is there a perennial wisdom that's the same in all of these traditions, East and West?

Needleman: Truth is truth, obviously, but that can be said in such a way as to make it into some flat, false ecumenism. To say that the same truth is in everything, that all is one, that the traditions are the same, can be totally useless, boring and meaningless. The differences are very important, and they're necessary.

Anthony: Why is that?

Needleman: Many reasons, but first of all, each tradition is in a cultural environment that it's dealing with. It's like the image of the mountain. There are many paths up the mountain, and they also start from different places around it. You know this image?

Wilber: Sure; the paths look different all the way up.

Needleman: They look different, but they're particularly different way back there at the bottom, where we are. One starts from the North Pole, and another starts from the jungle, and another starts from the desert; and the directions for following each path are very different than the directions for the others. If you follow the directions for a different path than the one you're on, you're going to die. Christianity, let's say, is the path that starts out in the desert, and the directions say, "Thou shalt carry much water; thou shalt wear light clothing." The directions for the path from the North Pole, Buddhism, say, "Thou shalt wear heavy clothing." They're both leading up to the peak, but if you obey one when you're in the other place, you're going to die. So, each tradition has a unique context in which it's trying to lead people to the universal truth.

To see the inner similarities of the authentic traditions takes a very highly spiritually developed person. It's a rather cheapened idea in our culture that they're all the same, they're all one. It took Ramakrishna, for example, living tremendous sacrifice for decades, to be able to say they're all the same, whereas now any doctoral candidate reading Schuon can say, "Well, they're all one." It's a very great, rare gift to be able really to understand how they're the same.

Anthony: Are you saying that the sense in which they're the same can only be experienced, that it couldn't be articulated or formulated?

Needleman: Well, I think it can be articulated, but it wouldn't be articulated, necessarily, in an abstract, discursive way.

Anthony: So you differ, then, from the writers in the *Studies in Comparative Religion* who seem to be claiming that they have articulated the common elements . . .

Needleman: They've done a marvelous work of articulating things within that kind of language. I think they're extremely interesting.

Anthony: It seems to me one thing they're up to is attempting to formulate what the wisdom traditions have in common, as a way of aiding people in discriminating between the true and false within their own tradition.

Needleman: Yes, but you cannot discriminate only through concepts. These are wonderful concepts that they've given, but you can't discriminate only with concepts.

I think the question really becomes, are we interested in learning about religion, or are we interested in learning about reality? I've always hoped that I was more interested in learning about reality, and to the extent that the study of religion can orient me toward that, it was good. I'm not a religious scholar, in that sense. I'm not interested in religion just as a phenomenon; I'm interested in whether it can help me to understand the real world.

The distinction of esoteric and exoteric is itself a very tough distinction. How you distinguish it may not be how someone else distinguishes it. Esoteric ideas are, among other things, ideas that help you to discover the truth for yourself, and not necessarily subtle ideas that you take from other people. To discover for yourself—that means you change, you become different. Or, as I put it in the article I wrote on Gurdjieff in *Consciousness and Tradition*, the esoteric concerns energy, the exoteric is form, concept, and all the rest of it. Anything that has to do solely with conceptual formulations, rituals, and formal observance . . .

Wilber: No matter how sublime.

Needleman: No matter how sublime, is exoteric.

Wilber: I like your distinction, because again, it cuts across literalism versus symbolism.

Anthony: So there are three different views on the universality of mysticism that have some kind of scholarly respectability, it seems to me.

Needleman: What does scholarly respectability mean to you? Scholarship is another word for science, isn't it?

Anthony: Modern scholarship, yes.

Needleman: Yes, the modern idea of scholarship is basically the revival of the idea, taken out of ancient Greek culture, of an impersonal, objective inquiry, as assessment of data. When it's applied to nature, it's called science. When it's applied to history or literature or ideas, it's called scholarship. But it's still science. The scholar has the same mindset as the scientist, only he's dealing with the non-material world. So, I respect scholarship, I'm in scholarship, I am a scholar up to a point, but when you come to questions of religion, there's a point beyond which the scholar, as such, cannot go.

Anthony: We're making the same point, because the point I'm trying to make, which I feel is complementary to what you've just said, is that there are at least three quite different positions that have some plausibility for people who call themselves scholars, on this issue of whether there is a universal mysticism. One is that there is a universal mysticism, and that its essence can be formulated. That's Frithjof Schuon and Aldous Huxley and others. Another position is that there is not a universal mysticism, and that the mysticism of the East and the mysticism of the West are quite separate, quite different things. Rudolf Otto argues this position, which is quite popular in the academic world. You seem to be formulating a third position that's somewhat different, and which strikes a deeper chord in me than either of these other two. You're saying, I think, that what mysticism is about, intrinsically, is actual transformation and transcendence, and that this is what is universal among authentic mystical traditions, although we can't formulate exactly what is going to produce transcendence in any specific cultural context, just as we can't formulate transcendence itself. You're saying that it's the actual process of transformation and transcendence that is the difference between esotericism and exotericism.

Needleman: Yes, I would settle with that. And when esoteric truth gets formalized, it has to be restated. But it's the ancient truth that goes back to the anteriority of mankind, and is always being restated in a way that breaks the patterns that formed around it in the past. Who knows what Ankhnaten did in Egypt or what some of the great Zen masters did? They blew up the thing. Buddha himself blew up the Brahmanic religion completely, exploded it, and yet he was obviously reconstituting it. Christ blew up the frozen Judaic situation, doing much more than reconstituting Judaism. He reconstituted things from a source of life that exploded everything that had accrued. It's not that the forms that had accrued were not useful, but they became exoteric. They were useful, necessary means for mankind to have ideals and so forth, but they did not necessarily lead to an intensive transformation of life.

Anthony: So you feel there is some value to exoteric religion.

Needleman: Of course I feel there's value. I don't think mankind could have existed without it.

Anthony: This distinguishes you from many contemporary writers.

Needleman: Maybe it does. I'd like to see them invent something that could hold learning and life together like the Christian church did. Most of our little experiments self-destruct or cause wars and violence within ten or twenty years.

Anthony: The picture that one gets from writings such as *The Aquarian Conspiracy* and from many humanistic and transpersonal writers is that exoteric religion is obsolescent, a thing of the past, and esoteric religion . . .

Needleman: Is the exoteric religion of the future.

Anthony: Yes, and we're going into a new age, now, and we'll all be mystics. What you're saying seems different.

Needleman: It may be true that in a certain sense exoteric religion as we know it has had its day. But, certainly, the new, exoteric religion of "esotericism" is not going to do much better. I mean, to drag in these esoteric terms and make them into mass religion . . .

Wilber: It's unilevel.

Needleman: Yes. I think that we're between religions. We're between traditions. It's a cliché, perhaps, but we are in an age of transition. Everyone says it, but this really is seriously true now. I think we've passed through something, and are at the beginning of something. I don't know if it's a new age, a better or worse world. I don't think anybody can say which way it's going to go. I think the New Age thinkers are overoptimistic and naïve about how good this is going to be. I'm not pessimistic, particularly, but it doesn't look particularly promising. There's almost nothing left of the old standards. The whole culture is in crisis at this point.

I find it in my work now, with the professionals in all fields. Everybody who's got any kind of sensibility is asking, why? What are we doing? Why are we doing it? Where is it going? Where do we get our values from? There's a pervasive quest for values, and the new religious movements are one expression of that, but it's all over the culture now. The new cultural hero is the seeker. One of the great cultural ideals of the 1980s will be the seeker. Not the finder. I think the seeker is the person who goes on seeking, who knows how to seek, who knows the conditions necessary for seeking.

Wilber: Can you talk a little bit about that impulse for seeking and some of the ways you see it coming out in the new religious movements? Is there any part of that seeking that you see as problematic? How could this seeking impulse go wrong?

Anthony: Or how could it go right? That is, what can seekers look for that would give them some kind of indication that the seeking is on the right track and has some promise to it?

Needleman: Well, it's tempting to try to say, but you never can get it quite so simply. But one of the things that interests me very much is the idea of the wish, the need, the desire for what is higher, as an organic part of the human mind, which has not been acknowledged in modern psychology. It's not so much that man has got a great Self in him, which he may or may not have, but he has a great need in him. And the need is the embryo of the Self; or the way the great Self appears in man, I think, is through the need. It doesn't appear through being wise and powerful, or through self-mastery and all that sort of thing, as you might gather from some of the literature. It appears as a restlessness, and a need, and a hunger that isn't satisfied by the things which most people claim satisfy them.

Wilber: Not so much a seer or a doer, but a wanter.

Needleman: Now, what should a seeker do? A seeker needs common sense, skepticism, and openness—all at the same time. We have to be open and skeptical at the same time. You can't be skeptical only, because then you're closed. You can't be open only, because then you're gullible.

Anthony: All things being equal, are you safer going into a group which has some continuous relationship to a tradition? Are you better off, for example, studying in relation to a Zen or Tibetan Buddhist, who is part of an unbroken lineage, than you would be by going into a movement like Scientology? Is having a teacher grounded in tradition important?

Needleman: But you can't just say, "traditional teacher." How do you know he's a traditional teacher? What are the credentials?

Wilber: Let's take something as an example that might not be on everybody's "Hit Parade"—the Unification Church. I suppose that you're no screaming fan of it, although you might not have anything against it. If somebody said, "From what you know about this, does this represent your understanding of an authentic religious involvement?"— your answer would be . . .

Needleman: No.

Wilber: And, could you elaborate at all?

Needleman: It would be hard for me to elaborate. A lot of it is intuitive, and a lot of it is what I've been able to surmise from the people I've met, from the pronouncements of some of the leaders, from the trouble they've gotten into, and from the kind of publicity they've created. I have a sense it's out of control. I have a sense of a lot of suggestibility, a lot of violence—not physical violence, but a kind of emotional agitation. And emotional agitation is, to me, almost a sure sign that the thing isn't transformative.

Wilber: Emotional agitation is not passion.

Needleman: No, not passion in the deep sense of the term, the love of truth. Emotionalism in religion is very dangerous. Emotions are a problem. Emotions are *the* human problem. And, as I said in *Lost Christianity*, just because an emotion has something called "God" at the end of it doesn't make it any less a problem—in fact, that makes it more of a problem. The chief problem of modern man is suggestibility, it seems to me. That is not my idea, it's Gurdjieff's. I find myself saying, "I don't think that's it" about any teaching that is basing itself on what I, rightly or wrongly, see as suggestibility.

It's a very subtle thing sometimes. Even from the beginning, when I was writing on new religions, I could never imagine what it was like to put on robes, smell incense, and see somebody sitting up on a throne. That must be very important in the tradition or the culture which it came from, but in this culture it gives people a very powerful suggestion: that you are religious, that you are on the way, that you are one step up to God.

The church has the same problem. If you walk into a church, emotions are immediately being suggested to you. Now, within the great context or tradition of monastic disciplines of the medieval period, and all the cultural forces that were part of living in that era, this must have been a very great and powerful and useful force in life. But when it comes down here now, you go in and you put your head down, and you begin to get emotional religion. I don't think that can go anywhere, esoterically.

Bruce Ecker: And yet you spoke of the value of higher feeling.

Needleman: Yes, but that isn't necessarily higher feeling. An ordinary emotion about a higher object is not a higher emotion. I can be craving God as much as I crave money. It's still craving. When the traditions speak of craving for salvation, that is of a completely different quality, a different vibration, and comes from a different part of your mind, your being, than do the ordinary desires.

Anthony: Is there any value for a seeker in submitting himself to a teacher who is viewed as being on a higher level of consciousness than himself?

Needleman: Certainly, a person needs the help of someone with greater being and knowledge than he has.

Anthony: That's interesting, because there's a common assumption that individual autonomy is the way to avoid most problems of spiritual seeking. As long as you don't submit yourself, as long as you maintain your own autonomy, then you won't have any problems.

Needleman: But man has no autonomy. Fallen man, or whatever we are, has no autonomy.

Wilber: Yes, I think that's the sane way to look at it. It's a peculiar bias among humanist and even transpersonal researchers that the devotional groups—or the ones that work through a master, Meher Baba, for instance, or Neem Karoli Baba—are necessarily a little bit suspect, whereas if you're in a non-devotional group, you're keeping your so-called autonomy. What they don't realize is that you might simply be keeping your ego.

Needleman: Yes, it's a very difficult subject. There is, first of all, a very healthy sense of, "I do not wish to be sucked in. I don't wish to be brainwashed, I don't wish to be at the mercy of something or someone, and give over." Something in man is free. Some little tiny thing—it's very much less than he thinks, and it's very much in a different place than he thinks it is. Without that, nothing can happen. But that's not the autonomy that people think they have. It's a very different kind of autonomy. That has to be deeply respected in any tradition or group, and that's very hard to do, because you have to have exact knowledge of where it is in people.

But then there is the other side: You can't do it by yourself. You must have help. I mean really—supernatural help, in a way.

Wilber: You can't get Autonomy with a capital A without theonomy.

Needleman: Right. So you've got two things, "autonomy" and "surrender," both of which are important. Again, it's a question of a finer feeling, of subtle perception and discrimination.

There is definitely a danger of submitting to a false guru, or even to a guru who's a great man but still doesn't know how to transmit. There are people who have attained great spiritual power but don't know how they got it and don't know how to give it to other people. And they make people think they're going somewhere, when they don't even know how they got there themselves.

Wilber: Could you say what you mean by false gurus?

Needleman: Well, somebody who picks up a great idea here and there, has a few mystical experiences and makes a career out of it. History is full of religious leaders whose spiritual authority is based on one big experience.

Anthony: Rudolph Otto calls them the illuminati mystics.

Needleman: Without derogating them, some of the people who founded sects within our Christian traditions may have been like that.

Ecker: So submitting to a false guru is a type of false submission.

Needleman: Yes—and then there's the other danger of people who feel they want to stay away from any submission, and that they're simply going to decide for themselves and do it themselves, and make up their own religion; people who, with all of the good intentions in the world, put together what they like out of various traditions, and make up a few things to cement them together. Many of the new "home grown" religions are of that variety, and to me, that often means trouble.

Wilber: So two major problems seem to be submission to false gurus, on the one hand, and overzealous autonomy, on the other: the former appealing to those who are too open or gullible, the latter to those who are too closed or skeptical. And the question of balance between extremes seems to come down, again, to what you've been talking about throughout this interview: an almost intangible, subtle perception and discrimination.

Needleman: Yes, indeed. More than that I don't know can really be said.

Editorial Commentary

"You cannot discriminate only through concepts." These words capture Jacob Needleman's central theme. He emphasizes that neither the scholarly study nor the practice of mystical religion can be fruitfully pursued through discursive rationality alone. The univocal, positivistic approach, so successful in the physical sciences, is insufficient to the task here. Mystical religion must be approached not just conceptually, but through a deeper resonance of meanings, symbolically—though not *merely* symbolically, not merely imaginatively. For religion to be transformative, its symbolically resonant forms must somehow stimulate the actual processes of spiritual realization in human beings, processes that inherently elude conceptual description.

In relation to the Anthony typology, Needleman's position corresponds closely to what Anthony and Ecker describe in Part 1 as multilevel multivocality, the appreciation of transcendental meanings without literalistically reducing them to mundane associations. At the other extreme is univocality, the literalistic, concretizing sensibility of well-defined, rational meanings, which generates unilevel religion. Intermediate is unilevel multivocality, which rejects univocal literalism but nevertheless fails to preserve the transcendental dimension of spiritual meanings, again reducing them to mundane ones. Needleman distinguishes implicitly among these three styles. He describes the spiritual teacher who exemplifies unilevel multivocality, the teacher who has "the most sophisticated, well-developed, conceptual understanding of all these things" but fails to have "the ring of truth," the deeper resonance of a living knowledge of transcendental meanings. However, as Needleman indicates in discussing the marks of the Buddha, not everyone is ripe for sensing this resonance or for "reading" spiritually symbolic meanings. The dilemma is that spiritual discrimination is beyond the reach of mere common sense, and that ordinary conceptual language is of no avail for imparting it. The resonant language of symbol and myth is necessary, but with this language one cannot assume a general audience. Of necessity, one's audience is limited to those who already have enough trans-rational spiritual discrimination to understand.

Needleman's reservations regarding the usefulness of rational-discursive concepts for describing religion become apparent each time Anthony solicits his opinion of the typology categories. After some initial protest that the unilevel versus multilevel and monism versus dualism categories cannot fully do justice to the matter, Needleman does approve of them as valid and useful to the extent that one can generalize at all in conceptual terms about mystical involvements. But a lingering point of contention between Needleman and Anthony remains: Can literalistic religious practice be transformative? We return to this point below.

The Anthony typology attempts to formulate criteria that can help people who lack subtle spiritual discrimination to avoid spiritual fraud and to recognize groups that competently foster spiritual realization. In particular, the unilevel and multilevel categories of the typology are defined substantively, in terms of observable qualities, and so provide predictive criteria for determining whether or not a group is likely to prove spiritually transformative.

The impossibility of teasing apart transcendental meanings from their cultural garb and capturing them in precise, univocal language makes it impossible for religious scholars to achieve a definitive comparison of mystical orientations. The universality of mysticism remains an open question as a scholarly issue. In Needleman's opinion, whatever may be the scholar's view, the various mystical traditions converge towards the same transcendent truth, although their convergence can only be apprehended transrationally and described symbolically, mythically. He has reservations, however, about the universality of Anthony's unilevel-multilevel distinction as a way of assessing the mystical authenticity of religious groups. Needleman regards the unilevel-multilevel dimension of the typology as applicable to the American new religions, but thinks it is probably not cross-culturally, universally valid. For the editors, this remains an open question. It seems possible that all authentic mysticism has the same epistemological structure, and if so, an epistemological criterion such as the unilevel-multilevel distinction could have universal sweep.

Needleman seems to identify authentic mysticism with a "transformation of energies." We agree, though we would add that from our viewpoint, there are valid mystical avenues that do not involve an explicit focus on the energy dimensions of consciousness. Ultimate mystical realization radically transcends energy just as it transcends matter and mind—according to Buddhist, Sufi, and Vedantic Hindu teachings—and, to use Needleman's image, not all routes to that mountaintop of gnosis require the seeker to work with energy *per se*. In these cases, the transformation of energies occurs as a natural by-product of spiritual practice, as in some multilevel technical approaches (such as Zen Buddhism) and in multilevel charismatic approaches (such as Meher Baba). Needleman's point is that valid mysticism profoundly affects the deeper structure of the seeker's consciousness, quite beyond the level of ordinary psychological processes.

As mentioned earlier, Needleman and Anthony appear to differ regarding the transformative efficacy of literalistic religions. Anthony cites univocality, or the matter-of-fact literalism of the rational-scientific sensibility, as one of the defining features of his unilevel category of nontransformative spiritual practice. Needleman cites as a counterexample how "somebody who is bowing down at a temple idol with all his heart and everything he's got, even though he's taking it literally, may be moving closer than some very sharp, sophisticated person who's saying, 'Oh, it's symbolic.'" It seems to us that both Needleman's and Anthony's viewpoints are valid, for on close consideration, they mean quite different things here by the word "literal." For Anthony, to relate to religious ideas and symbols through univocal literalism is to interpret them in terms of mundane meanings, which removes the transcendental dimension. Needleman himself provides a good example of this kind of literal-mindedness earlier in the conversation when he says that the thirty-two marks of the Buddha "can't be grasped literally." "To go look for someone who has arms that look like an elephant's trunk" is to be "looking in some external way," strictly in terms of mundane concepts that are well-defined, wholly understandable rationally, and therefore closed. In contrast, Needleman's worshipper who regards the temple idol as an actual divinity and bows down to it "with all his heart and everything he's got" is not reducing transcendental meanings to closed, mundane ones, but is, rather, encountering and responding authentically to a transcendental dimension that he regards as open-ended, alive, and pregnant with unfathomable meaning. Thus Needleman's worshipper does not relate to religious themes univocally, as if he exhaustively understood them in conceptual terms. That is our point. The worshipper's profound acceptance of religious forms at face value is the acceptance of transcendent mystery on its own inscrutable terms, without pretending to possess definitive understanding of what is accepted.[1] To embrace religious forms at face value in this way is not what is meant by "literalism" in both the study of the phenomenology of religion and in the multidisciplinary study of open versus closed belief systems and the influence of language on groups.[2] In our view, Needleman's worshipper exemplifies not literalism but faith and conviction, attitudes which are based on transrational, intuitive recognition of spiritual truth, independent of rational understanding. Thus Needleman's counterexample to Anthony's position regarding literalism is not actually a counterexample, as we see it.

Obviously, all spiritual and consciousness groups are bound to assume the truth of their own concepts, images, and practices. As Needleman puts it, one cannot always say of one's own religious forms, "Oh, it's a symbol." Therefore, the important question for a prospective member of a group is not whether the group accepts its concepts, images, and practices on face value, but whether or not it relates to these forms through univocal literalism, which does not allow for a transformative involvement.

Univocal literalism is the sensibility that marks most exoteric religion in the modern era. Still, Needleman assigns great value to exoteric Christianity in the history of the West. He agrees with new age thinkers that the exoteric framework has run out of life in the present period, and that we are now "between religions," but he differs sharply from the popular new age vision of cultural upliftment through mass esoteric sensibilities. He describes the spiritual future of Western culture as highly uncertain, except for seeing the image of the seeker as a central motif that will emphasize the importance of knowing how to keep the process of spiritual discovery alive, authentic, and ongoing.

Needleman does not fully spell out his view of the relationship between exoteric and esoteric religion. But what he does say seems consistent with Anthony's view that when an Avataric figure such as Jesus, Mohammed, or Buddha appears and spiritually enlivens a culture—breaking up encrusted, exoteric forms, as Needleman describes, with a fresh release of transcendental presence and meaning—the new, exalted sensibilities persist only for a few centuries. Invariably, culture increasingly subjects the transcendental meanings to rational formulation and elaboration until an exoteric consensus develops, along with an institutionalized split between majority exoteric and minority esoteric movements. The ongoing process of cultural rationalization, which has been described by the sociologist Max Weber, continues to erode the transcendence-mindedness of the exoteric religion until a thoroughly univocal-unilevel condition is reached, and a state of extreme materialism prevails culturally, as presently is the case.

The person who pursues esoteric, mystical realization requires, in Needleman's view, "the help of someone with greater being and knowledge than he has." On the issue of autonomy versus surrender to authentic spiritual authority, Needleman's position squares with our own. Autonomy as popularly conceived is a kind of self-deception. It may protect against false spiritual authority, but it also protects and preserves the seeker's false ego-self. Paradoxically, the true autonomy of the seeker's intrinsic being develops out of surrender to genuine spiritual authority. This view diverges from the blanket skepticism towards profound surrender that prevails in humanistic and transpersonal circles.

Needleman contributes to the other frameworks in this book with the concept of gurus who have undergone a genuine transformation of consciousness but do not know how they achieved it or how to enable others to achieve it, although "they make people think they're going somewhere." This concept implies that a spiritual master or teacher whose guidance proves ineffective is not necessarily devoid of inner attainment, and in that sense is not necessarily a charlatan. It also implies that the seeker has to discern not just the spiritual master who has truly attained, but the one who also can enable the seeker to attain.

Notes

1. On a related note, it has been a common misconception of people in literate, scientific cultures to view preliterate religious attitudes as consisting of conceptual beliefs. This is now widely recognized among anthropologists as a misunderstanding. In particular, anthropologists no longer regard myth as naïve belief, but as a participation in shared meanings of a quite different order than conceptual belief. Univocal literalism can occur only in a rational-literate cultural situation. Definitive conceptual interpretations of religious themes cannot exist in preliterate cultures, therefore "belief" as we know it does not occur. The postliterate student of preliterate religion has to refrain from reading himself or herself into the preliterate situation, and has to realize that the preliterate person lives within a totally different epistemological framework.

2. We refer to a very extensive literature that spans the fields of social psychology, linguistics, semiotics, sociology, and general semantics.

Conclusion

The dedicated reader has by this point considered a great many issues and arguments bearing upon our central theme: How can we distinguish true from false avenues to the realization of the highest, or deepest, in us? But let us take a realistic and truly pragmatic look at what happens in actual experience as we attempt to live spiritually and move somehow towards authentic realization, using all we have learned to make wise interpretations of spiritual teachings.

What happens is this: We err, and frequently. In unnoticed, insignificant moments, again and again we err, or forget, or delude ourselves. Minutes or decades later, we may realize what has happened, become conscious of it, catch ourselves. At that moment, we experience a sudden, sharp awareness of our fallibility, our lack of attainment, our weak attention, the crudeness of our understanding. We sustain a humiliation and a shock in these moments, making them unwelcome to the ego, skilled as it is at preventing such feelings from entering awareness. Frequent inner failures of attention and discrimination are inevitable; conscious recovery from them does not automatically follow. The capacity to feel these highly instructive and corrective humiliations, and to allow them to inculcate a genuine humility, is in our view crucial to the practical art of spiritual inner development.

Thus, disappointment is bound to come to the reader who thinks that the many criteria, guidelines, and points of discrimination in this book will enable him or her to avoid making spiritual errors. In fact, the view that one could achieve spiritual authenticity and smooth spiritual progress by straightforwardly applying a rational formulation of any kind is one of the chief errors we have focused upon. To hold that view is to be unconsciously defended against discovering the limitations and distortions inevitably present in one's current spiritual sensibility. The life of authentic spirituality does not always necessarily move smoothly forward and remain neatly under control; it has all the vicissitudes of any true adventure that goes far beyond the familiar: uncertainty, false trails, mistaken choices, physical, emotional, and mental hardships, and instructions misunderstood, misapplied or forgotten.

The pitfall of expecting to master spiritual life by using rational formulations results largely from a heavy cultural emphasis on "instrumental rationality," a sociological term denoting the utilitarian view of reason as the principle of efficiency in means-ends relationships. Instrumental rationality would turn all knowledge into a kind of technology—concrete, practical, efficient—but it is an approach that fails in the psychospiritual domain.

Instrumental rationality itself is one expression of a broader cultural emphasis on an ethic of individualism that again constitutes a major pitfall for Western spiritual aspirants. The founding myth of the modern era in the West is that of the individual's rebellion against the unjust authority of the collectivity.[1] Yet while the Western ethic overtly affirms that the route to freedom and fulfillment lies through individualism, the acceptable styles of individualism and the meaning of freedom and fulfillment have been defined by the collective culture. Even the widespread transition since the 1960s from objectivistic/externalistic values (the "culture of role") to subjectivistic/internalistic values (the "culture of self") has not changed this situation. It is an illusion to assume that by converting to subjectivism Americans transcend the cultural context; for most converts the culture still defines the style and goals of this "individualistic" subjectivism. Specifically, the culture provides images of fulfillment centering upon self-satisfaction, that is, abundant pleasure and comfort as a separate self. But it is the transcendence of the separate self state, not optimal satisfaction in that state, that we try to achieve when we travel authentic spiritual paths. The separate self state is the very condition of insecurity, unfulfillment, and suffering.

All visions of individualistic fulfillment offered and supported by Western culture are oriented around material success as the primary requisite condition in both objectivistic and subjectivistic perspectives, whereas authentic spiritual orientations regard material success as an entirely irrelevant index. Thus, any movement or group that mixes its vision of transcendence with images of heightened individualistic success and satisfaction probably constitutes a false path because it encourages a lack of awareness of the cultural assumptions distorting its interpretation of spiritual ideas.

In our view, then, the culturally prevalent styles of both objectivism and subjectivism (which correspond in the Anthony typology to unilevel dualism and unilevel monism, respectively) are unsuitable as frameworks in which to live a spiritual life. Given this situation, a reader might ask what sort of epistemology, what sort of truth claims are appropriate for transpersonal theorists and therapists in general, and in particular, what sort of truth claims—objectivistic or subjectivistic—are we making for the Anthony typology as the evaluative framework used in this book?

In order to answer this question we will review briefly the history of the dialectic between objectivism and subjectivism in Western culture (see also the Introduction and Part 1); it is this conflict between mainstream objectivism and an increasingly influential counter-cultural subjectivism that has characterized the modern era.[2] Subjectivist critiques were important in aiding individuals to transcend the reductionistic effects of objectivist culture and from the beginning were intertwined with mystical religion. Now that subjectivism has become a mainstream orientation, however, and a unilevel instrumental rationality still dominates our consciousness, it has become evident that in the present period truly liberating perspectives must transcend the dichotomy between objectivism and subjectivism. We have entered a post-modern era and it is now clear that effective critiques of the cultural imprisonment of consciousness must undermine both unilevel objectivism and unilevel subjectivism from within truly multilevel perspectives.[3]

A BRIEF HISTORY OF OBJECTIVISM AND SUBJECTIVISM

In *Beyond Objectivism and Relativism* (pp. 16–20) Richard Bernstein has argued that what he calls the Cartesian Anxiety has deeply affected Western culture since it assimilated the influence of René Decartes' argument that one's knowledge of the world must be built upon the bedrock of absolute certainty. The alternative to such objective certainty, according to Descartes, was total uncertainty, a terrifying moral and personal chaos. Thus from the beginning, objectivism, the perspective which Descartes favored, has been paired with subjectivism, an alternative which he viewed as a horrible danger.

It is unlikely that the Cartesian emphasis upon objectivistic certainty would have become a dominant cultural emphasis if it had not been combined with the scientific empiricism that gained prestige soon thereafter as a result of the immense influence of the physics of Isaac Newton and the scientistic philosophy of Francis Bacon. Within the scientific rationalism which became the dominant cultural perspective as a result of the

Enlightenment—and of the American and French revolutions which institutionalized the Enlightenment politically—objective certainty was to be achieved not through philosophical introspection—as in Descartes' perspective—but through paying close attention to the consequences of one's ideas in the material world—as in Newtonian physics.

These two cultural emphases, rationalistic certainty—what we have termed univocality—and empiricistic consequentialism, became the primary motifs in the bourgeois success ethic, which has dominated Western culture since the Enlightenment. Within the culture of role based upon it, individual success has been assumed to equal moral virtue; conformity to objective moral standards has been assumed to result in empirical or objective social status.

From nearly the beginning, the objectivistic success ethic that gained currency during the Enlightenment was viewed by important cultural minorities as antithetical to the achievement of the higher reaches of human nature. The perception that there was something fundamentally illegitimate in the new, objectivist sensibility from traditional religious, ethical, or aesthetic perspectives expressed itself in a variety of specific criticisms within the nineteenth-century Romantic counter-culture. Space does not allow an articulation of these counter-rational issues in any detail but we will mention them here in a very general way.

The Romantics focused upon flaws in both the univocalist and the consequentialist dimensions of the objectivist Enlightenment perspective. If formulations of knowledge are to be viewed as having only one meaning regardless of the level of consciousness of the person interpreting them, then the evocative or connotative dimension of meaning which had previously been viewed as the primary opening to transcendence in human consciousness would be eliminated as a factor in culture.[4] In addition, if moral virtue was assumed to be objective in the sense that its meaning could be read conclusively from its empirical consequences, then the tragic dimension of the Western sensibility would be consigned to the dustbin of history. Socrates, Christ, the Christian martyrs all died for their adherence to principles which would be thereby defined as false if material success were to be taken as the sole standard of objective truth.

Objectivism and subjectivism were defined from the beginning as mutually exclusive antitheses that exhaust the possibilities for human knowledge.[5] When the Romantics found that bourgeois standards of knowledge were not totally certain or objective, they therefore assumed that human meaning was to be found through embracing total uncertainty, or subjectivism. The subjectivist revolt, then, tended to identify transcendence with multivocality *per se* and with a vague, this-worldly pantheism. It remained unilevel because it assumed that all reality was to be found within one level of material consciousness, whereas the multilevel symbolic character of the medieval perception of the world assumed many levels of metaphysical existence—the Great Chain of Being—and many levels of consciousness capable of perceiving them. To oversimplify somewhat, whereas the Enlightenment sensibility was one of unilevel rationality, the Romantic sensibility was one of unilevel emotionality.[6]

The various heirs of the Romantic counterrationalist critique—Marxism, Freudianism, Existentialism, Artistic Modernism, Weberian sociology—have each focused upon different elements of the bourgeois pretensions to objectivist rationality.[7] Marxism undermines the claimed objectivity of the success ethic by arguing that the ethical merit of the capitalist world-view—which depends upon the interlinked notions of free will and the equality of opportunity in a democracy—are contradicted by the deterministic effects of the class system in industrial society.[8] Freudianism argues that internalized religious values (the super-ego) represent not objective religious truths but inauthentic compromises with oppressive collective demands. Moreover, the ego itself, the reality principle supposedly structured by the principle of objective rationality, is typically distorted in its assessment of reality by the underlying demands of individualistic selfishness (the id). Existentialism argues that conformity to supposedly objective social norms equals personal inauthenticity or bad faith rather than moral virtue. Human excellence consists in the free choice of one's values rather than adherence to social demands. Artistic modernism combined the Romantic, Marxist, Freudian and Existentialist critiques of bourgeois rationality into an artistic tradition that undermined the pretensions of bourgeois rationality in various dimensions. Finally, the modernist critique of the mainstream sensibility was given sociological expression by Weber's argument that rationalization per se, with its consequent disenchantment of the world, is a deeper problem for the modern sensibility than purely economic concerns. Weber argued that the domination of modern culture by instrumental rationality (the utilitarian redefinition of reason as the principle of efficiency in means-ends relationships) tends to disconnect humanity from the experience of ultimate value.

These subjectivist critiques of objectivism, integrated into what might be termed the modernist synthesis, formed the orienting belief system for an elite avant garde, which has gained in influence throughout the twentieth century. In the terms of the Anthony typology, the interpretive sensibility of the modernist perspective was unilevel rather than multilevel because it assumed that its ideological assumptions were valid for just one level of consciousness and that they would prove themselves through their empirical consequences. When enough people became converted to modernism, it would topple objectivist capitalism from within and usher in a brave new world of egalitarian, multivocalist, democratic socialism. Imagine the surprise of thinkers within the modernist *avant garde* when, as a result of the increased educational requirements of a post-industrial society, large masses of young people did in fact become influenced by the various multivocal critiques of capitalist democracy. Initially, the widespread social unrest of the 1960s gave promise of satisfying the utopian predictions of the literary modernist/ Marxist *avant garde*, but rather soon it became evident that the protests of the 1960s counter-culture—"modernism in the streets" in Lionel Trilling's contemptuous phrase—were anchored in too privatized and emotional a sense of outrage to serve as the basis for a new society.[9]

Since the 1960s it has become evident that the continued spread of pluralist values has done nothing to overturn the hegemony of instrumental rationality. Contemporary social experience demonstrates that the domination of the public sphere by highly systematized means-ends relationships structured by no value except that of efficiency is perhaps even more compatible with hedonistic subjectivism than with ascetic objectivism in the realm of private values. Narcissism, rather than authoritarianism, is the common cold of post-industrial society.

Given this analysis, social critics such as Christopher Lasch tend to see the monistic new religions, the most systematic expressions of subjectivist epistemology, as further extensions of narcissist culture. Contemporary mysticism, from this point of view, is simply the newest form of false consciousness, an ideology which mystifies and conceals the domination of consciousness by the reality of instrumental self-interest. Individuals may believe that they are achieving the transcendence of self through meditating at a Zendo on the weekends, but in their disciplined pursuit of rationalized self-interest in corporate offices during their work-a-day week, they manifest their true selves. Whether the official mainstream ideology is objectivist or subjectivist makes no difference to the domination of culture by instrumental rationality as long as the normal public business of society continues to be structured primarily according to the assumptions of materialistic efficiency.

As is obvious from our earlier analysis of unilevel monism, we too regard much, if not most, contemporary mysticism as merely another form of instrumental rationality. The literalistic interpretation of mystical doctrines in terms of their materialistic consequences does not really result in the transcendence of cultural controls over consciousness, but rather in the deepening of such control. Unilevel monism assumes, as did the *avant garde* modernist culture it drew upon for its inspiration, that the mainstream culture which was to be transcended was synonymous with objectivism. In fact, as we argued earlier, modernist culture has always needed objectivist culture as its exemplary antithesis in order to disguise its own lack of metaphysical content. By focusing most of its energies upon the discrediting of objectivist naïveté, and by painting itself with its vague emotional message as the natural antithesis to objectivist culture, modernism had, until the events of the 1960s, managed to sustain the illusion that it could serve as a self-sufficient framework for a new civilization. But since utilitarian reason continues to dominate the public sphere even after multivocality has become a mass perspective, the latter's pretensions to utopian self-sufficiency have become considerably less plausible. Nevertheless, unilevel monist groups—the great "Aquarian Conspiracy"—continue the covertly dualist strategy of basing their revolutionary status upon their claim to be the natural antithesis to the hegemony of mainstream objectivism, a hegemony that no longer exists.

POST-MODERN SOCIETY AND THE GREEK CATEGORIES OF KNOWLEDGE

The modernist period was characterized by the dialectic between mainstream objectivist values and elite subjectivist values. Since the 1960s, however, this dialectic has collapsed and the concept of the *avant garde* has disappeared as subjectivism became a mass perspective without altering the bottom-line reality of instrumental rationality. Within the resulting "post-modern" society, the production of artistic elites is no longer structured by reference to revolutionary values and is characterized by a non-systematic melange of styles, objectivistic realism mixing democratically with non-representational approaches.

Given the disintegration of the modernist synthesis, contemporary social critics have been attempting to develop an approach to knowledge that could aid in the liberation from instrumental rationality. Since both objectivist and subjectivist orientations have been shown to be compatible with instrumental rationality, critics have labored to develop a concept of knowledge which would transcend this dualism—that is, a type of rationality which would be neither objectivist nor subjectivist. We are thinking here specifically of Alasdair MacIntyre's radical reformulation of the philosophy of ethics in *After Virtue*,[10] of hermeneutical sociologists influenced by Gadamer, such as Robert Bellah,[11] of contemporary Marxist critical theory exemplified most prominently by the work of Jurgen Habermas[12]—and of a variety of other contemporary social thinkers sur-

veyed by Richard Bernstein in *Beyond Relativism and Objectivism.*[13]
These thinkers have resurrected classical categories of knowledge—originating in Plato and Aristotle—which relativize the antithesis between
subjectivism and objectivism.[14]

Most protagonists in the two-hundred-year-old dispute since the
Great Chain of Being was split into its "uniformitarian" (Enlightenment)
and its "diversitarian" (Romantic) guises have argued either that all
knowledge is objectivist or that all knowledge is subjectivist; either truth
equals total certainty or truth equals total uncertainty.[15] The Greek philosophers, however, rather than seeing all knowledge as being monolithic
in this way, tended to see knowledge as being of three different types,
involving different mixtures of certainty and uncertainty, depending
upon the particular roles it was to perform in human life.

The lowest form of knowledge was *techne* (often translated as technical rationality), a category somewhat similar to what we would call
technology—the application of pre-existing objective knowledge to well-
defined practical ends. Such knowledge was considered to be value neutral (or at most was structured according to the value of efficiency) and it
was thus only technical rationality that was considered to be objective in
the modern sense that it had equal meaning to people at all levels of
moral stature. According to the Greeks, such knowledge had a perfectly
appropriate though limited utility, the sort of knowledge that an artisan
could appropriately embody in the practice of his or her craft.

When misapplied to the human realm, however, *techne* is the
approach to knowledge which we have referred to as unilevel, that is,
instrumental rationality in either its objectivist or subjectivist guises.
Through scientistic analogy, human beings are viewed either as equivalent to essentially separate atoms interacting with each other only on the
basis of power or force, or as fierce animals competing for scarce
resources to determine the survival of the fittest. All values—whether
characterized as objectivist or subjectivist—apply to human beings with
mechanical uniformity and differences or levels of interpretation are
totally disregarded. When dualistic new religions are approached
through instrumental rationality, such mechanical univocal interpretation results in authoritarian collectivism—which denies the validity of
individual interpretations of spiritual ideals. When monistic new religions are approached through unilevel *techne*, collective ideals are totally
repudiated on the grounds that whatever is uncertain is thereby false.

The next-highest type of knowledge was believed to be *phronesis*
(often translated as practical rationality). The appropriate application of
such knowledge was within the realm of practical human affairs, of civic
and political activity. Because of the inherent complexity of a situation

in which individuals are both the subjects and objects of knowledge—both the knowers and the known—this type of knowledge could not possibly be understood as existing in a final and determinate form in the minds of all, independently of their level of moral stature.

The realm of *phronesis* could only be viewed as involving complete certainty if all human beings were viewed as possessing complete self-knowledge, an assumption which contradicts even the most casual empirical observation. On the other hand, human knowledge is not viewed as totally uncertain either. Rather, knowledge here exists in a form neither totally objective nor totally subjective in the modern sense of those terms. Knowledge apprehended through the mode of *phronesis* contains a universal element (interpreted well or poorly depending upon the spiritual maturity of the person glimpsing it) which is to be given fully determinate form only in concrete contexts. Thus the understanding of the conceptual content of ethical principles is viewed as only a first step in their practical comprehension. The living content of practical rationality is communicated primarily by means of traditions which provide many examples of its successful embodiment. It is only by such exemplary presentation in concrete contexts, combined with personal experience in the living of a virtuous life, that one comes to have a working grasp of its content.

Whereas *techne* applied within new religions results either in the complete denial of trans-individual ideals—as in unilevel monism—or in denial of the validity of the individual interpretation of such ideals—as in unilevel dualism—*phronesis* allows for the affirmation of spiritual ideals whose interpretation is neither totally certain nor totally uncertain. *Phronesis* points to the reality of transpersonal values without perpetuating dogmatic interpretations that encourage the repression/projection dynamic and allow members of unilevel dualist groups to escape responsibility for their own uncomprehended selfishness. On the other hand *phronesis* supports the validity of the individual interpretation of such ideals without thereby denying that such ideals truly exist and that they can be known in a more certain form at higher levels of consciousness—the characteristic flaw of unilevel monism, which encourages devotees to abandon efforts to transcend their own selfishness. Thus, *phronesis*, when applied within new religions in the manner we are suggesting, has characteristics which are convergent with multilevel approaches to spiritual values.

As normally interpreted by contemporary social critics, however, *phronesis* is primarily an intellectual, political orientation having no real potential to serve as the basis for the whole person's transcendence of instrumental rationality. This is so because these critics tend to neglect the role of *theoria*, the third type of knowledge specified by the Greek philosophers. Only by taking into account the complexly interdependent nature of *phronesis* and *theoria* can we formulate a full-fledged multilevel approach capable of aiding people in their total being to rise above the spiritually debilitating influence of contemporary culture.

This third type of knowledge, *theoria*, is sometimes misleadingly translated as theoretical rationality. A better translation might be transcendental wisdom or knowledge.[16] *Theoria* results from contemplation and involves knowledge of eternally existing unchanging reality, or what medieval thinkers referred to as the Great Chain of Being. At its highest level *theoria* involves knowledge of the *Nous*, the good, the absolute, wherein being and value mutually interpenetrate in a noncontingent manner. At its intermediate levels *theoria* involves knowledge of the eternal forms or archetypes that are derivative from the absolute being of the *nous* and have their shadowy representations in the material world. At its lowest level of application, *theoria* involves determinate knowledge of the practical ends or values which are only known in an incomplete and contingent manner by *phronesis*. (Paradoxically, such determinate knowledge on the lower levels of *theoria* can only be attained when the higher levels have already been mastered.) *Theoria*, as direct knowledge of ultimate truth, is the most real and comprehensive of the three types of knowledge, although from the modern unilevel sensibility it could be seen as the least objective; that is, awareness of its content is totally dependent upon the state of consciousness—we might say the level of consciousness—of its subject, and is not present at all in the great mass of people. Nevertheless, from our point of view *theoria* is the least subjective of the three types of knowledge since its content is the most certain and comprehensive once one has achieved sustained awareness of it.

As we have said, the neo-classical critics have tended to center their analysis of the problem of ethical knowledge in post-modern society upon the contrast between instrumental and practical reason, being rather silent upon the role of *theoria*. Doubtless in the context of an intact, non-decadent culture, a reemphasis upon practical rationality alone would be an effective strategy for revitalizing the integrity of human life. However, it is also probably true that when practical rationality has become as widely degraded to instrumental rationality as it has in this culture, it has done so because the ends or values assumed by practical rationality no longer have exemplary potency. Consequently, a primarily intellectual or political solution to the problem can do nothing to cure the condition in the absence of a fresh dispensation of such spiritual potency.

As Weber recognized, traditions tend to be revitalized in fundamental ways, not by intellectual analysis but by revelations of values that are made to seem new and relevant through their exemplification in the career of a human agent regarded as the embodiment of human/divine excellence—by charisma, in other words.[17]

Such charismatic figures, such human/divine agents, found traditions and revitalize civilizations by recombining values and being, subjectivity and objectivity in their own persons in ways which transcend the apparently insoluble contradictions between those spheres. Given the influence of such charismatic exemplars, practical rationality becomes viable again because the ends or values which must be taken for granted by it are given widespread acceptance. On the other hand, charisma has not been in its classical religious presentations (Christ, Socrates, Buddha, Mohammed) experienced by the participants in the cultures founded or reconstituted upon it as mere subjective or emotional potency. Rather, charisma has been experienced as the medium for the revitalization of a transcendental realm of knowledge, the realm of the Great Chain of Being—the realm of *theoria*, in other words. Thus, the resurrection of the Greek categories of knowledge seems helpful in an analysis of the problems of contemporary culture only if the category of *theoria* is taken fully into account.

It is not hard to see why *theoria* has been glossed over by the neoclassical social critics. Each of them hopes to achieve a critique that could be generally persuasive, at least within our own culture. The category of *theoria*, however, depends for its plausibility upon the acceptance of the existence of transcendental being and wisdom. Such faith in transcendental being and wisdom is by no means widespread, much less universal, in the current age. A critique of instrumental rationality which took it as given would necessarily doom itself to a restricted, a religious audience, as ours is cheerfully doing.

Having made it this far in our manuscript, you the reader are presumably willing to grant us that spiritual solutions are finally necessary for anything like a cure of the agony of soul caused by instrumental rationalization—which is at bottom a metaphysical disorder of consciousness. What then is the implication of our reemphasis on *theoria* for you, the spiritual seeker, given that we have already applied the concept of *phronesis* in a way that is convergent with multilevel spirituality? The correct relationship between *phronesis* and *theoria* in a multilevel spiritual perspective is suggested by this passage in Paul's first letter to the Corinthians in the Christian New Testament.

our knowledge is imperfect and our prophesying is imperfect. But when the perfect comes, the imperfect will pass away. When I was a child, I spoke as a child, I understood as a child, I thought as a child, but when I became a man, I put away childish things. For now we see through a glass, darkly; but then face to face; now I know in part; but then I shall understand fully, even as I have been fully understood.

The spiritual child in this passage is the Christian seeker, whereas the spiritual adult is his guide, Jesus the Christ, like whom he will some-day become. The seeker, who by definition has not yet achieved union with the divine wherein he or she will attain perfect knowledge, power, and bliss, is for now aware of the transcendental realm only through brief glimpses. The knowledge thereby imparted, although it may result in deep conviction in the existence of a transcendental reality, remains too incomplete for our interpretations of the nature of that realm to be cer-tain or infallible. The seeker can for now know only in part, as through a glass darkly, through the medium of *phronesis*. When the perfect comes—that is, union—the imperfect will pass away and we shall see face to face, we shall understand fully, through *theoria*. Through *theoria* we shall perceive the transcendental realm continuously rather than through brief glimpses, and our interpretations will become trustworthy and reliable.

Something equivalent to both the categories of *phronesis* and *theoria* is necessary within an authentic multilevel perspective. For its practical application such a perspective requires that seekers, who perceive pri-marily through *phronesis*, achieve relationships with those who have become perfect, or something close to it, that is, with spiritual masters who have mastered the realm of *theoria*. Because the seeker perceives the transcendental realm only in part, and his or her interpretations are thereby fallible, progress on the path, which is thin as the razor's edge, would be uncertain at best without the guidance of a real master. More-over, such progress results only from long and arduous effort, and the inspiration for such super-human effort usually can come only through the inspiration provided by a master who is an embodiment of transcen-dental wisdom, that is, *theoria*.

It is very important, then, for a seeker to find a guide who has actually achieved mastery of *theoria* rather than merely another form of *phrone-sis*. Although *phronesis* is a type of real knowledge, its unaided interpre-tations are too fallible to long withstand distortion by the powerful forces of the collective culture, dominated as it is by the misapplication of *techne* to the human and transcendental realms. *Phronesis* and *theoria* are complexly interdependent; *phronesis* requires a relationship with *theoria* in order to retain its integrity; a seeker requires a relationship with a real master in order to realistically hope for progress on the path.

To return to the question of whether the type of knowledge we are claiming to provide within this analysis is to be viewed as subjectivist or objectivist—of course it should be viewed as neither. The whole thrust of our analysis of new religions has been to argue that both subjectivism—in the guise of unilevel monism—and objectivism—in the guise of unilevel dualism—lead to the distortion of spiritual truth by subordinating it to cultural adaptation. Our development of the categories of unilevel and multilevel religion should itself be viewed through a multilevel lens. Our analysis should be used as an aid to the achievement of *phronesis*, a practical rationality which may aid discrimination and the achievement of spiritual authenticity in concrete contexts of application. The practical truth conveyed by *phronesis* is in turn dependent upon its relation to *theoria*, whose truth can, for the seeker, be at most glimpsed through multilevel eyes. The ends and values communicated by our framework are not fully determinable by understanding its conceptual content, but must be worked out more fully within concrete contexts of application. The examples we have given of the application of our point of view to specific groups are to be regarded as suggestive and heuristic rather than definitive. The value or quality of actual discriminations made with the aid of our categories will be at least as dependent upon the spiritual sensibility of the person making the judgment as they are upon the caliber of our analysis.

Perhaps the best that can be expected in an endeavor of this type is to aid in the crystallization of an awareness that was almost fully present already. So: Let those who have eyes, see; let those who have ears, hear.

Notes

1. The reader may find this reference to a history of Western *individualism* confusing, as previously we have asserted that mainstream Western values were, until recently at least, unilevel dualist and elsewhere have asserted that unilevel dualist values are *collectivistic* rather than individualistic. Actually, both statements are true in the context in which they are being made. Mainstream Western culture has gone through several stages since the Middle Ages, with each stage being more individualistic, or conversely less collectivistic than the previous one. The first post-Medieval stage was that of the Protestant ethic in the strict sense—in America the era of the Puritans. The second was the modern era, dominated by the spirit of capitalism. The third is the current, post-modern stage, which we have just begun, characterized by pluralism.

    Judgments of individualism/collectivism are relative to the scale established by these four cultural eras, with the medieval period representing the most collective pole and the contemporary pluralist period the most individualistic. Thus, when it is realized that civil religion sects affirm the values of the Protestant ethic stage of unilevel dualism, whereas the values of the modern era were that of the later spirit of capitalism, we can see that: (1) the three unilevel dualist categories that reaffirm Protestant ethic values—the modern mainstream, the Protestant ethic era and the civil religion sects—are each collectivistic when judged relative either to contemporary pluralist values or unilevel monist groups; and (2) all later cultural stages, including the unilevel dualist ones, are individualist when judged relative to the Middle Ages.

2. Modern society was characterized by an industrial economic base, mainstream objectivist values and elite countercultural subjectivist values. Post-modern or post-industrial society is characterized by an informational economic base, mainstream pluralism and an elite eclecticism no longer defining itself in opposition to mainstream values. See Jean-Francois Lyotard, *The Post-Modern Condition: A Report on Knowledge* (Minneapolis: University of Minnesota Press, 1984).

3. Familiarity with the history of this cultural dialectic between objectivism and subjectivism may aid readers in transcending it. As both depth psychology and mystical religion have taught us, before we can be liberated from social influences, we must become conscious of what they are. Cultural controls upon consciousness go very deep; they are apt to be most constraining when we believe that we have already transcended them in some direct and simple way, because then they become the most unconscious. The history of the successive stages of individualism in the West demonstrates that minority perspectives which present themselves as offering revolutions against cultural subjugation tend themselves to become institutionalized as the next unilevel mainstream norm. The individual's revolt against collective culture is itself the dominant tradition in the West. Consequently, we are never more controlled by our culture than when we have enlisted in the next revolution against it. If this book accomplishes nothing more than to help the reader become more capable of recognizing the polymorphous forms of unilevel culture and the depth of the problem of escaping from it and its psuedo-revolutionary entrapments, we shall be satisfied.

4. For the Romantic, human meaning is not primarily rational but *symbolic*. Where univocal rationality reduces the multiple levels of interpertation of a given text or situation to one dominant meaning, usually materialistic, symbolic approaches allow multiple interpretations of a given text to coexist and combine in consciousness, thereby evoking an awareness too complex or subtle to admit of literal paraphrase. At its best, such symbolic awareness affords glimpses of an ultimate realm within which the fundamental contradictions of human experience—subject/object, self/other, doing/being—are reconciled and integrated, whereas univocal approaches cut off consciousness totally from the transrational mode of apprehension and leave the self mired in conflict-ridden alienation.

5. See George Lakoff and Mark Johnson, *Metaphors We Live By* (Chicago: University of Chicago, 1980), Chapter 25, pp. 185–194, for a useful discussion of the definitional interdependence of objectivism and subjectivism in Western culture.

6. The content of the transcendence sought by the Romantics tended to be aesthetic rather than metaphysical. The impression that the Romantics had some positive message to offer came more from their critique of the bourgeois sensibility than from any ideational content in their own world-view. The effect of this contrast identity theme in the Romantics' critique of the bourgeois sensibility was to make the ulimate meaning of the Romantic perspective covertly dependent upon the utilitarianism it overtly condemned.

7. The general reader may be surprised that we view these modern movements as heirs of Romanticism. They are generally so viewed, however, by cultural and intellectual historians although tracing the ins and outs of these movements' agreements and disagreements with each other is very complex. They tend to share, however, a repudiation of the Enlightenment's subject/object dualism and of Kant's dictum that the noumenon, the "thing-in-itself," cannot be known directly. Most trace common roots to German Romantic philosophers such as Fichte, Schelling, Hegel, and Schopenhauer. For an excellent discussion of the Romantic character of these German philosophers see Harold Hoffding, *A History of Modern Philosophy Vol. II* (New York: Dover, 1955). For a discussion of the influence of German Romantic philosophy, particularly Schelling's, on the English Romantic poets, particularly Coleridge, see Owen Barfield, *What Coleridge Thought* (Middletown, CT: Wesleyan University Press, 1971). For a view of artistic modernism as basically Romantic in character see Morse Peckham, *The Triumph of Romanticism* (Columbia: University of South Carolina Press, 1970). For a discussion of Kierkegaard and Marx, the fathers of existentialism and communism respectively, as heirs of the Romantic philosophers, specifically as "the extreme development of the critical movement of the Hegelian left along the two lines of its chief concern, religion and socio-political thought," see A. Robert Caponigri, *Philosophy from the Romantic Age to the Age of Positivism* (South Bend, IN: University of Notre Dame Press, 1971), p. 138. Henri F. Ellenberger in *The Discovery of the Unconscious: The History and Evolution of Dynamic Psychiatry* (New York: Basic, 1970) asserts unequivocally that "Freud and Jung can be identified as late epigones of Romanticism" (p. 99) and provides an excellent discussion of Romanticism as the cultural background of modern depth psychology (Chapter 4). Weber's sociology is commonly viewed as existentialist and he was referred to by the modern existential philosopher Karl Jaspers as the "master" of modern existentialism. For the influence of Nietzsche on the development of Weber's thought see Chapter 7, Arthur Mitzman, *The Iron Cage: An Historical Interpretation of Max Weber* (New York: Grosset and Dunlap, 1969).

The general reader may also be surprised that we view these artistic, political, philosophical, and social scientific critiques of the bourgeois world-view as relevant to the formulation of *spiritual* standards. However, the interaction of these critiques with mystical, especially Oriental, spirituality has been apparent throughout their history in the modern era and their assumptions color contemporary American interpretations. These various critiques share with Oriental mysticism: (1) a repudiation of Enlightenment subject/object dualism and, conversely, an affirmation that man and nature are essentially one; (2) the view that unilevel discursive rationality imprisons humanity in a world of illusion, a world structured by the assumption of subject/object dualism; and (3) the view that transcendence of imprisonment in the world of illusion involves mastery of a transrational intuitive or symbolic mode of consciousness. A concise discussion of the contrast formulated within Zen philosophy between the imprisoning effect of discursive rationality *(vijnana)* and the liberating effect of intuition *(prajna)* may be found in Chapter IV, "Reason and Intuition in Buddhist Philosophy," in D. T. Suzuki, *Studies in Zen* (New York: Dell, 1955). This formulation of the contrast between a reductive, discursive rationality and liberating intuition would be accepted by most of the heirs of Romanticism. The extensive, explicit, direct influence of Oriental mysticism on the development of German Romantic philosophy has been documented by both Hoffding and Caponigri. The continuing influence of Oriental mysticism among the various modernist critiques may be inferred from this earlier influence, and is widely apparent, although in some cases, as in Marxist thought or Sartrean existentialism, it is obscured by an explicit repudiation of mysticism. Even here, however, the continuing influence of Oriental thought is rather transparent; for example, the dialectical logic of Marxism is taken from Hegel, who in turn developed it on the basis of Buddhist logic. See Thomas J. J. Altizer, "An inquiry into the meaning of negation in the dialectical logics of East and West," pp. 97–118, in Robert H. Ayers and William T. Blackstone, eds., *Religious Language and Knowledge* (Athens, GA: University of Georgia Press, 1972), and F. T. Stcherbatsky, *Buddhist Logic*, Vols. I and II (New York: Dover, 1962).

Similarly, Heidegger, to whom Sartre's work was greatly indebted, has explicitly repudiated Sartre's identification of Heidegger's position as atheistic—see Martin Heidegger, "Letter on Humanism," in William Barrett and Henry D. Aiken, eds., *Philosophy in the Twentieth Century*, Vol. II (New York: Random House, 1962). In his treatment of primordial being as prior to subject/object distinctions, Heidegger clearly writes in an intuitive tradition that includes both Romanticism and much Oriental mysticism. Not surprisingly, Heidegger has asserted—as Ken Wilber has also pointed out in his essay in this volume—"if I understand Zen scholar Suzuki, this is what I have been trying to say in all my writings." See Introduction to D. T. Suzuki, *Essays in Zen Buddhism* (London: Routledge and Kegan Paul, 1968).

Finally, the similarity among the epistemological assumptions of modern depth psychology, existentialism, and Oriental mysticism—or at least among their popular interpretations—should be obvious through the interpenetration of these three orientations within the humanistic and transpersonal psychology movements.

8. Of course, in some respects Marxism has itself been objectivist, its Romantic Hegelian heritage notwithstanding. The writing of the younger Marx is generally regarded as more humanist, whereas that of the later Marx and of his collaborator, Engels, are regarded as more scientistic, as is the orthodox Marxist-Leninist dogma of the Eastern bloc nations. Creative Marxist thinkers in the West, however, have been deeply influenced by Weber's argument that the anomic effect of instrumental rationality is a deeper problem for modern consciousness than economic injustice. Consequently, modern Western Marxists (Lukacs, the Frankfurt School, Philip Rahv and the literary Marxists clustered around the *Partisan Review*) labored to create a synthesis of Marxism and multivocalist artistic modernism which they believed would undermine the hegemony of instrumental rationality.

It was this multivocalist Marxist perspective, particularly as found in the work of Herbert Marcuse, that strongly influenced the development of the 1960s counter-culture, which in turn formed the cultural matrix for the growth of the new religions.

9. The best brief account we have found of the events described in this paragraph is Christopher Lasch's somewhat misleadingly titled article, "Modernism, Politics and Philip Rahv," *Partisan Review*, Vol. XLVII, No. 2, 1980.

10. Alasdair MacIntyre, *After Virtue: A Study in Moral Theory* (South Bend, IN: University of Notre Dame Press, 1981).

11. See Robert N. Bellah, "Social Science as Practical Reason," a privately circulated article; also "The Ethical Aim of Social Inquiry," in Norma Haan, Robert N. Bellah, Paul Rabinow, and William M. Sullivan (eds.), *Social Science as Moral Inquiry* (New York: Columbia University Press, 1983).

12. See especially Jurgen Habermas, *The Theory of Communicative Action: Volume I: Reason and the Rationalization of Society* (Boston: Beacon, 1984).

13. Richard Bernstein, *Beyond Objectivism and Relativism: Science, Hermeneutics and Praxis* (Philadelphia: University of Pennsylvania, 1983).

14. In *Religion in the Secular City: Towards a Post-Modern Theology* (New York: Simon and Schuster, 1984), Harvey Cox has argued that in order for religion to provide a sense of salvation or transcendence in the post-modern society, it must offer some form of transindividual knowledge. This is so because experiential-expressive liberal theology—which, since the early nineteenth century work of the German theologian Schliermacher, has based salvation on feelings or emotion rather than knowl-

edge—has lost plausibility in a post-modern society experienced as alienating despite its tolerance of subjectivist values. Cox's examples of approaches to spiritual knowledge that are experienced as offering salvation in this context are Evangelical Protestantism and Catholic liberation theology.

We agree with Cox's reemphasis on spiritual knowledge, although his examples seem problematic because they are both unilevel dualistic in terms of the Anthony typology. Better examples from our point of view would be multilevel mystical approaches as described in this book. In this connection, it seems to us that transpersonal psychology, with its emphasis on mystical or transrational knowledge, has advantages vis-à-vis both the unilevel subjectivist orientation of humanistic psychology and the unilevel objectivist orientation of mainstream academic psychology as a human science orientation that will aid individuals to transcend oppressive cultural influence.

Influential theorists associated with the transpersonal psychology movement, for example Ken Wilber and Huston Smith, have argued that the Great Chain of Being was the Western version of hierarchical ontology, that occurs in all the great religious traditions and thus constitutes a universal mysticism or perennial philosophy. It seems appropriate, then, that in self-reflection about its own knowledge claims, transpersonal psychology should resurrect the Greek categories of knowledge—*techne*, *phronesis* and *theoria*—particularly in view of the fact that the Greek philosophers were one of the two primary influences on the development of the concept of the Great Chain of Being (the other being neo-Platonic Christian theology).

Wilber has, in fact, in his epistemological essay "Eye to Eye"—in his book of the same title, *Eye to Eye: The Quest for the New Paradigm* (New York: Anchor Press/Doubleday, 1983)—utilized the medieval knowledge categories *cogitatio*, *meditatio*, and *contemplatio*, which are in some respect the heirs of the Greek categories *techne*, *phronesis* and *theoria*. The reader should note, however, that Wilber's treatment of these issues differs considerably from that of the neo-classical social critics referred to above and from that of this book as well. Wilber's treatment there was—as he himself now acknowledges—objectivist in certain respects, as he argued that a type of objective certainty was possible for experts in both the material empirical and the human social realms. Contemporary post-empiricist philosophers of science argue, however, that such certainty is not possible even in the empirical, much less in the social, realm; (see Bernstein, op. cit. and Richard Rorty, *Philosophy and the Mirror of Nature*, Princeton: Princeton University Press, 1970). We would argue that objective certainty is possible in any realm of knowledge only for those rare individuals who have completely transcended their egos and achieved union with the absolute. However, authentic faith in, conviction of, or commitment to trans-individual ideals is possible for non-perfected consciousness; it is that humble faith, born of the tension between trans-rational conviction, on the one hand, and the knowledge of one's own cognitive fallibility on the other, which is the essence of multilevel spirituality for those who have not yet achieved union with the divine.

15. See Chapter X of Arthur O. Lovejoy's *The Great Chain of Being: A Study in the History of an Idea* (Cambridge, MA: Harvard University Press 1935), for the classic description of the disintegration of the multilevel conception of the Great Chain of Being into its unilevel dualist (Enlightenment) and its unilevel monist (Romantic) formulations.

16. See Alan E. Blum's *Socrates: The Original and Its Images* (London: Routledge, 1978), for a book-length view of *theoria* interpreted as contemplative wisdom in the life and thought of Socrates.

17. In its earlier theological meaning "charisma" was defined as the revelation of the divine in a human agent. In its current popular usage charisma has come to mean merely subjective or emotional potency capable of influencing large numbers of people. This degradation of the concept of charisma from its multilevel spiritual to its unilevel contemporary meaning well illustrates the metaphysical color-blindness endemic in contemporary life. We, of course, are using charisma here in its original theological sense.

Index

Page numbers in **bold face** refer to a chapter by the subject, or a discussion with the subject. Numbers in parenthesis refer to note numbers on that page.

Ma Satya Bharti 32 (28)
MacIntyre, Alasdair 97 (20), 136 (4), 230 (18), 355, 365 (10)
Madsen, Richard 29 (13)
Maharaj Ji 10, 307
Maharishi Mahesh Yogi 20
Mahayana Buddhism 62, 89, 240, 323 (2)
manas 240
Manson, Charles 58, 69, 102 (43), 257
Marcuse, Herbert 30 (15), 98 (22)
Marin, Peter 18, 25 (1), 136 (2)
Marpa 48
Marsden, George M. 97 (20), 105 (62)
Marx 30 (15), 52, 98 (22), 353, 363 (7), 364 (7), 365
Maslow, Abraham 109, 238–240, 247, 279 (7)
maya 207 (3)
Mayer, J.P. 231 (26)
McClelland, David 141
Meher Baba 5, **48, 58, 78, 82, 86,** 103 (50), 105 (57, 59), **153–191**
Merton, Thomas 58 (3), 295, 300 (8)
Messiah's World Crusade 58
Miller, D. 27 (11), 30 (16)
Mills, J. 315, 319 (6)
Miltzman 363 (7)
Mohammed 263, 303, 359
monism 36–39, 58
Moon, Sun Myung 10, 17, 31 (24), 62, 253–254, 266, 307
Moral Majority 99 (27), 244
Mormons 99 (27)
Moses 213
Muktananda, Baba 86
Mullen, John Douglas 95 (11), 102 (45)
multilevel spirituality 36, 37, 40–44, 46, 58, 71–88, 92
multivocality 44–46, 92
Murphy, Michael x, 26 (9), **154–191**
Musgrove, Frank 30 (15), 99 (22)

Napoleon 307
Naranjo, Claudio 26 (9), 100 (33), 105 (58), 188, **193–209**
Needleman, Jacob x, 2–5, 25, 26 (5), 26 (9), 32 (40), 100 (29), 279 (4), **327–348**
Neem Karoli Baba 50, 86, 139, 342
Nelson, Marie Coleman 25 (1)
Nerman, Marshall 99 (22)
New Thought 62, 100 (30)
Newton, Isaac 351–352
Newtonian physics 172
Nicholson, Reynold A. 105 (61)
Nietzsche 29 (15), 98 (22), 309, 363 (7)
Nisargadatta Maharaj 298, 300 (9)
nous 358

Olin, William 11 (n), 102 (44)
Ornstein, Robert 25, 32 (41), 136 (2)
orthopraxy, zen buddhism and 214–216
Otto, Rudolf 72, 102 (46), 338, 343
Ouspensky 144
Owens, Claire Myers 97 (18)

Padmasambhava 195–196
Parsons 245
Patanjali, Bhagwan Shree 77, 104 (52)
Paul 359
Paul, Kegan 364 (7)
Peale, Norman Vincent 58, 69
Peckham, Morse 363 (7)
Pentacostal groups 69
People's Temple, The 10–11, 58, 60–62, 69, 92, 162, 179, 266, 286, 315, 334
Perls, Fritz 186 (2), 292
Phaeton 306
phronesis 356–361, 366 (14)
Piaget 238–239, 247
Piazza, Thomas 27 (11)
Plato 220, 356
Postman, Neil 96 (15)
prajna 364 (7)
Price, Richard 19, 194
Proust, Marcel 44
Psychosynthesis 15–17, 251, 253
psychotherapy 64–66
Puritans, American 55

Rabinow 365 (11)
Rahv, Philip 365
Reja Yoga 77, 83, 256
Ram 263
Ram Dass (Richard Alpert) 96 (12), 100 (33), 151 (2), 151–152, **153–191**, 275, 280 (23)
Ramakrishna Paramahansa 43, 48, 78, 86, 336
Rambo, Lewis 26 (9)
Reagan, Ronald 29 (12)
reality, describing 44–46
Reich, Charles A. 26 (2), 247
Reich, Wilhelm 186 (2)
Reimer, William 28 (12)
Reisman, David 27 (11), 30 (16)
Reisman, Paul 26 (9), **206**
Renzi, Eva 32 (27)
Richardson, James 94 (1)
Ricoeur 30 (15), 98 (22)
Riesman, Paul **170–171**
Rinzai School 229 (4)
Risch, Richard 136 (6)

About the Editors

DICK ANTHONY is a psychologist who specializes in the study of new religious movements from an interdisciplinary perspective. As Research Director of the Study for New Religious Movements and previously as a faculty member at the University of North Carolina, Chapel Hill, Anthony has been principal investigator of a number of research projects on the mental health effects of new religious movements. He is co-editor (with Thomas Robbins) of *In Gods We Trust: New Patterns of Religious Pluralism in America* and has published more than 50 articles on religious movements in professional journals.

BRUCE ECKER is a psychotherapist whose clinical and theoretical work in transpersonal psychology followed a lengthy career as an experimental physicist. His psychotherapy practice in Berkeley, California, includes family systems, couple, individual, and group work. The interplay of psychological and spiritual dynamics has long been one of his major areas of study.

KEN WILBER'S prolific writings articulating the transpersonal dimensions of psychology, sociology, anthropology, and physics have made him the transpersonal school's foremost theorist. Among his ten books are *The Spectrum of Consciousness, Up from Eden, Sociable God, Quantum Questions,* and *The Pathology of Consciousness.* After several years as Editor of the journal *ReVision,* Wilber is now General Editor of New Science Library, published by Random House.